INSIDE YOUR
HORSE'S
MIND

INSIDE YOUR HORSE'S MIND

*A Study of Equine Intelligence
and Human Prejudice*

Lesley Skipper

J. A. ALLEN LONDON

For Brian, the best of husbands

British Library cataloguing in publication data
A catalogue record for this book is available from the British Library
ISBN 0 85131 738 3
First published in Great Britain 1999
Reprinted 2001

J.A. Allen
Clerkenwell House
Clerkenwell Green
London EC1R 0HT

Designed by Paul Saunders
Illustrations by Rodney Paull

Typesetting by Textype Cambridge
Colour Separation by Tenon & Polert (H. K.) Ltd
Printed in Hong Kong by Dah Hua Printing Press Co Ltd

Contents

Acknowledgements

I should like to thank the following people for all the help and support they have given me, together with a great deal of valuable information.

In particular, I must thank Dr Marthe Kiley-Worthington for her encouragement and advice, as well as her immense generosity in making some of her scientific papers available to me.

Sylvia Loch has also been a continual source of support and encouragement; I must thank her especially for her advice on the chapters dealing with ridden work.

McTimoney practitioner Dana Green has also helped to keep my thoughts concentrated in the right direction with her extremely valuable in-depth knowledge and understanding of the equine musculo-skeletal system and her encouraging suggestions.

Biophysicist Dr Averil Cox has likewise been most helpful in providing technical information and clarification of various points.

Lynn and Sara Debnam have helped to keep me sane while wrestling with some of the concepts presented in this book. As well as providing me with some excellent material, they also allowed me the privilege of getting to know one of the sweetest-natured horses I have ever encountered – Mikenah – referred to in the pages of this book by her pet name of Tiff. In the relatively short time between her arrival at our yard and the completion of this book, Tiff has reaffirmed my belief in what I have written in these pages about the essential nature of horses.

My husband Brian and our Girl Friday Joanne Husband have, as always, shown infinite patience in listening to, and commenting on, my arguments and dissertations; without them this book would not have been begun, let alone finished. Lorraine Graham has likewise provided me with a 'sounding board' for many of my ideas.

My non-horsey friends Sue Coulthard and Antonia Harris have (as usual) also proved a valuable source of feedback in reading through my scribblings and commenting on their readability.

Among the many people who supplied me with information and advice, some of it of a technical nature, I must make particular mention of the following: Dr June Alexander, Rosemary Archer, Paul Belasik, D. Bothamley, Brian Checkland, Toni Cherrett, Sara Crozier de Roca, Dr Ian Dunbar, Melanie Gaddas-Brown, Jill Holding, Jane Littlefair, Heather Moffett, Sandra Nevin, Tommy Nevin, Gillian O'Donnell, Paul Hunting, Cheryl Procter, Jackie and Vicki Rowe, Graham Russ of Oaklands Veterinary Centre, Alison Sharp, Dr Rupert Sheldrake, Lisa Smith, Samantha Tobias and Jane Van Lennep.

For help with illustrations, my thanks go to: Herr Henric Brabec d'Ipra, Anita Chadfield, Sara Crozier de Roca, Lynn and Sara Debnam, Herr A. Eichinger of the Spanish Riding School Press Office, Anthony Fessler, Secretary of the Anglo-Austrian Society, Lorraine Graham, Antonia Harris, Mr J. J. A. Hohmann, Joanne Husband, Carina Jönsson, Dr Marthe Kiley-Worthington, Herr Klaus Krzisch of the Spanish Riding School, Bob Langrish, Jane Littlefair, Sylvia Loch, Anne Mattsson, M. Nuitjen-Hulsbosch, Senhor Arsenio Raposo Cordeiro, Lisa Smith, Brian Spencer, Eleanor and Roger Taylor, Samantha Tobias and Dr George Waring.

Thanks must also go to the staff of the London Library, Stockton Library, Cleveland County Libraries inter-loans service and the British Library for their patience, courtesy and efficiency in dealing with my numerous requests, and also to Ian and Jean Healey of the Sportingman's Bookshop in Devon (now incorporated into J. A. Allen) and the staff of Allen's Bookshop in London.

My undying gratitude goes to Caroline Burt and Jane Lake of J. A. Allen for their enthusiasm, faith, endless patience and encouragement, and to Lesley Young for proving a most helpful and understanding editor.

Last, but perhaps most important of all, my thanks go to all the horses I have known, some of whom I have counted as dear friends, while others have been simply acquaintances. In their way, they have all contributed to whatever little understanding I have gained of that wondrous species known as Equus caballus.

My thanks for permission to quote from copyright material go to: James Fleming of Alexander Heriot (Archer, et al., *The Crabbet Arabian Stud*; Lady Anne Blunt, *Journals and Correspondence*); J. A. Allen & Co Ltd (Brigadier-General Kurt Albrecht, *The Principles of Dressage*; Paul Belasik, *Exploring Dressage Technique*; Karin Blignault, *Successful Schooling*; Udo Bürger, *The Way to Perfect Horsemanship*; Dr Marthe Kiley-Worthington, *The Behaviour of Horses* and *Equine Welfare*; Sylvia Loch, *The Classical Rider*; Marquis MacSwiney of Mashanaglass, *Training from the Ground*; Nuno Oliveira, *Reflections on Equestrian Art*; Colonel Alois Podhajsky, *My Horses, My Teachers*; Dr Moyra Williams, *Horse Psychology* and *Understanding Nervousness in Horse and Rider*); Blackwell (Mary Bromiley, *Natural Methods for Equine Health*); Jonathan Cape (Desmond Morris, *Horsewatching*); Mary Daniels (Dominique Barbier with Mary Daniels, *Dressage for the New Age*); Deutscher Taschenbuch Verlag (Konrad Lorenz *On Aggression* and *King Solomon's Ring* [*Er redete mit dem Vieh, den Vögeln und den Fischen* © 1983 Deutscher Taschenbuch Verlag, Munich, English edition first published by Methuen, London under the title *King Solomon's Ring* © 1952 by Marjorie Kerr Wilson]); Dr Ian Dunbar ('Should You Let Sleeping Dogs Lie With You?', *Dogs Today* March 1997); Harvill Press (Stephen Jay Gould, extracts from *Bully for Brontosaurus* [first published in Great Britain by Collins Harvill Press 1991. Copyright © Stephen Jay Gould 1991] and *An Urchin in the Storm* [first published in Great Britain by Collins Harvill 1987. Copyright © Stephen Jay Gould 1987]); Heinemann (Vicki Hearne, *Adam's Task: Calling Animals By Name*); Hutchinson (Monty Roberts, *The Man Who Listens to Horses*); Sylvia Loch and *Horse & Rider* (various articles by Sylvia Loch which appeared in *Horse & Rider*); Manson Publishing (Jean-Marie Denoix and Jean-Pierre Pailloux, *Physical Therapy and Massage for the Horse* [tr. Jonathan Lewis]); Methuen (Mary Wanless, *Ride With Your Mind*); Peters Fraser & Dunlop (Tom Pitt-Aikens and Alice Thomas Ellis (*Loss of the Good Authority* © Tom Pitt-Aikens and Alice Thomas Ellis 1989), reprinted by permission of the Peters Fraser & Dunlop Group Limited on behalf of Tom Pitt-Aikens and Alice Thomas Ellis); Lucy Rees, *The Maze* and *The Horse's Mind* (© Lucy Rees, 1984 and 1995, reprinted by permission of the Peters Fraser & Dunlop Group on behalf of Lucy Rees); Professor Bernard Rollin (*The Unheeded Cry: Animal Consciousness, Animal Pain and Science* [now reissued in an expanded edition by Iowa State University]); Routledge (Mary Midgley, *Beast and Man*); University of Georgia Press (Mary Midgley, *Animals And Why They Matter*); Vintage (Jeffrey Masson and Susan McCarthy, *When Elephants Weep*); Weidenfeld & Nicholson (Stephen Budiansky, *The Nature of Horses*; Jane Goodall, *Through a Window*).

My further thanks go to the following for permission to reproduce illustrations from their books: Dr Marthe Kiley-Worthington and J. A. Allen, *The Behaviour of Horses*), Dr Steven Rose (*The Conscious Brain*) and Dr George Waring of the University of Southern Illinois (*Horse Behavior*).

Every effort has been made to trace copyright ownership of quotations or illustrative material used in this book. If anyone has a claim in this respect, they should contact the publishers.

Introduction

W HY DO WE NEED yet another book on equine psychology? The 1990s have seen an explosion of published work on equine behaviour, partly as a response to increased interest in a more thinking approach to riding and keeping horses, and partly because of the publicity given to the work of people such as Monty Roberts and the new breed of 'horse whisperers'. However, much of the recently published work has tended to concentrate on the simpler aspects of horse psychology, such as instinctive reactions, and has largely ignored the deeper question of what, if anything, horses might think about what goes on in their lives. One book which purports to be about the horse's mind actually devotes only one chapter out of 13 to that subject and even then the matter is dealt with rather perfunctorily! Such publications have also tended to place rather too much stress on the ideas of 'dominance' and 'pecking orders', which distorts our understanding of which aspects of their lives matter most to horses. Another distorting factor is the still common assumption that the horse is really a rather simple-minded creature, with a few basic needs and instincts, but nothing much in his head apart from these. Indeed, some writers go so far as to assert that horses are incapable of anything other than stock responses to certain stimuli.

Yet when we look closely at what horses actually do, we can see that this is far from being the case and that, both in their social lives and in their mental processes, they are really far, far more complex than is generally recognised.

It was in response to these distorting assumptions that I started to write this book. It began life as a series of magazine articles which attempted to examine such assumptions and to ask whether we are really justified in making them. I also tried to address the question of just what it is we are trying to teach horses when we train them under saddle, as this is an area abounding in misunderstandings. Like Topsy in *Uncle Tom's Cabin*, the size, number and scope of the articles eventually just 'growed', until it became clear that only a full-scale book could do justice to the subjects I was trying to cover. I am eternally grateful to Caroline Burt of J. A. Allen for having faith in my ability to tackle such a complex series of topics. It is an intimidating task to write about such subject matter when one knows that one will inevitably by criticised by laypersons for being too scientific, and by scientists for not being scientific enough!

In fact, it was the scientific aspect which made me decide on the current format. So much of what is written about equine behaviour, from both the lay and the scientific point of view, relies on certain basic assumptions which have seldom been questioned. A prime example of this is 'anthropomorphism' – what do people really mean when they use this term? Very few seem to have any clear idea, which is why I have discussed it in such detail in Chapter 4. Also built into current thinking about animal behaviour in general is a rather uncritical acceptance of what Stephen Jay Gould has called 'pop-sociobiology' or 'cardboard Darwinism': the explanation of all animal behaviour and motives in terms of evolutionary advantage. Chapter 3 explains why I believe that this, taken to the current extremes, can be disastrous to our understanding of equine (and, indeed, all animal) motivation.

It is because I feel so strongly that we must continually question and re-evaluate, and also because of the widespread tendency of observers to start from false or shaky assumptions, that I have divided this book into two parts. The first part examines some of the assumptions referred to above. It looks at the scientific study of animal behaviour in a wider sense, considering some of the methods used and questioning whether so-called scientific attitudes are necessarily all they seem. This might appear irrelevant to our subject, until one considers the extent to which such attitudes have influenced our thinking, not only about horses but about animals in general. Part I also considers some areas where 'received wisdom' and unwarranted assumptions have likewise had a detrimental effect on our understanding of animals (and therefore of horses). It amounts almost to a 'cleaning up' of concepts as it attempts to explain how some rather muddled concepts have led to some equally muddled attitudes.

In trying to clear up misconceptions, I may, of course, be guilty of creating a few of my own. I have tried very hard to avoid this; nevertheless, one cannot anticipate every possible interpretation of what one says and it is a risk one has to take. I felt it was necessary to include such explanations, but that it was best to place them in a separate section if the chapters on various aspects of equine thinking and behaviour were not to become impossibly bogged down by digressions into the reason for this or that scientific idea. While this section inevitably deals with attitudes towards all animals, not just horses, I hope the reader who is purely interested in the equine aspect will not jump straight to Part II as understanding of what is contained in Part II depends to some extent on having read Part I. From there, I go on in Part II to see what we can make of equine intelligence, emotions, social organisation, communication and learning; what matters to horses; how they vary as individuals; what we can teach them, and why such education is desirable from their point of view as well as ours.

As horses do not lend themselves to the kind of laboratory experiments so beloved of behavioural scientists, and controlled experiments are difficult to set up under natural conditions without altering the very behaviour being studied (a question considered in Chapter 3), I have, perforce, made much use of anecdotal evidence. Scientific objections to this, and refutations of such objections, are also given in Chapter 3.

Many excellent studies of horse psychology and behaviour have been at pains to point out that the horse cannot be judged by human standards, as he belongs to a totally different species, with different needs and priorities. This is all perfectly true, and it is equally true that many of the problems experienced with horses are the result of a failure to take into account these different needs and priorities. However, we should not take the fear of 'anthropomorphism' to extremes. It is also possible to err in the opposite direction: to insist too completely on the dissimilarity between the two species. The failure to apply what Dr Marthe Kiley-Worthington has called 'conditional anthropomorphism' – i.e. putting oneself in the horse's place, and asking: 'How would I feel in such a situation?' can lead to just as much unintentional misery for the horse as the other extreme.

I wish to try to address this imbalance and, in doing so, I hope to take our understanding of the horse one step further, by trying to comprehend how horses make sense of the world and what they regard as being of importance. I did not want this book to be just another catalogue of equine behaviour, so I have scarcely touched on many aspects which have been more than adequately covered elsewhere. For this reason I have had to assume a certain level of knowledge in my readers concerning the more basic aspects of equine behaviour. This book does not simply reiterate the arguments and conclusions of writers such as Owen MacSwiney, Marthe Kiley-Worthington, Lucy Rees, Henry Blake and others, although my conclusions overlap theirs at many points. Nor – let it be said right now – does it belong in the realm of what is often known as 'animal rights' literature, in spite of what I have written in later chapters about our moral obligations to the horses we keep for what is, after all, our own pleasure. This does not mean that I do not believe animals *have* rights; as it happens I do, at least in the sense that we owe them certain obligations (for a lucid, well-argued and balanced concept of animal rights, see Desmond Morris, *The Animal Contract*). I do believe that most people who maintain and set out a philosophy of animal rights do so out of respect for all forms of life, but all too often they defeat their own aims by employing arguments that are too simplistic, or too extreme, to evoke anything but derision or outright hostility. In addition, such people frequently shoot themselves in the foot by making proposals which, if carried out, would actually result in more, not less, animal suffering. This being said, I have drawn considerably on the work of several proponents of animal rights, in particular that of Bernard Rollin and Mary Midgley, who both avoid extremism and whose writings are a model of sanity and clarity in offering a counter-argument to those who would deny animals any consciousness, feeling or moral status.

Throughout this book I make reference to such concepts as 'classical riding' or 'classical horsemanship' and training. I am often asked for a clarification of these terms – what do such concepts mean? The word 'classical' has several definitions, but I feel the following one is most appropriate to our context: 'characterized by simplicity, balance, regularity and purity of form' (*Collins English Dictionary*); although 'harmony' would perhaps be a better word to use than 'regularity'. Classical riding and training are based on principles laid down in antiquity, which have stood the test of time. This means nothing more or less than the training and riding of horses in accordance with nature; working towards mutual understanding, rather than resorting to force, in helping to restore the horse's natural balance and enhance his paces under saddle. The horse is seen as a friend and partner, rather than – as so often happens – a rather stupid quadruped whose good nature and compliance may be turned to the rider's advantage in order to satisfy his or her ambition. The classical view is not, of course, restricted to those who call themselves 'classical', but the basic tenet of Xenophon's teachings is central to classical ideas: 'For what the horse does under compulsion . . . is done without understanding; and there is no beauty in it either, any more than if one should whip and spur a dancer. There would be a great deal more ungracefulness than beauty in either a horse or a man that was so treated.'[1]

Perhaps the whole ethos of classical riding may be summed up by saying that it is not just about technique. It is, if you like, holistic in its approach. By exploring every aspect of the partnership between horse and rider, it becomes, in effect, a philosophy, a way of life. It is because I feel very strongly that this kind of philosophy is essential if we are to understand horses and work in harmony with them that I have given it such prominence in those chapters which deal with communication, learning and training.

In my researches I have ventured into a number of worlds not usually associated with the training and keeping of horses, and I must ask readers to forgive me if I occasionally digress into the realms of history, philosophy, anthropology and even magic. All of these digressions have a purpose, as I hope to make clear by the end of the book.

I have also drawn on several fictional sources for inspiration. This may sound very unscientific and even rather sloppy until one realises that well-written fiction may sometimes provide just as much insight as scientific study. The great naturalist, and one of the founders of modern ethology, Konrad Lorenz, has this to say:

> Neither Selma Lagerlof's *Nils Holgersson*, nor Rudyard Kipling's *Jungle Books* contain anything like scientific truth about animals. But poets such as the authors of these books may well avail themselves of poetic licence to present the animal in a way far divergent from scientific truth. They may daringly let the animal speak like a human being, they may even ascribe human motives to its actions, and yet succeed in retaining the general style of the wild creature. Surprisingly enough, they convey a true impression of what a wild animal is like, although they are telling fairy tales. In reading those tales, one feels that if an experienced old wild goose or a wise black panther could talk, they would say exactly the things which Selma Lagerlof's Akka or Rudyard Kipling's Bagheera say.[2]

For this reason, I have not hesitated to draw from such books as Richard Adams's delightful novel *Traveller*, the story of the horse ridden by the great Confederate general Robert E. Lee during the American Civil War. It seems to me that the words which Adams, availing himself of the poetic licence referred to by Lorenz, puts into Traveller's mouth, convey a far greater sense of how a horse *would* think and feel than many a scientific treatise.

The Hopi, a native American tribe known as the 'people of peace', maintain that we live in the fourth of seven worlds; this one, like the previous three, will be destroyed by man's wilfulness. 'Only those who keep the tops of their heads open, acknowledging the spiritual forces that guide the processes of life, survive the destruction of each world to populate the next.'[3]

My hope is that what I have written will help us, like the Hopi, to keep the tops of our heads open.

Notes

1 Xenophon, *The Art of Horsemanship* (tr. M. H. Morgan, J. A. Allen, 1962) p. 62
2 Konrad Z. Lorenz, *King Solomon's Ring* (tr. Marjorie Kerr Wilson, Methuen, 1952), Preface, p. XVIII
3 Lucy Rees, *The Maze: from Hell to Hopi* (Bantam Press, 1995), p. 11

PART 1

Received Wisdom and Unwarranted Assumptions

CHAPTER ONE

Cleaning up Concepts

Too many people treat the horse as though he were
a machine, without ever realizing the fantastic world
that is his mind.

DOMINIQUE BARBIER

CAN HORSES THINK? If asked such a question, most horse owners would unhesitatingly reply, 'Of course they can think. How else could they devise so many ingenious ways to avoid work, unfasten doors and gates, and do a host of other things?' Yet so contradictory are our attitudes towards horses that the same horse owners, asked how intelligent horses are, would probably say that they are really not very intelligent at all. After all, if they were, they would never let us on their backs in the first place, let alone do such unnatural things as jumping five-bar gates or any of the other strange things we ask them to do.

Certainly, the views of some very eminent horsemen and women on this subject are uncompromising in the extreme. Elwyn Hartley-Edwards, in *The Encyclopedia of the Horse*, says, 'the horse is a creature of instinct, not of reason, which is a human attribute'[1].

And here is a passage from Jan May's book, *Equus Caballus: On Horses and Handling*:

To understand the horse thoroughly as a prerequisite to handling, one must realise that his brain has no capacity *whatsoever* for reasoning. He cannot, nor will he ever, have the ability for considered thought. His brain is merely a mechanism for guiding him from minute to minute through his world.[2]

According to May, the horse's waking brain functions solely according to stimulus and response, causing him to react appropriately, either to avoid danger or to seek the next blade of grass. If his mind registers a threat, he gallops off; and when he begins to eat, it is because his mind registers this as a pleasant experience worth repeating. In neither case is this a considered action, says May, only a reaction.

Elwyn Hartley-Edwards speaks further of the tendency of so many animal lovers to endow their pets with human qualities. He regards the dog as 'the extreme example of "humanization" being regarded by a large number of owners in the same light as a human child and endowed by them with human intelligence and imagination which it cannot possibly possess'[3]. The horse, he goes on, may not suffer humanisation to the same degree, ' . . . but without doubt he is popularly, and quite wrongly, thought to be an animal of high intelligence'[4].

The above statements were made by people with many years' experience with horses, who have earned a great deal of respect in the sphere of equestrianism, so one might expect their judgement to be reliable in this matter. But is this really all there is to a horse's brain? The experiences of a great many other horsemen and women, myself included, would suggest not.

Our horse literature abounds in instructional manuals offering advice on how to deal with problems in horses; and while some of these do acknowledge that horses may be able to think in a limited kind of way, many others deny vigorously that the horse can think at all, insisting that his brain is merely a mechanism and that he generally acts from blind instinct. The fact that so many equestrian trainers maintain this, in spite of evidence to the contrary (and often in spite of the contradictions inherent in their own treatment of horses), shows how pervasive this idea has become. If it were true, however, then it would be impossible to have any kind of meaningful relationship with our horses as one cannot have such a relationship with a machine (although some auto-enthusiasts would maintain that *they* do come close to having one). I can talk to my wordprocessor (and frequently do): I can coax and cajole it (when it is playing up); I can threaten and abuse it. Those who watched the TV comedy series *Fawlty Towers* will recall the glorious, hysterical moment when John Cleese, as Basil Fawlty, leaps out of his stalled car and thrashes it, yelling at it incoherently. But nothing I do to my wordprocessor will produce any response other than a purely mechanical one – garbage in, garbage out, as the computer people say.

Yet horses are clearly not like that. As every rider since the dawn of equitation knows, horses do have minds of their own. They have strong likes and dislikes, definite ideas about the way certain things should be done, and they frequently override their supposedly all-powerful instincts in situations that seem meaningful enough to them. Yet the mechanical approach denies the horse any ability to think, hope, love – indeed, to do anything other than respond to purely physical stimuli, fear or the lack of a stimulus for fear.

Whenever I am faced by assertions regarding the supposed inability of dogs, horses, etc. to think, I immediately want to ask, 'Why?'. What knowledge do we possess that enables us to state categorically that animals such as dogs and cats 'cannot possibly' possess certain qualities? As no one can enter into another creature's mind, we cannot know for certain what resides there. And as they do not have a spoken language (a matter of crucial importance, to which we shall return in later chapters), we cannot ask a dog or a horse direct questions that would verify or disprove theories about animal intelligence. We must perforce rely on more or less scientific observation; and as we shall see, 'scientific objectivity' is something of an illusion.

As Owen MacSwiney says, 'It is convenient to believe that the animals do not think at all, because a non-thinking entity makes no demands upon our conscience. It is too easy a way out'.[5] And as the very distinguished ethologist Dr Marthe Kiley-Worthington points out, there is really no scientific evidence to suggest that animals' brains do not work in essentially the same way as ours. But if this is so, how did there come to be such an insistence that animals generally 'cannot possibly' possess certain qualities such as intelligence, reasoning ability, the capacity for abstract thought, etc.?

A creature of instinct or of reason? Filly foal Imzadi takes her first steps, supervised by mother Kiri and watched by father Nivalis (right). Are they thinking about their relationship with her, or is their behaviour, as some insist, purely instinctive?

One of the main difficulties in exploring animal minds adequately has been a widespread reluctance on the part of biologists and behavioural psychologists to admit that mental processes play any part in determining behaviour, whether human or animal. This has led to some extraordinarily contorted thinking on the whole subject of animal behaviour, as the scientists involved try desperately to avoid charges of anthropomorphism.

This, I hold, is largely because not only they, but humans in general, have been at such pains to separate humans and other animals (for we forget, at our peril, that we *are* animals), to deny that we have anything in common, apart from some strange, superstitious notion of 'beastliness' (as when we say of a violent criminal: 'He behaved like an *animal*' – regardless of the fact that very few of the other social animals do behave like violent criminals). We have, in effect, become like aliens in our own world; and this has severely hampered and limited our understanding.

This is by no means simply a twentieth-century phenomenon. The thinking of people in general (in Western culture at least) about such matters as whether animals are intelligent and whether they have emotions, hopes, desires, etc. has been ambiguous for thousands of years. There is a popular belief that the Judaeo-Christian religion is largely responsible for teaching that animals cannot have souls, and that they are set on earth for people's use and pleasure; but this is only partly true. The Greek general, historian and philosopher Xenophon, writing in the fifth century BC, was in no doubt at all that the horse, at any rate, was capable of both thought and emotion. However, his compatriot, the philosopher Aristotle, believed that there was a 'natural order of things', and that plants were made for the good of animals and animals for the good of man (women came somewhere in between man and animals). He excluded animals from a life of reason; all things in nature had a purpose, and the sole purpose of animals was to serve man.

In the early Christian era, by contrast, there was no real tendency to separate the human race from the animal kingdom. Indeed, early theologians, such as St Maximus, St Irenaeus, St Ambrosius, St John Chrysostom, etc., stressed the unity of all creation, and said that animals were as much a part of that creation as man and therefore merited consideration and respect. The thirteenth century saw a shift in attitude, with the adoption of the animistic philosophy of the 'Angelic Doctor', Thomas Aquinas. This philosophy, a blend of the thinking of Aristotle with Christian theology, pervaded the teachings of the great medieval universities. Aquinas taught that animals were irrational, possessing no mind or reason, that they existed to serve man by divine providence, and that they therefore had no moral claims on humankind. This view of the status of animals has persisted to this day in the bulk of Christian (certainly Roman Catholic) teaching, although some Christians have put forward a very solid theological argument for granting animals a moral status.

However, Aquinas did not condone senseless cruelty to animals, nor did he insist, as later thinkers would, that animals were mere automata. In his philosophy, following Aristotle, it was taken for granted that all nature was alive, and that all living things had souls, even if only man's was immortal. But later changes in philosophical thought, during the Renaissance in the fifteenth and sixteenth centuries and the great scientific revolution of the seventeenth century, brought about a different attitude to nature. The French mathematician and philosopher René Descartes propounded a purely mechanistic view of the universe. All nature operated mechanically: everything – including the human body – was inanimate, except for the human mind, which was entirely separate from the body. Only human beings had conscious minds and conscious purposes.

As, in Descartes's view, animals were inanimate, mere machines, people had no moral obligation to them. Implicit in this idea was man's right to exploit 'the brute creation'. Some Cartesian disciples even specifically denied that animals could feel pain: if we beat a dog, they said, its cries no more prove that it feels pain than the sound of an organ proves that it feels pain when its keys are struck. Indeed, even today there are a number of moral philosophers who expend a great deal of effort in attempting to 'prove' that animals, not being conscious beings, do not merit our sympathy when they suffer pain, because they are not actually conscious of their pain!

Such notions were not allowed to go unchallenged; one of Descartes's most incisive critics was the great French writer Voltaire. 'Answer me, you who believe that animals are only machines,' he wrote. 'Has nature arranged for this animal to have all the machinery of feelings only in order for it not to have any at all?'[6] In *Le Philosophe Ignorant*, Voltaire again attacks Descartes because he:

> . . . dared to say that animals are pure machines who looked for food when they had no appetite, who had the organs for feeling only never to have the slightest feeling, who screamed without pain, who showed their pleasure without joy, who possessed a brain only to have in it not even the slightest idea, and who were in this way a perpetual contradiction of nature.[7]

– and the Cartesian view of animals has been challenged from that day to this. There have always been people who believed that animals did think, were capable of experiencing emotions, and that they had needs of their own. Great scientists and thinkers, such as Isaac Newton and the philosopher John Locke, also believed that animals shared the same capacity for feeling as humans, while 300 years ago John Ray wrote:

> It is a general received opinion, that all this visible world was created for Man; that Man is the End of Creation; as if there were no other end of any creature, but some way or another to be serviceable to man . . . But though this be vulgarly received, yet wise men now-a-days think otherwise. Dr Moore affirms, that creatures are made to enjoy themselves as well as to serve us.[8]

Indeed it was, paradoxically, the classical humanism of the seventeenth century that made possible the great flowering of classical horsemanship. In the introduction to her translation of Pluvinel's *Maneige Royal*, Professor Hilda Nelson says, 'As man became more aware of his own dignity and grandeur, so too, did he begin to look at other creatures as having emotions, being capable of pain and pleasure and, even if "devoid of a soul", at least having the ability to learn and remember.'[9]

The evolutionary theories that came out of the eighteenth and nineteenth centuries served only to emphasise the points made by Voltaire and others. Once the evolutionary continuity between humans and non-human animals had been established, it might have seemed impossible for anyone to deny that animals and humans had a similar, although not necessarily identical, capacity for thoughts and feelings. Charles Darwin never doubted this. His book *The Expression of the Emotions in Man and Animals* is still a fascinating study of the subject, while in *The Descent of Man* Darwin specifically states that 'there is no fundamental difference between man and the higher animals in their mental faculties'[10]. As scientist and philosopher Dr Bernard Rollin points out in his brilliant study of animal consciousness, *The Unheeded Cry: Animal Consciousness, Animal Pain and Science*, 'Evolutionary theory demands that psychology, like anatomy, be comparative, for life is incremental, and mind did not arise *de novo* in man, fully formed like Athena from the head of Zeus.'[11] As we shall see in Chapter 2, however, belief in this evolutionary continuity was later largely wiped out, not as a result of new scientific findings, but because of radical changes in scientific thought. For the greater part of the twentieth century animals have been regarded as almost purely biological phenomena, without thoughts, without emotions – and, in the thinking of many scientists and some philosophers, even without consciousness.

More recently, tentative recognition has been made in some quarters that animals in general are not only conscious but that many have complex emotional lives, and that a number of species (including horses) may have some understanding of abstract concepts. An increasing number of scientists (generally known as 'cognitive ethologists') have challenged the 'mechanistic' view of animals and produced some very compelling evidence in support of their ideas. Notable among them have

The classical humanism of the seventeenth century made possible the great flowering of classical horsemanship: M. de Pluvinel instructs the young King Louis XIII of France (from an engraving by Crispian de Pas, in Pluvinel's *Le Maneige Royal)*

been Donald R. Griffin in the USA and Dr Marthe Kiley-Worthington in Britain. However, comparatively little work has been done with horses in a domestic setting, and while much excellent work has been done in studying their behaviour in the wild, relatively little time has been devoted to finding out what, if anything, might actually be going on in their heads. Certainly, in the 1980s and 1990s a number of distinguished authors, such as Dr Kiley-Worthington, Lucy Rees and the late Marquis of Mashanaglass, Owen MacSwiney, have published some extremely good work on horse behaviour and psychology; while the Equine Behaviour Forum (under the aegis of Susan McBane) has done sterling work in compiling an impressive body of case histories. The work of Monty Roberts has also attracted much attention, as have the activities of a number of 'alternative' therapists, such as Linda Tellington-Jones, who advocate a much more empathetic approach than current equestrian orthodoxy generally encourages.

In spite of this, however, there is still a great deal of confusion among trainers, horse owners and horse lovers in general about horse intelligence, how horses learn and what is actually of importance to them. There is also, regrettably, too much reliance on 'received wisdom'. Explanations for equine behaviour are frequently put forward which are only tenable if one starts from certain basic assumptions which may or may not be correct, and too often these assumptions have gone unchallenged.

One might think that the huge advances in scientific knowledge made in the second half of the twentieth century would have led to a correspondingly large increase in our understanding of the equine mind. Indeed, some writers have gone so far as to assert that it is only with our modern scientific knowledge that we can hope to understand the horse. One such writer is Stephen Budiansky, who says, in *The Nature of Horses*, 'I would argue that at this late date in the shared history of man and horse it is *only* the objective tools of science that can sort out what millenniums of tradition, lore and wishful thinking have sometimes muddled'[12].

I disagree. Science (under which vague term I suppose one could group the whole paraphernalia of scientific research and scientific thought) can only give us information; it cannot tell us what to do with it. Sophisticated present-day veterinary medicine and the wonders of modern technology have certainly vastly improved our knowledge of the horse's physiological make-up, but what has science done for his mind? It is certainly true that scientific observation has helped to clarify many mysteries of equine behaviour (although in many cases they were only mysteries to those who had never taken the trouble to empathise with horses and find out what mattered to them) but, in the process, science has also smuggled in a great deal of its own contraband in the form of dogma based on received ideas. Scientific attitudes have served to obscure issues just as often as they have illuminated them but this has gone undetected because, in the popular view (and in the view of a great many scientists), science is 'objective'. As we shall see, however, scientists are just as prone to making false assumptions as the rest of us and once these have gained legitimate status they are remarkably hard to shift.

Humans have certainly been guilty of projecting a great many human hopes, desires and prejudices onto their perceptions about horses. But we do this about people as well: parents want their children to be bright, successful, charming, etc., and frequently face disappointment when their offspring fail to live up to their expectations. We want our friends to be loyal, and are devastated when they betray our trust. However, no sensible person would argue that, because of this, people are not *capable* of being bright, successful, charming, loyal (or whatever). While horses may not partake of all our thoughts, feelings, hopes and desires, as mammals we do share a great deal of our evolutionary heritage with them. They do not exist in some kind of blank, passive state, controlled solely by hard-wired instincts, waiting for events to happen and then reacting to them. They think, feel, make choices and act upon them. And while we may sometimes have been wrong in attributing certain thoughts and feelings to them (just as I may be wrong in attributing certain thoughts and feelings to someone I don't know all that well), this does not mean we have *always* been wrong in this respect. One of the reasons why horses have been so easy to domesticate is precisely because we feel intuitively that we have so much in common with them and that this makes communication possible, although certainly not always easy.

Horsemasters throughout the ages have undoubtedly been erroneous in many of their beliefs concerning the horse's mind, but one must ask, 'Are these errors any greater or more extensive than those committed by scientific thought?' Great horsemen, from Xenophon to Pluvinel, from la Guérinière to Steinbrecht, and so on right up to a handful of modern masters such as Nuno Oliveira, have managed to train horses to levels of performance seen nowadays only in places like the Spanish Riding School in Vienna. They were able to do this, not because of 'scientific knowledge' (other than their knowledge of the principles of equine movement and of training, handed down to them through generations and enhanced by their own genius), but because of their empathy with, and understanding of, the horse and what matters to him. Even Budiansky, committed as he is to the 'scientific' approach (whatever that might be) feels compelled to admit that: 'Successful training and schooling of a horse in any event has always relied as much on intuition, experience, and unconsciously honed instinct as on anything that science . . . can teach us.'[13]

Yet, as we shall see, the orthodox scientific approach rejects much of what the great masters believed about horses. In doing so it condemns itself to a straitjacket from which it is difficult to struggle free. How many scientists have trained horses to the levels achieved by masters such as la Guérinière or Nuno Oliveira? How many have even tried? American trainer Vicki Hearne says that, in her experience,

> . . . in obedience and riding classes, people with training in the behavioral sciences hadn't much chance of succeeding with their animals . . . the psychologists and philosophers had to bring their animals to me because they couldn't housebreak them, induce them to leave off chewing up the children or, in the case of horses, get them to cross the shadow of a pole on the ground.[14]

It is true that, in this respect, things have improved somewhat since behavioural scientists have largely abandoned their commitment to the stricter forms of behaviourism (discussed in the next chapter) but one must still ask why, if the scientific approach is the only valid one, so few scientists have actually achieved very much with the training of horses (one notable exception being Dr Kiley-Worthington who has trained not only horses but numerous other species with great success)? It can surely only be because they have either not felt it worthwhile to try, or (like the psychologists and behaviourists referred to above), they have overlooked some vital elements in their attempts at training, the most essential of these being the actual nature of the mind belonging to the creature they were dealing with.

In *The Nature of Horses*, Stephen Budiansky says that:

> Animal trainers – the successful ones, at least – have an intuitive sense, honed from long experience, of what makes an animal respond. The unabashedly anthropomorphic terms and concepts that nearly all good trainers use are not strictly speaking 'wrong'. They offer a way of thinking about an animal's motivation and behaviour that makes intuitive sense to us, and more important, that works in practice.[15]

Yet the unwritten implication here seems to be that, in some fundamental way, such talk *is* wrong, that it is only excusable because it serves a useful function (note that the author does not offer any explanation as to why the terms and concepts to which he refers are 'anthropomorphic'). If it is so difficult to train horses to a high level (or in some cases, at all) *without* talking and behaving as if they were capable of thinking certain thoughts and feeling certain emotions (and therefore taking these into account during the training), then one surely has to ask, 'Is this not because horses really do have such thoughts and emotions – or, at the very least, something so like them that any difference is not worth quibbling about?'

Writing about some of the assumptions made by scientists about the horse's mind, Dr Kiley-Worthington says,

> The 'scientist' will be trained not to think about whether or not the equine is able to do complex mental athletics, and is similar to humans. He already *knows* that equines do not have language, do not think, do not have self-awareness, and consciousness of themselves. The questions are not asked.[16]

It is perhaps noteworthy that many people with a scientific background have tried to deny the relevance of the kind of High School work with horses that the masters referred to in this chapter excelled in. This work has often been dismissed as an anachronism, a relic of the days when people held anthropomorphic concepts about 'noble' horses (the implication being, of course, that we now know better). How odd that those who are so ready to dismiss the work of true masters should, with all their scientific knowledge, fail to understand that such work is, above all, therapeutic for the horse (in restoring his equilibrium and strengthening him for his task of carrying a rider), and that the High School is merely the culmination of this work, not its sole aim. One cannot avoid the suspicion that it is their own lack of understanding of how such results may be achieved that leads to such disapproval. It is always easier to condemn what one does not understand than admit one's own perception is at fault.

As the next chapter will show, scientists are just as prone to jumping to what may be unwarranted conclusions (and often with less justification) as lay persons, but because of the commonly held perception of scientific thought being 'objective' and somehow above such foibles, this is rarely acknowledged.

The media revolution of the last few decades has brought undoubted benefits but one of

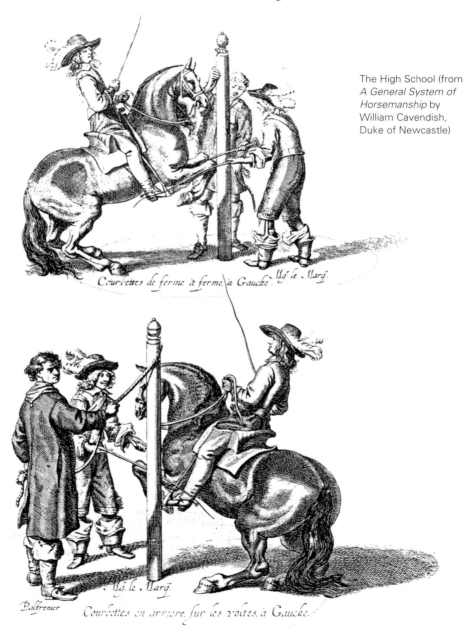

The High School (from *A General System of Horsemanship* by William Cavendish, Duke of Newcastle)

its less desirable side-effects has been to deprive people, by and large, of the ability to think for themselves. Increasingly, the popular press, television and such worldwide communication systems as the Internet feed us with prepackaged concepts in easily digestible chunks. These concepts are then accepted without question by millions of people, whereupon they become 'received wisdom'. Occasionally, lone voices are raised against this 'received wisdom'. These people are either elevated to the status of prophets, so that, in turn, their utterances become 'received wisdom', or else they are greeted with scorn and derision and soon are heard no more. Whatever receives wide coverage by the mass media becomes acceptable, regardless of its true merit, and questioning voices seldom get a hearing unless they are accompanied by a great deal of influence in the right places.

As far as popular literature dealing with equine behaviour is concerned, at the time of writing two main trends are emerging, which appear to be heading in opposite directions. At first sight this may seem to represent nothing more than a clash between partisans, as philosopher Mary Midgley puts it, 'of science and sympathy'[17]. That these different ways of thought need not be on opposing sides will, I hope, become evident by the end of this book. However, too often they are depicted as being so by people who have dug themselves into certain positions. One of these positions is often occupied by a particular type of popular journalist who may not be a specialist in equestrian matters but who writes about horses with an air of authority which tends to ensure they are taken notice of. These writers tend to adopt what is often called a no-nonsense approach to matters equestrian. They have little time for the enlightened academic approach to training and riding horses exemplified by, for example, Alois Podhajsky, even though they may have little knowledge or understanding of the principles involved. They have even less time for the empathic approach of people like Sylvia Loch and Lucy Rees, which they see as soft and sentimental. They are committed to what they see as 'scientific' views on evolution, relying heavily on the kind of uncritical acceptance of sociobiological explanations referred to in the introduction. The crime of 'anthropomorphism' is often mentioned by these writers. They also refer a great deal to 'dominance' and 'pecking orders', emphasising the aggressive and competitive side of the equine nature rather than the co-operative side. According to this way of thinking, horses respond only to threats, albeit mild ones; while the use of force is not openly advocated, the assumption is that sooner or later it will have to be employed.

The other main trend is exemplified by writers who may also be trainers or specialists in particular types of equine problem (whether physical or mental), and who adopt a more empathic attitude. While not precisely rejecting the 'scientific' approach, they tend to ignore it or play down its importance, relying instead on knowledge gained by personal experience and an intuitive understanding of the horse's needs. Unfortunately, in the process, they – or their adherents – may start to reduce this understanding to a type of dogma which stifles independent thought.

A third, less obtrusive position, which is adopted by more conventional equestrian writers, stands somewhere between these two extremes. These writers try to combine science with what they believe to be a sympathetic approach to training and behavioural problems, but, because they too often rely on 'received wisdom' and assumptions which may not be founded in fact, their good intentions frequently result in more, not less, confusion.

To some extent, these examples may represent the extremes of each viewpoint but the trends are very real and the hapless horse lover who seeks greater understanding may well feel that they have to choose among the different approaches. But as Mary Midgley says,

> Role-playing of this kind paralyzes our thinking because it makes thought seem unnecessary; the positions are ready-made for us. Once they have imagined themselves to be tough-minded, people are quite liable to accept the loosest and most vacuous ideas uncritically, provided they are put forward in the right contemptuous tone of voice, while those who have cast themselves as tender-minded sometimes accept very brutal suggestions, provided that they sound familiar and traditional.[18]

This tendency to rely on ready-made positions and on 'received wisdom' – whether of the long-standing kind or of the type laid down by the 'prophets' referred to above – and simply to copy what others have written without thinking it out for oneself, is to some extent understandable as not all writers have either the time or the means to undertake original research. None of us can be experts in every aspect of our chosen field of study. We all have to rely to a greater or lesser extent on the work of others and, where this lies in a field of expertise other than our own, to hope that the experts on whose writings one is relying have got it right. None the less, I believe it behoves all of us to question, constantly, such knowledge as comes our way. The evidence may be there: does it support the findings? Do the conclusions drawn necessarily follow from the facts presented? We may not all be able to do original research, but we do not have to be parrots. We all have the faculties for questioning.

In the end, I believe the only way to understand what may be going on in horses' minds is not to make arbitrary assumptions about what they *can't* think or feel but to look at what they actually *do*. As Jeffrey Masson and Susan McCarthy observe in their study of animal emotions, *When Elephants Weep*: 'Scientific humility tells us that we will probably never understand other animals completely. But if we do not begin by insisting that we already know what characteristics they do not have, we will understand a lot more.'[19]

Notes

1 Elwyn Hartley-Edwards, *The Encyclopedia of the Horse* (Octopus, 1977), p. 176

2 Jan May, *Equus Caballus: On Horses and Handling* (J. A. Allen, 1995), pp. 4–5

3 Hartley-Edwards, *Encyclopedia of the Horse*, p.176

4 Hartley-Edwards, *Encyclopedia of the Horse*, p.176

5 The Marquis MacSwiney of Mashanaglass, *Training from the Ground* (J. A. Allen, 1987), p. 47

6 Voltaire, F.A. de (J. Masson's translation), quoted by Jeffrey Masson and Susan McCarthy, *When Elephants Weep: The Emotional Lives of Animals* (first published by Jonathan Cape, 1994; vintage ed., 1996), pp. 33–4

7 Voltaire, (J. Masson's translation), quoted by Masson and McCarthy, *When Elephants Weep*, p. 34

8 John Ray, c. 1690, quoted by Lucy Rees, *The Horse's Mind* (first published by Stanley Paul, 1984; paperback ed., 1993), introduction

9 Dr Hilda Nelson, Introduction to *The Maneige Royal* by Antoine de Pluvinel (J. A. Allen, 1989), p. XIV

10 Charles Darwin, *The Descent of Man and Selection in Relation to Sex*, 1871, p. 448

11 Bernard Rollin, *The Unheeded Cry: Animal Consciousness, Animal Pain and Science* (OUP, 1990), p. 33

12 Stephen Budiansky, *The Nature of Horses* (Weidenfeld and Nicholson, 1997), p. 2

13 Budiansky, *The Nature of Horses*, p. 7

14 Vicki Hearne, *Adam's Task: Calling Animals by Name* (Heinemann, 1987), p. 43

15 Budiansky, *The Nature of Horses*, p. 79

16 Dr Marthe Kiley-Worthington, *Equine Welfare* (J. A. Allen, 1997), p. 82

17 Mary Midgley, *Beast and Man* (rev. ed., Routledge, 1995), p. 122

18 Midgley, *Beast and Man*, p. 122

19 Masson and McCarthy, *When Elephants Weep*, p. 214

CHAPTER TWO

The Appliance of Science

Nothing is more misleading than an
unchallenged false assumption.

DESMOND KING-HELE

WE LIVE IN A WORLD that is dominated by science. All around us are the products of modern technology: our food, our clothing, our houses, our modes of transport, our means of production, our recreation, even the water we drink and the air we breathe are affected by our technological know-how. There is, as a result, a tendency to forget that science and technology are not necessarily the same thing; that science is not all-powerful, that scientists are but human, and that scientific method is not infallible. Scientists themselves are apt to forget such truths and to persuade themselves that their pursuit of knowledge is pure and objective and that true knowledge can only be obtained by means of rigorous scientific method (whatever that might be).

Inevitably, perhaps, this view has meant that ordinary, everyday common sense – the wisdom distilled from personal experience – has tended to be ignored by science. After all, as scientist and philosopher Bernard Rollin points out in his book, *The Unheeded Cry*, some of the most basic common-sense views have been demolished by scientific discovery. Common sense says that the earth cannot possibly be a sphere, otherwise we should all fall off. Not so, says science: gravity is what keeps us anchored firmly to the earth. *Of course*, a stone dropped from a tower falls faster than a feather, says common sense: a stone is heavier than a feather. Not so, says science: it is the air resistance which makes the difference, not the weight of the stone. Clearly, if we had blindly followed the dictates of common sense, much valuable scientific discovery would have been rejected and we should still be sitting in caves. On the other hand, this does not mean that all common sense should be rejected. Science often deals with abstracts that have very little bearing on everyday life, and as Professor Rollin points out, we must never rely upon either abstract thought or common sense alone. 'Abstract reason and common sense must perennially engage each other in dialogue, and check each other's excesses.'[1] If we discard ordinary common sense, we reject the practical wisdom of the human race, which has withstood the test of time.

It is inevitable that scientists should, to some extent, separate theory from common sense, otherwise they would too often find themselves trying to reconcile incompatible ideas. But as Rollin says,

> What is pernicious is complete, systematic separation of theory, in philosophy *or* science, from common sense, as if they were two hats, so that when one wears one hat, one feels it necessary to totally disregard the other . . . Yet the desirability of such compartmentalization is a major theme in the ideology of modern science, at least in so far as science is an institutionalized social phenomenon.[2]

As a scientist, Rollin explains, one learns that values and common sense must be banished, for:

> They are epiphenomena, shadows, secondary qualities, as the data of the senses were to Lockean Newtonians in the eighteenth century. But when they are banished, there is nothing to check the excesses of scientism. If it violates common sense and ordinary sensibility for the physician to regard the human person as a biomechanical machine, then so much the worse for common sense – and, all too often, for the common man.[3]

And so much the worse for those unfortunate animals who have endured physical and mental torture in the course of experiments at the hands of scientists whose scientific training caused them to deny what their common sense told them – that the animals were suffering appallingly.

Of course, as we have seen, much that has been discovered by science does go against ordinary common sense. However, as Rollin points out, 'It is a very small step from noting the undeniable fact that much good science violates common sense to unconsciously making the less defensible claim that all good science must or ought to do so, or that such violation is the very essence of science.'[4]

This denial of the value of common sense has led to a number of scientific studies being carried out to 'prove' all manner of things that we all knew anyway – take, for example, the earth-shattering discovery that one's moods may be identified by one's facial expressions. I imagine that our most primitive ancestors all knew and made use of this knowledge; did it really require the time and expense of a 'scientific investigation' (which presumably received funding of some kind) to 'prove' it? As Bernard Rollin says,

> . . . in becoming a scientist, too often one must forswear what has not been arrived at by

the 'scientific method' (whatever that may be), and commit oneself totally to the pursuit of 'objectivity' (whatever that may be), which is generally construed as leaving no place for the accumulated wisdom of common sense unless it happens to have been transmuted into legitimate scientific knowledge by experiment or jargon.[5]

One of the problems that this causes for people like myself, who study animals (in my case, of course, horses), is that our observations and the conclusions we draw from them are likely to be dismissed as mere 'anecdotal evidence' and therefore not worthy of serious consideration. Jane Goodall, well known for her pioneering work in observing chimpanzees in their natural habitat at Gombe in Tanzania, tells how on one occasion she described to a group of ethologists how one of the chimpanzees had learned, as an adolescent, to stay behind in camp after the senior males had left, so that Goodall and her assistants could give him a few bananas for himself. She told how, in the beginning, Figan had given the game away to the older males by making loud, delighted food calls, but, on later occasions, after this had resulted in his bananas being taken from him, Figan learned to suppress his expressions of delight in order to enjoy his bananas in peace. Goodall had expected her audience to be as fascinated and impressed as she was. She had hoped for an exchange of views about Figan's undoubted intelligence. 'Instead,' she says, 'there was a chill silence, after which the chairman hastily changed the subject . . . Looking back, I suspect that everyone was interested, but it was, of course, not permissible to present a mere "anecdote" as evidence for anything.'[6]

It is true that there has, in recent years, been some modification of this view and certainly some organisations, such as the Equine Behaviour Study Circle (now known as the Equine Behaviour Forum – see Appendix III) have always welcomed anecdotal evidence from their members. The fact remains, however, that if one wants to be taken seriously in academic circles, one has to conform, unless one has a reputation so secure that any deviation may be regarded as mere eccentricity rather than a cause for outright dismissal of one's findings.

But how scientific is the rejection of anecdotal evidence? One of the principal pioneers in the systematic collection of such evidence, whose work is frequently cited as an example of how *not* to conduct an enquiry into animal mentality, is George Romanes, a contemporary of Darwin. Following Darwin, and making use of much of the latter's material (which he duly acknowledged), Romanes emphasised the evolutionary continuity of mental life. Like Darwin, he never doubted that animals have thoughts and feelings, but his work has been largely forgotten today, discredited by the scientific establishment. What caused this move away from the idea of evolutionary continuity of mind? What new evidence made science discard the work of Darwin and Romanes and insist upon the neo-Cartesian denial of animal thoughts and feelings that has persisted to this day?

When Bernard Rollin set out to examine this question, he was surprised to find no such evidence. What he did find was that:

. . . the evolutionary approach to animal consciousness had not been refuted empirically or logically, but rather, that it had been swept out of fashion by a confluence of factors, more rhetorical than logical, more sociological than empirical, more philosophical and valuational than scientific.[7]

In *The Unheeded Cry* Rollin discusses the philosophical and valuational bases for scientific change – in this case change which depends not upon some new discovery or evidence, but on what appear to be changes of fashion in thinking. These had to do with social and political upheavals as much as anything (indeed, we shall see in Chapter 3 that the current fashion for 'genetic determinism' – including the idea of the 'selfish gene' – has more to do with modes of thought currently fashionable in certain circles than it has to do with evolutionary truth).

Because, in spite of what scientists tell us, science is based upon philosophy, it is just as susceptible to changes in fashion as philosophical thought. So, at the beginning of the twentieth century, with these changes came the rise of behaviourism, with its rejection of the notion of consciousness. We cannot study mind, said the behaviourists, we can only study behaviour. And the only acceptable way to study behaviour was through rigorously controlled experiment. Behaviourists such as Watson and Skinner saw all behaviour as a matter of stimulus and response, of conditioning. Most 'conditioning' theory was based on the 'Skinner box', where rats, pigeons or other small animals could be taught that pressing a lever resulted in a pellet of food. The rats or pigeons (or whatever) were then taught to press the lever only in response to certain stimuli, such as a buzzer, or to avoid an electric shock, or both; there were any number of ingenious variations. The results were then applied indiscriminately to almost any species, including humans.

B. F. Skinner

It rarely seemed to occur to the scientists involved that this showed an insufficient respect for the differing characters of the various species, never mind of the individuals within such species. Nor did they appear to recognise that their findings, based on the results of carefully controlled experiments in highly artificial surroundings that no animal would naturally inhabit, might not reflect the animal's true behaviour or its capacity to learn. I do not think the equivalent – incarcerating human beings in small cells and rewarding them with food when they pressed the right lever, or subjecting them to varying degrees of torture if they did not – would tell us very much about human behaviour except that in extreme situations humans will do whatever they have to in order to survive and avoid pain.

One example of the absurdities which resulted from this was Skinner's attempt to explain children's acquisition of language as being a result of simple conditioning. The great linguist

Noam Chomsky poured scorn on this view, but as Bernard Rollin points out, even before this:

… anyone who ever raised a child knew that one cannot reinforce a child into speaking, that children speak when they are good and ready, and no amount of lollipops or spankings will affect this one way or the other. Yet so powerful is scientific ideology that it has no qualms about ignoring common experience. After all, say scientists, Newton and Einstein refuted common sense and common experience. Yes, one might reply, but there is only one Newton and one Einstein.[8]

(For a fuller discussion of the absurdities of pure behaviourism, see Mary Midgley, *Beast and Man*, and Bernard Rollin, *The Unheeded Cry* – two eminently sane and rational discussions about a difficult subject.)

The old-style 'strict behaviourism' may have faded away, but behaviourism in a milder form still flourishes, having found a rather uneasy bedfellow in the shape of sociobiology – the study of animal and human behaviour in relation to its survival value and evolutionary origins. Sociobiology has produced many insights into otherwise puzzling behaviour (although there are many fundamental weaknesses in the arguments put forward by the founder of modern sociobiology, E. O. Wilson, and his most devoted adherents; for a discussion of these, see Mary Midgley, *Beast and Man*, Stephen Jay Gould, *An Urchin in the Storm*, and Steven Rose, *Lifelines: Biology, Freedom, Determinism*). Given that the earlier proponents of behaviourism denied strenuously that behaviour could have any genetic origins, this might seem a rather odd situation, especially as some extreme supporters of the sociobiological viewpoint have equally strenuously maintained that all behaviour is genetically determined, even where it might appear to be learned or voluntary. However, many 'animal behaviourists' have shown that it *is* possible to steer a middle course between the two extreme positions. Both behaviourism and sociobiology have something of value to tell us about animal behaviour, *provided* one is not seduced into thinking that all behaviour is determined either by 'conditioning' or by evolutionary pressures, or that – if we accept that both play a role, as we surely must – we may quantify such influences by assigning percentages to them (such as 'temperament is X per cent heritable', or whatever). The whole issue is far too complex to be determined by some simple-minded 'nature *v* nurture' debate. Unfortunately behaviourism and sociobiological theory are often used as convenient pegs on which to hang difficult aspects of animal behaviour. Adherents of these views thus avoid having to think seriously about animal (and human) motivation.

What then shall we say about the arch-villain here, George Romanes, whose work is usually dismissed in standard works about animal behaviour as being hopelessly naïve, sentimental and anthropomorphic, a mere collection of anecdotes utterly lacking in scientific method? One can only assume that, for the most part, these critics have not actually read Romanes's work, but have simply repeated earlier criticisms. For when we read what Romanes himself has to say, we can see that he was working, not as a mere anecdote-monger, but as a serious scientist who approached his subject critically and methodically. This, indeed, was how people such as Darwin saw him; the latter respected and admired Romanes's work, as did many other prominent scientists of the day. So what was the basis of Romanes's method? Let the man himself tell us:

> First, never to accept an alleged fact without the authority of some name. Second, in the case of the name being unknown, and the alleged fact of sufficient importance to be entertained, carefully to consider whether, from the circumstances of the case as recorded, there was any considerable opportunity for malobservation; this principle generally demanded that the alleged fact, or action on the part of the animal should be of a particularly marked and unmistakable kind, looking to the end which the action is said to have accomplished. Third, to tabulate all important observations recorded by unknown observers, with the view of ascertaining whether they have ever been corroborated by similar or analogous observations made by other and independent observers. This principle I have found to be of great use in guiding my selection of instances, for where statements of fact which present nothing intrinsically improbable are found to be unconsciously confirmed by different observers, they have as good a right to be deemed trustworthy as statements which stand on the single authority of a known observer, and I have found the former to be at least as abundant as the latter. Moreover, by getting into the habit of always seeking for corroborative cases I have frequently been able to substantiate the assertions of known observers by those of other observers as well or better known.[9]

Bernard Rollin asks,

> Is Romanes's anecdote-sifting scientifically invalid? Does it require that we weaken and suspend ordinary canons of proof? Quite the contrary. What Romanes recommends that we do with the vast hodgepodge of data relevant to animal mentation is to apply to it the same sort of reasoning which we employ when we reconstruct historical events, write biographies, assess people's motives, their guilt and innocence in trials, defend ourselves against accusations, make judgements about people of whom we hear conflicting stories, and so on. In all these cases, what we do is to measure data against standard rules or canons of evidence and plausibility.[10]

This is precisely what Romanes did, and what I have done when using anecdotal material in this book.

However, this involves making use, not only of one's own observations, but of data provided by people who work closely with the animals concerned. This raises yet another bugbear – objectivity.

The objectivity of those who study animal behaviour in close proximity to their subjects is also often brought into question. The criticism of having lost objectivity by becoming too close to the animals they study has been levelled (unfairly) at people such as Wolfgang

Horses lead rich and complex social lives; only a fraction of the truth about them can be revealed in controlled experiments

Köhler and Jane Goodall, whose studies of apes have led to a much greater understanding of primate society. However, as Mary Midgley makes clear in her refreshingly sane essay on the roots of human nature (*Beast and Man*), it was the fact that people like Köhler and Goodall were so close to their subjects – were sufficiently *interested* in them – that the complexity and richness of apes' behaviour and social lives could be allowed to unfold. Such complexity, says Midgley:

> . . . will not emerge simply from isolated experiments, because it is a structural character-istic. People determined to 'explain animal behavior' on some simple scheme will always be able to find their own way of accounting for any isolated performance, however impressive, as mechanical, imitative, coincidental, or whatever. But this is vacuous, since 'explaining behavior' *must* refer to structural principles, therefore to long stretches of it and many partial parallels. It *is* relating it to a context.[11]

Because these creatures *are* complex, says Midgley, 'only a tiny fraction of the important truths about them can ever be seen in laboratories or expressed in control experiments'[12]. As I have already pointed out, the work of the Skinnerian school of behaviourists, while pro-viding a certain amount of insight into how some animals respond to specific stimuli, is very narrow in its application, and is of limited value in examining the real world in which most animals live. (How many horses do you know that live in a laboratory cage?) Attempts to

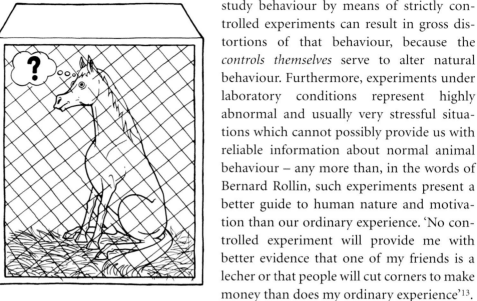

How many horses live in a laboratory cage?

study behaviour by means of strictly controlled experiments can result in gross distortions of that behaviour, because the *controls themselves* serve to alter natural behaviour. Furthermore, experiments under laboratory conditions represent highly abnormal and usually very stressful situations which cannot possibly provide us with reliable information about normal animal behaviour – any more than, in the words of Bernard Rollin, such experiments present a better guide to human nature and motivation than our ordinary experience. 'No controlled experiment will provide me with better evidence that one of my friends is a lecher or that people will cut corners to make money than does my ordinary experience'[13].

There remains one of the biggest obstacles of all to an understanding of animal behaviour and animal minds: the principle of parsimony. This principle, which has been elevated to the status of Holy Writ, is derived from Occam's Razor, the famous *dictum* of the fourteenth-century philosopher William of Ockham or Occam: 'Do not multiply entities unnecessarily.' Ockham intended this to apply to specific aspects of logical thought, but it is now applied to all kinds of scientific investigations. This reductive simplicity is often boiled down to the rather crude maxim, 'Do not look for complex explanations where a simpler one will do.' As Bernard Rollin points out, 'There are, of course, many questions to be asked regarding any such principle of parsimony or simplicity, the simplest being, "Why not?" What logical absurdity is generated by multiplying entities? And secondly, what counts as "unnecessarily"?'[14] Indeed, application of this principle can have some very odd effects. For example, if we relate this rule to the concept of evolution, we see that as an explanation of how things came to be as they are, this is far less parsimonious than the idea of the Creation. And it is not clear that it can sensibly be applied at all to the world of quantum physics, with its proliferation of 'entities' such as particles and their apparently eccentric behaviour.

With regard to animal behaviour, the principle of parsimony is usually invoked to reduce observed behaviour to a few simple concepts, such as 'conditioning' or 'closed instincts' (see Midgley, cited above). But we can also reduce human behaviour in this way, as the behaviourists did. Lloyd Morgan's famous canon (usually invoked in denials of animal intelligence), which says that 'In no case may we interpret an action as the outcome of the exercise of a higher psychical faculty, if it can be interpreted as the outcome of the exercise of one which stands lower in the psychological scale', was (if one reads his writings carefully) never intended as a denial of animal consciousness, awareness, thought, feelings, etc. Instead, it was meant as an antidote to those who had been too quick to discern the workings of higher reason in animals in cases where there was really insufficient evidence for such assumptions. Morgan himself was the first to admit that he might be wrong about this, and that it would cause him no grief if this should prove to be the case. And, rather ironically considering the use to which his 'canon' has been put, Morgan expressed his gratitude to Romanes, considering his death 'a loss to science which is irreparable'.

But how is it that men such as Romanes and Lloyd Morgan came to be so misrepresented? What happened to scientific objectivity? Regrettably, the history of science (which many scientists, sadly, do not bother to study) shows us that so-called 'scientific objectivity' is largely a very elusive thing indeed.

Ever since the seventeenth century it has been almost an article of secular faith that the Church represented dogma and a stultified, restricted view of the universe, while science represented the triumph of reason over superstition, of objectivity over blind faith. However, this is far from being the truth. It is tempting to believe that the history of science has been one long progression of learning, a gradual unfolding of knowledge as we advance towards ever greater understanding of the universe and of the world in which we live. In fact, science has been plagued by dogma and blind faith just as much as the Church (or any other religious organisation). There are countless examples of how, when new ideas (or radical reinterpretations of old ones) have been proposed, orthodox scientific opinion has leapt to squash such 'heretical' ideas. For instance, the idea of 'continental drift' (i.e. that, as the earth ages, the great continents are slowly drifting apart), is now accepted as scientific orthodoxy. Indeed, a whole new science, that of 'plate tectonics', has grown up around this idea. Yet when Alfred Wegener proposed this theory in 1915 it was met with derision, and it was not until decades later that discoveries were made regarding shifts in the earth's crust which made Wegener's ideas seem, all of a sudden, to be quite feasible after all. Many, many other scientific ideas have also been greeted with derision, dismissed out of hand, or have provoked outright hostility. The outrage which greeted Immanuel Velikovsky's startling proposals regarding the instability of the solar system (*Worlds in Collision*, published in 1950) seems more appropriate to an unthinking lynch-mob kind of mentality than to supposedly rational scientific thought. Without even seriously examining or debating the evidence put forward by Velikovsky, an academic pressure group persuaded Velikovsky's publishers to drop the book, whereupon it was taken up by another publisher and became a bestseller. Whether one agrees with Velikovsky or not is beside the point; the reaction of the scientific community in rejecting his ideas out of hand was unpleasant and irrational to say the least.

The noted British mathematician and space scientist Desmond King-Hele had this to say in the 1974 Halley Lecture at Oxford:

Academic learning is a marvellous edifice, permanent and satisfyingly interlinked, but even so, it may still be legitimate to define science as a thought-system that appeals to the scientists of a particular era, because it allows them to convince themselves that they are making some progress towards better understanding of natural phenomena. They programme their brains into a way of thinking, and then try to indoctrinate the innocent into the same mould, a process sometimes called education. Actions subversive of scientific orthodoxy are forcefully resisted, nowadays in the form of censorship, because scientific papers are sent to referees, good sound scientists who will veto anything revolutionary.[15]

Even without these academic pressures, certain theories may prove so attractive and so plausible that objectivity is compromised. There is the so-called 'Rosenthal effect', whereby the findings of observers and investigators match their expectations. As Bernard Rollin observes, 'if students are told before doing an experiment that one group of rats is smarter than another, they will report that that group learns faster than a second group, even when the groups are randomly selected'[16]. Thus 'objectivity' is frequently coloured by expectations; facts are often ignored because they do not fit into

Insights gained from everyday observation and experience: the Duke of Newcastle drew many inferences about the horses with whom he worked from observing such scenes as these (from Newcastle, *A General System of Horsemanship*)

a particular scheme of thought. And even when they *are* objectively gathered, facts need interpretation in order to make sense. The nature of that interpretation, and its findings, largely depend on who is doing the interpreting!

This should not be read, nor is it intended, as an attack on scientists or scientific thought. We need both, as science offers us a way of understanding the world that is bound up in every aspect of the way we live. However, we must also be aware that there are other ways of looking at the world, and as biochemist, historian of science and Professor of Biology Steven Rose points out, the fact that a piece of science or technology works does not necessarily mean that the theory on which it is based is true. Rose cites the case of Melanesians who apparently navigate their canoes accurately to islands a great distance away by regarding their boats and the stars by which they navigate as remaining still, while the sea moves past them.

So what we regard as true may very much depend on our viewpoint. Steven Rose says that the paradox of science is that: 'it claims to be able to provide us with something approximating to a "true" account of the material world, yet it can only do so while viewing that world through prisms provided by the experience and expectations of its practitioners'[17].

And those practitioners are but human, with human failings and foibles. Science is not a religion, its practitioners are not gods. They are as open to question and to being challenged as any of us.

In the context of our present study, if one looks carefully at the history of horsemanship, one thing is clear. Veterinary medicine and objective scientific field observations may have taught us a great deal about the physiology and external behaviour of horses, but the deepest understanding of them has not come from scientists but from those who – from Xenophon right down to Monty Roberts – have derived their insights from everyday observation and experience. I am not suggesting for one moment that we devalue science, or leave it behind, but it seems to me that we should make use of what it can tell us without worshipping it – and never, ever be afraid to question received wisdom, no matter from what source it is derived.

Notes

1 Bernard Rollin, *The Unheeded Cry* (Oxford University Press, 1990), p. 1
2 Rollin, *The Unheeded Cry*, p. 2
3 Rollin, *The Unheeded Cry*, p. 3
4 Rollin, *The Unheeded Cry*, p. 3
5 Rollin, *The Unheeded Cry*, p. 3
6 Jane Goodall, *Through a Window: 30 Years With the Chimpanzees of Gombe* (Weidenfeld & Nicholson, 1990), p. 12
7 Rollin, *The Unheeded Cry*, p. 53
8 Rollin, *The Unheeded Cry*, p. 20
9 George Romanes, *Animal Intelligence* (Kegan Paul, Trench, Trubner & Co., 1898), p. xi
10 Rollin, *The Unheeded Cry*, pp. 37–8
11 Mary Midgley, *Beast and Man* (Routledge, 1995), p. 224
12 Midgley, *Beast and Man*, p. 224
13 Rollin, *The Unheeded Cry*, p. 38
14 Rollin, *The Unheeded Cry*, p. 75
15 Desmond King-Hele, 'Truth and Heresy over Earth and Sky', 1974 Halley Lecture, Oxford
16 Rollin, *The Unheeded Cry*, p. 41
17 Steven Rose, *Lifelines: Biology, Freedom, Determinism* (Allen Lane, The Penguin Press, 1997), p. 24

CHAPTER THREE

Of Cardboard Motives and Selfish Genes

Things cannot be other than they are ... Everything is made for the best
purpose. Our noses were made to carry spectacles, so we have spectacles.
Legs were clearly intended for breeches, and we wear them.

VOLTAIRE, *CANDIDE*

WITH HIS TENDENCY to view everything as being for the best 'in this best of all
possible worlds', Voltaire's Dr Pangloss would have found himself very much at
home in the company of a growing number of evolutionary biologists who seek
to explain every facet of animal (and this includes human) physical structure and behaviour
in terms of evolutionary adaptation.

There is nothing wrong with this in itself as survival largely depends on adaptation of
some kind. However, the current trend in sociobiology is to mistake cause and effect: to treat
adaptation as the reason for, not the result of, evolution.

While this might not seem to matter very much, except to academics, in reality it has enormous implications for our understanding of behaviour, in particular of motives for behaviour. This is its relevance to our present study. As Mary Midgley says, 'if we are to understand
the behaviour of conscious beings, we must take their motives seriously and not try to
reduce them to something else'[1]. But this is what the 'strict adaptationists' (those who believe
that everything has an evolutionary purpose, and that that purpose must be for the best) try
to do. In this canon, everything an animal does must serve some adaptive purpose, no matter how futile or even destructive the behaviour might be.

The effects of this 'cardboard Darwinism', as Stephen Jay Gould (Professor of Geology and
Zoology at Harvard University) calls it, will be seen in later chapters as we see how distorted
interpretations of equine behaviour can become. 'Cardboard Darwinism' (or to give it yet
another name used by Stephen Jay Gould, 'pop-sociobiology' – 'speculative, story-telling

adaptationism', as Gould puts it) is not content merely to find some evolutionary explanation for animal behaviour; it must also demonstrate that, at some point, such behaviour must be advantageous. It seems there is no aspect of animal behaviour, no matter how disadvantageous, that cardboard Darwinism cannot weave some story around to 'explain' it in adaptive terms (for some examples, and critiques of 'adaptationism', see Stephen Jay Gould's collection of essays, *Bully for Brontosaurus*, and Mary Midgley's *Beast and Man*).

Ironically, one man who had no difficulty in accepting the odd blips and quirks that nature throws up was Charles Darwin himself. In *The Origin of Species* he wrote:

> Nor ought we to marvel if all the contrivances in nature be not, as far as we can judge, absolutely perfect, and if some of them be abhorrent to our ideas of fitness. We need not marvel at the sting of the bee causing the bee's own death; at drones being produced in vast numbers for one single act, with the great majority slaughtered by their sterile sisters . . . The wonder indeed is, on the theory of natural selection, that more cases of the want of absolute perfection have not been observed.[2]

As Gould points out in 'Cardboard Darwinism', the idea of 'adaptive optimality' (that everything is for the best in evolutionary terms) 'denies the structural integration of organisms by interpreting each part as a separate puzzle in good design'[3]. He demonstrates the error of assuming that because we know how a structure works now, we also know *why* it evolved. The general assumption among the purveyors of 'pop-sociobiology' is that if an anatomical structure – or a form of behaviour – exists, it must be adaptive in some way, otherwise it wouldn't have arisen in the first place. For example, Stephen Budiansky, discussing equine communication, says that one of the problems pointed out by evolutionary biologists 'is that a complex, cooperative system of communication would often appear to defy the rules of natural selection'[4]. But natural selection is a theory, not an immutable natural law; Darwin himself was perfectly willing to admit that natural selection might be only one of several evolutionary pathways. And there are no 'rules' as such, only a lot of more or less plausible hypotheses that are by no means universally accepted among scientists. Budiansky goes on to say, 'For a vocalisation to have evolved in the first place, it has to confer some survival value on the individual that is actually making the sound.'[5] Why? Might not a physical structure, or a form of behaviour, occur for other reasons altogether and persist not because it conferred survival value as such, but because it was not harmful enough to be eliminated by natural selection? Stephen Jay Gould points out the central flaw in statements such as Budiansky's, which follow the strict adaptationist line that all existing structures and behaviour must be adaptations with specific survival value. Gould says,

> I am willing to admit that harmful structures will be eliminated by natural selection if they cause enough distress. But the other flank of the argument is not symmetrical – it is not true that helpful structures must be built by natural selection. Many shapes and behaviors are fit for other reasons.[6]

Darwin himself, who, as Gould points out, 'was no mindless functionalist, but who struggled mightily to grasp the laws of structure', understood this as few of his adherents have. One theory often advanced is that unfused skull bones are adaptations specially evolved to permit the large heads of mammalian young to pass through the birth canal. But Darwin studied the skulls of non-mammalian species, and found that:

> The sutures in the skulls of young mammals have been advanced as a beautiful adaptation for aiding parturition, and no doubt they facilitate, or may be indispensable for this act; but as sutures occur in the skulls of young birds and reptiles, which have only to escape from a broken egg, we may infer that this structure has arisen from the laws of growth, and has been taken advantage of in the parturition of the higher animals.[7]

One suspects that Darwin would not have been impressed with some of the arguments advanced by pop-sociobiology in the name of 'strict Darwinism' – adherence to a rigid interpretation of Darwin's basic theories of natural selection. Sociobiological explanations have

gained such a hold over the thinking of many animal behaviour scientists that they are often presented as fact, not theory. Yet, as Steven Rose points out, what he calls 'Ultra-Darwinism' and sociobiological theorising rest on 'shaky empirical evidence, flawed premises and unexamined ideological presuppositions'[8]. Nevertheless, because of its appeal to a certain way of thinking, popular books on equine behaviour tend towards a rather uncritical acceptance of some of the wilder claims of sociobiology regarding motives (i.e. confusion of motives with long-term evolutionary results). For example, Paul McGreevy, Lecturer in Animal Behaviour at the University of Sydney Veterinary School, says in his book, *Why Does My Horse . . .?*, that: 'It goes without saying that the males and females of a species perform certain behaviours to attract a mate and to ensure the survival of their genes'[9]. Well, no one would quibble with the first part, but the second, relating to the survival of genes, is wildly speculative and acceptance of it depends on whether you regard gene-survival as the moving

Charles Darwin　force behind evolution. Yet here it is not presented as a hypothesis, but as fact.

Again and again we have the same confusion of motives. In the same book, discussing the acceptance of new members into a herd, McGreevy says, 'animals invest in the fitness of the group because it improves their own genes' chances of success, and the novel individual brings with it new genes that may capitalise on the work already put in by existing herd members'[10]. But they do nothing of the sort. The survival of individual genes would, at best, be a long term *result*; and as we shall see later in this chapter, the whole concept of 'gene survival' runs into serious difficulties. Passing on their genes is not, and cannot be, the actual motive of the animals concerned for behaving as they do. And the language used here – 'invest', 'capitalise', etc. – implies a degree of cost-benefit analysis of one's actions that would be remarkable in most humans, let alone horses.

Arabian stallion Nivalis, whose flashy trot is intended to impress the mare Tiff in the next paddock. Does passing on his genes really form part of his motivation in seeking a possible mate?

Advocates of pop-sociobiology usually argue that they are speaking metaphorically (for instance, they may say that no one really believes that animals go in for such calculation when deciding their actions; they merely behave as if they do), and we should know better than to take them literally. But the metaphors are seldom presented as such, and, as Steven Rose puts it, 'Sloppy terminology abets sloppy thinking.'[11] The sociobiologists' metaphors are often used carelessly, and are frequently based on assumptions about motives that seem to bear little if any relationship to the ordinary person's perceptions of reality.

One idea ostensibly repudiated in science is that life must have a *purpose*. One may not, for instance, talk about vague concepts such as a universal life-force. As we saw in Chapter 1, the mechanistic view regards organisms as inanimate machines whose organisation does not depend on any higher, non-material principles; this organisation is simply a matter of physico-chemical interactions. However, despite this, organisms are clearly driven by *some* kind of purpose – as is revealed by the instinctive behaviour of animals, such as nest building or migration. Since the mechanistic view denies the existence of souls or other life-principles, some other explanation has to be sought. As Mary Midgley, commenting on the notion of purpose, remarks, 'this idea, when officially outlawed, proves remarkably resistant and inclined to come back through the window'[12]. And as the radical biologist Rupert Sheldrake says, 'the soul has to be reinvented in a mechanical guise'[13]. In the nineteenth century, the germ plasm within a cell nucleus was identified as this 'inner organising principle'. With the recent explosion in genetic science, this role has been transferred to the genes. However, as Rupert Sheldrake says,

. . . far from being mere inanimate molecules, the genes have been endowed with all the properties of life and mind. They are even supposed to be selfish. The living world is thought of as a capitalist economy, and the individualistic, selfish and competitive characteristics of man taken for granted by free-enterprise economic theories are then projected on to the genes.[14]

We have here a fine illustration of Desmond King-Hele's description of science as 'a thought-system that appeals to the scientists of a particular era'. The mechanistic world-view seemed appropriate in an age when machines appeared to offer a means towards a future Utopia; in our free-market-driven economic climate, where the Western world seems to be run not by politicians but by accountants, the idea of the 'selfish gene' is undoubtedly attractive to some. According to this theory, living organisms are nothing but 'throwaway survival machines' for the 'selfish' genes, which will adopt all kinds of strategies to ensure their survival and transmission from one generation to the next.

When people such as E. O. Wilson or Richard Dawkins (whose book, *The Selfish Gene*, has exterted a great deal of influence on both scientific and popular thought), talk about living organisms being merely the vehicles for their genes, they inevitably tend to do so in ways that make it sound as though the genes themselves are engineering our existence. They, of course, deny vigorously that this is what they mean: Dawkins in particular protests that he is speaking metaphorically. But the language they use is so loaded (e.g. references to 'selfish genes', descriptions of ourselves as merely 'throwaway survival vehicles for our genes') that one wonders why, as Dawkins especially is writing for a lay audience, they feel the need to use it at all, if it is not in fact what they *do* mean.

'Such language is much odder,' says Mary Midgley,

. . . much less defensible even than Life-Force talk. The Life-Force was a name for something mysterious, vast, and structural; remarks about it were clearly remarks about how the universe in general works. Genes and DNA, by contrast, are precise names given by scientists to specific little bits of complex goo. And little bits of goo, however complex, cannot design or engineer anything.[15]

Stephen Jay Gould, commenting on the view of bodies as mere 'survival machines' for the genes, says,

I find little defensible in this view. Selection cannot 'see' genes, and can only work through the differential birth and death of organisms. Nearly all genes have multiple effects, many irrelevant to adaptation. Bodies are not an inventory of parts produced by individual genes, but integrated structures that cannot always be changed piecemeal by the dictates of selection. Organic forms are not an array of optimal adaptations to their immediate surroundings, but complex products of history, not always free to change in any direction that might 'improve' them.[16]

Clearly, this criticism also extends to the idea that animals do whatever they have to in order to ensure the survival of their genes. As Mary Midgley asks, why should the proliferation of the genes be the purpose of existence? 'It seems . . . irrational to pick on any stage of the species's continuation as containing the point of the whole thing.'[17]

Steven Rose goes even further than this. In *Lifelines* he exposes the essential vacuousness of the idea of the genes as representing the whole point of our existence, by showing that, far from the genes directing and shaping an organism's destiny, it is the cells themselves which 'instruct' the DNA which bits of 'information' it carries to switch on and off, and when (as not all genes are always active). Emphasising the role of any organism's life history in shaping its development, he further argues that:

> The present instant of our, or any organism's life, is simply inexplicable biologically if considered merely as a frozen moment of time, the mere sum, at that moment, of the differential expression of a hundred thousand genes. Each of our presents is shaped by and can only be understood by our pasts, our personal, unique developmental history as an organism.[18]

In any case, as Rose further points out, the sociobiologists' gene is not a biological entity, but a metaphysical construct, as each 'original' DNA molecule will have been diluted millions of times by newly synthesised molecules in the course of the countless cell divisions that occur between conception and adulthood. 'When the new adult mates and generates offspring, the odds against the DNA they acquire containing any of the molecules present at its parents' conception are unimaginably great.'[19] Rose explains that what is meant, in the biological sense, by the preservation and transmission of genes, is not the persistence of the DNA molecules, but the replication of form as there is no actual chemical or physical continuity. 'To speak, even metaphorically, as if the DNA had an "interest" in its own accurate replication is to traduce the complexity of the biochemical processes, to introduce a metaphysical notion of "the gene" which the chemical structures of DNA themselves belie.'[20]

Equine chromosomes: are these the whole point of any creature's existence?

While much observed animal behaviour seems (or can be made) to fit in with the 'selfish gene' idea of evolution, many animals persist in acting in ways which appear to defy evolutionary sense. A typical example of this is the altruism shown by many species, including the human. Take the not uncommon occurrence of one human risking his or her life to save another. According to the 'selfish gene' way of looking at things, this would only occur if the rescuer and the rescuee were genetically linked, so that saving one organism would ensure the continuance of those genes, even if the other organism were destroyed in the process. Of course, this does often happen; one only has to think of a mother risking her own life to save that of her child. However, it just as often happens that the parties involved are not remotely related; and this can be the case in the animal world too. At simpler levels, caring for the young is a collective responsibility among the hunting dogs of Africa; while among some primates, unrelated 'baby-sitters' will often look after youngsters in the absence of their parents. Such examples of 'baby-minding' are also very common among feral cats (and some domestic ones). I have observed similar phenomena among horses; an example is given in Chapter 8. Furthermore, feral bands of horses have been observed to adopt orphaned foals.

As Peter Evans says in *Ourselves and other Animals*, 'It is hard to see what evolutionary purpose is served by expending effort on someone else's offspring, thereby limiting the resources available for the care and development of one's own.'[21]

The problem is that E. O. Wilson, from whose work much of the theorising about 'selfish genes' is derived, based his theories on a study of insect societies, which are quite unlike those of social mammals. When he – and others writing in the same vein – talk about 'genetic fitness' (the chances of an individual leaving offspring), they do so in terms which seem totally divorced from reality. If reproductive success – leaving as many offspring as possible – were really the sole purpose of any creature's existence, why all the paraphernalia of social living? Why not just have a creature that did nothing but reproduce? The reproductive drive is indeed a powerful one, but it is not all-powerful. Many animals choose not to reproduce even when they have the opportunity to do so (anyone who breeds dogs or horses can testify to this). Moreover, for thousands of years humans have expended a great deal of thought and ingenuity in preventing, or at least restricting, that 'proliferation of their genes' which the 'genetic fitness' imperative is supposed to ensure. As Steven Rose comments,

> Even the most hard-line of ultra-Darwinists manifestly do not conduct their own lives according to their own ultra-Darwinist precepts, by sparing no efforts to maximise their inclusive fitness. How do they account for this apparent genetic failure on their part?[22]

Richard Dawkins explains it thus: 'We are built as gene machines . . . but we have the power to turn against our creators. We, alone on earth, can rebel against the tyranny of the selfish replicators'.[23]

Colourful language, to be sure – but does it actually mean anything? For any such claim as Dawkins is making to have any validity ('We, alone on earth . . .'), we would have to know everything there is to know about the social and reproductive behaviour of every species on earth — and we have no such knowledge. Even those species we *have* studied in any detail (pitifully small in number), continually overturn our assumptions about them as new observations are made. Steven Rose points out the fundamental flaws in Dawkins's argument:

> Either we, like all other living forms, are the products of our genes, or we are not. If we are, it must be that our genes are not merely selfish but also rebellious, building the pheno-typic structures that give our brains and our culture the power to contradict the orders of some of the other replicators embedded in every cell of our bodies. And as our brains are the product of evolution and did not fall independently from the sky, nor were they gen-erated by a highly un-Darwinian massive mutational leap, there must presumably be at

least a germ of rebelliousness in the genes of our near evolutionary neighbours too. The selfish genetic imperative is hoist with its own petard.[24]

The thinking which leads so many scientists to cast all animal and human behaviour in the purely 'selfish', harshly competitive mould is not scientific but philosophical. The product of several centuries of Egoist philosophy, this mode of thought holds that no creature acts except for its own benefit. But although it is true that acts of altruism and compassion often do benefit those who perform them, this is not universally the case. Nor do animals 'trade' or 'invest' in certain behaviour (even humans are seldom this calculating); they simply do whatever has proved successful in maintaining their lifestyle (and sometimes they do things that work against this. For a thorough discussion of this philosophical stance, see Mary Midgley, *Beast and Man*, Chapter 6 'Altruism and Egoism', in which the author dissects the weaknesses of the Egoist philosophy, and is severely critical of its application to sociobiology).

However, it is this philosophy that has informed most thinking about natural selection. The 'struggle for survival' was the central theme of Darwin's work, although the phrase 'survival of the fittest' was not originally his. This 'struggle' is usually interpreted as a bitter and sometimes bloody battle, with organism pitted against organism in pitiless competition. 'Struggle' was a term Darwin used for convenience; as he said, two animals may indeed struggle with each other in a time of dearth, but a plant on the edge of the desert may also be said to struggle against the drought. Unfortunately, the importance of the former type of struggle, of competition – the 'war of all against all' – has been exaggerated in Western thinking about natural selection. The role of co-operation, while recognised to some extent, has been downplayed in contrast to the view of nature as 'red in tooth and claw'. Even Darwin, who did recognise the immense importance of co-operation among social species, tended to overemphasise the significance of competition. We must remember that even before he started to study natural selection in the wild, he was very much influenced by the doctrines of Malthus who maintained that as populations grow in prosperity, this prosperity will result in an increase in rates of reproduction which will, in turn, lead to conflict as the population exceeds the available food supply. However, Malthus's theories, although superficially plausible, are based on some very shaky premises. According to Malthus, those who are better off will have more offspring. But history shows us that the very opposite is the case: the better off tend to have *fewer*, not more, children – hence the saying that the rich get richer and the poor get children. Nevertheless, Darwin based his theory of natural selection on Malthus's ideas of competition for dwindling food supplies. Moreover, Darwin's theory was further developed after he had visited the tropics, an area packed with different species and affording ample opportunities to observe competition at work in nature. If Darwin had pursued his studies in, say, Siberia, he might have drawn different conclusions, as did the Russian anarchist Prince Pyotr Kropotkin. The latter is usually depicted as an amiable, unscientific idealist who interpreted the concept of natural selection according to his own ideals of co-operation and mutual aid. But as Stephen Jay Gould shows in his essay 'Kropotkin Was No Crackpot' (in *Bully For Brontosaurus*), this is far from being the case.

Kropotkin was certainly influenced by his own, to some extent national, preferences, just as Darwin was influenced by his view of life in a small, crowded island. Kropotkin's visions of mutual aid and co-operation must have stemmed in part from his cultural heritage: Russia in the nineteenth century was vastly underpopulated, with the majority of the populace belonging to the peasant class. Peasant life revolved around the *mir*, or village commune (it is noteworthy that the word *mir* can also mean 'world' or 'peace'). Co-operation rather than competition had always been at the heart of Russian peasant life for therein lay their security; as the old saying had it, God is in Heaven, and the Tsar is far away. Furthermore co-operation was essential in a country whose harsh climate meant that the 'struggle for survival' was waged not against other creatures, but against the land itself. Malthus's doctrines made no sense in such an environment. As Stephen Jay Gould says, 'We all have a tendency to spin universal theories from a limited domain of surrounding circumstance. Many geneticists read the entire world of evolution in the confines of a laboratory bottle filled with fruit flies.'[25] A bit further on, contrasting Kropotkin's experience with that of Darwin, Gould adds, 'An Englishman who had learned the ways of nature in the tropics was almost bound to view evolution differently from a Russian nurtured on tales of the Siberian wasteland.'[26]

But it was not so much the case that Kropotkin's political ideals influenced his view of nature; rather, it was the other way round. As part of his military service he spent five years in Siberia, from 1862 to 1866, and used this opportunity to study the geology, geography and zoology of this vast land. At that time he sought confirmation of Darwin's theories about competition between organisms in the struggle for survival, but found little evidence in their favour. What he found instead were frequent examples of co-operation and mutual aid in coping with the harshness of the environment. In *Mutual Aid*, written in English while in exile in London, Kropotkin wrote:

Two aspects of animal life impressed me most during the journeys which I made in my youth in Eastern Siberia and Northern Manchuria. One of them was the extreme severity of the struggle for existence which most species of animals have to carry on against an inclement Nature; the enormous destruction of life which periodically results from natural agencies; and the consequent paucity of life over the vast territory which fell under my observation. And the other was, that even in those few spots where animal life teemed in abundance, I failed to find – although I was eagerly looking for it – that bitter struggle for the means of existence among animals belonging to the same species, which was considered by most Darwinists (though not always by Darwin himself) as the dominant characteristic of struggle for life, and the main factor of evolution.[27]

Gould comments,

. . . I would hold that Kropotkin's basic argument is correct. Struggle does occur in many modes, and some lead to cooperation among members of a species as the best pathway to advantage for individuals. If Kropotkin overemphasized mutual aid, most Darwinians in western Europe had exaggerated competition just as strongly.[28]

So when we read explanations of animal behaviour which emphasise intense competition, with its accompanying strife, we should ask, is this really what is going on? Or are the writers merely repeating the standard Darwinian line (as we have seen, not necessarily shared by Darwin himself), exaggerating the extent and severity of competition?

One of the greatest distorting factors of all cites survival itself as constituting the single aim of all organisms. A wildlife programme on TV recently informed viewers solemnly that: 'The sole purpose of any animal's life is survival.' The circularity of this argument is obvious: the animal lives in order to survive. Well, if it is living it *is* surviving. So what? Surviving as long as one is able may certainly be an aim in life, but it can scarcely be the *only* one. If survival is the name of the game, we need never have advanced beyond the amoeba as these have been around longer than almost anything else. As Mary Midgley points out, since the amoeba reproduces by division, 'its first members are in a sense still here in person. There's survival for you.'[29]

This whole question of motives and philosophical stances needs a book to itself, and Mary Midgley has admirably addressed these issues in *Beast and Man*. As she says, 'The motivation of living creatures does not boil down to any single basic force, not even an "instinct of self-preservation".'[30] It is, instead, she says, a complex pattern of separate elements, roughly balanced according to the species.

> Creatures really have divergent and conflicting desires. Their distinct motives are not (usually) wishes for survival or for means-to-survival, but for various particular things to be done and obtained while surviving. And these can always conflict. Motivation is fundamentally plural. It must be so because, in evolution, all sorts of contingencies and needs arise, calling for all sorts of different responses. An obsessive creature, constantly dominated by one kind of motive, would not survive.[31]

E. O. Wilson quite rightly pointed out that we need to make use of the evolutionary perspective. But as Midgley also points out, it is equally necessary that we should be 'capable of dealing with the foreground – of abandoning the long perspective and looking directly at the motives of individuals'[32].

While I have no problems with accepting the biological and evolutionary basis for much of our behaviour and that of non-human animals, and, indeed, find this basis most helpful in understanding that behaviour, it cannot stand as *the* explanation without gross distortions of motives. Furthermore, I do not see how we can say that *any* of our actions are motivated by any evolutionary drive, except from an impossibly remote standpoint. We can legitimately introduce this long view as part of our explanation but it must be made clear that it does not constitute the whole explanation. As Mary Midgley says,

Kruger does not have to work to find food, nor does he have to spend his days avoiding predators. If survival is his sole aim in life, what remains?

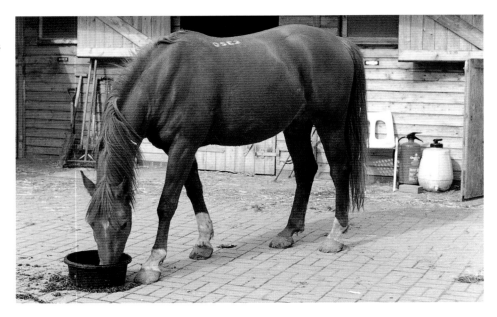

Motives have their importance in evolution and their own evolutionary history – but they have also each their own point, and it is virtually never a wish to bring about some evolutionary event, such as the maximisation of one's own progeny. Confusion between the aims of individuals and the 'aims' of evolution – if there can be said to be such things – is ruinous.[33]

Notes

1 Mary Midgley, *Beast and Man*, p. 117
2 Charles Darwin, *The Origin of Species*, 1859, p. 472
3 Stephen Jay Gould, *An Urchin in the Storm* (Penguin, 1990), p. 48
4 Stephen Budiansky, *The Nature of Horses*, p. 130
5 Budiansky, *The Nature of Horses*, p. 130
6 Gould, *An Urchin in the Storm* p. 49
7 Darwin, *The Origin of Species*, p. 197
8 Paul McGreevy, *Why Does My Horse . . .?* (Souvenir Press, 1996), p. 18
10 McGreevy, *Why Does My Horse . . .?* p. 74
11 Rose, *Lifelines*, p. 116
12 Midgley, *Beast and Man*, p. 89
13 Rupert Sheldrake, *The Rebirth of Nature* (Century, 1990), p. 79
14 Sheldrake, *The Rebirth of Nature*, p. 79
15 Midgley, *Beast and Man*, pp. 90–1
16 Gould, *An Urchin in the Storm*, pp. 66–7
17 Midgley, *Beast and Man*, p. 93

18 Rose, *Lifelines*, p. 157
19 Rose, *Lifelines*, pp. 212–13
20 Rose, *Lifelines*, p. 213
21 Peter Evans, *Ourselves and other Animals* (Century Hutchinson Ltd, 1987), p. 97
22 Rose, *Lifelines*, p. 213
23 Richard Dawkins, *The Selfish Gene* (Oxford University Press, 1976), p. 215
24 Rose, *Lifelines*, pp. 213–14
25 Gould, 'Kropotkin Was No Crackpot', in *Bully for Brontosaurus* (Penguin, 1992), p. 332
26 Gould, 'Kropotkin Was No Crackpot', p. 333
27 Prince Pyotr Kropotkin, *Mutual Aid*, quoted by Gould, 'Kropotkin Was No Crackpot', pp. 335–6
28 Gould, 'Kropotkin Was No Crackpot', p. 338
29 Midgley, *Beast and Man*, p. 153
30 Midgley, *Beast and Man*, p. 168
31 Midgley, *Beast and Man*, p. 168
32 Midgley, *Beast and Man*, p. 142
33 Midgley, *Beast and Man*, p. 142

CHAPTER FOUR

The Great Heresy

Anthropomorphism is a remarkable concept. It may be the
only example of a notion invented solely for God, and then
transferred unchanged to refer to animals.

MARY MIDGLEY

Can you imagine trying to communicate with an alien species from outer space without first trying to establish what you have in common?

If one group or individual wants to establish peaceful relations with another group or individual, they first of all try to establish some common ground, some basis of mutual understanding from which they can explore other possibilities. They will, if they are intelligent enough, acknowledge differences where these become apparent; but unless these differences are likely to lead to a conflict of interest they are usually ignored in favour of similarities. It is upon these similarities that mutual alliances are built.

But suppose that one party insisted that the two had nothing in common and that the other party was stupid and incapable of rational thought, and that these assumptions were based almost entirely on their lack of a common language. How much genuine understanding would there be in such a case? How much mutual understanding would arise from such an attitude?

Not much, one might think. Yet it is precisely such an attitude that has been held for some considerable time, by otherwise intelligent people, in the realms of animal behaviour. It is this attitude that I want to set in its more general context, before going on to relate it specifically to horses.

I refer to the idea that to attribute subjective experiences, emotions, self-awareness, etc. to animals is 'anthropomorphism'. Just as it was once heretical to attribute immortal souls to animals, now the new heresy is 'anthropomorphism'. In one context this is an attempt to preserve the *status quo* – the supposedly unique position humankind holds within the animal kingdom. At its most innocent it is a (perhaps laudable) attempt to prevent the ignorant from treating animals as if they were humans, with human needs, thoughts and responses. This kind of anthropomorphism ranges from the quite mild and harmless (lonely old ladies talking to their cats as if they could understand every word) to the wildly inappropriate (overprotected, pampered lap-dogs treated like human companions, with their own wardrobes and accessories, elaborate living accommodation, and irrelevancies like canine beauty parlours and hotels, but deprived of any kind of life natural to a dog).

However, there is a darker side. Humans have always had a tendency to use animals as symbols of human vices and virtues and to attribute to them qualities which they may or may not possess: thus we have the cunning fox, the gentle lamb, the treacherous serpent, the brave lion, the noble horse . . . (as it happens, horses *are* noble – at least many of them are – but that discussion belongs in a later chapter). This is all very well so long as it is recognised that it *is* only symbolic. Unfortunately, humans also have a tendency to forget where symbolism ends and reality begins and this has led to some monstrous cruelties and injustices, such as wolves being skinned alive in medieval France as 'punishment' for their 'savagery' in killing in order to eat. Animals used to be considered, in some societies at least, as having precisely the same moral values as humans: therefore the wolves referred to above were considered to be fully morally responsible if they killed a human, no matter what the circumstances. Even now there is a tendency to divide animals into 'good' species and 'bad' ones. Whales are perceived to be 'good', and Great White sharks are perceived to be 'bad'. For what reason? For being sharks? Individual animals of all species may have good or bad characters, or behave in ways that are desirable or not, depending on the species. Fratricide among wolves, for example, would be an unspeakable crime, but not among hyenas. This does not make hyenas worse than wolves, just different. They have their own codes of conduct; but humans tend to apply *human* standards and to judge according to those standards. This is not so much anthropomorphism as *anthropocentrism* – the belief that humankind is the measure of all things.

The same anthropocentrism leads otherwise intelligent people to expect large, powerful dogs to put up with having their ears pulled by small children, as if they should 'know better' than to retaliate when the ear-pulling (or whatever) annoys them beyond endurance. The result is all too often the tragic mauling of a child and the unjust punishment of the dog. The punishment is unjust because it assumes that the dog is vicious, when, in fact, all it has done is to react as it would with one of its own kind when pushed beyond a certain limit. Some (rare) dogs may indeed be naturally vicious but the number of truly vicious dogs is comparable to the number of truly vicious horses (a problem I shall discuss further in Chapter 14). Neither species acts in a 'vicious' manner without good reason – according to their own species's code of behaviour at any rate.

So we do animals – in particular those animals who share our lives most intimately, namely dogs, cats and horses – no favours by judging them according to human standards; but to acknowledge this is very far from denying them any thoughts or emotions in common with humans. Yet this is precisely what happens.

The 'anthropomorphite heresy' is as old as the Christian religion and was held by certain very early Christians who believed that God had a human shape. The word 'anthropomorphic' derives from the Greek *anthropos*, man, and *morphos*, indicating shape or form, from *morphe*, shape. The heresy lay not in attributing the wrong shape to God, but in the attribution of any shape at all. This was the sense in which anthropomorphism was used right up to the nineteenth century, when it was rather suddenly extended to include the attribution of human qualities to non-human animals. My *Collins English Dictionary* defines anthropomorphism as 'the attribution of human form or behaviour to a deity, animal etc'[1].

The new heresy is to assign human characteristics to animals. 'Just as humans could not be like God, now animals cannot be like humans (note who has taken God's place).'[2] Philosopher John Andrew Fisher says that:

The use of the term 'anthropomorphism' by scientists and philosophers is often so casual as to almost suggest that it is a term of ideological abuse, rather like political or religious terms ('communist' or 'counter-revolutionary') that need no explication or defense when used in criticism.[3]

As Masson and McCarthy point out, 'To accuse a scientist of anthropomorphism is to make a severe criticism. It is regarded as a species-confusion, an unprofessional merging, a forgetting of the line between who one is and what one is observing, between subject and object, womanish.'[4]

So great a heresy has the idea become of attributing subjective states, such as thoughts or emotions, to animals, that investigation of such subjective states has become a scientific taboo. 'As a result,' says Masson:

. . . none but the most prominent scientists risk their reputations and credibility by venturing into this area. Thus many scientists may believe that animals have emotions, but are unwilling to say that they believe it, and unwilling to study it or encourage their students to investigate it. They may also attack other scientists who try to use the language of the emotions.[5]

Jane Goodall describes how, when she first started her study at Gombe in 1962, it was simply not permissible in ethological circles to talk about an animal's mind, nor was it considered proper to speak of them having a 'personality' – even though everyone knew that animals do have their own unique characters. One respected ethologist, says Goodall, 'while acknowledging that there was "variability between individual animals", wrote that it was best that this fact be "swept under the carpet". At this time ethological carpets fairly bulged with all that was hidden beneath them.'[6] Goodall goes on to say:

How naïve I was. As I had not had an undergraduate science education I didn't realize that animals were not supposed to have personalities, or to think, or to feel emotions or pain.

I had no idea that it would have been more appropriate to assign each of the chimpanzees a number rather than a name when I got to know him or her. I didn't realize that it was not scientific to discuss behaviour in terms of motivation or purpose. And no one had told me that terms such as *childhood* and *adolescence* were uniquely human phases of the life cycle, culturally determined, not to be used when referring to young chimpanzees. Not knowing, I freely made use of all those forbidden terms and concepts in my initial attempt to describe, to the best of my ability, the amazing things I had observed at Gombe.[7]

This straitjacketing approach not only stifles proper enquiry, it condemns many scientists to the use of words and expressions which make their writings almost unreadable to anyone with the slightest feeling and concern for language. We find that even when writing for a lay readership scientists shy away from the use of language which, to any non-scientist, would seem appropriate to describe the behaviour of animals.

According to this taboo an animal cannot be said to be frightened; instead, it shows flight behaviour. It does not feel affection; it displays courtship or parental behaviour. It is not angry; it exhibits aggression. A horse is not curious; it shows investigative behaviour. So we are told that:

When an animal has voluntarily stopped drinking (in lieu of disturbing or distracting external stimuli) and has begun to engage in some other behaviour, we can usually infer that its water need has been satiated. In anthropomorphic terms, the animal is no longer 'thirsty'.[18]

Even if we accept the dubious premise that we can never have any knowledge of an animal's subjective state, 'thirst' is surely as much a physiological state as it is a subjective one. If my throat is dry because of lack of water, I may say that I am thirsty; this is a description of my physical state, not just of how I feel about it. Can we really say that the physiological state of animals (or, at least, of most mammals) when deprived of water is so different from that of humans that a whole new set of concepts is called for? If it *is* so different, then how can scientists justify applying the results of experiments on animals to humans? And if it is not, why is it anthropomorphic to use terms such as thirst or hunger or whatever?

Mary Midgley points out that zoologists, when observing the behaviour of frightened birds or fish, do not find that:

. . . everyday descriptions like 'alarm' suddenly lose their application, or lead to wrong predictions, and that a new set of terms needs to be invented. Embarrassment about the use of such words is not scientific. It is metaphysical. The words arouse suspicion, not because they are useless, but because of a philosophical view about what they might commit us to.[9]

And this philosophical view is that if we apply to animals terms which are normally used to

According to behaviourists, a horse cannot be said to be curious; instead it shows 'investigative behaviour'. Foals at Carlton Bank Stud in North Yorkshire investigate Brian

describe emotions or states of mind, we are thereby laying claim to precise knowledge of that animal's subjective experience – and this is unscientific. But are we really making any such claim? Of course we are not, any more than I am claiming to know exactly how you feel when you say that you are hungry or thirsty or tired. To say that we know exactly how an animal feels would be, as Mary Midgley puts it, 'wild'. But, as she goes on to say,

> . . . it would also be wild in talking of human beings. Even when we know most clearly that another person is alarmed, or has seen the river, we can never share their experience. The barrier to sharing it is already a complete one with human beings, so it cannot be made any more complete by adding the species-barrier to it. We may suspect that the dog's experience would actually be more different from ours than another person's would. But that suspicion is irrelevant, since an impossibility cannot be made more impossible . . . The problem here is not about anthropomorphism, but about Behaviourism, and it arises already on the human scene. The barrier does not fall between us and the dog. It falls between you and me.[10]

To understand your experiences, I can only extrapolate from my own and surmise that your experience is probably very similar to mine. As Nick Humphrey says: 'for all I know no man other than myself has ever experienced a feeling corresponding to my own feeling of hunger; the fact remains that the concept of hunger, derived from my own experience, helps

Jane Littlefair with Arabian filly Chynaas Tee. Chyna evidently likes to be close to Jane – are we wrong in making such an assumption?

me to understand other men's eating behaviour'[11]. To recognise, and hopefully understand, mental and emotional experiences in others (whether human or non-human) is to recognise patterns, and both humans and non-human animals – 'nature's psychologists', as Nick Humphrey puts it – do this all the time. Indeed it is inconceivable that any social species could survive if it did not. In every social interaction it is necessary to be able to 'read' others' states of mind and emotion and this necessity transcends any 'species-barrier'. It is present in the daily life of those of us who live, work with and train animals. We may make mistakes with this, as indeed we do with other humans, but the fact that we do make these mistakes does not render the process of recognising others' mental states invalid. 'Indeed,' says Bernard Rollin, 'it is by virtue of the fact that mentalistic attributions to people and to animals work most of the time that we are able to identify far-fetched or implausible cases that don't work!'[12] And if you handle big, strong, potentially dangerous animals like horses (dangerous not because of any inherent aggression, but simply because of their size and strength), you have to get it right at least a good part of the time, otherwise accidents will happen – indeed, they happen a great deal more frequently in cultures where there has been insufficient respect for, and understanding of, the horse's mental and emotional needs.

If this is true of horses, it is even more true of elephants who still play a huge working role in the economies of several countries. These working elephants can still only be successfully handled by *mahouts* who have very close and life-long relationships with them. As Mary Midgley says:

> Each mahout treats his elephant, not like a tractor, but like a basically benevolent if often tiresome uncle, whose moods must be understood and handled very much like those of a human colleague. If there were any less expensive and time-consuming way of getting work out of the elephants, the Sri Lankan timber trade would by now certainly have discovered it.[13]

As Midgley points out, the *mahouts* may very well have certain beliefs about their elephants which are false because they interpret some aspects of elephant behaviour by relying on an inappropriate human pattern.

But if they were doing this about the basic everyday feelings – about whether their elephant is pleased, annoyed, frightened, excited, tired, sore, suspicious or angry – they would not only be out of business, they would often simply be dead. And to describe and understand such moods, they use the same general vocabulary which is used for describing humans.[14]

As far as popular literature about horses is concerned, cautions against the error of anthropomorphism abound, but rarely is this matter properly discussed. Instead, the reader is given vague warnings which in some cases the authors themselves then proceed to ignore! A good example of this is afforded by Henry Blake who, in *Talking with Horses*, says that in order to communicate with horses: 'We must learn to think and react as the horse thinks and reacts, and guard against the sentimentality of anthropomorphism: that is, against endowing the animal with human characteristics.'[15] But he does not say why anthropomorphism is 'sentimental' (as with the unfortunate wolves of medieval France, it can be anything but), nor why animals and humans cannot share certain characteristics. Later in the book he says:

> You have only to watch a bunch of wild horses in the field together to see that their reactions and behaviour are completely alien to those of the human being . . . Horses, no matter how friendly, will often kick and bite each other, *as human beings will argue with each other* [my italics], but it is always an instantaneous reaction and it is over in a moment or two. A horse is not human and the greatest barrier to the understanding of any animal is anthropomorphism, that is to say, attributing human personality and behaviour to animals.[16]

Readers may note the glaring inconsistency in this passage, contained in the phrase '*as human beings will argue with each other*'. Even as the author is warning us against attributing human personality and behaviour to horses, he is making a comparison between their behaviour and ours. If equine behaviour were truly as alien as he says it is, then such comparisons would be pointless, just as many scientists still believe they are. But horses are not alien beings from another planet, any more than we are; they are mammals, as we are, and we share an evolutionary continuity because of that. The main difference is that we are predators and they are prey animals; we are tool-using cave-dwellers descended from tree-dwellers, and they are creatures of the open plains, running animals descended from inhabitants of the forest floor. This means, of course, that we approach many matters from a radically different point of view, but having a different point of view does not mean we have nothing in common. Our task is surely to find out what we *do* share, while trying to understand the things that we don't, and trying to see things from the horse's perspective. Indeed, throughout his book Blake ignored his own advice, constantly drawing parallels between horses and humans — and he did this because it was often the only way to make sense of what was going on. He may sometimes have been mistaken; but he could scarcely have reached the degree of understanding that he did if he had truly believed that horses were utterly alien in their behaviour and personality.

The author with Tiff (Mikenah). Are horses really so alien to us that we can never have any insight into their thoughts and feelings? (Brian Spencer)

Some opponents of the modern heresy of anthropomorphism, while conceding that it can help with predicting animal behaviour, insist that this simply means that animals have evolved to *act* as if they thought and felt, because this makes evolutionary sense. Masson and McCarthy cite the case of a female cheetah who, on fearing that a lion may attack her cubs, runs towards the lion to lure it away from the cubs. According to the 'evolutionary sense' theory this does not mean that the mother cheetah fears for the lives of her cubs; it only means that she has evolved to act – for survival purposes – *as if* she feared for their lives. As Masson and McCarthy observe rather tartly, 'To speculate that leaving more off-spring is the ultimate cause of her behaviour is permitted. Not permitted is to speculate that fear for their lives is its proximate cause, far less about how she may feel seeing the lion grabbing them.'[17]

This is surely an example of 'cardboard Darwinism'. I would ask how the theory outlined above can possibly explain why young chimpanzees who have lost their mothers can quite literally die of grief? How could merely acting *as if* they were grieving for their mothers (and dying in the process, in spite of efforts to save them) possibly make evolutionary sense? Nor is it only chimpanzees who exhibit such grief. Horses, as we shall see, can be similarly affected by the loss of a companion, as can many other species. Jeffrey Masson and Susan McCarthy rightly ask, 'Why is it so impossible to know what animals feel, no matter how much or what kind of evidence there is? How is knowing about their feelings different, in truth, from the assumptions made routinely about the feelings of other people?'[18]

Nor is it at all clear to me why so-called 'anthropomorphism' should be so much more objectionable than 'mechanomorphism' – the attribution of the properties of machines to humans and animals alike. Scientists routinely describe animals (and humans) as 'machines', and refer to the 'mechanics' of biological function or to the 'mechanics' of this or that aspect of behaviour. It is quite clear that to many of them animals are indeed nothing more than biological machines. Yet despite the superficial resemblance of many biological functions to the workings of machinery, neither humans nor animals are at all like machines: as Mary Midgley points out, only machines are like machines. So 'mechanomorphism' would seem to be much less defensible than 'anthropomorphism' but how often do we hear of scientists being castigated for the heresy of 'mechanomorphism'?

Curiously enough, while modern ethologists tend to avoid any terms that may smack of the dreaded anthropomorphism, one of the founders of ethology was by no means so reticent. In his popular writings at least (if not in his scientific papers) Konrad Lorenz wrote unashamedly of the emotions of the animals he studied, in particular of his beloved greylag geese and of the jackdaws who so often shared his life. In the delightful *King Solomon's Ring* he tells of one low-ranking female jackdaw who, having become the consort of the troop leader, did not hesitate to take advantage of her rise in status:

But that little jackdaw knew within forty-eight hours exactly what she could allow herself, and I am sorry to say that she made the fullest use of it. She lacked entirely that noble or even blasé tolerance which jackdaws of high rank should exhibit towards their inferiors. She used every opportunity to snub former superiors, and she did not stop at gestures of self-importance, as high-rankers of long standing nearly always do. No – she always had an active and malicious plan of attack ready to hand. In short, she conducted herself with the utmost vulgarity.

You think I humanize the animal? Perhaps you do not know that what we are wont to call 'human weakness' is, in reality, nearly always a pre-human factor and one which we have in common with the higher animals? Believe me, I am not mistakenly assigning human properties to animals; on the contrary, I am showing you what an enormous animal inheritance remains in man, to this day.[19]

In fact, we can only sensibly describe the attribution of subjective experiences to animals as anthropomorphic if we can say with certainty that animals cannot have them. Unless we want to take the extreme sceptical position of the solipsist who denies the possibility of all knowledge save that of one's own existence (for all I know I might be the only person who actually thinks or feels anything; I might be imagining all the rest) we cannot make any such assumption. As Bernard Rollin points out:

No rational person would apply the term 'good-natured' to a day of the week, but many sane, rational, and intelligent people in most cultures and during most historical periods have applied mental-state terms to animals. It is possible that they have been wrong in so doing; but it is certainly not a fallacy unless one begs the question by assuming what one needs to prove: namely, that animals are the sorts of things to which such terms cannot sensibly be applied. And how can the common sense of science do this when whole segments of scientific research, while denying the tenability of mentalistic attribution to animals, must in fact presuppose it in order to do their work?[20]

It is worthwhile recalling that it is not so long ago in historical terms that many educated Europeans dismissed the physical and emotional sufferings of the poor, and of other races, with the belief (often quite genuinely held) that 'they don't feel things as we do'. This was how a great many of the people who, in Hitler's Third Reich, committed terrible crimes against Jews, Slavs, Gypsies, etc. rationalised what they did; they persuaded themselves that the people they killed and tortured were sub-human, and therefore did not suffer as true Aryans would. Too often people assume the same about animals. One is reminded of Shylock's great plea for justice in *The Merchant of Venice*: 'Hath not a Jew eyes? Hath not a Jew hands, organs, dimensions, senses, affections, passions? . . . If you prick us, do we not bleed? If you tickle us, do we not laugh? If you poison us, do we not die?'[21]

Surely, then, the only way we can truly understand the actions and motives of non-human animals is to accept that they too have thoughts and feelings. Our task is to discover, through open-minded observation, what these thoughts and feelings might be.

Notes

1 *Collins English Dictionary*, 2nd edition, 1986, p. 63
2 Jeffrey Masson and Susan McCarthy, *When Elephants Weep*, p. 44
3 J. A. Fisher, 'Disambiguating anthropomorphism: an interdisciplinary review' in *Perspectives in Ethology* 9 (1991), p. 49 (quoted by Masson and McCarthy, *When Elephants Weep*, p. 44)
4 Masson and McCarthy, *When Elephants Weep*, p. 45
5 Masson and McCarthy, *When Elephants Weep*, p. 45
6 Jane Goodall, *Through a Window*, pp. 11–12
7 Goodall, *Through a Window*, p. 12
8 G. Hatton, 'Ingestive Mechanisms and Behaviours' in *The Behaviour of Domestic Animals*, (ed. E. Hafez, Baillière Tindall, 1962), p. 102
9 Mary Midgley, *Animals and Why They Matter* (University of Georgia Press, 1984), p. 129
10 Midgley, *Animals and Why They Matter*, p. 130
11 Nick Humphrey, 'Nature's Psychologists', *New Scientist*, 29 June 1978, pp. 900–3
12 Bernard Rollin, *The Unheeded Cry*, p. 30
13 Midgley, *Animals and Why They Matter*, p. 115
14 Midgley, *Animals and Why They Matter*, p. 115
15 Henry Blake, *Talking with Horses* (Souvenir Press, 1975), p. 39
16 Blake, *Talking with Horses*, p. 155
17 Masson and McCarthy, *When Elephants Weep*, p. 49
18 Masson and McCarthy, *When Elephants Weep*, p. 49
19 Konrad Lorenz, *King Solomon's Ring*, p. 152
20 Rollin, The *Unheeded Cry*, p. 25
21 William Shakespeare, *The Merchant of Venice*, Act III

CHAPTER FIVE

Is There Anyone There?

... having no reason to believe something is
not the same thing as having a reason to doubt it.

VICKI HEARNE

THE WRITERS OF THE phenomenally successful science-fiction TV series *Star Trek* created a number of convincing alien races, some more or less humanoid in character, others less so. Of those appearing in the series' second incarnation, *Star Trek: The Next Generation*, one such species created an unforgettable impression: the Borg. What 'Trekkie' could hear without a shiver the words, 'We are Borg. Resistance is futile. You will be assimilated'?

The key words here are, '*We are Borg*'. What made the Borg so terrifying was not simply their appearance (half humanoid, half machine), but the fact that they lacked all individual awareness. Their minds were simply part of the Borg collective consciousness. They could not conceive of individual minds, individual needs; the needs of the collective were all they knew. To humans such a lack of individuality, of self-awareness, is utterly and frighteningly alien. This is one reason why some kinds of mental illness – or degenerative diseases such as Alzheimer's disease – fill the average person with dread: the thought of losing oneself is unutterably terrifying.

Yet, curiously, behavioural scientists, psychologists and philosophers have been at great pains to deny animals any sense of self, status as rational beings, or even consciousness. As we shall see, this has profound implications for our relationships with animals, and in particular for those who most closely share our lives – in this instance, horses. For now, however, let us see whether the idea that animals lack consciousness or self-awareness actually holds water.

First, what do we mean by 'self-awareness'? I suspect that this largely depends on one's status in life. For some it may mean nothing more than the recognition of oneself as an individual, instead of a mere unit of consciousness in a collective. For others it may mean the ability to look inside oneself and ask questions such as, 'Who am I? What do I think about *this* or *that*? What do I *feel* about it?'

Cogito, ergo sum: 'I think, therefore I am'. This famous statement, made by René Descartes, sums up his belief in human uniqueness. He placed everything of value in the mind, separating mind and body utterly. The body was simply a mechanism. His concept of *being* was restricted to his mind ('I think, therefore I am'). In Descartes's view, animals did not *think*, they were merely automata, without souls, operating without consciousness. Therefore, by implication, they were not creatures it was possible to be conscious of 'being'.

René Descartes

The reasons for Descartes's beliefs were twofold: lack of consistently intelligent performance on the part of animals, and their lack of spoken language. Descartes maintained that apparently intelligent performances by animals were not proof of real intelligence, because at other times the same animals would act in a stupid fashion. However, as Mary Midgley points out in *Beast and Man*, humans also show this lack of consistency. She cites the case of a horse that, cleverly finding its way home, still takes fright at something that is not in fact dangerous. On the other hand, a man who realises that there is no danger may nevertheless fail to find his way home. As Midgley says, 'Relatively stupid conduct by a fairly intelligent being on an off-day is not in the least like the stupidity of a machine. A car cannot even try to find its way home; a clock will not make even a bad shot at identifying danger. Stupid solutions show a consciousness of the problem.'[1]

Midgley concludes that, for this and other reasons, most people today would probably not think of animals as unconscious. Nevertheless, a great many scientists (particularly those engaged in experiments involving animals), some behaviourists and some philosophers do devote a considerable amount of effort to attempting to 'prove' that animals are not conscious. Some biologists and psychologists maintain that even humans are not conscious, in the sense that while we think we are acting from conscious choice, in fact our actions are pre-determined either by conditioning or genetic 'programming' (depending on which school of thought they follow).

But as Mary Midgley, again objecting to such interpretations, argues,

. . . if the seemingly intelligent actions of the higher animals are never really intelligent, what are they? Notions of mechanical, imitative, or reactive explanations are usually held in the background of such discussions as if they were the obvious and simple ones. I believe they are, on the contrary, incoherent and obscure as explanations of what actually happens. They would never have been put forward except to save a received theory from disaster.[2]

– the received theory being, of course, that of animals as unconscious automata acting according to innate 'programming'.

This was why some Cartesians denied that animals feel pain, that a sudden drawing away from pain did not mean they actually consciously *felt* anything; it was purely a reflex. This argument has, in fact, been used quite recently to demonstrate that animals, however real their pains might be, do not deserve our sympathy as they are not 'conscious' of feeling such pains!

In this context, a parallel is often drawn between animals and infants. The latter have often been regarded as not conscious because we do not appear to retain very early memories. It is salutary to reflect that until well into the second half of the twentieth century it was widely believed that it was unnecessary to anaesthetise infants and babies because, not being fully conscious beings, they did not feel pain! It was, instead, routine to give them curariform drugs which paralysed their muscular activities but did not provide relief from pain. At the age of two and a half, I too was a victim of such thinking. Two of my milk teeth needed extracting but the dentist (following orthodox thinking) did not deem any kind of anaesthetic necessary. Apparently, although I have no recollection of it, I screamed the surgery down and was afterwards (not surprisingly!) terrified by the sight of a dentist. My mother vowed never to put me through such an experience again and set about finding a sympathetic dentist. She was lucky enough to find not one, but two: the Walker brothers, who both had a way with children which, if it did not exactly make a visit to the dentist something to look forward to, at least made it less of an ordeal for a child who was by now almost pathologically frightened at the thought of having anything whatsoever done to her teeth. I still have fond memories of 'Mr Bob' and 'Mr Jim', but to this day I am a pathetic, quivering bundle of fear whenever the prospect of even a routine visit to the dentist looms.

The point to remember about all this is that I have no actual memory of the original trauma itself; I only know what I was told by my mother and grandmother. However, this cannot be because, as some scientists and philosophers would have it, I was not yet a fully conscious being. I have distinct memories of another incident which happened even earlier in my life, when I accidentally left a favourite toy on a bus and my mother spent an entire afternoon trying to retrieve it (she succeeded). I don't, however, remember something else which happened at about the same time; my mother recalled me standing up in the bath, with a collection of stuffed toys and dolls ranged round the edge, wagging my finger portentously and saying solemnly, 'Now – say after me – *hip-po-ta-mus!*' She found this hilarious coming from a two year old, and it is certainly not the kind of thing that an unconscious, or even semi-conscious, being would do (and my mother was not the kind of person who would invent such a tale, either). Yet until the age of about three I have very few memories other than odd ones such as the incident with the lost toy. This does not mean, however, that

I was not fully conscious of early experiences at the time they occurred. It must be that, for some reason, humans do not easily retain very early memories.

In fact, it seems that we do lose some of our memory capacity as we grow older. The so-called 'photographic' or 'eidetic' memory is much more common among young children than it is in older children or adults; it becomes comparatively rare after puberty. Neurobiologists have suggested that this may be because a 'filtering' process is necessary to enable the brain to classify and store relevant data, while discarding what is irrelevant. The experiences of those adults who have retained an eidetic memory suggest that to remember absolutely everything would make life extremely difficult, if not impossible, as all kinds of irrelevancies constantly intrude upon the consciousness and interfere with thought processes.

In spite of this, negative conclusions about animal consciousness have been justified on the grounds that, even if we rightly regard animals (or at least the higher mammals) as sentient beings, capable of feeling pain, of having beliefs, expectations and desires, we can only count them as 'conscious beings' if they are not only capable of holding beliefs but also of thinking about those beliefs and reporting on them!

However, this idea only holds water if we deny that any form of animal communicating counts as real 'communication' – i.e. signalling with the intent of the signals being received and understood – and, as we shall see, this simply does not make sense.

Part of the problem in determining the nature of 'consciousness' lies in the fact that there is considerable argument as to whereabouts in the brain this 'consciousness' resides – if, indeed, it resides anywhere in particular. One popular view held by neurophysiologists is that it is the reticular formation – situated near the base of the brain where it joins with the spinal cord – that is the seat of consciousness. The reticular formation is responsible for the brain's general state of alertness; when it is damaged, unconsciousness results. However as Roger Penrose, Rouse Ball Professor of Mathematics at Oxford University points out in his brilliant, provocative book, *The Emperor's New Mind*, one problem with this, which seems to worry a great many people, is that the reticular formation is, in evolutionary terms, a very ancient part of the brain. If, he goes on to say, all one needs to be conscious is an active reticular formation, then frogs, lizards and even codfish are conscious! Penrose himself does not regard this last argument as problematical. What evidence do we have, he asks, that lizards and codfish do *not* possess some low-level form of consciousness? What right do we have to claim that only humans are 'aware'?

the reticular formation

Is the reticular formation the sea of consciousness?

Are we alone, among the creatures of earth, as things whom it is possible to 'be'? I doubt it. Although frogs and lizards, and especially codfish, do not inspire me with a great deal of conviction that there is necessarily 'someone there' peering back at me when I look at them, the impression of a 'conscious presence' is indeed very strong with me when I look at a dog or a cat or, especially, when an ape or monkey in the zoo looks at me.[3]

This sense that there is 'someone there' is precisely what leads many people to reject the notion that other creatures, especially the higher mammals, do not share with humans a conscious presence, a highly developed sense of self. In any case, why should the matter be regarded as an 'all-or-nothing' proposition? Why should there not be different levels of consciousness, of self-awareness? As Mary Midgley puts it, a sharp division into 'all-or-nothing' does not make evolutionary sense. 'For if it were true, there would have to have been a quite advanced point in animal evolution when parents who were merely unconscious objects suddenly had a child which was a fully conscious subject. But that situation makes no sense.'[4]

Evolution, as Bernard Rollin says, entails continuity. Humans share with other creatures enzymes, proteins, functions and structures. 'It would be evolutionarily odd,' says Rollin,

> . . . if consciousness had emerged solely in humans, especially in light of the presence in other creatures of brains, nervous systems, sense-organs, learning, pain behaviour, problem-solving, and so on. Continuity and small variation constitute the rule in living things. If someone wishes to violate the principle of continuity and assert quantum jumps between animals, while remaining a proponent of evolution, the burden of proof is on him.[5]

The second part of Descartes's thesis about animals hinged on their lack of capacity for language, and therefore for abstract, contemplative thought. But, as we shall see, language is not a prerequisite of conscious, complex thought; indeed, it can sometimes hinder thought processes, interrupting and distracting the mind with its idle chatter. None the less, the principal argument against the possibility of horses, or any other mammal (with the possible exception of the higher primates and some cetaceans, such as dolphins and killer whales), having the ability to think as we understand thinking, or indeed to be self-aware, hinges on the fact that we use what we call 'language' and they do not.

As a species, we are unique in having a clearly structured, *spoken* language. Other species do, of course, use vocal means of communication; but ours is by far the most sophisticated. We depend on our use of language to such a degree that we tend to forget the extent to which we also rely on body language and facial expression to 'flesh out' the bones of verbal communication (one reason why telephone conversations can be fraught with misunderstandings is that we cannot see the other person's reactions to what we are saying, or read their possible response from their body language, before we ever say anything). We therefore find it very difficult to conceive of a state of mind where thinking does not involve the use of language. This has led many otherwise very intelligent people to assume that a species that does not have language as we know it cannot be capable of rational thought; cannot, in other words, *think* in a structured way, but can only act *instinctively*.

However, communication, no matter what form it takes, can only be effective if it is *understood*, and understanding means receiving and interpreting. This is an interactive process, not merely a passive one; a creature capable only of automatic, pre-programmed responses would be incapable of interpreting the signals made by others who form part of its social group (it might also help prey animals to be able to interpret the signals sent out by potential predators!). Mary Midgley stresses that communicating: 'is conveying information and social attitudes. And this is something that it makes sense to talk only of conscious beings as doing.'[6]

In the case of horses, communication is both complex and subtle; its nature and extent are examined in Chapter 10. Even so, the fact that it is non-verbal (although sometimes vocal) is often cited as 'proof' that the horse cannot be a rational creature, any more than any other non-human animal.

Even Descartes had to recognise that this posed a problem. People born as deaf-mutes, he said, can count as rational beings because they 'usually invent for themselves signs by which they make themselves understood to those who are usually with them'[7].

But – and here is the whole point – dogs, horses and many other animals also *make themselves understood to those who are usually with them* – and this includes members of their own species, humans, or totally unrelated species. As we shall see, there is no such thing as a standard automatic response. The communication has to be interpreted, in other words *thought about*, yet this is consistently denied by people who appear to feel that the sky would fall on them if they admitted that other species can experience rational thought and can communicate in a rich, subtle and complex manner *without* the need for verbal language.

If we do recognise this, can we really claim that the spoken word is the only valid form of language, or at least of communication? If we include signing as a form of language (as Descartes did, in an indirect sort of way), then surely a kinaesthetic or visual form of communication must also be included?

Albert Einstein

Even if it is not, what evidence is there that language is essential for thought? Do any of us really 'think' in words all the time? Albert Einstein, in a letter to the noted French mathematician Jacques Hadamard, wrote:

The words or the language, as they are written or spoken, do not seem to play any role in my mechanism of thought. The psychical entities which seem to serve as elements of thought are certain signs and more or less clear images which can be 'voluntarily' reproduced and combined . . .'[8]

The eminent scientist and explorer Francis Galton stated quite unequivocally that he did not think as easily in words as otherwise, and that he found it a great drawback in explaining himself. After working hard and arriving at results that were perfectly clear to himself, he found that when he came to express them in language he felt this clarity slipping away, and that he wasted a vast amount of time in trying to find appropriate words and phrases.

Hadamard himself wrote: 'I insist that words are totally absent from my mind when I really think . . . I fully agree with Schopenhauer when he writes, "thoughts die the moment they are embodied by words". '9

Roger Penrose says that these examples accord very much with his own thought-modes. In *The Emperor's New Mind*, he says:

> Almost all my mathematical thinking is done visually and in terms of non-verbal concepts . . . the difficulty that these thinkers have had with translating their thoughts into words is something that I frequently experience myself. Often the reason is that there simply are not the words available to express the concepts that are required.'10

Penrose also goes on to say that when he has been concentrating intensely for some time on mathematics, and someone suddenly engages him in conversation, he has found himself almost unable to speak for some seconds.

This is from a man who has just taken his readers on a dazzling tour of relativity theory, quantum mechanics, cosmology, fractal geometry and many other concepts that are mind-boggling (at least to the lay person) in their complexity! If such minds as these do not require language for their most complex ideas (and, in fact, seem to find it a positive disadvantage), can we really claim that lack of language debars animals from the realms of abstract or conceptual thought?

As moral philosopher Dr Stephen Clark said in a symposium on self-awareness in domesticated animals:

> . . . ordinary discourse precisely distinguishes things that merely move and things that behave; 'behaviour' is only possible for a creature with an inward dimension, with its own real perception of the world . . . there is something it is like to be a cow, as there is not to be a tractor. Tractors don't have points of view, cows do; there is a way things look to a cow.11

However, some philosophers object that it is fruitless to try to imagine what it might be like to 'be' a horse or a dog or cat (or whatever), on the grounds that it is impossible to 'be' any of these things. One can only 'be' something, they argue, if one can imagine what it would be like not to 'be': i.e. if you could imagine non-existence, what it would be like to cease to 'be'. This, they claim, it is impossible for an animal to do as animals have no concept of death.

But how can they be so certain? The lack of language rears its ugly head yet again. How could one imagine a concept such as death, or non-being, without language? Moreover, how could one convey such an idea to others? They argue that there is no evidence to support the idea that animals have any such concept.

I do not see why one could not have a concept of death without language. Animals often witness the death of other animals; they must be able to distinguish a lifeless body from a living one (the fact that some prey animals sometimes 'play dead', and get away with it, is no argument against this proposition; humans pursued by other humans also, on occasion, 'play dead' – and they too sometimes get away with it). If animals see others of their kind die regularly (as they must in the wild) there is no reason to suppose that they do not accept it as something that happens to all, in time. Some species mourn their dead companions; elephants have been seen to do this in the wild, and horses, dogs and cats definitely show distress at the loss of a close companion. They may not always know that the departed one has died, although often they do; and there is no reason to suppose that they cannot imagine a state where one ceases to exist. There is evidence (considered in Chapter 15) that horses at least can imagine alternatives to their present state of being, or mind; why should this not extend to the concept of death?

The argument that they cannot report such a state of mind is to my mind – especially in view of what has been said about communication – vacuous. To those who take the trouble to listen to what they are saying, animals can and do report all kinds of states of mind, and those who truly pay attention to them seldom have difficulty in understanding. This is especially so with horses.

Finally, we must consider the question of self-awareness. As we have seen, this could be considered, at its most basic level, to be simply a matter of recognising one's own individuality (in a way that the fictional, *Star Trek* Borg, for example, could not). On a more complex level, one sign of self-awareness could be insight into the thoughts of others: the ability to recognise, for instance, that one has certain information that others do not have, thus clearly differentiating one's own perceptions from those of others. It is often supposed that very small children do not possess this ability as they readily appear to believe that if they cannot see someone, that person cannot see them either (as with a two year old covering her eyes, thinking that she is hiding herself). According to this theory, it is not until around the age of seven that children develop the capacity to realise that they may know things that others do not. However, any number of children develop the concept of hiding, either themselves or treasured belongings, at a much earlier age than this (I know, because I did so myself) so this does not seem to me very convincing.

It has been almost routine to assume that animals (other than, perhaps, certain of the great apes, and possibly whales and dolphins) do not possess the conceptual ability required for such insight into the minds of others. Vicki Hearne describes how, in comparative psychology and animal behaviour classes, students had to be 'cured' of the habit of supposing that animals might hide from one another (as she says wryly, 'I have never known a hunter to be successfully cured of this habit of mind.'[12]) Hearne comments,

I was deeply intrigued by this, for what in the world was the puppy doing under the bed when you returned home to find an unwelcome monument on the broadloom, if not hiding? But it was pointed out to me what a great and anthropomorphic mistake it was to say or think this. In order to be hiding, whether from predators or from the vexed owner of the carpet, a creature would have to have certain logical concepts that animals simply couldn't have.[13]

– including, as stated above, self-awareness. Only the insight given by self-awareness – that is, the insight that other creatures do not necessarily know what the individual knows (and therefore do not know the individual's whereabouts) – could tell the animal that it was necessary to hide.

To the average person this sounds barmy. One might think, 'But *of course* animals hide from one another. Prey animals do it all the time. Cats hide from dogs; dogs hide from small children who they know are likely to torment them.'

Ah yes, is the answer, but these actions are merely instinctive; they do not provide evidence of conceptual thought. In attempting to prove this, scientists and philosophers are prone to making extraordinary assumptions. Philosopher Peter Carruthers cites the case of squirrels burying caches of food as examples of purely instinctive behaviour (i.e. 'closed' instincts in operation). He asks, if this behaviour is evidence of real planning rather than being purely instinctive, why is it that other squirrels do not watch as the food is being buried, and then come and steal it?[14]

Well, in fact, they do just that. People who make a point of observing squirrel behaviour report that caches of food are regularly broken into by other squirrels who have watched to see where they are buried. Indeed, I have frequently seen this behaviour myself, as there is a large colony of grey squirrels in the cemetery less than a hundred yards from where I live, and the dogs and I often stop in the course of our walks to watch the squirrels going about their business. One may see that, as they dig and bury, the squirrels often pause and look round to see if they are being observed (they are, of course, by us, but, as non-squirrels, apparently we don't count).

Why does a dog bury a bone? For later on, of course. But why bother to bury it, if the dog did not *know* that only he was aware of its whereabouts? There is surely no point in secreting something away if every Fido, Rover and Rufus also knows where your treasure is buried. But if *only you* know where it is, then Fido, Rover and Rufus cannot get their teeth into it. There are also numerous well-attested examples of horses making strenuous efforts to let humans know that something is wrong (one such example is given in Chapter 7). If the horses in question were not aware that the humans concerned did not share their knowledge, then why bother to communicate? Surely this is evidence of insight into the minds of others: awareness of knowledge that others lack.

Yet an extraordinary amount of mental effort has gone into 'proving' that animals do not possess such insight. One case cited by Vicki Hearne is that of a laboratory experiment in which octopuses would hide behind glass in full sight of a predator. This was used as an example of purely instinctive behaviour as, obviously, the octopuses were incapable of working out that the predator could still see them. This is certainly one way of looking at it but, as Vicki Hearne points out, the researchers ignored not only questions about the vision of octopuses and their predators, but also the other, glaringly obvious possibility: that in the absence of anything else to hide behind other than the glass, octopuses might just feel safer getting behind anything they could, whether the predators could see them or not!

Far more convincing are experiments carried out with Bonobo apes, in which the experimenter is directed to hidden food whose whereabouts he does not know, but which is known to the apes. This is certainly evidence that Bonobo apes, at least, possess sufficient insight into the minds of others to realise that not everyone else shares the same information. But what about other animals – non-primates? After all, Bonobos are probably genetically the closest creature on earth to humans. Does this mean, as has often been supposed, that only primates are self-aware? How do we test self-awareness in other creatures?

The difficulty lies in devising appropriate tests that would 'prove' once and for all that certain animals are at least self-aware. One such test, which has been tried on various primates, is the recognition of oneself in a mirror. Some of the primates did well in these tests, clearly appearing (after some initial familiarisation) to recognise their own images. But would a dog or a horse?

How do you know, when you see yourself in a mirror, that the person you are seeing is *you*? Quite simply, you know because at some point in your life you learned that the shiny surface you were looking at was reflecting your own image. Most of us learn this as babies or as very small children, so that it passes into the realm of things we 'know' without really having to think about them. But think of all those stories of the early explorers coming into contact with 'primitive' peoples who had never seen mirrors. Many of these 'primitives' reacted with amazement and even horror at the sight of themselves in a mirror. They did not immediately recognise their own images; as, indeed, why should they? They were often convinced that somehow a living person (or his spirit) had been trapped inside the mirror (the same interpretation has often been put on photographs). In the past this was often taken as a sign that these peoples were intellectually inferior; otherwise they would have 'recognised' themselves in the mirror. But is it really a sign of intellectual inferiority? Of course it is not. It simply means that, for such peoples, knowing what one looked like was a matter of inference (from the evidence of one's own senses and from feedback from other people), not of the evidence of one's own eyes, and that such knowledge was not especially relevant to one's lifestyle. If you had grown to adult life without ever seeing a mirror, or any comparably reflective surface, and had no concept of such things, would you necessarily recognise your own image in similar circumstances? I should doubt it very much. Although in the mirror experiments referred to earlier chimpanzees appeared to recognise themselves, gorillas did not. How plausible is it that chimpanzees are self-aware, yet gorillas, with their intelligence and social complexity, are not?

It is not clear whether my dog recognises his own image in the full-length mirror that hangs in the hallway of our house. When he was a puppy he used to bark at it, even growl at it; now he simply ignores it. He does, however, recognise other dogs on TV (so much for the prevalent idea that dogs cannot recognise two-dimensional images). This is not simply a case of reacting to smallish, moving objects. Whenever a dog appears (even if it is a still picture), he makes a dive for the TV set, going at it with little darting runs and snapping at the screen, not aggressively but purely in excitement. The only other animals on TV that cause him to react in this way are horses. Cats are a matter of curiosity, but no great deal of reaction. Horses, however, provoke excitement of a different kind; he seems worried by them (just as he is when he encounters them in the flesh). This tells me that not only can he recognise two-dimensional images, he can also discriminate between different species within those images.

What about horses? I have never shown my horses a TV set, so I do not know how they would react to one. However, Zareeba, Kruger and a horse we used to have called Mo have all seen themselves in a mirror. Mo does not react to the sight of his own image, possibly because he is used to it; he has often been ridden in indoor schools with mirrors. Zareeba and Kruger, on the other hand, have had relatively little exposure to mirrors. The first time they were ridden in an indoor school equipped with mirrors, we were careful to ensure that they did not catch sight of themselves suddenly, and so rode them up to the mirror and let them look at themselves in it. On seeing themselves for the first time, both seemed intensely interested; not startled, as one might expect them to be, simply curious, reaching out to sniff the mirror. Once they had accustomed themselves to this unusual sight, they seemed to lose interest. I have seen other horses react in the same way, including a stallion being loose schooled in a big indoor arena, again equipped with mirrors. This stallion halted in front of the mirror, reached out and sniffed it, and spent quite some time watching himself in it.

Do horses recognise themselves in a mirror?

One could make several separate cases from this. It could be argued that the horses' lack of interest once they had grown used to the mirror indicates that they do not recognise themselves, and that this works against any ideas that they might be self-aware. On the other hand, one could just as easily argue that they *did* recognise themselves, or that they worked out that as the horse in the mirror was not a 'real' horse, it must be a reflection of themselves. The stallion's reaction would seem to support this argument; his interest in the mirror suggests that he did at least recognise a 'horse' image. However, given the normal reaction of a stallion to other horses, if he believed the mirror image actually to *be* another horse, it would be most unlikely that he would react to it so passively. Some horses are not so passive; Sara Debnam reports that her Arabian stallion Balthasar becomes extremely vocal when he catches sight of himself in a mirror!

Of course it could be that the horses did not recognise the mirror image as being a horse at all and were only curious about something that appeared 'different'. If this were the case, it would still not prove that horses are not self-aware; it could just be that their eyesight is not particularly well adapted for recognising reflected images.

The fact that such a simple piece of information can be interpreted in several different ways without too much mental effort (you may be able to interpret it in many other ways) illustrates the difficulties facing ethologists when they are trying to piece together the manner in which various animals interpret the world around them. Personally I think that experiments with mirrors may well be irrelevant as they are not an intrinsic part of a horse's way of life, and that we must look at other aspects of equine behaviour, such as social interactions, to determine, as far as we can, the level of their self-awareness. I think this also applies to most other animals.

Psychologist Dr Roger A. Mugford, writing about 'problem' dogs, says in this context that:

> It is argued elsewhere . . . that the dog is socially skilful, is very adept at communicating its feelings to human observers and is rather clever at manipulating its social and physical environment. But these are not uniquely canine traits; many other species of animals would doubtless be able to do the same if they were given the opportunity. And what if one compares the capabilities of a highly evolved social animal like the dog/wolf with man, that most self-consciously aware of animals? Evolutionary theory predicts that there will be few sharp discontinuities in the natural world, and it would be strange if man had the monopoly in self-awareness . . . The present writer finds that it is helpful to consider self-awareness as the concept of an individual in relation to time – past and future. If one can anticipate certain of one's needs – say for food, shelter, companionship, etc.) *and manipulate matters* so that the needs are fulfilled, then one is self-aware. Many . . . 'problem' dogs . . . are very capable of manipulating the present for some future gain, so they must be self-aware. For the present writer, it is very humbling to find dogs manipulating human beings, like good psychologists, and very well aware of their own tomorrow.[15]

Horses, too, can be manipulative in this sense in a domestic setting. Our stallion Nivalis loved being hand-fed as a foal because of all the attention he got in the process. Now he still tries to insist on me, Brian or Joanne holding his feed bucket up for him, preferably near the door so that not only is he receiving all our attention, he can also see what is going on in the yard while he eats. He does not achieve this by being aggressive or demanding, but by looking pathetic and downcast and pushing his feed bucket disconsolately about the stable until someone comes and holds it up for him. I was soft enough to go along with this until I realised that he was busy training us to wait on him hand and foot (he would also have us hold his water bucket up for him if he could). We compromised by hanging a portable manger over his door so that he could still see everything that was going on and feel himself to be the centre of attention.

There are countless other examples of how horses train their owners and riders to comply with their wishes. Throughout this book I shall be stressing co-operation with the horse, rather than confrontation; but sometimes confrontation is necessary as the lesser of two evils – as when horses try to manipulate us into situations that are potentially damaging, psychologically if not physically, for both horse and human. Mary Wanless cites the case of riders who never confront the horse:

Nivalis likes us to hold the feed or water bucket for him

These are the nice, polite riders, who defer to the horse, and let him choose how and where he goes. One rider I know found her horse so much more comfortable on one rein that she soon stopped riding on the difficult rein altogether. Having successfully organised this, the horse may go on to decide that he does not like cantering, or does not like leaving his fellows. When the rider colludes with the horse, she encourages him to become nappy . . . until he finally decides that he does not even want to go out of the yard.[16]

Very often horses learn a manipulative strategy as a form of self-protection. Horses who have come to dislike, say, being groomed because of rough handling in the past, may kick out or bite in protest. If they learn that doing this means the disliked activity is discontinued, they may bite or kick even when groomed by a sympathetic handler. They may also go on to train their handlers not to attempt *any* activity the horse dislikes, no matter how necessary it may be for his health and comfort! How we can handle such a situation is touched upon in Chapter 16, but it does show how horses can manipulate us to bring about conditions they desire. They are sometimes far better at training humans than we are at training them!

Professor Donald R. Griffin, one of the pioneers of the study of animal cognition, has this to say:

It seems to me that if we assume that an animal can be aware of some objects that have obvious importance in its life, we are making a very *un*parsimonious assumption if we conclude that it can never be aware of that creature about which it receives by far the most sensory information, the animal from whose proximity and impact it never escapes, namely itself. Indeed, if we allow a considerable awareness of an animal's environment and its companions, but deny it any self-awareness whatsoever, we are forced to postulate that the abundant information that impinges on its brain from its own body is all barred in some special way from reaching its awareness. Such a limitation seems both implausible and maladaptive, for information about itself is at least as important to an animal as information about anything else, if not more so.[17]

If we follow the reasoning that common sense dictates, then we must surely conclude that horses *are* self-aware, although much more investigation is required before we can assess the degree of this self-awareness. The trouble is that the kind of scepticism that science applies to animal consciousness and thought can rapidly reach the stage where it stifles all genuine enquiry and understanding. As Vicki Hearne points out:

. . . Western faith in the beauties of doubt and refutation . . . is, in its place, a virtue, but like any popular notion, it is rarely in its place and tends to run amok and lead to the curiously superstitious notion that to have no reason to believe a proposition is the same as having a reason to assert that the proposition is false.[18]

To put it another way, absence of evidence is not necessarily evidence of absence.

Notes

1 Mary Midgley, *Beast and Man*, p. 210
2 Mary Midgley, *Beast and Man*, p. 217
3 Roger Penrose, *The Emperor's New Mind* (orig. pub. OUP, 1989; Vintage paperback ed., 1990), p. 494
4 Midgley, *Beast and Man*, p. 217
5 Bernard Rollin, *The Unheeded Cry*, p. 32
6 Midgley, *Beast and Man*, p. 115
7 René Descartes, 'Discourse on Method' quoted by Midgley, *Beast and Man*, p. 233
8 Albert Einstein, quoted by Penrose, *The Emperor's New Mind*, p. 548
9 Jacques Hadamard, quoted by Penrose, *The Emperor's New Mind*, p. 548
10 Penrose, *The Emperor's New Mind*, p. 549
11 Stephen R. I. Clark, 'Awareness and Self-Awareness' in: *Self-Awareness in Domesticated Animals*, Proceedings of a workshop held at Keble College, Oxford 7th & 8th July 1980, ed., D. G. M. Wood-Gush, M. Dawkins and R. Ewbank (The Universities Federation for Animal Welfare, 1981), p. 13
12 Vicki Hearne, *Adam's Task*, p. 7
13 Hearne, *Adam's Task*, p. 7
14 Peter Carruthers, *The Animals Issue: Moral Theory in Practice* (Cambridge University Press, 1992), p. 135
15 Dr Roger Mugford, 'The Social Skills of Dogs as an Indicator of Self-Awareness' in *Self-Awareness in Domestic Animals*, p. 43
16 Mary Wanless, *Ride With Your Mind* (first pub. Methuen, 1987; Hamlyn ed., 1995), p. 131
17 Donald R. Griffin, 'The problem of distinguishing awareness from responsiveness' in *Self-Awareness in Domesticated Animals*, p. 7
18 Hearne, *Adam's Task*, p. 12

PART II
The Horse's Mind

CHAPTER SIX

Perfectly Rational Horses

> Some . . . are pleased to say, that horses are void of
> understanding, because men get the better of them: but when
> the horse gets the better of the man, which frequently
> happens, is the man then void of understanding?
>
> WILLIAM CAVENDISH, DUKE OF NEWCASTLE, *c*.1658

AS WE SAW IN Part I, one of the main difficulties in exploring the horse's mind adequately has been a widespread reluctance on the part of biologists and behavioural psychologists to admit that mental processes play any part in determining behaviour, whether human or animal. This has led to some extraordinarily contorted thinking on the whole subject of animal behaviour, as the scientists involved try desperately to avoid charges of anthropomorphism. Some behaviourists and philosophers argue that animals cannot make conscious choices. They would say that if a horse is startled it does not choose consciously to take action: it merely reacts. The response is therefore an unconscious one. At the beginning of Chapter 1 I quoted a book on horse handling as saying that the horse has no capacity for reasoned thought whatsoever, nor will he ever have this capacity. However, on the next page the author says, 'The horse has *much feeling* but little *understanding*. This means that he is governed by instinct and that rational thought plays very little part in his actions. A horse is, therefore, less intelligent than a dog, although his memory is far superior.'[1]

Now, either the horse has some capacity for rational thought or he has not. Rational thought either plays a part in his actions or it does not. You cannot, on the one hand, say that he has no capacity *whatsoever* for reasoned thought and then, within a few paragraphs, say that rational thought plays 'very little' part in his actions. Such inconsistency illustrates the widespread lack of clarity in current thinking about the horse's general intelligence and, in particular, his reasoning capacity.

As for the assertion that horses are less intelligent than dogs, all I can say is that anyone who maintains this has not met a dog like our late Doberman, Cooper. A dog of great charm, and endearing in his goofiness, he was, nevertheless, undoubtedly one of the stupidest dogs in canine history. I have never known any horse to approach him for sheer blissful idiocy.

In any case, this kind of argument is a specious one, particularly as regards horses. The horse's *instinctive* response to, say, fear is to remove himself from whatever is causing the fear. In domestic horses that have been well handled in early life, however, this instinct is modified; if it were not, we could scarcely get near them, let alone ride them. The horse can *choose* not to react to fear. If a horse trusts his handler sufficiently, he will follow them even into what he perceives to be danger, because the degree of trust overcomes the fear. He is not, therefore, responding merely to 'instinct'. He is making a choice – and it is precisely on this degree of choice that trainers such as Monty Roberts base their whole philosophy of handling.

A serving stallion can be taught quite easily that it is inappropriate for him to leap on any mare he fancies, except at the proper time (indeed, stallions quickly learn this for themselves if they are allowed to run out with mares). In this way, mature serving stallions that have been well educated in such matters can be ridden out in mixed company, even with mares that are in season. The point is that they, too, are making a choice about their behaviour. The stallion knows that he feels an instinctive urge to mate with an in-oestrus mare but, because of his education, he chooses not to (note that he still has a choice: if he really wanted to jump on a mare then neither you nor I, nor all the king's horses and all the king's men, could stop him). Choice is by its very nature a matter of thought!

We ourselves make these kinds of choices all the time. We learn not to express certain instinctive urges (at least most of us do!) in circumstances where it is inappropriate to do so; indeed it may be said that sometimes we make such a good job of this repression that all kinds of neuroses result. This learning, even though it is conditioned, is still to a great extent a matter of *choice*. In any case, what we call 'instinct' is a vastly complex subject which is far from comprehensively understood. The term 'blind instinct' is often used to indicate that a creature has acted without conscious thought, and that this somehow renders its thought processes inferior to the 'rational' thought processes of the superior human brain. But instinct, or innate behaviour, or 'genetic programming' – the terms used vary according to the school of thought being followed – is not simply a matter of fixed 'programming' or 'hard-wiring'. It is tempting to take the analogy with computers to extremes and think of animal brains as being like ROMs – genetically programmed read-only memories. At the level of some very simple organisms this may well be the case, although even flatworms have been found capable of a limited type of learning. However, the more complex the creature, the less such a concept can apply. The term 'closed instinct' refers to a specific behaviour pattern fixed in every detail by genetic programming; good examples of this are certain types of birdsong and the 'dances' of honeybees. Even where the creatures who are programmed in this manner have been reared in total isolation from others of their kind, they will still reproduce the behaviour pattern in precise detail, without any conditioning of the type described in Chapter 3. For more complex animals, however – particularly those with intricate social organisations – such fixed behaviour patterns would be totally inadequate, as stereotyped responses would not enable the animal to select behaviour or a course of action *appropriate* to the situation. Indeed, when we see animals such as horses performing stereotyped behaviour, we know from this that something is wrong, precisely because their normal behaviour is *not* simply a series of fixed responses (some theories about the causes of stereotypic behaviour in horses are discussed in Appendix I).

'Open' instincts, on the other hand, are still 'programmed' genetically but in a more general way; the outlines are there, so to speak, but the details must be filled in by experience. As Mary Midgley observes,

> Even quite simple animals . . . perform activities where the gap left for experience has to be much larger, yet the general aim is still innately determined. For instance, in such general locomotive tendencies as the one to *come home* – which is common to many animals, including some very simple ones – an indefinite and unpredictable variety of ways of traveling, routes to be followed, and kinds of possible obstacle has to be provided for. Yet the creature must still have a general ruling motive. It cannot just wander at random till something 'reinforces' a movement, since this is the surest way to an early death . . . So 'programming' includes a number of strong *general* tendencies, for example, to get home, to seek water, to hide by day, and to avoid open spaces. And the more complex, the more intelligent creatures become, the more they are programmed in this general way, rather than in full detail.[2]

Midgley cites the example of cats who retain the instinct to hunt even if they are never taught to do so or if they never observe another cat hunting; if given the opportunity, they will hunt even when they are well fed. However, their hunting activities are not just a series of stereotyped movements; they encompass a wide range of behaviour. Cats also learn from their hunting experiences, thus improving on their past performances.

In horses, too, general tendencies, such as the recognition of potential predators (even though they may never have seen a predator, much less been attacked by one) and flight from possible danger, have been genetically 'programmed'. But as we saw at the beginning of this chapter, such 'programming' can be modified. In a domestic situation, horses can become accustomed to all manner of sights and sounds. Through the process known as 'habituation' (to which we shall return in Chapter 11), they come to tolerate situations which their genetic 'programming' tells them to avoid.

This adaptability has led some observers to conclude that the instincts themselves have been 'bred out' of horses, so to speak, by the process of domestication. The German psychologist Oskar Pfungst (of whom more anon) wrote in 1911 that, with domestication:

> . . . in their habits they have become adapted largely to suit our needs . . . But with the loss of their freedom they have also gradually been deprived of the urgent need of self-preser-

vation . . . Chained in stalls (and usually dark stalls at that) during three-fourths of their lives, and more than any other domestic animal, enslaved for thousands of years by reins and whip, they have become estranged from their natural impulses, and owing to continued confinement they may perhaps have suffered even in their sensory life.[3]

Apart from Pfungst's unduly gloomy (and parochial, as he was describing the conditions peculiar to a specific era, not to the whole of history) view of human-equine relations, he was quite simply wrong here. Horses are far from 'estranged from their natural impulses'; a failure to understand this has led to untold misery for all parties concerned, not to mention a great many avoidable accidents. When we subject horses to (for example) excessive restraint, we invite resistance because we are asking them to overcome the most powerful aspect of their innate 'programming': their flight responses. These will be discussed in more detail in the next chapter; here it is enough to say that for a prey animal like the horse, being deprived of the ability to remove itself from potential danger is one of the worst things that can happen. That is not to say they cannot tolerate restraint in moderation, but if prolonged or too severe it can provoke strong, and in some cases violent, resistance. The success of such trainers as Monty Roberts is based on their ability to recognise such innate tendencies and to work with them rather than against them. Horses are adaptable, but they are not infinitely so, any more than we are!

Pfungst was also wrong in believing that horses necessarily suffer in their sensory life as a result of domestication. So much depends on the environment in which horses (and any other mammals, including humans) live. We are all a product of both our genetic inheritance and our lifetime experiences; and the development of the brain (and with it sensory experience) depends not only on what we inherit but what we do with it.

With regard to actual brainpower, however, what does the horse inherit? One argument frequently advanced to demonstrate the inferiority of the equine intellect is the size of their brains, especially in proportion to their bodies. Pfungst quotes a French physiologist who, on dissecting a horse's brain, said, 'When I saw your proud look and beautiful neck, I hesitated a moment before mounting upon your back. But now that I have seen how small is your brain, I no longer have any qualm about using you.'[4] Any number of would-be riders have expressed the same kind of views; and I should imagine that many of them have later deeply regretted that they so shamefully underestimated their equine 'servants'! In any event, Pfungst disagreed with the physiologist.

We may say that the brain of the horse, compared with that of the ape, or even that of the dog, represents a relatively low type of development. But owing to the rapid changes in the views, often contradictory, concerning the nature of the nervous structures and processes underlying the thought process, any conclusion based on such views would be premature.[5]

Even so, the concept of the horse's brain as being relatively undeveloped is still widely held and often repeated in a humorous context. Former eventer Julian Seaman has described the horse's brain as being about the size of a golf ball, while in an article which appeared in the October 1996 issue of *Riding* magazine, entitled 'Basic Instincts', journalist Dylan Winter referred to the horse's 'primitive little brain'. Even in serious books about horse training, the horse's brain is often misrepresented in this way. Karin Blignault, in her otherwise excellent book *Successful Schooling*, says, 'The horse has a fairly primitive brain which is more dependent on sensory information than is the case with the highly developed human brain (cortex).' [6] But a 'fairly primitive' brain would, in effect, be little more than a continuation of the most primitive brain of all, the brain-stem. This continuation of the brain-stem (itself an extension of the spinal cord) was formed by the olfactory lobe which consisted of cells that analysed smells and divided them into categories, e.g. food, and whether it was good or bad to eat, a potential mate, or danger in the form of an enemy. Other cells then passed messages to the nervous system, causing the body to react appropriately. From this there developed other 'lobes', so that the primitive vertebrate brain probably consisted of three such lobes: the forebrain being concerned with smell, the midbrain with vision, and the hindbrain with movement and balance. By the time mammals appeared on the scene, the cortical brain, the great mass of tightly packed nerve cells, had already developed. As for the neocortex, the 'thinking' brain – *all* mammals have one! So to describe the horse's brain as 'fairly primitive' is not only misleading, it is just plain wrong.

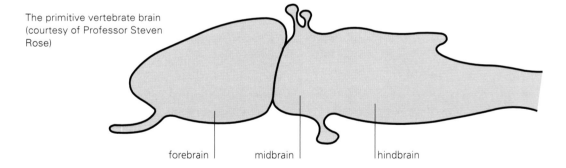

The primitive vertebrate brain (courtesy of Professor Steven Rose)

forebrain   midbrain   hindbrain

It is this 'thinking brain', the neocortex, that houses all the higher brain functions. Grey in colour, it forms an outer layer on top of the bulk of the brain tissue, which is white. The appearance of this grey neocortex, with all its convolutions (see the illustration above and on page 67), led the great mathematician Alan Turing to describe the brain as resembling nothing so much as a bowl of cold porridge. The grey matter consists of nerve cells, or neurons, which are responsible for the brain's processing activities; the human brain contains literally billions of these neurons. This is in part due to the sheer size of the human brain. But how important is brain size in determining intelligence?

At one time it was believed that the absolute size of the brain was all-important. This seemed to confirm (and sometimes created) a great many prejudices; in particular it was

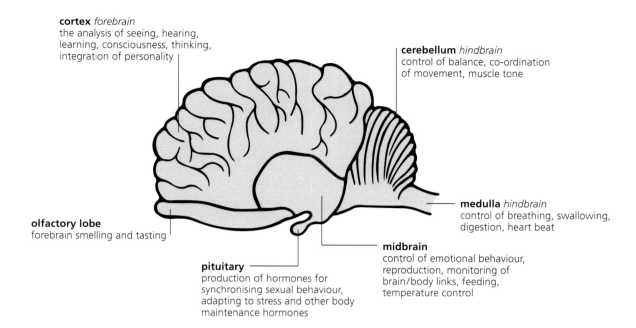

cortex *forebrain*
the analysis of seeing, hearing, learning, consciousness, thinking, integration of personality

cerebellum *hindbrain*
control of balance, co-ordination of movement, muscle tone

olfactory lobe
forebrain smelling and tasting

medulla *hindbrain*
control of breathing, swallowing, digestion, heart beat

pituitary
production of hormones for synchronising sexual behaviour, adapting to stress and other body maintenance hormones

midbrain
control of emotional behaviour, reproduction, monitoring of brain/body links, feeding, temperature control

The equine brain (courtesy of Dr Marthe Kiley-Worthington)

seen as significant that the brains of women were generally smaller than those of men. Then the brains of some of the larger mammals, such as the great apes, whales and dolphins, were examined and found to be comparable in size to the brains of humans. So, clearly, absolute size would not serve as a means of assessing real or potential brain-power. It was then considered that the ratio of the brain volume to the bodyweight determined intelligence; in other words the more intelligent the species, the greater the brain capacity in proportion to its body size, so as to provide an excess of brain cells for non-essential brain-activity – i.e. abstract thinking. However, as Dr Marthe Kiley-Worthington wryly observes, the trouble with this argument is that, when it is followed through, a tree shrew comes out much brighter than *Homo sapiens*, although, as she also points out, 'he may be for all we know!'[7].

There are further problems with this. The average human brain has a capacity of approximately 1,400 cc, but the brain of the great French novelist and winner of the 1921 Nobel Prize for Literature, Anatole France, had a capacity of only 1,000 cc (Nobel Prize winners are not noted for being intellectual duds). Moreover, the brain capacity of Neanderthal man may have been at least 2,000 cc (although, of course, Neanderthal man was bigger and heavier than Cro-Magnon man, from whom we descend). However, as Dr Kiley-Worthington says, even if the principle of relative brain size does not always hold sound, 'nevertheless we would expect a horse to have a bigger brain that us because of its large body. In fact its brain is comparable to ours.'[8] Indeed, if we look at the illustration on page 68, we can see that the horse's brain is much larger than the dog's, about the same size as that of a cow, and slightly smaller than that of a human; and we can also see that it has a great many convolutions,

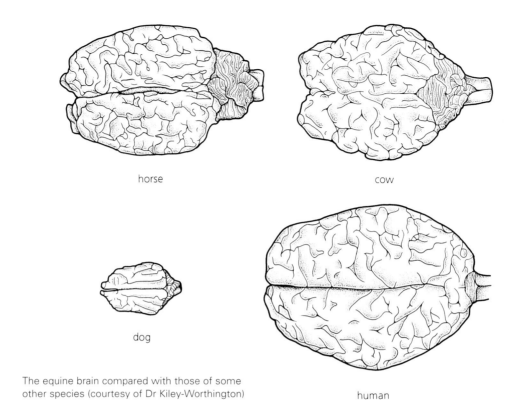

horse

cow

dog

The equine brain compared with those of some
other species (courtesy of Dr Kiley-Worthington)

human

more even than the human brain. So even if the horse's brain is, relatively speaking, on the small size, it is far from being the tiny, primitive structure so often referred to.

One hypothesis which may help to put this in perspective is that it is not so much the relative size of the brain (although this is still significant) that is important, as the volume of the cerebral cortex. The more convolutions there are, the greater the number of neurons and a corresponding rise in processing power. However, it does not automatically follow that all of this processing power will be available for what we refer to as 'thinking'. It depends on the amount of the cortex that is 'committed' – for example, to the kind of 'programmed' or 'wired in' behaviour referred to earlier in this chapter. As we have seen, while some aspects of equine behaviour are certainly 'wired in' (as are certain aspects of all mammalian behaviour, including that of humans), horses' general behaviour is not of the fixed or stereotypic kind as, although certain tendencies are innate, they can be modified by experience. This means that horses have much more of their cerebral cortex free for non-essential processing than, for example, marsupials, whose neocortex is almost all occupied by motor functions.

Some people believe this also to be true of horses. Stephen Budiansky says, 'The good news is that horses have a relatively large brain for an animal of their size. The bad news is that they use most of it just to keep their feet in the right place.'[9] He goes on to say that this may be something of an exaggeration but not much, as the sheer range of movement of which horses are capable creates a huge demand for what he calls 'hardwired controls' in the central nervous system. However, this is somewhat misleading as it is largely the hindbrain – the cerebellum, which sits to the rear of, and slightly below, the forebrain or cerebrum – that is responsible for muscle tone, co-ordination and fine control of movement, and balance. The cerebellum also has a cortex, and this cerebellar cortex has even more convolutions than the cerebral cortex. In horses the cerebellum is exceptionally large and well developed and it is this, rather than the cerebral cortex, which controls and fine-tunes those wonderfully graceful and athletic equine movements. If we look at the illustration below, we can see that the areas of the cortex associated with voluntary movement in the horse are in proportion to the areas which govern sight, smell, hearing, etc.; this leaves a considerable portion of the cerebral cortex free for non-essential thought processes.

So the relatively small size of horses' brains should not fool us into thinking that they are deficient in brain power. As Marthe Kiley-Worthington comments, 'The horse does have an extraordinarily well developed cerebral cortex, and we must wonder what goes on there, if the dog (whom we often consider is more intelligent and quicker to learn than the horse) can make do with a very much less developed fore brain.'[10]

She goes on to say,

. . . we must not underestimate how well they use this fore brain. It may just be also that there are all sorts of other things going on in their heads which we at present do not know or understand. I would suggest therefore that we must be very cautious when dismissing horses as rather stupid animals. Maybe it is we who are stupid in our not being able to understand them . . . we are very much less proficient at reading their language than they are at ours![11]

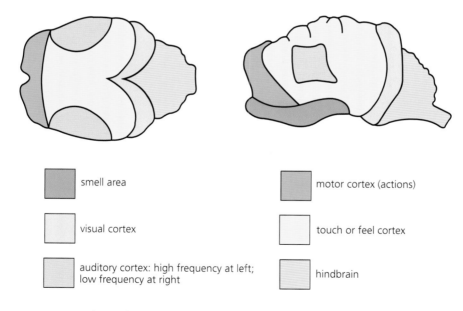

	smell area		motor cortex (actions)
	visual cortex		touch or feel cortex
	auditory cortex: high frequency at left; low frequency at right		hindbrain

Areas of the equine brain (courtesy of Dr Kiley-Worthington)

One of the main difficulties in testing the comparative intelligence of different species lies in the impossibility of devising tests that are universally applicable. Every species, including the human, is better at some things than at others. We have only to look at the work of really good tracker dogs to see this: their ability to discover and follow a scent trail is as mystifying to us as our lack of ability even to detect scent would no doubt be to them. As Vicki Hearne puts it:

> For dogs, scenting is believing. Dogs' noses are to ours as a map of the surface of our brains is to a map of the surface of an egg. A dog who did comparative psychology might easily worry about our consciousness or lack thereof, the way we worry about the consciousness of a squid.[12]

It is not enough to argue, as many would, that 'scenting' is not a sign of intelligence, merely of instinct: intelligence takes many forms, and the tracker dog's ability to 'read' a scent is dependent on the dog's powers of analysis, just as the horse's ability to 'read' body language is evidence of an equally impressive analytical power – as we shall see later in this chapter.

In any case, as Dr Kiley-Worthington points out, 'intelligence tests' really only test the ability to do such tests; and both humans and animals get better at them with practice. In order to gain some true idea of the intelligence (or otherwise) of any species, we have to rely on observations of its behaviour in the kind of situations in which it normally finds itself.

Thinking horsemen and women have always been aware that it is useless to punish a horse for any misdemeanour unless the punishment can be administered immediately – and that means immediately, not even a few seconds later, otherwise the punishment will not be connected with the misdemeanour. This is often taken to be proof of the horse's lack of reasoning power, and (it is said) it is because of this same lack of reasoning power that we must take care to ensure that aids or commands are given as clearly and consistently as possible.

But is this really the case? What if a human were placed in the same position as the horse? Suppose you are a process worker, performing a specific task, and orders are being shouted at you in a foreign language which you may or may not properly understand. Let us further suppose that you make some error of which you are blissfully unaware. The supervisor starts shouting, 'You idiot! You've got it wrong!' But what have you done wrong? The supervisor does not explain, but simply keeps on shouting that you're an idiot, you've got it wrong. Do you think you would have the remotest idea what you had done wrong unless the reproof were directly connected to the error?

Another example of how reasoning breaks down in the face of incomprehension and lack of information was given in a TV programme, *Dogs with Dunbar*. In this programme Dr Ian Dunbar demonstrated how unreasonable are the demands we often make on our animals' capacities for understanding. He asked a member of the audience to take the part of a dog being 'trained'. Without being given any prior clues, the human 'dog' had to respond to Dr Dunbar's command. This command consisted solely of the words, 'Do it!'. No other clues or information were given, and the hapless 'dog' spent several minutes trying to guess what Dr

Dunbar wanted while the trainer kept repeating the command, 'Do it!'. Eventually the 'dog' guessed correctly that Dr Dunbar wanted her to 'sit', but this was purely guesswork and not the result of a carefully reasoned thought process on the lines of, 'I am a dog; dogs are expected to sit; therefore he probably wants me to sit.' Even if the dog knew that dogs (the trained variety anyway) are generally required to sit on command, there was no way of reasoning that this was what was required in this particular situation, except by a system of trial and error. Indeed the human 'dog' did not arrive at the solution by any kind of reasoning; it was purely a lucky guess and that in spite of the fact that this was a human of at least average intelligence who did know that dogs are generally required to 'sit'! How unreasonable it is, then, to deny dogs (and horses) the power of reasoning simply because they cannot achieve what even humans, with their supposedly superior reasoning ability, cannot do!

It could be argued that dogs are perfectly capable of knowing why they are being punished; for example, if a dog pees on the carpet he is quite able (if he has been so taught) to recognise that he ought not to, and of understanding that that is why he is being punished. Most horses do not, on the face of it, appear to have the same recognition of misdemeanours (although this question will be considered in Chapter 9), which is one reason why their intelligence is often compared unfavourably with that of dogs.

The truth is that as the horse cannot understand or speak English (or any other language, even though he can be taught to associate words, and even phrases and whole sentences, with certain things or actions, and with specific stimuli, places or people), we must communicate with him in his own language: body language and the language of touch. As he is very much better at interpreting these than we are, our attempts to communicate with him in this way are apt to be very clumsy, especially by his standards. Inevitably, then, unless we have a superb command of our bodies and can prevent any involuntary actions, we are likely to be sending all kinds of unintentional signals to the horse, even when he is standing still and we, to all intents and purposes, are sitting still on his back. Some horses are so sensitive that even an involuntary movement on the part of the rider can be interpreted as an aid. A member of the Lusitano breed society, writing in the spring 1997 issue of *Luso News*, described riding a Portuguese bullfighting horse as a bizarre experience in which an involuntary twitch or cough was likely to send the combination off in the opposite direction at Mach 3! Is it the case, then, that where the horse has done something wrong he has necessarily been disobedient or failed to reason that his action was incorrect? Or is it simply a breakdown of communications? If we refuse to give the horse the benefit of the doubt and insist that he is either disobedient or stupid, just who is showing the lack of reasoning power?

Of course, I am not suggesting that horses are all so devoid of guile or malice that they are always and inevitably blameless, but knowing what is genuine disobedience or inattention and what is a simple breakdown of communication is part of the art of horsemanship. Just how subtle an art this is will be seen in later chapters. We must always ask ourselves whether we have been sending the right signals.

A story frequently used to illustrate the sheer *wrongness* of imagining that horses (for example) can think as we do, let alone communicate their thinking (and which, incidentally, proves the point just made about horses' ability to read body language), is that of Clever Hans. Hans belonged to a German, Wilhelm von Osten, who believed he had stumbled upon an equine genius. Hans could respond to various questions, either by pawing the ground a certain number of times with a hoof, or by indicating letters of the alphabet with his hoof. Many experts came to examine Hans and could find no evidence of trickery, of the giving of subtle 'cues'; Hans would still give the right answer if von Osten was not present. However the psychologist Oskar Pfungst felt that it might be more profitable to study the *questioner* rather than the horse. Pfungst discovered that Hans could not give the right answer if he could not see the questioner, or if the questioner did not know the right answer. Furthermore, he would *always* give what the questioner thought was the correct answer, even if the latter tried to remain quite still and not give any 'cues'. It became clear that Hans was reading the most minute changes in the questioner's breathing, facial expression (even the tiniest involuntary twitch of the nostrils or of the eyebrows), general postural tone, etc. and deducing the correct answer from these almost imperceptible changes that took place as the correct answer was reached. In other words, he was interpreting body language with a perception and accuracy that almost defies the human imagination; and from this he was working out when to give the desired response. Yet this truly astounding feat is commonly

Clever Hans

referred to as the 'Clever Hans' fallacy which, as Vicki Hearne says, is 'the fallacy of supposing that the animal "really" understands words or symbols when what the animal is doing is "merely" reading body language'[13].

Hearne herself will have none of this. In relation to this visual reading of body language and to what she calls the horse's 'intricate kinesthetic language', she speaks of:

> . . . a humbling realization that when we talk with horses, we are talking into a kind of intelligence we can just barely have any understanding of, partly because we communicate with horses largely through touch . . . Hence horses have continually to forgive us for what must seem to them to be extraordinarily blunt and clumsy communication, most of the time.[14]

Part of the problem is that different people mean different things when they speak of reason. Philosophers, psychologists and behaviourists have all been deeply influenced by Descartes when they define 'reason' as one of the things which sets humans apart from the rest of the animal kingdom. Mary Midgley states the problem clearly enough:

> Part of the trouble certainly is that Descartes, like Plato, saw pure, speculative reason of the logician's or mathematician's kind as lying at the core of human life – so that he was really defining man not so much by his consciousness or general intelligence as by his capacity for mathematics. But this again is a special view of what *matters* in life, of what our ambitions should be. It is not the normal meaning of reason.[15]

'Irrational' suggests a fundamental confusion about what is important. Animals – and especially horses – are seldom really confused in this way unless they are not particularly intelligent as measured against others of their own kind. The confusion may rest with those who assert that reason is a solely human attribute!

Reasons for denying that horses are capable of conceptual thought are usually, as with consciousness, based on the lack of a structured, spoken language. However, we have already seen that a lack of such language does not prevent conceptual thought; indeed, in some cases language is inimical to it. Common sense tells us that horses must have certain general concepts, at least – at the most basic level, concepts such as 'a creature that looks like *this* is dangerous'. A generalised, reflex action would not do, or horses would be forever fleeing from shadows. They need to be able to discriminate *this* class of animal or *that* type of terrain from others. And for this, as well as for more complex concepts that occur within their social interactions (such as friendship, for example) words would not, of course, be necessary. Pictures, and feelings, would be more than adequate.

Indeed, pictures can sometimes be far more eloquent than words. Philosopher Colin Wilson draws attention to this in discussing the controversial works of maverick Egyptologist René Schwaller de Lubicz. In writing about hieroglyphics (perhaps the best known form of picture writing) Schwaller argued that words are like the kind of blurry photographs one sees in three-dimensional photography; only when one views the photographs through special goggles does the image come to life.

One actually has to see three-dimensional photography of a high quality to appreciate fully what Schwaller is getting at here. A friend who is very skilled at stereo photography once showed me some photographs he had taken in the Grand Canyon. The 'flatties', as stereo photographers call conventional two-dimensional pictures, were spectacular enough but conveyed only a suggestion of the grandeur and scale of those massive cliffs. Then he invited me to put the stereoscopic viewing goggles on and showed me some stereo slides of the same landscape. The first shot looked down into the abyss from the top of the Grand Canyon, and I almost fell off my chair, my head whirling with vertigo. The whole landscape came alive, so that one felt one could reach out and actually touch the rocks. This was the closest one could get to actually being there.

In this way, Schwaller says, hieroglyphs are far more alive than mere words. 'Each hieroglyph', he says, 'can have an arrested, conventional meaning for common usage, but it includes (1) all the ideas that can be connected to it, and (2) the possibility of personal comprehension.'[16]

Schwaller argues that this three-dimensionality was a characteristic of the ancient Egyptians. I have already argued that there is no real evidence that the brains of other animals work in a fundamentally different way from ours. If ancient man's mind worked in a similar way to that of the more complex non-human mammals, then this suggests that, if early man thought in pictures rather than words, there is no reason why non-human animals cannot do so; and no reason why their thoughts cannot encompass at least moderately complex conceptual thought.

In fact, there is now considerable evidence that they are, indeed, capable of forming concepts, of generalising and reasoning. Experiments carried out by Dr Evelyn Hanggi of the Equine Research Foundation in the USA have shown, among other things, that horses can understand the relationship between object A and object C, if A is larger than B and B is larger than C. This work, which has barely scratched the surface of what Dr Hanggi believes may be the true capabilities of horses, demonstrates that they can certainly perform exercises in logical deduction – precisely what so many people are at pains to assure us horses cannot do!

Egyptian hieroglyphs

This sign is known as a *determinative*, a meaning-sign used with words for anything going into or coming out of the mouth. It has literal meanings (e.g. speaking, eating) or metaphorical meanings (expressing thoughts, emotions, etc.); it also encompasses activities associated with these, as in call out, summon

I am not suggesting that horses are *necessarily* capable of higher levels of reasoning or conceptual thought; that would be to raise unfair expectations of them (although for all we know they may well have far greater mental powers than we, with our limited means of communication with them, can even guess at). But surely we can give them credit for possessing at least some reasoning power. Humans lose nothing of their uniqueness by admitting this, as our conceptual powers still far exceed those of even the most complex non-human mammals. As Mary Midgley says, 'if the talk is of elephants, we can do justice to the miracle of the trunk without pretending that nobody else has a nose'[17].

Horses can show signs of reasoning ability in any number of ways. Susan McBane records the case of a mare who became entangled in a wire fence. She got a hind leg inside a loop of loose wire and when she moved forward she realised her leg was not free.

> She attempted to move the leg two or three times but felt the wire on it each time. Her owner was about to go out and extricate the mare when she noticed her stop and stand quite still for a few seconds. The animal looked back to the left, then to the right (it being the left leg that was caught). She then lifted her off-hind leg and, feeling for the wire carefully, put the hoof down on the loose wire, pressing it to the ground. This left the near-hind leg free. The mare then stepped slowly and carefully forward with the near hind, released the wire by lifting her off hind and, moving that forward a step, too, looked round again and finally walked off to graze elsewhere; a clear example of connected thought and the ability to work out the result of certain actions.[18]

Many horses would have panicked in such a situation, but this is not a sign of lack of intelligence and reasoning power, just of the fact that, to a horse, getting a leg or a foot trapped is one of the worst things that can happen, because it prevents the possibility of escape. Humans, too, tend to panic in such situations – even the most intelligent of them. There must be many more instances such as the one described above which go unobserved or unrecorded because they do not have any visible consequences.

Alois Podhajsky's great Lipizzaner stallion Pluto Theodorosta gave evidence of the same kind of intelligence. Retired from the Spanish Riding School at the age of 29, he found his retirement lacking in excitement. The door of his box was always open, so one day the stallion decided to go for a walk. The stallions of the Riding School are kept in the Stallburg in Vienna, a part of the Hofburg complex separated from the famous Winter Riding School by a busy side street. To get to the Riding School the stallions have to cross this street and the traffic is always halted to enable them to do so. On this particular day, Pluto Theodorosta trotted through the great courtyard of

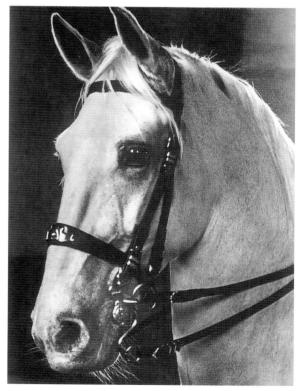

Pluto Theodorosta
(Courtesy of Mme Eva Podhajsky and Sylvia Loch)

the Stallburg and out into the narrow street. The groom who raced after him was appalled to see a bus bearing down on the stallion. 'But Pluto Theodorosta paused, waited until the traffic had passed, and crossed the street when he had convinced himself that there was no danger.'[19] The whole point here is that the stallion was *not* just repeating what he had always done in the past. Whenever they had crossed that road previously, the stallions had not waited for the traffic; *the traffic waited for them*. Had Pluto Theodorosta simply been following the habit of a lifetime, he would not have waited; he would have assumed the traffic would automatically stop for him. He did not do so; he waited and judged for himself when it was safe to cross.

A friend in Cornwall, Lynn Debnam, sent me a videotape of her Anglo-Arab gelding Pharlight Gambler playing with a child's football. Pharli was trying to catch hold of the football between his teeth but of course the ball kept spurting away from him every time he put pressure on it. Frustrated by his inability to get hold of the ball, Pharli went down on his knees and attempted to hold the ball between his forelegs so that he could get a purchase on it with his teeth. Unfortunately, because he was unable to press his forelegs close enough together to grip the ball properly, it kept squirting out from between them, flying backwards through his hind legs. Pharli would then leap to his feet, disentangle himself from the ball and the game would begin again. This surely suggests that horses may be prevented from solving certain problems not so much by a want of reasoning power, but by limitations imposed by their lack of manipulative ability. As primates we tend to forget just how much of our own enormous capacity for problem-solving by reasoning is tied up in this very manipulative ability; indeed, our superior reasoning power may well be a direct result of that ability. Pharli's amusing game with the football also suggests that greater reasoning power is something that all horses *potentially* possess, but that it needs developing by enriched experiences (a concept explored further in Chapter 16). Horses who are allowed to indulge in play of this kind almost always seem far brighter than those who are not; in Pharli's case he seemed to be saying to himself, 'If *only* I could get hold of this thing' – and, failing to get hold of it in his teeth, he tries: 'What if I clasp it between my knees?' What is this if not reasoning?

As with consciousness and self-awareness, reasoning does not have to be a case of 'all-or-nothing'. After all, at its most basic, rational thought is only a way of trying to make sense of a universe that often seems far from rational. Horses also have a need to make sense of things; this is manifested in their willingness to keep on trying to find some kind of coherence in the demands we make of them. When that coherence is missing (as it too often is), some horses will cope as best they can. Others, more sensitive or more intelligent, will break down (in the psychological sense). As Vicki Hearne says, 'the horse's drive to make sense of things is as strong as ours – call it "reason", in the way Hume had in mind when he remarked that reason is just another instinct'[20]. Owen MacSwiney maintains that the horse uses intelligence to meet most situations. 'The society into which it has been forced by domestication, being contrary to the animal's natural society, creates problems with which it can only come to terms by its powers of observation, memory, ability to understand and assimilate, and its general intelligence.'[21]

This use of the horse's 'general intelligence' often involves finding solutions to problems in ways that go far beyond the simple, reactive level of mental activity proposed by Jan May. One of our horses did this in a way that can only be described as creative. At the time, the horses were being kept at livery while our own stables were being built. During the autumn, one of the stable roofs began to leak badly and the yard owner was waiting for a spell of fine weather to get up there and repair it. So badly did the rain come in during a heavy downpour (and there were a few that autumn) that, in the meantime, Mo, a horse of great wisdom and worldly experience, was compelled to wear a New Zealand rug in his stable. Mo got fed up with the way raindrops kept falling on his bed and flooding his stable so he started dragging his empty feed bucket under the leak to catch the drips. The yard owner watched him do this several times and drew our attention to it so that we could see for ourselves. If this is not thinking and planning, I do not know what is; and I know there are many horse owners whose horses have demonstrated similar thinking and planning capabilities, in spite of all the theories that tell us horses cannot do such things.

Take, for example, our gelding Kruger. We have a pretty informal arrangement in our small yard: on occasions, when the horses are out in the field, while we are working in the yard and can thus be on hand to prevent any traffic jams, squabbling or accidents, the horses are allowed to wander freely in and out of the yard. Kruger is a horse of great charm and personality, but he is driven by his belly. After the horses have been out for so long, Kruger will wander in, apparently nonchalantly, and investigate all the mangers to see who has left some food from the morning feed. If the others are well out of immediate range, say, down at the other end of the field, he will take his time, wandering into each stable in turn and rooting out the scraps. If, on the other hand, the others are still quite near, he will only visit those stables whose occupants are most likely to have left something. Nivalis the stallion usually leaves a few scrapings; Roxzella, Nivalis's mother, sometimes leaves a bit but more often does not. The gelding Zareeba (Kruger's half-brother) never does; nor does the mare Kiri or her offspring Toska. Kruger always finishes off with Roxzella's stable because it is at the end of the block and he can peer round the corner periodically to see if any of the other horses are coming in and are likely to challenge his scavenging activities.

He has developed this a stage further. If the hayracks have been filled by the time he comes in, after investigating the likely mangers for leftovers, he then visits every stable in turn and eats as much as he can out of each in the space of time he judges he has available before he is either discovered by the other horses or chased out by us. He does not, however, eat any of his own; he saves that for later.

This tells me that Kruger is not merely responding to some stimulus but has made a conscious decision to come in and scavenge for food. (I might add that he is not in any way underfed, just extremely greedy.) He has worked out who is likely to wander in and pinch some of the leavings (reasoning from observation); he has learned from experience who is likely to have left some food; he believes that if he does not keep watch some of the others might wander in and beat him to some of the leavings; and he clearly comes in hoping to find some scraps, even though experience has taught him (a) that while the others do often leave some they do not invariably do so, and (b) that depending on what we are doing in the yard at the time, we may or may not chase him back out again. He has also learned to be opportunistic: to grab a bit of everyone else's hay while preserving his own for later. Kruger is observing, drawing conclusions, formulating a strategy and then acting upon it. In other words, he is *thinking*.

Rationality is more than mere cleverness or logic. It includes having the right priorities and knowing what matters. Computers are logical, they can even be called clever, but they are not *rational*. They do not know what is important unless they are specifically told; they cannot work it out on their own. The truly remarkable thing about the story of Clever Hans – and the one point which is most often overlooked – is not just that Hans was able to distinguish and interpret the body language of his audience with such devastating accuracy. It is that, among all the jumble of signals that the audience were quite unconsciously sending (by which I mean all the inadvertent twitches, shifts of position, etc. that anyone will make even while attempting to sit still), Hans was able to distinguish and read those that were truly relevant to his task. He knew what *mattered*.

Notes

1 Jan May, *Equus caballus*, p. 5
2 Mary Midgley, *Beast and Man*, p. 53
3 Oskar Pfungst, *Clever Hans (The Horse of Mr von Osten)*, (tr. Carl L. Rahn; orig. published by Henry Holt and Co., New York, 1911; re-published by Holt, Rinehart and Winston, Inc., 1965), p. 242
4 Pfungst, *Clever Hans*, p. 218
5 Pfungst, *Clever Hans*, p. 218
6 Karin Blignault, *Successful Schooling: Train Your Horse With Empathy* (J. A. Allen, 1997), p, 79
7 Dr Marthe Kiley-Worthington, *The Behaviour of Horses in Relation to Management and Training* (J. A. Allen, 1987), p. 38
8 Kiley-Worthington, *The Behaviour of Horses*
9 Stephen Budiansky, *The Nature of Horses*, p. 147
10 Kiley-Worthington, *The Behaviour of Horses*, p. 38
11 Kiley-Worthington, *The Behaviour of Horses*, pp. 38–9
12 Vicki Hearne, *Adam's Task*, p. 79
13 Hearne, *Adam's Task*, p. 5
14 Hearne, *Adam's Task*, pp. 106–07
15 Midgley, *Beast and Man*, p. 212
16 René Schwaller de Lubicz, quoted by Colin Wilson in *From Atlantis to the Sphinx* (Virgin, 1996), p. 201
17 Midgley, *Beast and Man*, p. 206
18 Susan McBane, *Behaviour Problems in Horses* (David and Charles paperback ed., 1994), pp. 61–2
19 Colonel Alois Podhajsky, *My Horses, My Teachers* (originally published in 1968 as Meine Lehrmeister Die Pferde; tr. by Eva Podhajsky, J. A. Allen, 1997), p. 152
20 Hearne, *Adam's Task*, p. 108
21 Marquis MacSwiney of Mashanaglass, *Training from the Ground*, p. 47

CHAPTER SEVEN

Creatures of Emotion

...I do not deny that beasts feel; what I deny is, that we may not consult our own advantage and use them as we please, treating them in the way which best suits us; for their nature is not like ours, and their emotions are naturally different from human emotions.

BARUCH SPINOZA, *ETHICS*

COUNTLESS PEOPLE, AMONG them many extremely intelligent and far from inhumane individuals, have accepted without question the position set out in the quotation above, from the works of the seventeenth-century Dutch philosopher Spinoza. The latter was not writing from any special scientific knowledge; on the contrary, he was profoundly ignorant of the most basic facts regarding the majority of non-human animals. There are many reasons for believing that Spinoza was wrong, on both moral grounds (is it really right for us to treat other creatures in any way we please, without consulting their needs and feelings, just because they are in some way different from us?) and on factual grounds (are the emotions of non-human animals really so different from human emotions?). With regard to our present subject we are perhaps fortunate that, because horses are domesticated, we have so much material ready to hand for study. On the other hand, this material has not always been used wisely. Here, as everywhere, we must be wary of making unwarranted assumptions and of accepting unquestioningly 'received wisdom'.

As we saw in Chapter 4, a surprising number of people (including, until recently, most scientists), would go further than Spinoza and assert that animals cannot feel emotion as we know it. Even people who actually keep horses may believe this to be the case; or they may believe that only certain animals feel emotions. A friend was telling me recently that a lady who keeps her pony at livery with them said, after a conversation on the subject, that she didn't realise that horses had feelings like dogs and cats do and that they could become devoted to their owners! But emotion is not something reserved for humans with their better developed brain power. The emotional centres of the brain developed millions of years ago from the primitive olfactory lobe. From this olfactory lobe there developed new areas of the emotional brain. These, collectively known as the limbic system, surround the primitive brain stem. Psychologist Daniel Goleman has described the different parts of the limbic system as looking like bagels with a bite taken out at the bottom where they join the brainstem.

With the development of these new centres of emotion, animal life became much more varied and flexible. Instead of simple, automatic reactions, the evolution of learning and memory brought with it the ability to discriminate and thereby to make choices. The neocortex – the thinking brain – developed from this discriminatory centre, and its effects were to add a greater number of nuances to emotions.

This means that emotions cannot be separated from mental activity, because the limbic system is linked to the neocortex by means of a complex neural 'wiring' system. Thoughts and emotions are indivisible from each other, as even when we think we are being totally objective, our emotions guide our thoughts. Daniel Goleman, in his compelling study of what he calls 'emotional intelligence', maintains that the general view of intelligence, which exalts the IQ as measured in rather arid intelligence tests and holds that emotions have no place in rational thought, is a narrow view of intelligence. It ignores the 'wash of feeling that gives life its flavour and its urgencies, and which in every moment biases exactly how (and how well or poorly) information is expressed.'[1] He goes on to say, 'Emotions enrich; a model of mind that leaves them out is impoverished.'[2]

This applies to animal life just as it does to humans. The development of the limbic system and its neural links with the neocortex came many millions of years before humans appeared on the scene. Ironically, much of the research that has led to greater understanding of how the limbic system interacts with the neocortex, and how this affects emotional responses, has been carried out on mammals such as rats, so we can scarcely say that emotion is a purely human quality!

The big question, therefore, is not whether other animals experience emotions, but *what* emotions they feel and in what degree. We cannot say, with Spinoza, that their nature is not like ours and their emotions are naturally different from human emotions; given the continuity between humans and other mammals, this would not make evolutionary sense. It does seem to be the case that because of the larger number of connections in the human brain which link the neocortex with the limbic system, we really do have an ability to feel the widest range of reactions to our emotions, as well as a greater number of nuances and subtleties. But let us not forget that other animals (including horses) also have complex 'wiring', as well as an enlarged neocortex. The fact that we have an advantage in this respect does not entitle us to dismiss the emotional lives of other animals, nor to claim that we cannot know anything about what they might feel. Of course, we can never know exactly what another creature feels; as we saw in Chapter 4, this is as true as of other humans as it is of animals. What we can do is look at their lifestyle and see what emotions would be appropriate to it. We can also study their behaviour to see what emotions reveal themselves, either in actions or in physiological reactions.

The problem here is to identify basic emotions and their many subtle variations. Daniel Goleman says, 'I take *emotion* to refer to a feeling and its distinctive thoughts, psychological and biological states, and range of propensities to act.'[3] As Goleman points out, there are hundreds of emotions, each with its own variations and nuances – far more than we actually have words for. Theorists argue over which emotions – if any – can be identified as the basic ones from which all others stem, but this problem need not concern us here. Attempting to catalogue and describe all the emotions (together with their many ramifications) that horses may possibly feel would take a book in itself, so all I have done here is to look at some of the more basic emotions, such as fear, anger, love and sadness. Jealousy and friendship are made up of all of these elements and so have also been included. Other emotions, such as pleasure and pride, are dealt with in later chapters. For now let us see how important their most basic emotions are to horses.

Daniel Goleman reminds us that the word emotion comes from a Latin root meaning 'to move', suggesting a tendency to act. We are constantly reminded that horses are prey animals, creatures of flight, whose defence consists of running away from danger, rather than standing and fighting as a predator might. This is true, but it is only one side of their nature, albeit an important one. To say, as some writers have done, that this one quality is what governs the mentality of domestic horses and ponies is to ignore the fact that *no* species is governed by one quality alone. Nevertheless, for the horse as a prey animal, fear is an exceptionally powerful emotion. I would hesitate to describe horses, as numerous others have done, as

The alarm posture: Roxzella starts and snorts at something in the distance

'defenceless'; it does not seem an appropriate word to describe any creature that can crush bones in its teeth and kick down a brick wall with its hind feet. Even so, a horse finds it difficult to use these weapons against predators if the latter can get hold of the horse's nose, bite at its legs or jump on its back. The horse will lash out desperately when cornered, but the best policy is always to avoid being caught in the first place. So the horse's first defence from danger is to run away, then, from a safe distance, halt and evaluate the nature of the danger. This safe distance, or 'flight distance', varies with the situation. In feral horses it may be as much as half a kilometre, though usually less; in well-handled horses in a domestic setting it may be as little as a few metres, depending on the cause of the alarm. If the source of that alarm is not immediately nearby, the horse may stand immobile for a few seconds, head raised in the classic 'alarm' pose, while he decides what to do. Then he will either 'stand down' the alert or he will take flight. In those first seconds of alarm the limbic system floods the body with hormones that fix the horse's attention on the cause of the alarm, preparing him for instant action.

Anger is another emotion which can lead to instant action: the swift attack with the teeth, the lightning kick from the hind foot. But while horses often display *aggression*, this is not necessarily the same as anger. Aggression may be nothing more than mild annoyance; the annoyance felt by a horse, for example, when another invades his personal space (an area extending around him for approximately two to three metres, into which only intimate friends and family are allowed) uninvited. It may lead to nothing more than a warning: a lift of a hind foot (if you don't go away, I might – just might – kick) or the laying back of the ears. What appears to be annoyance may not even be that; it may be part of some other behaviour,

'Go away!' Nivalis (here shown as a yearling) annoys Mo

such as the peculiar posture known as 'snaking' – head and neck extended, swinging the head from side to side – shown by stallions when moving their mares away from other groups or possible danger. Some people have interpreted this as a display of annoyance on the part of the stallion but this is unlikely, unless he is annoyed because the mares are not responding or are moving too slowly! Paul McGreevy says in his book, *Why Does My Horse . . .?* that this is a rather anthropomorphic interpretation: '. . . stallions may *seem* annoyed to the human observer, but we cannot be sure what emotions they experience'[4]. But as we saw in Chapter 4, we cannot be sure what emotions other humans experience either! We can only interpret what we see and hear. It may be that in this particular context annoyance is not what we are seeing, but when a stallion – or any other horse – is truly angry there can be no mistaking it. Full-blown anger tends to be an instant reaction. The heart-rate increases, and the body is primed for action by hormones such as adrenaline – the classic 'flight or fight' reaction. Horses who are really angry seldom pause to give warnings. Our stallion Nivalis is as sweet-natured a gentleman and as easy to handle as one could ever wish for. Yet I have seen him change in an instant, from being relaxed and calm, to a bundle of murderous rage on suddenly seeing a hated rival. Had my husband ignored Nivalis's earlier signs of annoyance at the sight of this other horse, on the grounds that we can never be sure what horses are feeling, he would have been unprepared for this reaction, and he – as well as the two horses – might have been seriously hurt.

Because aggressive behaviour is relatively obvious, it has been all too easy for observers to 'home in' on this aspect and assume that it has greater significance than may actually be the case. The nature of friendly interactions may be far less readily apparent and, indeed, may sometimes only be obvious to people who are intimately acquainted with the animals concerned. If alien observers were to eavesdrop on some human family conversations, they might easily conclude that aggression and dominant behaviour were the mainstays of human family life, and in some cases they would be right, but this would ignore the myriad far subtler threads and ties which hold human families together – such as ties of love and affection – which, ultimately, may be far more important than any aggression its members may occasionally express towards each other. In short, it would be a very crude and incomplete analysis of extremely complex behaviour; and so it is with animals in general, and horses in particular.

Nevertheless, animal behaviourists often seem obsessed with displays of aggression, not only because these are generally so obvious, but also, perhaps, because humans seem desperate to point out that while we are a very aggressive species, so are other species of animals. One question often asked is why are stallions aggressive? A far better question would be, under what circumstances are stallions aggressive? One cannot say stallions are basically aggressive, because no creature is *basically* any one quality. Certain qualities may predominate in different circumstances. It is not, for example, true that stallions will invariably show aggression to other horses. Any number of people have found that, providing there are no mares about, and the horses concerned have been properly brought up and allowed to form social bonds with other horses, it is possible to turn serving stallions out together with geldings or even with other stallions without mishap; they simply form into the kind of 'bachelor band' which will be referred to in the next chapter. A friend from Cornwall, Sara Debnam, not only turns their gelding Pharlight Gambler (mentioned in Chapter 6) out with her stallion Balthasar, she also rides Balthasar out while leading Pharli!

Aggression is only one aspect of a stallion's emotional make-up, albeit a necessary one. Stallions are aggressive in much the same circumstances as any other mammal: when they feel threatened, when their families are threatened or because of frustration (when this type of aggression is turned on a third party not connected with the source of the frustration or annoyance, it is known as 'redirected aggression'). In the case referred to above, Nivalis felt threatened because he had come to regard this other horse as a potential rival. Many other

Pharli with Sara Debnam and Balthasar (Lynn Debnam)

species are aggressive in defence of their territories but, as the next chapter will show, horses are not territorial in this sense. Nor do they generally have scarce resources to defend so, apart from their personal space, they defend what means most to them. In general this means their friends and family.

As we shall see in the next chapter, horses' social lives revolve around their family groups, and the friendships they form within those groups. In domestication, because family groups are comparatively rarely kept together, friendships form with other horses from outside the family, as well as with animals of other species, including of course humans. The bonds formed within these friendships can be very deep and very strong, and we must not ignore or underestimate them if we value our horses' emotional well-being. Yet such is the obsessive fear of anthropomorphism that we are often encouraged to do just that. Paul McGreevy says, 'Anxious to avoid anthropomorphism, ethologists tend not to use the term "friendship" for non-sexual bonds that can be observed between horses. Instead, they favour expressions such as "preferred associates", "affiliates" and "peers".'[5] Recognising that he is writing for a non-scientific readership, McGreevy does go on to say that: 'In deference to the purists I too will try to remember that I am a scientist, but I have retained the title of this section [i.e. 'Friendship'] so that everybody knows what I am referring to.'[6] However, in spite of this con-descension, he does not say *why* it is anthropomorphic to use such terms as 'friendship'; he appears to assume that this should be self-evident.

Friends: Arabian gelding Zareeba and Connemara foal Dandy

Friends: Zareeba and Golly, a 32-year-old Shetland

In the same way, we are told by another author that: 'In domesticity, one horse left on its own may appear to be pining for its friend and indeed this may be so; but it is not because it misses friendship as we know it, but rather because it is disliking its solitary state.'[7] How easy it is to dismiss relationships which may be of immense importance to the horses concerned! There are countless examples which prove that it is not simply some generalised 'herd instinct' that makes horses pine for departed companions; in many cases the horses in question are not left on their own but have other companions, yet they clearly miss their special friend who is no longer there.

The fact that such friends may sometimes quarrel leads to some strange conclusions. McGreevy says in this respect that:

It is probably because 'friendship' is the wrong word to describe what is going on that equine friendships seem curious to human observers. For instance, antagonistic interactions are more common between affiliated horses, but these exchanges are less aggressive than with less bonded individuals.[8]

But this is exactly what happens in human friendships! Who are you most likely to quarrel with? Those closest to you! The history of any normal human relationship is marked by countless ups and downs. The stronger and more lasting the bond, the more likely it is that there will be frequent, if minor, disagreements; people who spend a lot of time in each other's company are bound to have their differences. I see no reason why the same phenomenon, observed in horses, should be in any way remarkable. Nor do I see why the term 'friendship' should be considered wrong in such a context. Friends are those for whom we feel special liking and affection and whose company we like to share. In what way is it supposed to be different for horses?

Where family groups are kept together, the clannish nature of horses means that the strongest bonds of friendship are usually to be found within that group, although, as with every aspect of life, equine or human, there are any number of exceptions: our Arab mare Tiff (Mikenah) and her half-brother, the stallion Balthasar, simply don't like each other. In general, however, the strength of this family bond must never be underestimated. We have only to see what happens when close family members, or old friends, are reunited after a period of separation. I shall never forget the day my Arab gelding Zareeba and his half-brother, the Arab x warmblood Kruger were brought together again after a two-year separation. I had brought Zareeba as a two year old direct from his breeder; before that he and Kruger (a year younger than Zareeba) had spent most of their time together. Just over two years after I had acquired Zareeba, my husband decided to buy Kruger as well.

When we brought Kruger home, he and Zareeba started to whinny out to each other as soon as Kruger was off the wagon. Turned out together in our sand arena for the first time, they spent ages running around together and playing in that rough, coltish manner which alarms those who do not realise that no actual aggression is involved. Then they settled down to groom each other, their delight in their reunion evident in every aspect of their body language. Since that day they have never spent more than a few hours apart.

Such is horses' need for companionship that horses kept on their own can suffer severe emotional deprivation. Where a congenial equine companion cannot be provided, many

Brothers indulging in rough play: Kruger and Zareeba

horses still manage to form close relationships with animals of other species. For this
reason thoughtful one-horse owners try to
provide a suitable stable or field companion
for their horses. Sheep and goats, being relatively peaceful creatures, are great favourites.
Lisa Smith recalls how an Arab mare she
used to have became extremely attached to a
nanny goat Lisa had provided as her companion. Shaka-Dari would not travel to a
show unless the goat could go too! When the
goat gave birth to twins, Shaka-Dari became
very fond of them too and would lie down in
the field with both kids beside her.

This need for companionship has led
some writers to express the belief that horses
only bond with humans (or other animals) if
equine company is not available. Stephen

Shaka-Dari with twin kids (Lisa Smith)

Budiansky says, 'Our horses' affection for us, their owners, is unquestionably real, grounded
in a basic instinct to form friendship bonds; it is slightly bruising to our egos, though, to realize that they bond with us only for lack of better company.'[9] But this is not really true,
because even horses that have as much congenial equine company as they could possible
want may still form very strong bonds of affection with their human handlers, riders and
trainers. Arab horses, and those generally termed 'Iberian' (i.e. Andalusian or pure-bred
Spanish horses; Lusitanos; and Lipizzaners) in particular are very 'human' oriented horses,
who will gladly – and voluntarily – leave their equine companions to spend time with their
human friends. The extent to which they do so depends, of course, on a number of different
factors – not least the degree of empathy which exists between such horses and the humans
in their lives.

Horses who lead rich and full social lives with other horses may also have close friends
among other species, such as cats. Several of our own horses, particularly Zareeba, are very
partial to cats and never seem to mind a small furry body rubbing up against their legs. The
late Lady Wentworth, breeder of some of the finest Arab horses of this century, recalled how
one of her stallions was very fond of a stable cat which used to sleep in his manger. At feed
times, the stallion would very gently take the cat in his teeth by the scruff of its neck and
equally gently deposit it on the floor. But while many accounts exist of horses making friends
with cats, goats, sheep and various other animals, there seem to be relatively few examples of
friendships between horses and dogs. This may be because dogs are among the horse's natural predators and this tends to make horses very wary of them. Even so, while some of our
horses have remained either indifferent or actively hostile to our dogs, others have responded to them in a friendly manner. Toska has never been fond of dogs, but when we acquired

Zareeba and Tigger: one cat
is good company . . .

. . . two are even better.
Zareeba with Tigger and
Gizmo

Brian and Kruger enjoying a scratch

our Doberman, Max, he and Toska developed a most unlikely friendship. Max (rescued by the RSPCA from a compound) had never seen horses before he came to us. He was afraid of them and acted aggressively toward them. After a few weeks, though, he started to make friendly overtures to them, unfortunately by jumping up and trying to lick their noses. As catching hold of the nose is how some predators immobilise horses in the wild, horses have an instinctive tendency to back off from – or respond aggressively to – what they see as an assault. But Toska, the least likely of all of our horses to make friends with a dog, did not seem to mind Max licking his nose and face, and after a while even seemed to welcome the dog's presence. One day my husband arrived at the stables to find the kickover bolt of Toska's stable flipped back. Certain that he had secured the bolt the night before, he was worried that intruders had got into the yard, although that seemed unlikely with Max loose about the place. Then, having secured Toska's stable again, Brian saw Max pawing at the door, trying to get in to be with Toska and, in the process, knocking the bolt back!

Some of our horses (such as Zareeba and the foal Imzadi) have actually sought contact with dogs, with varying results. Our late Doberman, Cooper, seemed to appreciate the attentions of the horses who did like him, being quite happy to sit still while they licked and whiffled at his back, nibbled at his tail, etc.

Unlike the stable cats, however, who relish and reciprocate such attentions from the horses, Cooper reacted in a purely passive way. Zareeba likes dogs and tries desperately to make friends with them. Cooper liked Zareeba in turn, and responded to his friendly overtures by leaning up against the horse's legs or touching noses with him, but the communication problem came when Zareeba invited Cooper to groom him by licking his back or whiffling at him with his mobile, prehensile muzzle. Cooper tolerated this, but with a look of puzzlement, as if to say, 'Darned if I know what this creature wants, but I'll go along with it anyway.' As mutual grooming with a friend is an extremely important part of Zareeba's life, he must have wondered why Cooper did not reciprocate; after all – as we shall see – the cats and humans in his life all do!

Indeed, mutual grooming plays a very important part in the social lives of horses. The whiffling actions of the very mobile muzzle and lips, nibbling with the teeth, and occasionally licking (although the latter is more usually seen in mares with newborn foals and courting stallions) of the coat – all of these can be gentle, vigorous or even quite rough, depending

on the circumstances and the horses involved. Mutual grooming, or allogrooming (as behavioural scientists call it), serves not only to clean the skin of debris, loose hair, dead skin, etc. but also, by virtue of its intimacy, to cement bonds between friends and family alike. It has also been shown to reduce the heart-rate of the horses involved, which has led some observers to conclude that it is not, as is generally supposed, a sign of friendship but mainly – or even solely – a means of reducing aggression. A recent study of the one remaining truly wild horse, *Equus przewalskii*, seemed to confirm this. However, the behaviour patterns of Przewalski horses with regard to grooming are quite different from those of *Equus caballus*, the domestic horse, so it seems perverse to use the former as a model for interpretation. Besides, such a conclusion simply does not make sense.

Zareeba and Roxzella enjoying a mutual scratch
Below Mother and daughter: Kiri and Imzadi (Antonia Harris)

While mutual grooming undoubtedly has a role to play in reducing tension, and with it aggression, this cannot be its main function. Mutual grooming is most frequent, and most prolonged, between horses that are already bonded by family ties or affection. The average amount of time horses spend grooming each other appears to be between three and ten minutes, while two of our horses, Zareeba and Roxzella, who are very devoted to each other, sometimes spend up to 20 minutes or more in intense grooming activity. Further, while some mares may sometimes show aggression towards their foals, many others never do and yet they and the foals still groom each other. If it were truly the case that mutual grooming really serves to deflect aggression, why would a foal who had never experienced aggression from, nor observed aggressive signals in, humans seek to groom with both me and my husband, as Imzadi did when she was only a few hours old?

Here, as elsewhere, the 'egoist' model described in Chapter 3 acts to distort motives. Following the egoist train of thought, Paul McGreevy says, . . . 'like most animals, horses have not evolved to give each other something for nothing'. Commenting on the fact that horses like to have their heads rubbed, he points out that it is rare for a horse to stand and allow another horse to rub his head on their flank. 'This is because, in such a T-shaped arrangement, they cannot be certain that the favour will be reciprocated.'[10] But this is simply not true. I have seen numerous horses rubbing their heads on others in this way; one of the little ponies turned out in the field belonging to the riding school next door used to rub his head against the side of a huge Thoroughbred colt, who would stand good naturedly while pint-sized Aero relieved his itch. Only the day before writing this, as I was walking up the road towards our stables, I saw two ponies, regular companions, standing at right-angles to each other, one of them planted firmly while the other rubbed his head on her neck. Among our own horses the Arab stallion and his dam regularly groom each other, and I have frequently seen Nivalis go up to Roxzella and rub his head vigorously against her shoulder. Roxzella will, in turn, do much the same to her boyfriend Zareeba. She approaches him at right-angles to his body, and steadying herself against his flank, rubs her head up and down his back ecstatically, while the long-suffering gelding simply stands there, bracing himself against the pressure of Roxzella's weight.

I think this explains why so many horses do *not* appear to tolerate such one-sided grooming: the pressure exerted by a horse indulging in a vigorous head-rub is considerable and more than enough to send an unprepared human flying. While horses can obviously take a great deal more than this before they, too, are thrown off balance, they still feel unbalanced by it and this must be a very unpleasant feeling for a creature whose whole sense of security centres on his ability to balance himself. To allow a companion to groom in this way, a horse must feel a great deal of affection for that companion, which would explain why I have only ever seen it among horses who are very close to each other emotionally. So if your horse wants to rub his head against you (and you don't mind a few bruises) take it as a sign of affection, brace yourself hard against something solid, and feel flattered that your horse considers you a friend who will tolerate such rough treatment!

By the same token, if our horses show signs that they would like us to indulge in mutual

Zareeba uses the author as a scratching post

grooming with them, we should respond to this if we want to cement our relationship with them. Some horses can be quite rough but others are surprisingly gentle. Among our horses Zareeba, Nivalis and Kruger come into the latter category; all three of them can give the back of one's neck a wonderful massage with their gently whiffling, mobile muzzles – as effective as the hands of any masseur!

Sometimes one must be prepared for a horse to ask (by way of body language) to be groomed in ways that may not appeal to everyone. If an unsuspecting person for whom Zareeba has developed a liking should go into his box and give him a friendly scratch on the neck, they may be disconcerted to have the horse swing round abruptly whereupon they find themselves presented with a large equine backside. They might miscontrue this as threatening but they would be very much mistaken: it is Zareeba's way of telling one that he wants his backside scratched.

Many horse owners report that their horses seem to enjoy licking their hands (and sometimes their faces as well). The approach which denies horses any feelings of affection will insist that this is a purely biological action: as humans have a considerable amount of salt in their sweat, this is a horse's way of trying to obtain extra salt. This is no doubt true to an extent; from being a very young horse Zareeba has shown a tendency to lick my hands and as many other horses do this with me I have often thought that I must have very salty skin. However, Zareeba has not one, but two salt licks in his stable, both of which are regularly, but not excessively, used. And as he does not, on veterinary evidence, have an abnormally high salt intake requirement, there must be some other explanation. Having spent countless hours watching the social interactions of horses with each other, as well as the interactions of horses with humans, cats, dogs and other animals, I have come to the conclusion that horses lick each other, humans, cats and dogs, etc. *because they like to do so*. Because the usual grooming actions – nibbling, whiffling and scratching – are relatively obvious, it is easy for the observer to concentrate on these and to overlook more subtle actions, such as the delicate licking actions carried out by some horses with a favoured partner. Stallions lick and nibble their mares during courtship. Mares lick their foals tenderly, and so on. Zareeba and Imzadi used to lick the Doberman Cooper's back. The stable cats are very fond of going into Zareeba's stable where they curl up in the straw next to him, trusting him to be careful enough not to stand on them. It used to puzzle me why one cat in particular would regularly come out of Zareeba's stable with his head, neck and part of his back soaking wet; I used to think that if he fell in the water bucket with such monotonous regularity, he must be a singularly stupid cat – and why was it always the same parts of him that were wet? Then one day I happened to see what was going on: this particular cat had a habit of sitting on Zareeba's back, licking his withers and combing out the long mane hairs that grow on the top of the withers. Zareeba had started to reciprocate and was giving the cat a good wash! As a horse's tongue is not only much bigger but much wetter than a cat's, the result was a very soggy moggy.

Zareeba likes to lick humans: shown here with Joanne

As the distribution of feline sweat glands means that a cat's coat hair is unlikely to be salty, and as dogs do not sweat, it is difficult to see how a horse could be motivated to lick them by a need for salt. Licking would seem, in this context, to be a purely social action, performed as part of a grooming ritual with someone whose company the horse enjoys – a compliment, if you like. So if a strange horse licks you, he may indeed only be after the salt on your hands. On the other hand, he may be trying to make friends – so take it as intended that way and you may be surprised by the response.

Even the sex lives of horses are far more complex than we are generally led to believe. The received wisdom about animal sexual relations is that if they are not exactly nasty, brutish and short (although they may be all three), they are at best seasonal (with the exception of those of some apes), and involve only a primitive instinct to mate. It is assumed that no emotional involvement is felt.

Indeed, it is widely assumed that animals in general are incapable of romantic love. Writing about animals who mate for life, J. Benyus says,

It's important to remember . . . that these animals are not displaying 'true love', but simply following the dictates of their genes. They are survival machines, and their mission is to multiply their own genes in the gene pool. If a male felt that his partner could raise young without him, he'd be off in a flash. But this would not be abandonment in our terms, and we need not feel sorry for the female. Both are pursuing their own game plan that will lead to the best positioning of their genes – a pursuit that is adaptive and, therefore, beautiful.[11]

Commenting on the previous passage, Jeffrey Masson and Susan McCarthy have this to say,

> Whatever their scientific view of human coupling may be, most people would not accept this as an accurate way of looking at their own loves and families, far less of their emotional motivations, yet where the difference on this point lies between animals and people is not stated. The fact that an animal is described as a machine on the one hand, and as a creature that may ponder whether its partner can raise young alone on the other, is only one inconsistency in this passage.[12]

Yet, because they express the currently fashionable, sociobiological 'survival machine' explanation for animal behaviour, such gross distortions of animal motives are often accepted uncritically.

One of the main reasons for denying animals a capacity for romantic love may be that among humans it has often been considered to be such a rarefied emotion that it only occurs at certain times, in certain cultures, and (dare one say it?) among certain classes. We saw in Chapter 4 how, until relatively recently, it was often assumed among the more educated classes in Western Europe that the 'lower classes' 'don't feel things as we do'. Similarly, it has often been claimed that romantic love was unknown among less privileged people. In the 1970s I remember reading a historical treatise on love which maintained that romantic love was a product of the nineteenth century; the same book claimed, in all seriousness, that sex as a pastime rather than a means of reproduction was invented in the 1960s. Others have stated that romantic love was an invention of the Middle Ages. Such views make complete nonsense of huge chunks of human history and have ignored the mass of evidence, whether archaeological, historical or literary, that romantic love has existed in all cultures, at all levels of education, from prehistoric times. Yet anthropologists have, until relatively recently, simply assumed that, in the words of anthropologist William Jankowiak, this type of behaviour was 'culture-specific'. Researchers had 'assumed' – as they seem all too prone to do – that romantic love did not exist in the culture they were studying, so they simply did not look for evidence of it, nor did they ask questions about the kind of activities often associated with romantic love, such as clandestine affairs, elopements, suicides over love affairs, etc. Yet all these things occurred in the cultures they studied – they simply didn't bother to follow them up.[13]

That romantic love – or something so close to it that it is scarcely worth giving it another name – does occur in animals rapidly becomes clear from the number of case-studies of different species cited by Jeffrey Masson and Susan McCarthy in their ground-breaking study of animal emotions, *When Elephants Weep*. The few ethologists who have not been intimidated by the fear of being found guilty of the heresy of anthropomorphism have never doubted its existence among animals. Konrad Lorenz argued in favour of the evolutionary continuity which makes it seem far more likely than otherwise that animals in general are capable of falling in love in the same way as humans (and he is not just talking about purely sexual attraction). In *King Solomon's Ring* he says:

And if I have just spoken of a young male jackdaw falling in love with a jackdaw female, this does not invest the animal with human properties, but, on the contrary, shows up the still remaining animal instincts in man. And if you argue the point with me, and deny that the power of love is an age-old instinctive force, then I can only surmise that you yourself are incapable of falling a prey to that passion.[14]

What about horses? Do they fall in love, as jackdaws, geese and parrots, as well as many different species of mammals, do?

According to Henry Blake, 'it is unusual for anything except sexual attraction to be involved in the mating of horses'[15]. But if we watch their behaviour, I think we must conclude that horses do fall in love. Strictly controlled breeding conditions are the rule in a domestic setting, and mares and stallions are frequently given little or no choice in the matter of a mate. The fact that they will still mate with each other – and that stallions can be taught to mount a dummy 'mare' for artificial insemination purposes – is often taken as proof that instinct alone is at work and that horses are incapable of emotional involvement at such times (although I do not think any species which exhibits such a predilection for sexual 'toys', such as inflatable rubber dolls, has any right to pass judgement in this matter). Also, one has to consider how many such matings are, in fact, rather forced, in many cases with neither mare nor stallion allowed to court each other as they would in a free-ranging situation.

Whether allowed this element of choice or not, mares and stallions can still display very strong likes and dislikes in the matter of potential mates – and they can make these preferences known in no uncertain manner. Countless breeders have stories to tell of how mares or stallions have fallen in love with specific members of the opposite sex and will not look at another. My own Arab mare Roxzella ran out with a stallion for several years. Their relations were perfectly amicable but Zella positively refused to have anything to do with the stallion sexually. Nor, when she was sent away to stud, did the stud staff have any greater success in persuading her to accept a very handsome Thoroughbred as a mate. Eventually she went to another Arab, and this time she decided that this was the one for her! A former stud manager recalls how one mare she had in her care was equally determined not to succumb to any stallion presented to her. After endless rejections, they turned her out with a stallion who ran with his mares. Elaine went into the field one day to find this mare, who previously would not entertain a stallion anywhere near her, standing with her head over the stallion's back, blissfully happy and relaxed. From her whole demeanour, Elaine said, it was clear that the mare had quite simply fallen in love with him.

Given the choice (which few are), stallions too can be extremely discriminating in the selection of a mate. The refusal of stallions to mate with mares with whom they have grown up, even where they are not related, may be a natural inhibition that safeguards against close inbreeding and the consequent narrowing of the gene-pool. In many cases, however, one cannot discount the possibility of simple personal dislike. Some stallions show preferences – or dislikes – for mares on account of their colour. Lady Anne Blunt of the famous Crabbet

Arabian Stud recounted how her grey stallion Azrek only became excited by mares of the same colour as himself. This widely reported phenomenon is usually explained in terms of the stallion being reminded of his dam's colour, and in some cases this may be so. But it does not explain our own stallion's preference for bay mares, as his own mother is grey, as he is himself. However, Nivalis was born bay and has only very gradually turned grey. It seems that, in his case, he associates bay mares with his own colour – perhaps another argument that horses are indeed aware of themselves! My niece's stallion Losker, who is bay, dislikes bay mares and prefers chestnuts. Other stallions can show all kinds of preferences in mares, some of them apparently eccentric, but clearly of great importance to the horses concerned.

It is not only females and entire males who can fall in love. Geldings can be smitten too. When we first brought Roxzella home, Kruger was struck by the proverbial *coup de foudre*. When the mare was first turned out into the field and trotted out with her incredible airy, floating action, Kruger simply stood on the other side of the fence, eyes popping out, with a goofy expression on his face. He never took his eyes off her and at the first opportunity attached himself to her. For over a year she was the light of his life, and he has never shown the same interest in any other mare.

At one time we had an old gelding, Mo, who was clearly in love with Kiri, my husband's hunter mare. They were constant companions, grooming each other almost exclusively (although Mo would occasionally condescend to allow Zareeba and Kiri to groom). They went everywhere together, lay down side by side in the field and, if out of each other's sight for even a few minutes, would call hysterically for each other. If Kiri, when in season, showed any interest in the geldings next door, Mo would become extremely jealous, driving her away from the fence and generally berating her for flirting. When Kiri went away to stud, Mo became very dejected, calling for her incessantly, losing his appetite and generally showing no interest in any kind of activity. When Kiri eventually returned, Mo was beside himself with joy and this made us decide that we could never part with him because it would be cruel to separate him from Kiri permanently. However, matters resolved themselves because once Kiri had her foal, although she and Mo were still very good friends, the intensity had gone out of their relationship. Kiri had her foal to think about, and Mo had the distraction of playing with our young Arab colt Nivalis. Eventually Mo went to a wonderful home where he is in his element among a group of mares – all his!

It is usually assumed that geldings lose all stallion characteristics and that they will take on the voice and demeanour of a mare, but this is only true in some cases. Much seems to depend on whether the horse had reached sexual maturity when he was gelded, and, of course, on the individual horse. Some geldings, no matter at what age they were gelded, retain a great many stallion-like characteristics, particularly in their behaviour towards mares. I remember a pony belonging to my sister-in-law, who would jealously herd the mares away from the other geldings, or, having attached himself to one pony mare in particular, would drive her away from the others and not allow them anywhere near her.

However, while some geldings clearly retain some sexual feelings, they do not always seem to remember how to follow them through. Mo would behave to Kiri when she was in season exactly as a stallion would, nibbling and licking her and generally teasing her. Kiri would stand for him, just as she would for a stallion. Then it was as though he just couldn't remember what came next; he appeared to lose interest and simply wandered off, leaving his lady love flat and quite clearly extremely frustrated!

Other geldings evidently *do* remember what comes next and, in the right circumstances, have no hesitation in acting upon their knowledge. Some equine behavioural scientists maintain that it is extremely rare for a gelding actually to serve a mare properly, but this phenomenon may be more common than is generally realised. I have seen it happen myself, several times. On one such occasion, we were visiting another horse-owner one day when he happened to glance through the window which looked out onto one of his paddocks, and remarked, 'That gelding's been serving the filly all day.' We looked out and, sure enough, there was the gelding quite clearly serving a young mare. As no harm was being done, and both the horses seemed happy enough, the owner was not bothered. It is not true, either, that geldings who do manage to serve mares are invariably rigs. The gelding just referred to certainly was not. Nor is it true that geldings who retain sexual feelings are necessarily rigs. My own gelding Zareeba is defintely not a rig, yet he behaves towards the mares Roxzella and Tiff just as a stallion would. In fact, this is an example of how horses can have repressed feelings which do not surface until the conditions are right.

Zareeba was gelded at the age of two, when he was already sexually mature. Two weeks after being gelded he did serve a mare, fortunately without any untoward consequences. He seemed to settle down after that and, apart from a slight hankering after a pony mare kept at the same livery yard, showed no real interest in mares. When, at the age of four, he was moved with our other horses to our own property, he never showed more than a passing, friendly interest in Kiri, the only mare we had at the time.

When we acquired Roxzella, all this changed. To begin with, Roxzella was attracted to Kruger who, as described above, fell violently in love with her. But this affair was of short duration. Either Kruger was too boisterous for her or she was too unpredictable for him – who knows? Whatever the reason, they lost interest in each other and Roxzella started to become friendly with Zareeba. They spent more and more time together and eventually became inseparable companions. Zareeba's attitude changed. He became very protective towards Roxzella, sometimes chasing other horses away when they attempted to approach her. I was surprised by the degree of aggression he showed as he very rarely displays aggression to any living creature, except to other horses when he was protecting Nivalis as a foal, and that had been only on odd occasions. This behaviour reached its peak when the riding school next door turned a three-year-old colt out in the field adjoining our land. The colt immediately started to flirt with Roxzella, which Zareeba did not like one bit. If Roxzella wandered over to the fence in response to the colt's interest, Zareeba would come galloping full tilt from wherever he had been grazing, screaming his head off, to intervene. Normally the friendliest of horses, he has since then also shown similar hostility towards a gelding who broke through into one of our fields. When this happened, none of the other horses showed any aggression whatsoever; they and the intruder (whom they already knew over the fence) settled down immediately to graze peacefully. But when the gelding ambled over to Roxzella, showing no more than a friendly interest, Zareeba instantly launched an attack, teeth bared and mouth open for a savage bite. The gelding quickly got the message and retired instantly. Zareeba, honour satisfied, broke off the attack and returned to his lady-friend's side.

It is not true, either, that horses only take an interest in each other sexually at certain times of the year. Dr Marthe Kiley-Worthington has for some years been experimenting with a system of running a vasectomised stallion with mares, thus allowing them a more natural lifestyle without the complications of too many foals. 'One of the interesting consequences,' she writes,

> . . . is that the mares appear to encourage sex and copulation from the stallion, and in some cases this has continued throughout the year. Interestingly enough it looks as if the mares are happy to have sex with him when they have been separated and returned and even when, according to their cycling they should not be in season. Whether they are having sex at other times than just when in season remains to be confirmed.[16]

There is some evidence that this does occur. I have heard numerous reports of mares allowing stallions to serve them when they are not in season, and Dr June Alexander, who breeds both Arabs and Welsh Cobs at her Okeden Stud, told me of a mare she had who would willingly stand for the stallion only a matter of hours before foaling! These may be far from isolated instances; relatively few observations have been made to see whether stallions and mares who run together do copulate other than just when the mare is in season. Certainly, there are numerous instances among other species where copulation takes place outside the female's 'season', and not just among primates. Female cats who have been spayed will sometimes have sexual relations with tomcats if they like them enough; this has occurred with several of my own cats. There may be many other such examples throughout the animal world, but so widely has it been assumed that sex is a purely seasonal matter that little investigation has been carried out.

Regarding her experimental group, Dr Kiley-Worthington continues, 'what is very clear is that sex is frequent and appears to be extremely important to both the stallion and the mares. After all why should it not be as important to them as it is to humans? Perhaps more so, if they are such emotional creatures.'[17]

If horses can love, can they also feel jealousy? This is an ambiguous emotion, with elements of love, fear and anger all bound up in it. Love for another may be accompanied by fear that a real or imagined rival will steal the affections of the loved one; the result may be anger, directed at one or both of the other parties involved. For some reason which is not at all clear, some people seem reluctant to accept that jealously is an emotion which horses might feel. For example, in Paul McGreevy's book *Why Does My Horse . . .?* an enquiry into a horse's behaviour towards his owner's boyfriend ends, 'I know horses can't be jealous'[18], while Léonie Marshall, in *Your Horse's Mind*, says, 'Jealousy is not an emotion one would attribute to horses'[19], and then goes on to give an example of behaviour which, in a human, would quite clearly be a sign of jealousy! In neither of these two cases is any explanation given as to *why* horses should be incapable of such an emotion. I suppose that if one denies that horses are capable of love and friendship, one must also believe them free of jealousy. Why is it permissible to state on the one hand that we cannot be sure what emotions horses feel, and on the other to deny them the ability to feel specific emotions?

In any case, there is plenty of evidence that horses *do* feel jealousy – sometimes painfully so. Nivalis and Toska used to be the best of friends until my husband (with whom Nivalis has an exceptionally close relationship) started to lunge and long-rein Toska. At the same time, Toska's mother gave birth to Nivalis's foal, which cemented the stallion's relationship with her. Nivalis not only resented Toska's still evident affection for his mother, he also resented Brian paying too much attention to Toska. Nivalis felt threatened on two fronts: his relationship with his mare, and his relationship with his human. Had he been older and more mature, he might have been able to cope with this better, but his self-confidence had not yet formed to that extent. Unable to get at his perceived rival, he would take his frustration out on the nearest person (usually me) – not in a violent manner but simply by becoming nippy and generally a pain to be around, quite unlike his normal gentle, well-mannered self. We have had to be extremely tactful in handling this situation, as a jealous stallion is no joy to deal with. Nivalis still dislikes Toska, and probably always will, but at least he no longer objects quite so much when he sees Brian paying attention to Toska – so long as someone is there to make a big fuss of him and tell him how wonderful he is! If that is not jealousy, how then can we describe what is going on in any way that actually makes sense? If a human were to behave in such a way on seeing one of his closest friends not only making up to his wife or girlfriend, but also threatening to take away his best friend, we should have no hesitation in saying that he was jealous. Why should it be different for horses?

If horses can feel love, and consequently jealousy, it follows that they can also experience a varying range of emotions, from sadness to real grief, on being parted from friends and those they love. As I mentioned in Part I, it is often stated that animals cannot know the concept of death – at least, of their own death. However, there is no real evidence to suggest that this is correct. Some species may understand that they, too, will one day die; some may not. We have no way of knowing for certain, but the reactions of some animals on approaching a slaughterhouse do at least suggest that they have far more understanding of such things than we like to believe. It would be comforting to think that they have no notion of their approaching deaths but this is an assumption I do not think we have any right to make.

Just because horses in a domestic setting do not always appear to feel grief or distress over their dead companions, we should not assume that they are incapable of such feelings. In many cases, lack of reaction to another's dead body may simply reflect lack of experience. In the wild, animals inevitably witness deaths among their family, group, mates or other companions. In domestic situations, where groups tend to be less stable (in some cases constantly changing), horses may never see the dead body of another horse. How many humans, if kept socially isolated and never having had the concept of mortality explained to them, would immediately recognise death on seeing a body for the first time? In any case, the apparent indifference of some horses to dead companions may not be indifference at all, but a modification of an instinct which, in the wild, would tell them not to linger near a dead body as it might be dangerous to do so. Commenting on the reactions of domestic horses to the dead body of another horse, Tom Ainslie remarks, 'If a horse dies in its pasture, the other occupants stay as far away from the corpse as they can possibly get. They probably associate all death with predatory attack, fearing that the latter may still be near.'[20]

Certainly zebras, whose social organisation is very similar to that of *Equus caballus*, can show grief for their dead offspring. It has been noted that zebra stallions remain on good terms with their adult sons. During one study of wild zebras, researchers wanted to mark a stallion who was still living in his father's herd at the age of four and a half but, unfortunately, the anaesthetic dart killed the young stallion. The latter's father came over to the body repeatedly and tried to rouse him. Later that day he was seen roaming from herd to herd for hours, calling for his son.[21] This might mean that he had not grasped the fact of his son's death; it could equally mean that he was emotionally unable to grasp immediately that *his* son was dead. After all, many humans also show an inability to accept the fact of a loved one's death until some considerable time after the event. In any case, the fact that the zebra stallion was clearly distressed by the death of his son tells us something about the emotions equines feel at such a loss. Donkeys, for example, can become so attached to companions that the loss of such a companion can deprive the bereaved donkey of all will to live; in such circumstances donkeys have been known literally to die of grief.

Mares suffer grief at the loss of their foals; this is evident in their behaviour and their whole demeanour. Our Arab mare Tiff's mother, Bel, went into a deep depression when one of her foals was born dead. How easy and convenient it is for veterinary surgeons and behavioural scientists to dismiss this as 'merely' the result of hormonal activity. We do not doubt that human mothers feel such grief for their dead children; what evidence is there that mares do not have similar feelings?

Behavioural scientists, as we have seen, often feel obliged to provide some sociobiological explanation for every type of behaviour. Paul McGreevy, for instance, notes that among free-ranging horses, if a suckling foal dies, its dam will often resume nursing the previous year's foal. 'In this way she enhances the viability of her genes, which she has already passed on to the surviving foal.' This may be the ultimate *result*, but it does not begin to explain either the mare's current motivation or her feelings about the matter. McGreevy seems to acknowledge this, as he adds rather tentatively, 'One could argue that it gives the mare both physical and emotional comfort.'[22] One could indeed, and to most people this is by far the most likely explanation. There is no need to retreat to some remote evolutionary viewpoint in order to explain such behaviour.

A friend told me of her Arab stallion's reaction when the mare with whom he ran out, and who was in foal to him, gave birth prematurely to a foal which did not survive. Their owner had gone to the field as normal to check on the horses, and was very disturbed when only the stallion appeared to greet her, looking extremely distraught. He kept running up to her, then running back down the field, and repeating this as if trying to tell her something. She found the mare in another part of the field, greatly distressed, having given birth prematurely to the foal which had either been stillborn or had died soon after birth. It turned out that the horses had been disturbed by farm machinery in the next field and, in her fright, the mare had gone into labour. The stallion was very upset and persisted in trying to protect the body of the dead foal. When the farmer who owned the land came to bury the foal, the stallion tried to prevent him from carrying out the burial.

In addition, many horse owners have noted the reactions of their own horses to the death of a close companion. In some cases, where the bereaved horse has not actually seen the companion horse's body, he or she may simply assume that the other horse has gone else-where and may act in a very distressed manner, looking for the missing one and calling out to him or her. In other cases, particularly where they have actually seen the body, they may simply become very distressed. Jane Littlefair, whose Arab gelding Sultan Shahryar I had known since the day of his birth, reported to me that when she lost her old mare Sultan was distraught at the loss of his friend. He did not look for the mare or call out to her; he simply became very dejected and would not allow his owner to have anything to do with him. Jane said to me, 'It was as if he blamed me for the mare's death.' Eventually he recovered and regained his former trust in, and affection for, his owner, and he now has a new female com-panion whom he adores; but for a while he was a very unhappy horse indeed.

Sometimes depression following the loss of a companion may not be readily apparent; it may manifest itself in physical symptoms, the cause of which may appear to be something quite different. A friend of ours has a pretty young Arab mare whom – like Sultan – we have known since she was a tiny foal. Annie is an extremely laid-back horse with a lovely sweet nature; calm and sensible, yet sensitive enough to make her a joy to work with. She and Sandra had lots of fun together, doing several competitive trail rides, and Sandra was look-ing forward to taking Annie on other, more advanced long-distance rides.

Then in 1997 disaster struck. Annie developed mud-fever; her legs started to swell up like balloons and, in spite of all the vet's and Sandra's best efforts, the condition continued to worsen. After six months of this, Sandra was at her wits' end; she had spent a fortune on vet's bills. Annie had been treated with an assortment of creams, gels and lotions, and pumped full of antibiotics – and still the condition was getting worse. By this time poor Annie was going almost demented whenever anyone attempted to touch her hind legs, and started lash-ing out even at Sandra – a most uncharacteristic reaction for this mare.

Finally, in desperation, Sandra decided to try alternative medicine, and after reading of successes with conditions like mud-fever, she contacted an aromatherapist. The aromather-apist discussed with her every aspect of Annie's condition, her diet, the way she was kept, etc., then she asked, 'Is she under any stress?' Sandra was unable to think of anything in Annie's current way of life that could be causing her stress. Then the aromatherapist asked, 'Has she recently suffered the loss of a companion?' Sandra was stunned. 'Of course, yes,' she said, and told the aromatherapist how, in April 1997, her other young mare, Millie, had tragically had to be put down after contracting acute grass-sickness. Millie and Annie had been very close companions. The aromatherapist said she believed the trauma of her loss had compromised

Annie's immune system and this had lowered her resistance to the bacteria which cause the condition. As a result of aromatherapy treatment, within a matter of days Annie's seemingly intractable condition began to improve. Within weeks it had almost disappeared, and shortly after that Sandra was able to start ridden work with Annie again.

Was the aromatherapist right? I think she was. Where a more reactive horse might have appeared listless and depressed after losing a friend, in laid-back Annie grief took the form of loss of resistance to infection. Of course, other factors could also be involved, yet the vets who treated Annie could find no specific reason why her mud-fever should prove so impossible to cure. One is tempted to ask why they did not consider the same possibility as the aromatherapist, but while most vets undoubtedly do a good job, theirs is a huge field of study and, like doctors, they are generally trained to treat the symptom rather than the patient. In spite of an impressive body of evidence, there has been considerable resistance from the medical profession as a whole to accept the role that the emotions play in precipitating, and curing, illness. Indeed, until the 1970s medical scientists believed that the brain and the immune system were entirely separate. Since then, however, researchers have found pathways from the central nervous system to the immune system; they have also found that hormones (such as adrenaline, noradrenaline, cortisol and prolactin, as well as endorphins which act as natural pain-killers) which are released in times of stress have a strong effect on the immune system. The temporary suppression of the immune system which results from the release of these hormones may act, in the short term, to conserve the energy required for action appropriate to the crisis. But if the stress is constant the effects on the immune system may be long-lasting, leaving the body prey to all manner of viral and bacterial infections.

The mind, the emotions and the body are thus not separate from each other but form an integrated whole. If we want to keep our horses healthy and sound, we cannot ignore their emotional needs. Daniel Goleman calls 'emotional intelligence' – the wise use of emotion as a guide to appropriate behaviour – a 'basic flair for living'. Just as with humans, the horse whose emotional life is disturbed will not be able to interact properly, either with his human handlers or with other horses. This is often the reason why horses become bullies, misinterpreting even neutral actions as being filled with hostile intent, and reacting with inappropriate aggression. Emotional distress may show itself in the performance of stereotypes (see Appendix I), usually (and inappropriately) known as 'stable vices'. Or the horse's physical health may suffer. As in Annie's case the immune system may be affected, or the horse may suffer from frequent bouts of colic. Many other illnesses may also be caused, or at least made worse, by emotional stress.

It is important to remember, too, that emotional distress affects the ability to learn and to perform well. 'When emotionally upset, people cannot remember, attend, learn, or make decisions clearly. As one management consultant put it, "Stress makes people stupid," '[23] – and precisely the same applies to horses.

So if we want our horses to stay sound, live longer and make full use of their potential, we must learn to recognise their emotions and use what Dr Marthe Kiley-Worthington has called 'conditional anthropomorphism'. This does not mean treating horses as humans, but recognising what is of importance to them, trying to see things from their point of view, and imagining, 'If I were a horse, how would I feel if . . .'. Recognising a continuity of emotional experience among different species – as well as the differences – is only the first step towards understanding.

Notes

1 Daniel Goleman, *Emotional Intelligence* (Bloomsbury, 1996), p. 41
2 Goleman, *Emotional Intelligence*, p. 41
3 Goleman, *Emotional Intelligence*, p. 289
4 Paul McGreevy, *Why Does My Horse . . .?* p. 211
5 McGreevy, *Why Does My Horse . . .?* p. 139
6 McGreevy, *Why Does My Horse . . .?* p. 139
7 Léonie Marshall, *Your Horse's Mind* (Crowood Press, 1996), p. 16
8 McGreevy, *Why Does My Horse . . .?* p. 109
9 Stephen Budiansky, *The Nature of Horses*, pp. 84–5
10 McGreevy, *Why Does My Horse . . .?* p. 183
11 J. Benyus, *Beastly Behaviors: A zoo lover's companion* (Addison-Wesley, Reading, Mass., 1992), p. 52
12 Masson and McCarthy, *When Elephants Weep*, p. 98
13 Masson and McCarthy, *When Elephants Weep*, pp. 112–13
14 Lorenz, Konrad, *King Solomon's Ring*, pp. 152–3
15 Henry Blake, *Talking With Horses*, p. 54
16 Dr Marthe Kiley-Worthington, *Equine Welfare*, p. 282
17 Kiley-Worthington, *Equine Welfare*, p. 282
18 McGreevy, *Why Does My Horse . . .?* p. 91
19 Marshall, *Your Horse's Mind*, p. 102
20 Tom Ainslie and Bonnie Ledbetter, *The Body Language of Horses* (William Morrow and Co. Inc., New York, 1980), p. 49
21 cited by Masson and McCarthy, *When Elephants Weep*, p. 104
22 McGreevy, *Why Does My Horse . . .?* p. 72
23 Goleman, *Emotional Intelligence*, p. 149

CHAPTER EIGHT

Harmony and Disharmony: Social Organisation

Leadership is not domination, but the art of
persuading people to work toward a common goal.

DANIEL GOLEMAN

WHAT MAKES A HORSE co-operate? Any number of trainers and riders have expressed the opinion that horses must be stupid creatures to allow humans on their backs in the first place, let alone to do all the other unnatural things we require of them. As we have seen, however, horses as a species are far from stupid.

We must therefore seek the answer elsewhere, and it lies in one of the most misrepresented and misunderstood aspects of equine life: the fact that the horse is, above all, a social creature.

So how do horses organise their social lives? Virtually every modern book on the training and management of horses stresses that horses are herd animals and that they have a well-defined social hierarchy. This is usually referred to as a 'pecking order'. 'By nature the horse is a herd animal and this strong pull in his character invariably prompts him to join a group where a hierarchy, or pecking order, exists. This hierarchy fulfils the essential needs for protection of each individual horse, giving the herd its order, strength, and leadership.'[1] This view of equine social organisation is so widely accepted that few people would question it, although some more thoughtful souls might wonder whether the use of such terms as 'pecking order' are really appropriate, as we are considering large grazing herbivores and not a group of farmyard chickens. That being so, *are* such terms appropriate? Is the view of equine society quoted above the correct one, or is it an oversimplified stereotype?

One does not have to read too much of the scientific literature on animal behaviour and social organisation to realise that many of the writers seem to have what almost amounts to an obsession with hierarchies and dominance. Prior to the twentieth century, comparatively little had been done by way of studying animals in their natural habitat, and little was known about their social organisation. Since the beginning of the twentieth century, however, many wide-ranging studies in comparative psychology have been carried out and the middle years of the century saw the rise of the new science of ethology. All kinds of animals were studied and the idea of social dominance emerged as a result of observations of domestic fowl made by the Norwegian naturalist Schjelderup-Ebbe in the early 1920s. He noted that aggression between any two birds within a flock was unidirectional: if one bird pecked another, the other bird would not respond in kind. Schjelderup-Ebbe therefore considered the aggressor to be the 'dominant' individual, and the one on the receiving end of the aggression was labelled the 'subordinate'. He believed that this overt aggression was the key to social organisation in domestic fowl. 'Between any two birds', he wrote in 1922, 'one individual *invariably* had precedence over the other', and further, 'In this case Z is the despot, the superior being, the tyrant, he has the power and may use it as he pleases.'[2] Because it was first documented among domestic fowl, this clearly defined hierarchy became known as a 'pecking order'.

As studies of animal societies increased in number and scope, hierarchical organisation was also found in many other species and soon the phrase 'pecking order' was being used in a widespread, rather careless manner to describe virtually any social arrangement where some kind of hierarchy was observed. Another popular phrase was 'dominance hierarchy'; so that one can scarcely pick up a book on animal behaviour without finding references to dominance hierarchies of one kind or another. Observations of aggressive – or as animal behavioural scientists would put it, 'agonistic' – interactions between domestic horses, and also in feral horses living in natural groups, led the observers to conclude that horses, too, were hierarchical and that dominance played a prominent part in their social organisation.

But how true is this? Does dominance really play such an important role in equine society? At first sight it would seem that it does and that the bulk of the scientific literature is correct. In recent years, however, doubts have set in in many quarters about the reliability of many of the observations regarding dominance hierarchies in general. The idea of such hierarchies is naturally very appealing to scientists who, understandably, like to be able to categorise observations. But nature is neither so tidy nor so obliging. As Masson and McCarthy point out in *When Elephants Weep*, ethologists studying dominance hierarchies can find it frustrating when they are unable to determine whether one animal is dominant over another. They often seem to conclude that if studies are carried on long enough, or more extensively, some kind of true ranking will emerge. It rarely seems to occur to them that 'hierarchy' may not be an accurate way of describing that particular social organisation. 'It is as if they hope that the relations between animals gathered at a waterhole can be as neatly quantified as those of academics gathered before a granting agency.'[3]

Masson and McCarthy go on to note that: 'The notion of observing a group of animals engaged in mysterious interactions and extracting a tidy hierarchy which generates testable predictions has great appeal for scientists. Sometimes the idea that hierarchies are inevitable and prove certain things about humans is also part of the appeal.'[4]

It is also important to realise that most of the major studies of dominance, which have shaped theories about its function in the social organisation of non-human animals, have concentrated on birds or primates (especially the latter), and the results then applied to mammalian societies in general, often without regard to differences in habitat and lifestyle. Dr Marthe Kiley-Worthington says, 'The organisation of many mammalian societies described primarily in terms of a "dominance hierarchy" may be an unwarranted, and possibly an inaccurate over simplification which has not always been carefully assessed.'[5] She goes on to point out that this dispute is not new, problems with the concept of dominance in large herbivores having been identified a number of years ago (e.g. Kiley-Worthington, 1977; Syme and Syme, 1979). In spite of this, most observers have assumed, and described, dominance hierarchies; but they do not always make it clear how they have measured these hierarchies. When they do, the measurement has usually been based on the rather crude system of counting the number of threats made by one horse to another, then 'ranking' the results. The context of these threats – which would surely tell us how relevant they are to social organisation – has rarely been recorded in detail.

Before we can see whether the idea of a dominance hierarchy is really relevant to equine society, we need to look beyond the rather crude notion of a pecking order and try to understand what is meant by dominance and what its function is.

Generally, if one individual always responds submissively to another individual at the start of any aggressive encounter, we may say that this is a 'dominance relationship'. In a detailed critique of theories about dominance, Irwin S. Bernstein distinguishes dominance *relationships*, which occur between two animals, from dominance *hierarchies*, within which an individual's rank may be located.[6] Why do dominance relationships, or dominance hierarchies, arise? Among primates at least, several major functions of dominance have been identified. Syme and Syme, following Rowell (1974), define these functions as follows:

- **Leadership:** 'Dominant animals are assumed to be leaders . . . In primates, for instance, this involves active roles in group defence, policing internal group strife, and leadership in terms of the geographical movement of the group.'[7]
- **Sexual priority:** 'Social dominance is assumed to be of evolutionary significance in that sexual priorities can be observed for dominant animals in terms of both sexual behaviour and reproductive success.'[8] In addition, as noted above, it is assumed that dominance gives priority of access not only to potential mates, but to such commodities as food, water, territory, personal space, etc.
- **Reducing aggression:** 'Formation of a dominance hierarchy reduces the level of aggression within a group; once the dominance-subordinance relationship is established physical aggression is restricted to threat rituals from which the subordinate readily retreats.'[9]

In order to see whether these assumptions hold true for horses, we must first look at how free-ranging horses organise themselves when allowed to do so without human intervention.

When James Feist and Dale McCullough carried out their detailed observations of groups of feral horses living on the Pryor Mountain Wild Horse Range in the western USA, and compared these with similar observations of other feral groups, they were struck by the extent to which the same social organisation occurs within such bands. This is in spite of thousands of years of domestication, in which horses have commonly been kept in far from natural conditions, and selectively bred for certain behavioural characteristics. 'Despite this period of manipulation by man, once horses manage to escape and live in a wild or semi-wild state, the typical wild social organisation emerges.'[10]

Above Family group: Tiff, Bel and Pharis. Even though Pharis was not Tiff's father, they adored each other (Lynn and Sara Debnam)

Right Family and friends (Anne Mattsson)

This 'typical wild social organisation' is not, as is generally believed, the large, rather anonymous herd. Smaller bands of horses may come together sometimes to form a larger, temporary 'herd' but, in general, such herds are found only in places where human intervention either upsets the ratio of males to females, or actively ensures the creation of a larger group. The form of organisation horses seek for themselves when left entirely to their own devices is the much smaller family group consisting of a stallion, one to five mares (three being the average number) and their immature offspring. The latter stay with the family until they become sexually mature, when they usually leave the group (or are kicked out by the stallion) and form groups of their own; although in some cases they may remain with the family group much longer than this. Fillies may leave the group to go in search of a mate, while colts may either search for potential mates or form 'bachelor groups'; even these are seldom large, generally consisting of up to three or four colts, but sometimes as few as two. We do not know exactly how long such groups remain stable, but it appears that the adults of a family group frequently stay together for many years. Individual groups do come into contact with other groups, often at watering places, but they generally keep their distance.

So how do concepts of 'dominance' fit into such an organisation? Until relatively recently it was almost universally assumed that a herd of horses was led by a dominant stallion. R. H. Smythe wrote: 'one horse, almost invariably a stallion, places himself at the front of a herd or drove of horses and stays there by virtue of general acceptance'[11]. However, after the publication of studies of free-ranging horses which seemed to contradict this idea a new myth arose: the leadership of a herd was no longer assumed to be a dominant stallion but, instead, a dominant mare. 'In the case of herd hierarchies in general, the boss of the herd is far more normally a matriarchal mare rather than a stallion.'[12] 'In the wild it is the dominant mare of the herd, and not the stallion, which makes all the decisions.'[13] It may seem odd that I have called this idea a myth, yet, in fact, there are three myths here: that of the 'dominant stallion'; that of the 'dominant mare'; and – most pervasive of all – that of the leader, or 'boss' – the latter concept expressed in rather rigid terms by R. H. Smythe, describing the supposed social order which ruled horses in the wild:

> When the 'boss' stood still and listened, the others did likewise. When the 'boss' decided it was an appropriate moment to make a rapid getaway, or even to make a leisurely move into some other neighbourhood, the others all followed without question. When the 'boss' called a halt, all came to a standstill together.[14]

More recently, other authors have stated that: 'In equine society there is a leader: one horse which is the boss, and which the others respect and obey.'[15] All these ideas are part of 'received wisdom' about equine social organisation; and none of them stands up to close examination.

Part of the problem is that 'leadership' is rather a woolly concept. Syme and Syme define the characteristics of social leadership as 'the control of aggression between individuals within the group, and the protection of other members when the group is faced with threat or predation[16]. *Spatial* leadership, which governs movement from place to place, has been defined mainly by studies of primate behaviour. The definition of spatial leadership as given by Kummer (1971) is summed up by Syme and Syme: 'A spatial leader is an individual within a group who decides the direction and time of group movement throughout the group's home range. Although some animals may occasionally try to lead the group, members will not move until the leader does.'[17] Leadership, according to Feist and McCullough, 'can be expressed either by the taking of initiative by one animal with the others following, or by the active driving or herding of the group by a stallion'[18]. In their study, leadership by initiative was recorded in 159 cases during movements from place to place, or going to and from water. Of these, 106 (66.7 per cent) were led by the stallion, and 53 by a mare. Of the 53 cases in which a mare assumed leadership, seven were in response to the nearness of other harems, and nine were due to unnatural disturbances. In these 16 cases the stallion herded the group, directing its movements. 'Thus, in only 23.3% of the observed cases was the mare solely responsible for leadership.'[19]

Ebhardt (1954) reported that stallions were the common leaders among Icelandic pony bands. Hall (1972), studying the Pryor Mountain Wild Horse Range, regarded the most consistent leaders to be dominant mares. Tyler (1972) found that adult mares were the leaders among New Forest ponies (Hampshire, England). However, Tyler herself acknowledged that her findings were skewed by the fact that there were very few stallions in the New Forest, and these were periodically moved around or removed altogether. 'From the small number of cases where stallions were associated with mare groups and because of the unstable nature of these relationships due to man, it was not possible to conclude whether the stallion as the dominant member of his group was the leader.'[20]

Klingel (1964, 1967) reported that among plains zebras the oldest mares appeared to be the leaders in group movements, but the stallion was still the dominant animal. Klingel also recorded that among mountain and Hartmann's zebras leadership when moving *to* water was assumed by the stallion but taken over by the dominant mare when moving *away* from water. This pattern was also occasionally observed by Feist and McCullough. Berger (1977) found that in walking *to* water stallions led on 32 occasions, mares on 24. In walking *away* from water, out of 52 observed walk patterns, stallions showed temporary leadership 15 times, mares 19. Feist and McCullough describe how, when members of the group other than the stallion became excited or disturbed by something, they would whinny to attract the stallion's attention. If he did not see any cause for alarm, and remained calm, the rest of the group did likewise. They conclude that: 'Both initiative leadership and herding behavior in the harem show that the stallions are the principal leaders and they direct most of the movements of the groups.'[21] In his book *The Man Who Listens to Horses* Monty Roberts makes numerous references to 'dominant mares', and indicates that he equates their dominance with leadership, but he does not say how he measured this dominance or how he defined leadership; and he gives no more than vague details about the social organisation of the groups he studied. Valuable as his observations are in relation to what is important to horses, they do not really tell us anything useful about equine social organisation.

All we can really determine, then, is that 'leadership' (however it is defined) is not the sole property of either sex but may at various times be assumed by mares or stallions.

Regardless of sex, can 'leadership' be assigned to a dominant horse? Feist and McCullough report that groups approached water in single file on a trail, with either the stallion or a mare leading. The return to feeding areas would be conducted in a similar fashion, although they might graze along the way. Mares who reached the water first were often those who were lactating. Tyler observed that when the New Forest ponies moved from daytime grazing areas into the valleys in the evenings, when they reversed these proceedings in the mornings, or when they moved to other drinking places, they would sometimes move as much as a mile without grazing. These moves could be initiated by any member of a group, even by an immature pony. They usually walked in single file; order was not always constant, although there was some evidence that dominant mares and their families led the way. However, if the group was alarmed they would all gallop away alongside one another, with no obvious leader. This is consistent with the flight behaviour seen by Berger who says, however, that when the terrain was flat, horses did follow each other, although different horses assumed leadership at different times. Berger also says that among the bands he observed:

No one horse served consistently as a leader during walking patterns to or from the spring . . . the origin of a leader for a walking pattern frequently was the individual that merely assumed the initiative and walked. When others followed, the lead horse continued, but when there were no followers, which often was the case, the horse soon stopped.'[22]

Feist and McCullough remark that: 'We were unable to determine a hierarchy among the mares of a group with regard to position in movements. However, observed leaders were usually older mares or mares with foals or yearlings.'[23] Berger, as in his comments quoted above, insists that: 'At no time was complete leadership shown for any individual stallion or mare within a band.'[24]

So much for the myths of 'dominance' equating to 'leadership' among horses. However there are other aspects to leadership which we have not yet discussed; notably its role in 'policing' aggression and protecting other members of the group. These will be considered when we come to look at alternative views about the roles of individuals in equine society. For now, let us look at the remaining bastion of dominance theory: the function of dominance in ensuring priority of access.

It is usually presumed that dominant males will enjoy greater reproductive success (being able to mate with more females). From the writings of (predominantly male) animal behaviourists and ethologists one might think that females were entirely passive, having little or no say in the matter, but this is far from being the case. Among hamadryas baboons dominance status may be less important to the reproductive success of a male than the preference of a female. Shirley Strum observed that, with olive baboons, the more aggressive and 'high ranking' a male was, the less success he had in getting females to mate with him. Nor did such aggressive males fare any better when it came to getting the best food.[25] Similar situations have been described in other species, such as lemurs and langurs, while in his celebrated study of cats, Paul Leyhausen notes that even when a tomcat is successful in fighting off a rival, the queen is just as likely to choose the defeated male as to choose the victor[26] – and as anyone who has ever observed cats in such a situation knows, the choice is very definitely the female's. The same applies in many other species.

But what of horses? Do mares invariably go for the more dominant types? Do they, indeed, have any choice in the matter? We have, of course, already considered this question in Chapter 7. Even so, it might well be the case that a more dominant stallion would have more success in fighting off (or scaring off) rivals than a less dominant individual, while an aggressive young stallion might have more success in either winning young unattached mares or in enticing mares from another band. These are distinct possibilities, yet there is very little conclusive evidence one way or the other. According to Feist and McCullough, out of 82 observed encounters between stallions of different groups, 37 were the result of the nearness of other groups. Twelve fights were caused by attempts on the part of a harem stallion to gain a mare from within another harem, while four other fights were part of attempts by stallions to recover mares that had become separated from the harem (only one such attempt was unsuccessful). So from this limited data it would seem that the greater part of the aggression between stallions was the result of attempts to protect existing groups, rather than to gain access to mares from other groups, although clearly this did happen. This correlates with other studies which have found that stallions appear to concentrate more on maintaining group cohesion and stability than on enlarging the size of their harems.

Berger found a direct relationship between harem size and what he called 'interband stallion rank' (a rather crude ranking of stallions in relation to stallions of other bands); however, he also noted that when the number of foals was subtracted from the groups there was negligible difference between the stallions in the middle rank. In any case, the number of stallions in this study (four in all) is hardly sufficient to give proof one way or the other. Much more observation needs to be carried out on feral bands in a wide range of locations before we can make any assumptions regarding the relationship of 'dominance' to access to potential mates.

What about defence of territory? Various studies of feral and semi-feral groups have shown that horses are not territorial in the sense of laying claim to specific areas. They defend their group and their personal space rather than a defined 'territory' and it is not uncommon for the ranges of two or more bands to overlap considerably.

This leaves only priority of access to resources such as food, drink and shelter; for many animal behaviourists dominance is unquestionably linked with access to such resources. Paul McGreevy says, 'most hierarchies are established in relation to food resources.'[27]

He further says that:

Free-ranging horses are usually familiar with the seasonal disappearance of food sources, and it is at times of relative paucity that rank can mean the difference between surviving and perishing. The horse that demands access to the best of what food is available is less likely to suffer illness and is also the least likely to be lethargic when escaping a potential predator.[28]

As with the other assumptions examined so far, we must ask what evidence is there that this is really the case?

The study of the Tour du Valat herd of Camargue horses made by Wells and Goldschmidt-Rothschild gives no real evidence of dominance affecting access to food and water. The authors content themselves with the observation that: 'Headthreats . . . are given to subordinate individuals in more general situations such as grazing, seeking shelter and maintaining individual distance.'[29] However, they give no data from their study which would support this statement.

Berger makes no mention of dominance in relation to feeding; while Clutton-Brock et al., in their study of Highland ponies, merely state that: 'Apart from increasing the frequency of interaction, the provision of food had little effect on the social structure of the group.'[30]

Feist and McCullough record no correlation between dominance and access to food. With regard to drinking, they observe that: 'Threats were used at the water holes to gain drinking space, although for the most part group members were tolerant of each other in this circumstance.'[31] They also note that: 'As each horse finished drinking it would wait for the rest of the group to finish when all moved away together.'[32] As all had thus had the same amount of opportunity to drink (because the rest of the group would wait for them), a dominance hierarchy would not seem to confer any benefit here.

In the context of competition for scarce resources, it is interesting to note that, during Stephanie Tyler's celebrated study of New Forest ponies, hay was supplied to the ponies in winter to provide competition so that large numbers of threats could be recorded in a short time – far more than would be observed during 'normal grazing, when *competition was negligible*'[33] [my italics]. How does this lack of competition fit in with McGreevy's picture of rank as a matter of life and death?

The same lack of competitiveness dogged Grzimek when he conducted his early experiments in determining rank in horses. As Syme and Syme comment,

Observing insufficient aggressive behaviour in a non-competitive situation he then recorded the response of 29 young stallions to restricted food in a bucket and eventually obtained enough data for an hierarchy. Even in this competitive setting the horses were extremely tolerant of each other and possible situational variation in dominance relationships was noted.[34]

I have observed the same kind of tolerance among our own horses, even on the part of those who would most aggressively defend their personal space or their heap of hay. This tolerance seems most evident among close friends (as one might expect), but in our group at least these friends do not necessarily display similar levels of aggression, which does not correlate with the findings of Clutton-Brock and others that horses tended to associate most with other horses of similar rank. Thus we find Kruger (high levels of aggression) sharing his haylage with Zareeba (low aggression); Roxzella (high aggression) sharing with Zareeba (low aggression); Zareeba with Tiff (both low aggression); Tiff with Imzadi (who as an immature horse defers to the older mare); and Mo (high aggression) with Toska (low aggression) – Mo even going so far as to allow Toska to nibble at a mouthful of haylage he himself was in the process of eating! Our stallion Nivalis made a particular friend of one of the riding school ponies who spent the summer of 1997 in the field adjoining ours. They would spend hours grazing on opposite sides of the fence, noses actually touching on occasions; but not once, in hours of observation, did I see the slightest sign

Zareeba and Kruger sharing hay

Below Roxzella and Zareeba graze very close to each other

of aggression, even though they were often grazing the same patch of grass and that summer the grass was very sparse. Zareeba and Roxzella may often be seen grazing, nose to nose, in just such a way; while Lynn and Sara Debnam, whose late Arabian stallion Pharis used to run out with their other Arabian stallion Balthasar and another Arabian, the gelding Merlin, report similar observations. Pharis and Merlin were particular friends and would graze side by side, so close that they were almost nibbling the same blade of grass. I have several times observed Nivalis's daughter Imzadi, as a foal, cheekily poking her nose into the manger hung over Nivalis's stable door, from which he was contentedly eating his breakfast. His response to this impertinence was to allow her to eat a few mouthfuls then gently push her away, as if to say, 'That's enough; this is, after all, *my* breakfast.' The mare Tiff is often allowed to wander freely about the yard and is sometimes fed there in the open. On one recent occasion she and the rest of the horses were having their dinner; Tiff finished hers and wandered over to Nivalis's stable where he was still eating. Tiff stuck her nose in the stallion's manger and proceeded – just as Imzadi had done – to munch away at his feed. Nivalis's only reaction was to stretch out and nuzzle her neck, the intoxicating pleasure of her company evidently overcoming any concerns about his dinner!

Some experimenters have adopted the rather crude approach of Grzimek and attempted to 'rank' horses by presenting them with food in a bucket and recording who ends up with it. In this situation, says McGreevy, it is the dominant horse who always ends up with the bucket. But what is actually being measured here? Given the examples of food-sharing related above, does this really tell us anything other than how important food is to a partic-

Imzadi and her father Nivalis share a handful of feed

ular individual? And given that this may bear little or no relation to that individual's actual bodily needs, is there really any 'sociobiological' significance to this? McGreevy acknowledges that all that would be established is which horse is dominant in what he calls an 'isolated food-related hierarchy'[35].

The bucket test referred to above has often been conducted after systematically depriving the horses of food. However, as with Tyler's provision of hay to provoke competition between the New Forest ponies, the creation of such artificially competitive situations exposes the main problem of approaching the study of social interactions in this way. Like the laboratory experiment, such an approach distorts the very behaviour it is supposed to be clarifying. Those who make use of it appear to assume that if they place their subjects in extreme situations, often quite unlike those they would encounter in the free-ranging lifestyle natural to them, the 'true nature' of equine social interactions will somehow be revealed. In the same way there is an odd, almost superstitious notion that only in extreme conditions will the essential truth about human nature reveal itself. This is such a widespread idea that it has become almost a convention of novels, plays and films. It is true that such extreme conditions will often reveal unsuspected aspects to a person's character, but this tells us only about reactions to specific situations; it does not give us a complete picture of that person. Should we conclude, therefore, that because under unnatural, extreme conditions aggression may increase, and with it tendencies for certain horses to dominate others, this represents the 'true' nature of horses? Of course we should not, any more than we should conclude that humans are 'naturally' brutish and nasty because of their behaviour in similarly extreme conditions.

In this context Mary Midgley considers, in *Beast and Man*, anthropologist Colin Turnbull's observations of a tribe called the Ik. These unfortunate people have had their traditional hunting and gathering grounds taken away from them, and are starving, without any hope of relief. As a result their traditional way of life has broken down completely, and they behave towards each other (including their children) in an extremely brutal manner. Turnbull says that the Ik teach us that our much vaunted human values are not inherent but merely part of the ways in which society ensures its survival, and that they are luxuries which, like society itself, can be dispensed with.

They do nothing of the kind, says Midgley.

What they teach us (if we need to learn it), is that any society of living things can be destroyed if it is hit hard and persistently enough. In the process of destruction its more complex and advanced capacities will probably tend to go to pieces before its simplest and most primitive ones. That will not show that they were not inherent. Nobody doubts that a bee's complex instinctive capacities are inherent. But if bees are systematically deprived and harassed to death they will stop their more complex operations before they stop crawling around and trying to feed and occasionally sting . . . Social animals cannot live the life they are fitted for at all without their own form of society. The demand for it is as deeply inherent as is the demand for one's own future safety.[36]

The lack of altruism that Colin Turnbull noted among the Ik was, Midgley suggests, scarcely surprising as they had been in a desperate situation long enough to ensure the selection of those interested only in surviving. They are, as she points out, a dying society. 'But what does it mean to suggest that everything else in their lives was a *luxury*? Is the idea that only extreme situations are real and serious? If so, most of life is unreal; what sort of unreality is this?'[37]

Of course, most horses are not in anything like such a desperate situation; nevertheless we must face the fact that, given the way so many are kept – in imbalanced, often single-sex groups where there may be frequent changes of companions and little chance to form the deep bonds so necessary to horses, and in (to them) cramped conditions – we should not be surprised if they react to this by becoming more aggressive and even bullying other horses.

What of other resources, such as shelter? Horses do not generally need to compete for hiding places as they escape from predators by fleeing, not by hiding. Except in forest areas (not a truly equine habitat in any case), they do not crowd into small areas for shelter but, instead, make use of other features of the terrain, such as rocky outcrops and large hollows in the ground.

Finally, what about the role of dominance in reducing aggression? This might indeed be of value where there is a distinct linear hierarchy (i.e. A dominates B who in turn dominates C). In such a hierarchy each individual knows his or her place. At least, that is the theory, and in some animal societies it appears to work like that. But what about horses? Can a linear hierarchy be established from dominance relationships between individuals?

In his experiments with buckets, Grzimek managed to establish such a linear hierarchy but that was in one context, in fairly large, single-sex groups. As such a situation is highly artificial, it does little to enlighten us about equine social organisation. (How much would an alien from another planet learn about human social organisation by studying only, say, the *harēm* of a Turkish sultan?) In their study of Camargue horses, Wells and Goldschmidt-Rothschilde established a dominance hierarchy from the distribution of headthreats (i.e. aggressive signals made with the head alone). However, this does not really tell us anything useful about the context of such threats; and in any case this particular 'herd' had a much lower ratio of stallions to mares than would be found among truly feral horses. This is relevant because Feist and McCullough could not establish any kind of 'dominance hierarchy' among the mares in the groups they observed. They concluded that this was because of the strong dominance shown by the stallions (although even this varied considerably; some stallions were very relaxed and tolerant). Montgomery (1957) studied ten horses for a total of 14 hours and found what ethologists call a 'triangular relationship' (A dominates B who dominates C who in turn dominates A). One might question whether 14 hours is a long enough time for observation; nevertheless, this is interesting given that many writers insist that simple linear hierarchies are the norm among horses. Clutton Brock et al. did not find a linear hierarchy among the Highland ponies they studied. They concluded that:

> . . . the study supported Gartlan's (1968) emphasis on the complexity of social structure and the inadequacy of dominance in explaining many variations in social relationships. In neither group was the hierarchy fully linear, and there was no obvious explanation of the irregularities which occurred. Moreover, dominance was apparently unrelated to the frequency with which individuals were observed in different positions in the group and to the number of times they were involved in grooming sessions.[38]

This latter observation is interesting as many writers have assumed that mutual grooming is related to dominance. Some insist that it is usually the subordinate partner who initiates the grooming session; others that it is the dominant partner. Certain authors evidently cannot decide on this question. On page 144 of *Why Does My Horse . . .?* Paul McGreevy says that the more submissive member is most likely to initiate the exchange (of mutual grooming); but on page 183 he says that it is usually initiated by the higher-ranking individual in a pair!

Some writers maintain that linear hierarchies are found in small groups (as one might expect). One might, indeed, find a linear hierarchy in a group of three horses (A›B›C). Not surprisingly, such hierarchies have been observed in bachelor groups. However, one might just as easily find, as Montgomery did, A›B›C›A. In any case, to draw any conclusions from this (other than the obvious one, that some horses are more aggressive than others), one would have to know the *context* in which aggression was shown — and this has not often been considered.

From this brief glimpse at some of the findings of various studies, we can see that the relevance of dominance to equine societies is by no means clear-cut. We see that linear hierarchies emerge in some situations but not in others. Some behavioural scientists have proposed that linear hierarchies may be disrupted by what they call 'coalitions': two horses forming an alliance against a more dominant horse and effectively 'deposing' him. This has certainly been observed in primate societies but, while I am not saying it does not happen in groups of equines, I have been unable to find any evidence to support the idea of it being a significant feature of such groups. Given that linear hierarchies appear to be unimportant in truly feral groups (except, as noted, in bachelor groups – although even here their function is largely undefined), it is difficult to see how they could be so important in reducing aggression and maintaining group cohesion (indeed, in Feist and McCullough's study it appeared to be the stallion who was mainly responsible for this, although they do not give details about exactly how he did so).

Dr Marthe Kiley-Worthington, who has spent many years observing the social interactions of domestic groups of horses, comments that: 'Circularities in a hierarchy will indicate individuals' changes as a result of either or both "mood" (emotional change) or context, and therefore indicate little but individual differences and roles rather than some overall explanation of the society's working.'[39]

Dr Kiley-Worthington points out that one of the benefits of group living is that it can increase the acquisition – and passing on – of social and other skills.

The acquiring of ecological knowledge and its passing on through generations to increase survival is likely to be of prime importance to prey species. Knowledge of the topography, where to run if chased to reduce the chances of capture, feeding sites, what to eat, availability of water at different times of the year, cognitive maps of the home range and detailed knowledge of the potential sheltering sites with different wind directions, must be learnt and this knowledge may well be passed on through the social group . . . Such 'cultural' knowledge could be built on through generations even without verbal or written language, and thus each individual in a social group does not have to 'invent the wheel' herself, although she may be able to improve on its building. Thus the 'culture': movement patterns, spatial distribution, even perhaps, relationships within the group, and so on, will change as a result of an individual's input . . . even 'innovation' may occur. In this way ecological and other non-social knowledge will be extended throughout the social group.[40]

The importance of such 'cultural' knowledge has been shown in other herbivorous species, notably elephants; the killing of older females who possessed this knowledge has proved disastrous for the survival of younger members of the social group.

The maintenance of group cohesion thus becomes paramount, as the most experienced and knowledgeable members of the group may hold the keys to its survival. In the model of the 'dominance hierarchy', if horses usually respond to aggression by withdrawal or avoidance (as is generally supposed), then group members are less likely to learn much from each other as social interactions are thereby decreased. On the other hand, if aggression is met with aggression, this would serve to disrupt the cohesion of the group.

Dr Kiley-Worthington suggests that an alternative view of equine social organisation might be that affiliative and 'deflammatory' behaviour, which serves to reduce conflict and excitement within a group, is what keeps that group together. This would aid the individual by strengthening social bonds and increasing the possibility of him or her gaining both ecological knowledge and understanding of the individuals within the group, as well as passing that knowledge on to other individuals.

These conclusions are the result of many years' observation of Dr Kiley-Worthington's own horses, including a specifically designed study. She and her team of trained observers recorded social interactions between 13 Arabian, part-bred Arabian, and Welsh horses and ponies: one stallion, seven mares, two yearling fillies, two geldings and one colt foal. They were observed and the observations recorded for a total of 1,779 horse hours in three field situations of differing sizes, over a period of six months. The results were analysed using a specially designed computer program. (For a full description and analysis of these observations, see Kiley-Worthington, 'Communication in Horses: Cooperation and Competition' — going to press at the time of writing.)

This study took account of two factors not often considered in other studies of equine behaviour. These are:

- The total number of interactions in which an individual is involved, either as a recipient or a performer/initiator of social interactions. Dr Kiley-Worthington calls the measurement of this the 'total social involvement' score for that individual. It indicates the extent to which an individual is socially involved with the group.

- The individual's score as either (a) a performer or (b) a recipient of social interactions. Dr Kiley-Worthington found these two parameters to be of some importance in understanding the social organisation and the role of individuals within it. She also identified two aspects of this social organisation which add far more to our understanding of horses than the usual rather rigid concepts of 'dominance': these are the 'tit-for-tat' response, which she likens to Charles Kingsley's famous maxim 'be done by as you did', and the opposite, which encourages co-operation: 'do as you would be done by'.

The findings led Dr Kiley-Worthington to conclude that as a result of assessing all the various behaviours observed in this group: 'the important organisational parameters are not the metaphyscal "dominance hierarchy", but rather other variables in which activity hierarchies can be constructed'[41]. She lists these as:

- the total amount of *social involvement*;

- the degree to which the individual is a '*performer/initiator of social interactions*'; or

- a '*receiver/responder*' (i.e. one who generally receives or responds to social interactions rather than initiating them);

- individuals may be '*stickers*' – those who behave in a way that deflates aggression and act to encourage group cohesion, and 'do as you would be done by'. All of these 'sticker' behaviours are more common than 'splitter inflammatory/dispersive behaviour;'[42]

- one or two '*splitters*' who avoid others more, act aggressively, inflame situations, and whose actions tend to disperse the group.

It emerges from this study that friendly actions ('affiliation') are the most successful way of showing interest and not being either ignored or avoided. Aggression was responded to mainly with avoidance or ignoring but in 25 per cent of cases the response was aggression. Dr Kiley-Worthington suggests that:

> This 'be done by as you did' aggression might ensure that individuals do not become unchallenged 'dominant' individuals or 'hawks' when behaving in a way which could endanger the cohesion of the group. In other words that an unchallenged 'dominance hierarchy' (in terms of priority of access and competition), rather than being an important organisational parameter of the society, threatens the cohesion of the group.[43]

On the other hand, a potentially co-operative and compromising approach ('do as you would be done by') could increase the cohesion and stability of the group – which, as we have seen, could have important implications for its survival.

Dr Kiley-Worthington concludes that instead of trying to explain this equine society in terms of a rather vague dominance hierarchy based on competition (which in free-ranging equine societies has, in any case, little relevance), we should consider other organising features. She argues that the idea that a dominance hierarchy always reduces aggression has not actually been shown to be the case. She proposes that the equine society in her study should be considered more as a unit of co-operative individuals. 'The majority of the behaviour, and the majority of the individuals in this society behaved to encourage cohesion of the group and deflate potentially inflammatory/dispersive situations.'[44]

She points to the 'do as you would be done by' – you scratch my back (or bite me) and I will scratch yours (or bite you) – aspect of the results.

This would be a sensible strategy to foster cooperation and cohesion since it will control 'hawkishness'. Any inflammatorily behaving miscreant (hawk) instead of being avoided, even 'respected' and thus 'getting away with it' (becoming 'dominant') and consequently becoming more aggressive, inflammatory and dispersive in his behaviour, has a fair chance of being aggressed back (25% of performed aggression is responded to with aggression).[45]

Dr Kiley-Worthington does not claim that this is a definitive study of equine social organisation; rather, that it could be used as a basis from which to explore the latter in terms of a somewhat more subtle, complex organisation than the rather crude dominance hierarchy so often assumed. Some methods of horse management may create a situation rarely encountered in the wild: conflict within a group over food and water, or overcrowding, leading to increased aggression. In such groups, as Dr Kiley-Worthington pointed out in her earlier work, *The Behaviour of Horses*, it may indeed be possible to work out a dominance hierarchy based on aggression. But, she adds, 'an increase in aggression may well lead to a more obvious and better developed dominance hierarchy, but do not let us conclude from this that a "dominance hierarchy" is very important in normal horse society'[46]. She concludes that: 'the relationships between horses are just as complex as between people, and to describe them in simple terms, such as "dominance hierarchy" is inadequate and pointless'[47]. She goes on to say that she has known, studied, handled, trained and ridden her own group of horses and watched them and their offspring grow up for many years, 'and I suppose I know them as

You scratch my back. . . Nivalis, Joanne and Lorraine enjoy a scratch

well as anyone knows a group of horses. Yet I still cannot describe a "dominance hierarchy". There is indeed an aggressive hierarchy. But what does this tell us about how each relates to every other?'[48]

Having spent hundreds of hours observing our own horses' interactions with each other, I can only echo Dr Kiley-Worthington's words. What does the presence of an aggression hierarchy tell us? Only, as I have already remarked, that some individuals are more aggressive than others. Even this depends on context: of our adult horses Kruger and Kiri are aggressive about food and personal space but interact comparatively little with other horses in other contexts. Roxzella is aggressive over food and personal space and will be aggressive in defence of her friends (see Chapter 15). Zareeba and Nivalis, on the other hand, seldom become aggressive about food and personal space but will become positively ferocious in the defence of their friends, family or vulnerable youngstock. It seems far more profitable to study personality profiles than to attempt to construct dominance hierarchies from such complex and variable interactions. (See page 122 for a chart of aggression related to context among our own group of horses. This was based on a total of 540 hours' observation over a period of six months).

Ah, yes, the believers in dominance will cry, but what about the reactions of established groups to new horses? Scientists and lay persons alike frequently point to the hostile behaviour that horses in an established group often display towards newcomers as a prime example of the importance of social rank. This hostility is usually explained by the idea that each time a strange horse is introduced into a group it is necessary for the pecking order to be re-established. It is even claimed sometimes that this process is necessary after a horse has been absent from the group for a relatively short time, as in the case of a riding school horse being taken out of the field for a lesson. However, my own observations do not tally with this. Our land borders a field belonging to the local riding school and when their horses are turned out again after a lesson, or after being away at a competition, there may be a little excitement for a few minutes but nothing that would suggest any kind of re-establishing of pecking orders.

I believe the true explanation of hostility towards newcomers is much more closely related to human social responses in such a situation. We should not find anything strange in this; many social species have very similar attitudes towards new members of their group. The parallel I am drawing is with the traditional human village in the days when these were small, tightly knit communities in which everyone knew everyone else (and their business), everyone had social roles to play and there was a comforting (if sometimes rather stifling) stability within the group. Such communities do still exist in the Western world, although they are becoming scarcer and scarcer. At one time they were the norm in country life, and in many other areas of the world they are still the rule rather than the exception.

When a stranger (with or without family) moves into such a community, he or she is likely to be treated, if not with open hostility (although this does sometimes occur), then certainly with suspicion and coolness. This is not because the inhabitants of such communities are any more hostile or unfriendly than anyone else; it is to do with the maintenance of stability within the group. After all, the community knows nothing about the stranger. They may be

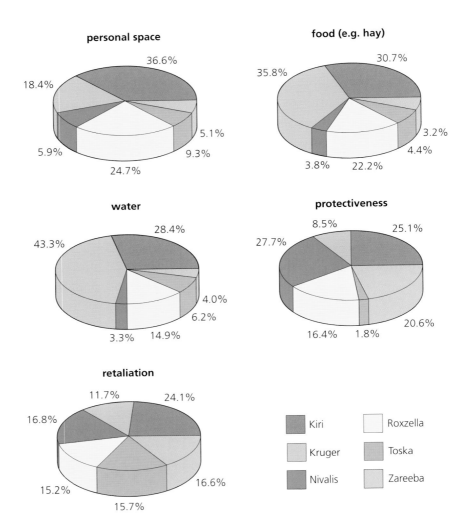

Chart of aggression related to context

a potentially disruptive influence, destroying the balance of the group. And the importance of this balance should not be underestimated for it has deep historical roots. In the days before the establishment of a central authority, the safety of a community depended on unity within that community, and as this state of affairs existed (and in some parts of the world still exists) for far longer than any other, it is a deep-rooted way of thinking. So it may be some time before the stranger is accepted and even longer before he or she is fully integrated into the group.

If we reflect on the importance of stability within the group to equine communities, we can see that many of the same considerations apply here. The stranger is avoided or treated with hostility until his or her reactions and general demeanour have been assessed. Once the group is assured that this newcomer will not upset the balance of their society, then he or she will be welcomed without fuss. Clearly, if we think of equine groups in terms of social roles rather than hierarchies based on aggression, there will be some sorting out of roles within a group whose members have changed, but there is no need to invoke crude ideas of pecking orders. Horses are much more subtle than that.

One of the factors that may help to explain why there is less aggression among feral horses than among many groups of domestic horses is that of space. This, rather than the idea of priority of access, may help us to understand some of the instances of threatening behaviour observed in feral groups. For example, Berger based the hierarchy ranking of the horses he studied mainly on their behaviour while drinking. 'The rank of a horse within a band became most apparent during drinking for two reasons. First there was a limiting resource (e.g. water) and, second, there was only a limited amount of space at the fountain. Thus, freedom of movement was restricted.'[49] I think this lack of space is far more important than is often realised. As prey animals, horses need to feel part of a group but they also need personal space; crowding gives them less room to manoeuvre and a feeling of being trapped – a situation that is highly stressful to any prey animal. Behavioural scientists have often approached this from the point of view of horses needing to be able to escape from possible aggression on the part of their companions. This is obviously important but from my own observations of small, stable groups of horses, I believe there is another factor which is equally important: the element of choice. Where the group is stable, horses will seldom graze at any distance from their companions. Among our own horses, if we turn Zareeba, Roxzella, Kruger and Toska out in the same field, they will spend most of their time fairly close to each other. They have the choice – to stay with their companions or to move elsewhere. But put too many horses in a relatively small space (remember that to a creature whose home range in a feral state would encompass anything up to 40–50 km^2 or even more, even a 16-hectare field is small!) as is the norm for domestic horses, and this will inevitably increase aggression as invasions of personal space become more frequent. If, in addition, these companions are often changing, the resultant lack of stability can seriously undermine the spirit of co-operation that is natural to horses.

The same phenomenon may be seen in humans, particularly in offices where too many people work side by side in a cramped space. Even the most good-natured and co-operative of individuals can become short-tempered and obstructive in such situations; while the problems of urban high-rise developments are too well known to need documenting here. Yet in small, stable communities, where everyone knows each other and has established a relationship with them, the effects of such crowding are somewhat mitigated. If we cannot avoid keeping our horses in (to them) small enclosures, we should at least ensure they have congenial companions and allow them to form long-term bonds!

Stephen Jay Gould has written about what he calls 'the hold of theory upon our ability to observe' and in Chapter 2 I mentioned the so-called 'Rosenthal effect' where researchers find exactly what they expect to find. One cannot avoid the suspicion that this is sometimes what happens when horse-owners enthusiastically report dominance hierarchies in groups of domestic horses, which appear to match exactly the descriptions of such hierarchies in popular equestrian literature. This is no reflection on either the integrity or the intelligence of such people; it is merely an instance of a universal human tendency.

If we must think in terms of dominance, then I would suggest it is time we moved away from the idea of crude aggression. As much behaviour that is usually described as 'dominant' is not, in fact, aggressive but merely assertive (and there is a huge difference in meaning here), why not use that word which is much more specific and need not involve concepts of either aggression or bullying?

This may be largely a question of semantics but I think it matters, as the use of such words colours our attitudes. When trainers of the calibre of Monty Roberts or Richard Maxwell use words such as 'dominant', one need have no fear that they will abuse that concept. However, the less subtle or empathic observer may well do so, which leads to the kind of bullying attitudes which should have no place in our relationships with horses. To return to the point made at the beginning of this chapter: if we consider the nature of equine society we should not be at all surprised that horses allow us to manipulate them, but this has nothing to do with notions of dominance or of hierarchies. Belief that it does means that we have to hold contradictory and incoherent views about horses' response to authority — as we shall see in the next chapter. If we approach the training and handling of horses using concepts such as 'dominant' and 'dominance', or the wildly inappropriate 'pecking order', and, from this, insist on assuming the role of 'boss', should we be surprised if – as so often happens – the horse fails to respond as we expect since we are invoking ideas essentially alien to him?

If, on the other hand, we accept that concepts such as dominance hierarchies are inadequate to explain the complexities of equine society, what implications does this have for our relations with horses? Does it invalidate other concepts, such as leadership, which have proved so effective in handling and training horses? Not at all. We ask horses to share our world and, as I shall argue in the next chapter, we are in charge, whether we like it or not. If we were to attempt to live with a feral herd, on their terms, I hope we should have the humility to accept the leadership of horses in matters where they have far greater wisdom than we do. In our world, we are far more aware of its dangers and possibilities than horses are, so here they need our leadership and guidance. So long as we are not seduced by some feeble vision of 'boss and subordinate' and, instead, think of the relationship as more of a partnership, with ourselves holding the controlling interest but with ample room for input from the horse, we shall not go far wrong.

If, instead of trying to subdue the horse, we start from concepts of co-operation and friendship, all kinds of possibilities become real. As Marthe Kiley-Worthington has said, we should make sure we are liked, not dominant!

Notes

1 Jan May, *Equus Caballus*, pp. 3–4
2 Schjelderup-Ebbe, quoted by G. T. Syme and L. A. Syme, *Social Structure in Farm Animals* (Elsevier, Amsterdam, 1979), p. 3
3 Jeffrey Masson and Susan McCarthy, *When Elephants Weep*, p. 73
4 Masson and McCarthy, *When Elephants Weep*, p. 78
5 Dr Marthe Kiley-Worthington, 'Communication in Horses: Cooperation and

Competition' Publication 19, Eco-Research and Education Centre, University of Exeter. In press at time of writing.

6 Irwin S. Bernstein, 'Dominance: The baby and the bathwater', in *The Behavioral and Brain Sciences*, 1981, no. 4, p. 420

7 Syme and Syme, *Social Structure in Farm Animals*, p. 4

8 Syme and Syme, *Social Structure in Farm Animals*, p. 5

9 Syme and Syme, *Social Structure in Farm Animals*, p. 5

10 James Feist and Dale R. McCullough, 'Behavior Patterns and Communication in Feral Horses', in *Zeitschrift für Tierpsychologie*, no. 41, 1976 p. 367

11 R. H. Smythe, *The Mind of the Horse*, (J. A. Allen, rev. ed., 1972), p. 15

12 Susan McBane, *Behaviour Problems in Horses*, pp. 92–3

13 Lesley Bayley and Richard Maxwell, *Understanding Your Horse* (David and Charles, 1996), p. 45

14 Smythe, *The Mind of the Horse*, p. 32

15 Bayley and Maxwell, *Understanding Your Horse*, p. 9

16 Syme and Syme, *Social Structure in Farm Animals*, p. 75

17 Syme and Syme, *Social Structure in Farm Animals*, p. 76

18 Feist and McCullough, 'Behaviour patterns and communications in feral horses', p. 357

19 Feist and McCullough, 'Behaviour patterns and communications in feral horses', p. 357

20 S. J. Tyler, 'Behaviour and social organisation of New Forest ponies' (*Animal Behaviour*, 1972, monograph 5), p. 131

21 Feist and McCullough, 'Behaviour patterns and communications in feral horses', p. 358

22 Joel Berger, 'Organizational systems and dominance in feral horses in the Grand Canyon', *Behavioral Ecology and Sociobiology* 2, 1977 p.145

23 Feist and McCullough, 'Behaviour patterns and communications in feral horses', p. 358

24 Berger, 'Organizational systems and dominance in feral horses in the Grand Canyon', p. 139

25 Shirley Strum, *Almost Human* (New York, 1987), cited by Masson & McCarthy, *When Elephants Weep*, p. 77

26 Paul Leyhausen, *Cat Behavior: the Predatory*

and Social Behavior of Domestic and Wild Cats (trans. B.A. Tonkin, Garland STPM Press, 1979), pp. 256–7

27 McGreevy, *Why Does My Horse . . .?* p. 193

28 McGreevy, *Why Does My Horse . . .?* p. 193

29 S. M. Wells and B. von Goldschmidt-Rothschilde, 'Social behaviour and relationships in a herd of Camargue horses' in *Zeitschrift für Tierpsychologie*, no. 49 (1979), pp. 363–80

30 T .H. Clutton-Brock, P. J. Greenwood and R. D. Powell, 'Rank and relationships in highland ponies', in *Zeitschrift für Tierpsychologie*, 41 (1976), pp. 213–4

31 Feist and McCullough 'Behaviour patterns and communications in feral horses', p. 349

32 Feist and McCullough, 'Behaviour patterns and communications in feral horses', p. 341

33 Tyler, 'Behaviour and Social Organisation of New Forest ponies', p. 122

34 Syme and Syme, *Social Structure in Farm Animals*, p. 58 See also Grzimek's own observations in *Man and Animal*, ed. Heinz Friedrich (Paladin, 1972), p. 45

35 McGreevy, *Why Does My Horse. . .?*, p. 195

36 Midgley, *Beast and Man*, p. 300

37 Midgley, *Beast and Man*, p. 300

38 Clutton-Brock et al., 'Rank and relationships in Highland ponies', p. 214

39 Kiley-Worthington, 'Communication in Horses: Cooperation and Competition'

40 Kiley-Worthington, 'Communication in Horses: Cooperation and Competition'

41 Kiley-Worthington, 'Communication in Horses: Cooperation and Competition'

42 Kiley-Worthington, 'Communication in Horses: Cooperation and Competition'

43 Kiley-Worthington, 'Communication in Horses: Cooperation and Competition'

44 Kiley-Worthington, 'Communication in Horses: Cooperation and Competition'

45 Kiley-Worthington, 'Communication in Horses: Cooperation and Competition'

46 Dr Marthe Kiley-Worthington, *The Behaviour of Horses*, p. 139

47 Kiley-Worthington, *The Behaviour of Horses*, p. 146

48 Kiley-Worthington, *The Behaviour of Horses*, p. 146

49 Berger, 'Organisational Systems and Dominance in Feral Horses', p. 135

CHAPTER **NINE**

Authority or Tyranny?

When you are incoherent in your notions about an animal
you are working with, things do not go so well with the animal.

VICKI HEARNE

ONE OF THE GREATEST obstacles to our understanding of the horse and a true dialogue with him, has been an over-reliance on concepts of dominance (as outlined in
the previous chapter) and a misunderstanding of the nature of authority. For much
of the history of the human/horse relationship, the horse has been seen as an adversary to be
overcome, a naturally fractious creature whose spirit it was necessary to break in order to
render him tractable and fit for service. Hence we have the term 'breaking' for the preliminary stages in the horse's education; and very often this has been all too appropriate an
expression. In his autobiography, *The Man Who Listens To Horses*, Monty Roberts gives a
vivid account of the procedure known as 'sacking out'. This usually involved several horses,
which might scarcely, if ever, have been handled before. They were driven into a crush where
headcollars were fitted, then tied up to the corral fence. The handler then stood in the middle of the corral with a heavy tarpaulin or weighted sack which was attached to the end of a
rope. This sack was thrown over the backs and around the legs of the already terrified horses,
who pulled back against the ropes, fighting desperately to get away from this dreadful thing
that threatened them and from which there seemed no escape. This barbarous procedure
would be repeated over and over again, often for several days, during which time a saddle
was put on. The horse was then subjected to further restraint and terrorisation. This went on
for up to three weeks until the horse could eventually be ridden, the brutal treatment continuing unabated. Its purpose was to break the horses of any resistance – hence the term
'breaking'. Sometimes this was a literal description of what happened, as horses frequently
injured themselves in their frantic struggles to escape.

The evident cruelty of this method made the young Monty Roberts determined never to inflict such abuse on a horse. His subsequent observation of how horses in a natural group control and discipline each other, and his 'join-up' method of starting green horses, are now well known and are described in *The Man Who Listens To Horses*. Yet mistrust of such reliance on the horse's co-operation is still deeply ingrained in many people. Young Monty's own father insisted that nothing good would come of it, and even though Monty has started literally thousands of horses using this method, old Mr Roberts insisted to his dying day that one day a horse would 'get' his son. To date this has not happened, yet despite Monty's success, the old method of sacking out is still used to a considerable extent in the Western USA.

The usual explanation given for the popularity of this method is that in the days of the great cattle barons, when the cowboys of the West depended on their horses to an even greater extent than they do now, they needed a method that would give fast results, no matter how rough and ready; they simply did not have time for more refined and humane ways. Yet Lucy Rees, author of *The Horse's Mind*, demonstrated in a TV documentary shown by the BBC in 1986, *To Ride a Wild Horse*, that it was far quicker to 'break' (or as Monty Roberts would say, to 'start') a horse by gentle methods than by brutality. While the cowboys who insisted on breaking their horses with ropes were still struggling, Lucy Rees was riding her mustang stallion about freely. Nevertheless, in spite of the fact that rather less extreme methods are generally in use in Europe, the ignorant and those with closed minds continue to treat the horse as a potentially savage creature who cannot be trusted to co-operate willingly and without the use of force on the part of his handler.

It has not always been so. All over the world, and in all ages, there have been horsemasters who understood the true nature of horses and how to handle them without inflicting fear or pain: the Native Americans of the plains, the *bedu* of the Arabian peninsula, and the Osmanli Turks immediately come to mind, while in Europe the greatest masters of equitation, from Xenophon in the fifth century BC through to the present day, have practised the 'gentle art'. Even in the times of the crusades – an era scarcely characterised by its humaneness – we find many accounts of the love of crusaders for their horses and the gentleness with which they treated them. In the seventeenth century the famous Duke of Newcastle, often unjustly regarded as an advocate of cruel methods, considered (in common with most of his contemporaries) that fear was the principal motivator in both man and beast. Nevertheless, he insisted that the horse must be cherished and treated with gentleness, and indeed if one reads his writings carefully there is very little in them that runs contrary to the spirit of Xenophon and his like.

This attitude, while by no means universal on the continent of Europe, was far more widespread there than in the English-speaking countries, where methods of 'breaking' horses were often extremely rough. Few people these days would openly advocate such methods, yet I know of any number of 'trainers' who still resort to some appalling practices behind the closed doors of indoor schools, in various attempts to force the horse into submission.

Clearly, the continuing use of forceful or abusive methods of compelling horses to submit to the trainer or handler has its roots partly in a desire for quick results; in equestrian com-

petition, most specifically in the dressage arena or the showring, it is too often superficial impressions which count. But there is another, perhaps even deeper-seated reason. How often, especially in badly written fiction, do we read of riders 'dominating' proud horses – especially stallions? The same

Backing without tears: Joanne sits on Nivalis for the first time. A scratch on the withers helps, and Nivalis reciprocates by grooming the back of Brian's neck

thing can be seen in films, where horses are often seen being ridden in an extremely rough manner, supposedly showing off the rider's skill in forcing such a powerful creature to submit. Perhaps this has its origins in an age-old human desire to subdue nature: to the popular imagination, what could be a more compelling image of nature subdued than a proud, fiery horse dominated by a human?

A number of authors have expressed doubt as to whether the horse recognises the authority of his handler/trainer/rider.

> Many people consider discipline and physical restraint the keystones to managing a horse. 'Teach the horse who's master: don't let him get away with it.' Horses certainly learn to avoid pain, but whether they understand the concept of master, or of outwitting authority, is another matter, and one that reaches as deep into our evolution as theirs.[1]

As we saw in Chapter 6, it is generally accepted that dogs, when properly educated in matters such as house rules and permissible behaviour, are quite capable of understanding when they have done something wrong, and even apologising for it in advance of the owner realising that a misdemeanour has been committed (for an excellent explanation of the role of contrition in canine society, see Desmond Morris, *Dogwatching*). Horses, on the other hand, are usually held to be incapable of recognising when they have done something wrong, let alone expressing contrition. In Chapter 6 I questioned whether, as is often claimed, this really points to the horse's lack of reasoning ability, or whether it is merely a sign that communications have broken down. Are horses capable of distinguishing right from wrong? They are, of course, but it is *their* right and wrong that we have to consider, not ours. We have to remember that equine society, like canine society, has its own rules of behaviour, and that our ideas of what is acceptable may not be the same as the horse's!

As for the concept of authority, the problem is that a great deal of thinking on this subject is rather muddled. I believe that this is largely the result of social attitudes which colour our dealings, not only with other people but with non-human animals too. One of the most noticeable features of Western social life in the second half of the twentieth century has been the breakdown of all forms of authority. This process began much earlier, around the time of the First World War (1914–18), when the old social orders began to break up and all Europe was in a state of upheaval. The breakdown was accelerated during the 1950s and 1960s through the proliferation of a number of protest movements, most notably the anti-Vietnam War movement in the USA and various manifestations of student unrest. Some of these movements were relatively peaceful; others encouraged civil disobedience which often spilled over into overt violence. Most notorious of all were the so-called 'revolutionary' organisations, many of which had no constructive political agenda but held as their central aim the destruction of all forms of authority. Very often this aim permeated, in a diluted form, the educational establishments of various countries. In April 1969 the London *Evening Standard* printed an account of a 'progressive' kindergarten in what was then West Germany where one of the main ideals was to develop in infants a 'healthy contempt' for authority.

In their excellent enquiry into the causes of juvenile delinquency, Tom Pitt-Aikens and Alice Thomas Ellis address this question of the breakdown of authority. As Alice Thomas Ellis reminds us, when Hitler and Stalin destroyed the old social order, both the Nazi and the Communist regimes actively encouraged children to betray their parents in the name of 'the cause' ('the cause' being either National Socialism or Communism). The whole concept of authority was thus rendered meaningless, as Ellis puts it: 'morally and spiritually destitute, a deformed and monstrous rootless growth'[2]. How could children have any respect for the authority of their parents if betrayal of that authority was presented as not only acceptable but desirable?

The rejection of the idea of authority, then, has its roots in the all too evident tyranny of various regimes. Much of Western liberal thought throws its hands up in horror at the idea of submitting to any kind of authority, let alone imposing it on others. In some countries, parents and teachers have abdicated authority to such an extent that children are often expected to discover their own values, instead of having these 'imposed' upon them by others. Discussion of the consequences of this attitude belongs elsewhere, and this issue has been admirably covered by Hannah Arendt in *Between Past and Future*, where she points out with chilling clarity how this abdication of authority results in less, not more, freedom. For our present purposes, however, it is enough to see how contempt for authority, or a misunderstanding of its true nature, can cause confusion and incoherence.

For some, a romantic attraction to the idea of anarchy and the rejection of responsibility for one's actions leads them to view all authority as something to be resisted. For others, equally romantic, authority in whatever form represents a dark force that must be overcome, lest it lead to totalitarianism and the horrors of the labour camp and the gas chamber.

Yet there is a vast difference between legitimate authority and the authoritarianism which both the revolutionaries and the liberals reject. Tom Pitt-Aikens defines authority thus: 'Authority may be confused with both *influence and authoritarianism*, but I shall here define authority as "that which within a definite area may allow, disallow or insist upon change, with or without any further references".'[3] We should understand that here he is talking about a *specific* kind of authority, i.e. that invested in those who have the legal responsibility for children. As we have the same kind of responsibility to the domestic animals in our care, we may as well use this definition here. Pitt-Aikens goes on: 'Influence, however, may be effected over any area and may have to make reference to someone or something else, while authoritarianism is simply a particular brand of authority that exists at the expense of freedom.'[4] It is this latter concept that is usually confused with true authority, and in this lies the problem. This confusion is not easily disentangled because the misconception has become too widespread. As a consequence, 'authority' is now almost a dirty word in some circles, even among people who should know better.

What does all this mean for the thinking horseman or woman? It means that we had better get our concepts sorted out, since, as trainer Vicki Hearne has pointed out, 'When you are incoherent in your notions about an animal you are working with, things do not go so well with the animal.'[5] But this incoherence is deeply rooted in the horse world and it has proved just as difficult to eradicate there as elsewhere. The confusion of authority with authoritarianism has led some people to insist on total obedience from the horse at all times, such obedience often being exacted by harsh treatment if the horse refuses to comply. At the least this results in a very oppressive regime. Others, appalled by the idea of subjecting a horse to any kind of discipline, have fled to the other extreme and allowed the horse to do more or less as he pleases. In between, there are countless people who manage to achieve a more balanced approach and who have a sane, orderly relationship with their horses. But far too many horses lead a miserable existence, either hemmed in by too many restrictions or, alternatively, suffering the uncertainty of not knowing what behaviour is acceptable and what is not.

As we have already seen in the previous chapter, the issue is further clouded by an obsession with 'dominance' which afflicts large numbers of those devoted to the study of animal behaviour.

If it is true that horses do not understand the concept of authority, then it would indeed be unreasonable to expect them to understand concepts of crime and punishment. If we accept the pervasive idea that equine society is based on some kind of dominance hierarchy, however, this makes nonsense of such claims. What would be the point of a dominance hierarchy if a lower-ranking horse did not accept the higher-ranking horse's authority (I use 'authority' here in the sense in which it is normally used in such a context – almost as a synonym for domination)?

This attempt to reconcile two incompatible ideas leads to some very strange contradictions. For example, in *Why Does My Horse . . .?* Paul McGreevy says that: 'Horses resent demonstrations of authority. They have evolved to recognise rank only in disputes over resources like food and water.'[6] It is not at all clear what the author means by 'demonstrations of authority', but given the context in which this phrase appears in the book (i.e. a discussion of the ways in which humans often 'discipline' horses, most commonly by means of physical punishment), he appears to have in mind the kind of crude authoritarianism so readily confused with true authority. Yet, later in the book, discussing the reasons why horses tolerate being ridden, he cites the view that the natural gregariousness of horses enables them to put up with humans 'because they see them as dominant companions. This could be a useful way of understanding horses' submission to bossiness on the part of riders – in horse-to-horse terms tyranny and dictatorships are seen as tolerable by subordinate individuals.'[7]

This is incoherent. You cannot on the one hand say that horses resent demonstrations of authority, then on the other claim that they see tyranny and dictatorships as 'tolerable'! Demonstrations of 'authority' are nowhere so heavy handed or oppressive as under a tyrannical dictator – and this applies just as much to equine society as it does to humans. Besides, where does this leave us? If horses resent demonstrations of authority, how do we set about training them? Following the line of reasoning in the quotations given above, we would have to make ourselves 'dominant companions'. But as the concept of 'dominance' given here is evidently that of the tyrannical dictator, and as (as we saw in Chapter 8) dominance is, in this way of thinking, largely displayed through aggression, this does not actually help us very much. Besides, if horses have really 'evolved to recognise rank only in disputes over resources like food and water', why should they take any notice of a trainer, as there is no such resource in dispute in this situation?

As we shall see in Chapter 11, the kind of thinking which places emphasis on dominance very often also emphasises the role of 'negative reinforcement' in training – defined by McGreevy as 'the introduction of an unpleasant event to increase his [the horse's] willingness to perform a given behaviour! '[8]. So for the trainer who follows this mode of thought, it must seem that (in spite of the warning about horses' resentment of demonstrations of authority) the only possible way forward is by coercion; and unfortunately this is all too often the path that is chosen. I do not for one moment suggest that Paul McGreevy is advocating coercive or bullying methods of training horses; nevertheless, his comments about 'tyranny and dictatorships' could so very easily be taken to mean just that.

The consequences of such methods can be devastating for the horse (and in many cases for the handler). Some horses do submit to coercion, although they can scarcely be said to lead a satisfactory existence. Others will not submit under any circumstances; these are the stuff of great horse stories. Unfortunately for them, the ending is seldom as happy as in those stories, unless they are fortunate enough to fall into the hands of someone like Vicki Hearne or Lucy Rees. In *Adam's Task* Vicki Hearne describes the rehabilitation of a crazy mare called Drummer Girl. This mare was psychotic and dangerous; her first action on emerging from her trailer on arrival at Hearne's yard was a deliberate attempt to maim her new trainer. Hearne says that in deciding how to proceed, 'a number of options simply weren't available. If, for example, I were to approach her believing some febrile nonsense . . . about training as coercion, then my beliefs would be manifest in my body as I approached the mare, and she, reading this, would plain old kill me, that's all, if she could find a way'[9]. Some horses, subjected to coercion or domineering attitudes, *do* find a way to kill or maim their tormentors. Sylvia Loch tells how, many years ago, she witnessed a magnificent stallion being ridden in a very aggressive manner. The horse was being prevented from moving freely by draw reins, a severe curb bit and some kind of martingale as well. The rider was 'clearly afraid of its boisterous power and rode it in the most aggressive but nervous way possible, spurring it forward in one instant only to punish it in the mouth the next'[10]. The horse, not surprisingly, seemed about to explode. Sylvia Loch learned from the rider's assistant that this rider treated all his horses like this; she was not surprised to learn, a few months later, that this particular stallion had killed him.

Some horses, while stopping short of actual slaughter, still manage to inflict considerable damage. I have personally witnessed an Arabian stallion, driven to despair by coercive training and attempts to 'dominate' him, attack his handler savagely. There have been countless similar incidents, some of them actually occurring in the showring.

While mares and geldings can and do suffer from such attempts at domination, it seems to be stallions who are most likely to be treated in such a manner. This must surely spring from the idea that as stallions are generally supposed to be aggressive and 'dominant', such qualities must be controlled or suppressed by the use of the same 'dominance' and aggression on the part of their human handlers in order to 'show them who's boss'. But, as Sylvia Loch says, 'Some stallions are so humiliated by bad treatment . . . that they turn in on themselves rather than on the perpetrators of their discomfort.'[11] She recalls one stallion who turned to self-mutilation following intensive dressage training with a harsh trainer. This self-mutilation was so bad that in the end he had to be put down. 'Even castration failed to change the way he felt about himself; yet he had been a wonderfully calm and talented horse previously.'[12]

A Lipizzaner stallion called Maestoso Sitnica was more fortunate, although before he found his sanctuary with Lucy Rees he was violent and dangerous. Bred in Yugoslavia and trained in Germany for dressage, he passed through the hands of various trainers in Europe, gaining more and more of a bad reputation on the way as being almost impossible to handle.

> He would not be caught in the box, would not be bridled, could not be led nor mounted. He knocked people down, ran over them, crashed through barriers and created havoc. He had no fear of, nor respect for, anything. The scars and lumps on his head bear testimony to the efforts made to control him.'[13]

He could not be turned out as he could jump well and fences in any case meant nothing to him. He was extremely difficult to exercise as he was so explosive. Lucy Rees recognised that his problems stemmed not from fear but from the need to escape pressure. Her strategy for his rehabilitation required careful planning, making use of Maestoso's natural vigour, intelligence and curiosity, and constant thought on her part. 'Yet,' says Lucy Rees, 'we made steady progress, and finally he came to believe that whatever I wanted to do must involve something good for him in the end, and he became patient, willing and extremely interested in my ideas.'[14] She goes on,

> Maestoso's problems stemmed from his immense strength, stamina and energy, coupled with unbending pride. Met by a domineering attitude and relentless overtraining, these made him violent and dangerous, as if he felt he was fighting for his life. After two or three years of exercise and freedom . . . his remarkable gentleness and nobility made it almost impossible to believe he was the same horse.[15]

I hope these examples have made it clear – if such clarification is still needed – that for horses in general – and for horses like Maestoso Sitnica in particular – 'tyranny and dictatorships' are *far from* being acceptable. This is not how horses think of their relationships with other horses; belief that they do results all too often in the use of coercion. This does not have to take the form of physical abuse; it can simply be a relentless insistence on obedience, or a refusal to allow the horse any freedom of expression. Vicki Hearne says, 'I don't mean that you can't coerce horses, only that if you do, you will end up, if you are lucky, with a dull, unenthusiastic mount, or if you are unlucky, with a Drummer Girl emerging murderously from the trailer.'[16]

So if coercion and domination both carry with them the seeds of disaster, how then can we approach the training and handling of horses? We could, of course, try the other tack and attempt to train the horse simply by making ourselves liked. However, mere liking, while obviously desirable, does not ensure either attention or obedience. There has to be something more. Respect, of course, will supply part of this deficiency but, again, respect on its own is not enough. I can respect someone without feeling the slightest inclination to follow their requests (although I might pay attention to them). We must seek our answers from within equine society, but they do not reside in any 'dominance hierarchy', real or imagined. Instead, they spring from those very aspects we identified in the previous two chapters as being of the utmost importance to horses: friendship, affection and co-operation.

As we have seen, it was rejection of the brutal methods he saw being used to 'break' horses that set Monty Roberts on the path to discovery of his join-up method. His father was mystified when the young Monty, set the task of 'breaking' a couple of youngsters, asked for a few days in which to get to know them. 'To get to *know* them?' Mr Roberts asked. He clearly thought this was some kind of insanity. Allowing his son to go ahead, he warned him against any 'fancy business'. 'A horse is a dangerous machine, and you'd be wise to remember that. You hurt them first – or they'll hurt you'[17] – and such attitudes are still very much alive, in certain quarters at least.

Young Monty, however, was not to be deterred. He took the horses to a round pen and followed them about, trying to get them to allow him near them. As he says, he didn't really know what he was doing, but after three days, to his surprise, one of the geldings started to follow him around. He found he could reach up and put a saddle on the horse's back – all without any of the pain and brutality associated with the 'breaking' practices normally used by his father.

Sadly, Mr Roberts senior was not impressed – in fact he was furious, and beat his son with a length of chain. If anything were required to convince young Monty that this was *not* the way to proceed, this was it. 'It was a lesson in how *not* to win respect and allegiance; instead it only enforced a reluctant obedience and instilled fear.'[18]

Some time after this happened, Monty had the opportunity to observe how horses themselves instil respect in others.

What he saw, while watching the activities of a free-ranging herd, was how an older mare, a real matriarch, disciplined a very badly behaved young colt who was making life a misery for some of the younger horses. The mare had been watching the colt's bullying tactics for some time, moving a little closer to him every time he misbehaved. Finally he attacked a full grown mare. The matriarch who had been watching him launched herself at the colt, knocking him off his feet. She did this twice, then drove him out of the herd. She then took up position, watching for any signs of the colt trying to get back in.

The colt was clearly very miserable out there on his own. 'He walked back and forth, his head close to the ground, executing this strange, uncomfortable gait several times. It looked like a sign of obedience, similar to a bow made by a human being.'[19]

The old mare did not let the colt back into the group until he had fully expressed his contrition by way of his body language. Then, not only was he allowed back in, but the mare made a great fuss of him, grooming him and paying him lots of attention – just as if he were the Prodigal Son.

> He sinned a few more times, but she always drove him out and kept him out there before letting him back in and welcoming him into the group with extensive grooming. The third time he sinned, he practically owned up and walked out there himself, grumbling about it but accepting his fate.
>
> Then he came back in and stuck to the group like glue . . . For four whole days the dun mare had made the education of this awful brat her number one priority, and it had paid off.[20]

Apart from the insight this gave Monty Roberts into the body language of horses, this story is important because of what it tells us about the horse's need to *belong*. The worst thing that could happen to a wild horse – from a purely practical point of view – is isolation from the group; a lone horse is easy prey for big cats and wolves. That is the evolutionary underpinning of equine sociability. Of course, that is not the whole picture. Just as important as actually being *within* the group is *acceptance* by the group. The old mare did not just let the colt

If we take the trouble to bond with horses . . . Brian and Toska

back in; she positively welcomed him. When he was allowed back into the group after his last 'sin', the colt not only behaved himself, he went out of his way to be nice to everyone, almost to the point of making a nuisance of himself. Simply being safe from predators was not enough. The importance that horses attach to friendship and affection meant that he had to feel wanted and accepted; that was far more important to him than getting his own way by being obnoxious. This, and not submission to any kind of 'bossiness', is why the horse will willingly accept so many of the strange things we ask him to do. If we take the trouble to bond with him, he *wants* to be with us, to participate in what we do – in other words, to be part of our 'group', even if it is only a group of two!

And what of the mare who was doing the disciplining? Monty Roberts uses the term 'dominant mare', but not in the usual, rather careless sense in which both scientific and lay persons tend to use such terms, and which was outlined in the previous chapter. Indeed, Roberts's whole method rejects any idea of 'dominance' in such a sense. This was no authoritarian dictator, bossing and bullying the herd around. The other horses respected this mare because she was old and wise and knew all the risks; she also knew what was right and where the limits of acceptable behaviour are drawn. Her authority stemmed not from a domineering attitude (for she was only aggressive to the colt when he was being aggressive to others – 'be done by as you did'), nor from any kind of 'tyranny' or 'dictatorship': it derived from her experience, wisdom and judgement. This is the kind of authority we need in our dealings with the horse. As Lucy Rees says, 'A horse gives you his loyalty because your steadfast good sense, especially at times when his small courage fails him, impresses him, not because you dominate him. If you are safe and unafraid, he wants to be in the same place.'[21]

Certainly, there are times when a true leader must dominate. As Tom Pitt-Aikens points out, if danger threatens or swift action is required, autocratic decisions may be called for. He uses the metaphor of a sinking ship: when the ship is going down, it is not appropriate for the passengers and crew to start discussing what must be done; it is for the captain to decide when to abandon ship. A good military commander might call a council of war to seek the advice and opinions of his senior subordinates on strategic matters but he cannot afford to waste time on such a conference when an instant decision has to be made. Similarly, if the group is threatened, the stallion, whose job it is to protect the group, must be able to count on instant obedience to his signals. As Vicki Hearne says, we exert this kind of authority over one another all the time, 'or at least we had better do so if only to be able to say "Duck!" at the right moment. If our authority is weak, if we haven't taken responsibility for it, we *won't* say "Duck!" at the right moment, or the person so addressed may not duck.'[22]

What does she mean by taking responsibility for our authority? Among other things, she is saying that we must recognise the need for such authority, but also that such authority must have both coherence and integrity. Suppose, says American trainer Paul Belasik, you have an appointment with someone who is always late. If you arrive on time, you will waste time waiting, time that could be better spent doing other things. Do you still bother to arrive on time? 'Of course, you must. This imbues your action with an integrity.' And this integrity, as he says, is not dependent on the outcome. 'You take care of your own integrity. You try to arrive on time, all the time. Your intentions are clear. Your commands have integrity'[23]. But if we go about shouting 'Duck!' just to impress people, then our commands have neither coherence nor integrity, and after a time such commands will quite rightly be ignored. If the commands we give the horse lack these qualities, should we be surprised if he too ignores them? Vicki Hearne points out that: 'the ability to exact obedience doesn't give you the right to do so – it is the willingness to obey that confers the right to command'[24].

The word 'obey' itself derives from two Latin words, *ob* (to, towards) and *audire* (to hear, learn, listen, attend to). It is thus associated with the act of *paying attention*. As well as ensuring that the horse wants to be with the trainer, it also means that he is *listening*. Indeed, when good trainers say that a horse is 'listening' to his rider, they mean it in just the sense it is used here – that the horse is paying attention. Focusing the horse's attention on the handler or rider is – provided always that the latter's commands have the required qualities of coherence and integrity – a very powerful way of ensuring the horse's obedience. So many cases of 'disobedience' stem from the fact that the rider's or handler's commands *do* lack those qualities. If, at the same time, the horse is subjected to training based on punishment rather than reward, he may well feel that doing nothing is the only sensible response to an incoherent demand.

Extremely important in establishing and maintaining the horse's trust and complicity, and his faith in our authority, is that we must not be arbitrary. We must not, for example, punish the horse because we are in a bad mood, but because he has done something to deserve it (and we must be absolutely sure about that). La Guérinière says, 'Above all, a horse should never be chastised out of foul mood or anger, but always with complete dispassion.'[25]

Following from this, we are usually told that our treatment of the horse must be consistent. We must not reward or punish certain behaviour at some times but not at others, otherwise the horse will feel confused and insecure. However, perfect consistency is simply not possible without also introducing inflexibility and injustice. We could only be utterly consistent if we could say 'this behaviour' (whatever it might be) is *never* appropriate, no matter what the circumstances, or that another behaviour is *always* appropriate (again without regard to circumstances). But we cannot say these things without perpetrating monstrous injustices; and those riders and trainers who believe they are being consistent when they always punish the horse for bucking, say, or refusing to jump, or who insist on total, mechanical obedience in dressage tests, or whatever, are not being consistent, merely inflexible. They are failing to accept what Vicki Hearne calls the 'burden of judgement' which handling and training horses morally entails.

It is really far more important that we should treat the horse with consistency *according to the context*. Horses are very good at reading contexts. Their social lives teach them when a certain behaviour is appropriate and when it is not. So (provided it is made clear to them) they are perfectly capable of understanding that they may do X (whatever 'X' might be) in *this* context, but not in *that* one. It just is not true that lenience in some aspects leads to law-

Paying attention: Nivalis stands up for Brian

lessness in others. It all depends on whether we have taken responsibility for our authority, as described above, and on how coherent that authority is.

An example of *incoherent* authority is that which insists it must always be right. Tom Pitt-Aikens points out that: 'Delinquents rightly hate and mistrust the authority that is pathologically determined to be one hundred per cent certain that it is right – as if this could ever be!'[26] While the majority of horses will certainly not start off as delinquents, an incoherent authority that either refuses to take charge or, having taken charge, then insists it must always be right, will very likely drive them to delinquency. Yet much of the advice given out by 'experts' seems to advocate just this kind of pseudo-authority. For example, a speaker at an equestrian conference, talking about the phobia many horses have about getting their feet wet, said there was absolutely no reason why a young horse should make a fuss about paddling in shallow water. In fact, from the horse's point of view, there is every reason. You and I may know that it is only a puddle, at most a couple of centimetres deep, but to the horse it could be a bottomless well, and he is not about to find out by risking a test which might lead to his destruction. It takes a great deal of courage for a horse to put his foot into something unknown. Horses brought up in boggy areas may not be so bothered about puddles, and of course feral horses quickly learn from their group companions which water holes are safe and which not, but some horses really object to going through puddles. This is not stupidity or obstinacy in most cases, but a reflection of the fact that, to the horse, his feet are all important. If they get trapped or if he puts them in a hole (which a puddle might well be), he is

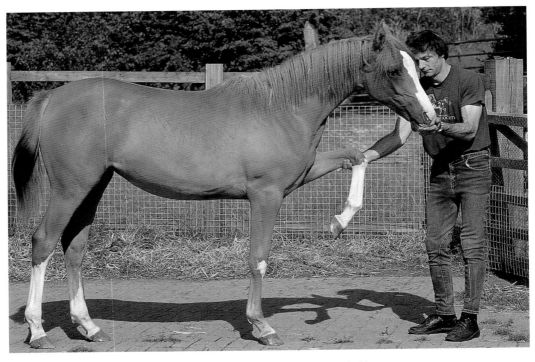

Trust: Imzadi freely gives Brian her leg to hold up

defenceless; he cannot run away. Hence the objection many horses show to having their feet picked up: they feel restrained and trapped – the worst position a horse can be in from his point of view. We must also consider that many horses have an abhorrence of being splashed, to the extent that many of them will not urinate on a hard surface. The more thin-skinned horses are likely to be particularly fussy on this point, as urine splashes can cause skin irritation.

To insist on a horse going through puddles without taking all of this into account (and devising ways to neutralise the objection without resorting to coercion) is not a measure of authority, it is just plain ignorance. The people who advocate such insistence seldom tell us how many battles they have fought – and either lost, or won by force – with horses whose sense of self-preservation (or dislike of being splashed) is stronger than their respect for this pseudo-authority or their fear of any punishment.

It is one thing to say that the horse should obey without question if our demands are reasonable, but we must always ask ourselves, *are* our demands reasonable from the horse's point of view? Too many good horses have been ruined by their handlers' insistence on always being right, on winning arguments instead of addressing the real problem. Tom Ainslie tells the story of a promising filly, of a sweet and tractable nature, whose legs received several cuts in a race. She was kept stabled while the cuts were healing. When she was judged well enough, she was taken out to the track for exercise. The filly refused to go. She fought like a totally wild horse and it took half an hour to reach the track – a trip that would nor-

Trust: Imzadi with Brian

mally have taken just a few minutes. When they reached the entrance to the track, she reared up and flipped over backwards and her rider narrowly escaped serious injury. Tom Ainslie comments,

> The filly would have gone willingly to the track for a strengthening gallop if her handlers had understood the psychological effects of a week's confinement. They should not have rushed her back to arduous work before giving her a chance to enjoy her release from the stall. But they treated her conventionally. That is, they overlooked the difference between a horse and an automobile. A repaired car goes where it is driven. But the horse has a brain that generates feeling and preferences.[27]

The filly associated being saddled, ridden and taken to the track with a stressful activity to which she was not yet ready to return.

> Had the balking filly's people been more concerned with her long term well-being than with winning an argument, they might have understood what was on her mind. They would then have taken her for a leisurely walk and let her browse and roll. They would have spared her the psychological and physical rigors of a workout until two or three days of diversion and light exercise had helped her recover from the distress of confinement.
>
> Why did they not accept that easier and more productive alternative? Why did they prefer to traumatize the animal in a fight? Perhaps they were unaware of their options. More probably they did not care to lose dignity in the ancient battle for supremacy over a supposedly pea-brained species. So, they pushed a perfectly decent horse around the bend.[28]

All kinds of red herrings are usually introduced into discussions about control and obedience, including the usual behaviourist arguments that allowing a domestic animal licence will mean a revision of the hierarchy, usually to the detriment of the human. But how true is this?

Let us look at the question of control from a wider point of view. In the 1997 March issue of the monthly magazine *Dogs Today*, a discussion was carried on about whether a dog should be allowed to sleep on its owner's bed. Behaviourist David Appleby believes that allowing the dog on the bed could cause problems by creating an environment where the dog came to believe he had a higher status than his owners. Dog trainer Ian Dunbar disagrees. 'Whether a dog is allowed on the couch or bed should be up to owners,' he says. 'The dog must understand the rules and that the owner is always in control. My philosophy is to allow a dog a lot of comforts and a lot of freedom, but with lots of rules.'[29] He goes on to say, 'People often confuse the issue of who is in control with other little red herrings, such as who should eat first, who should go upstairs first and so on – situations where the owners' lack of control manifests itself.'[30] Dunbar believes that problems which arise with dogs who have been allowed on the bed are a manifestation of a control problem, not the cause of it, and that once the control problem has been resolved the dog can sleep where he or the owner likes. Basic obedience training (which, if it is done properly, most dogs love) will sort out the matter of control. 'If your dog likes you, he'll do what you ask him, so you remain in control,' says Dr Dunbar. 'This way, you don't get into the terrible situation of having a miserable dog whose life is full of petty rules. Let your dog sleep comfortably – wherever that may be.'[31]

I believe the same philosophy is appropriate to horses. Rather than insisting on absolute control and obedience at all times, we should be concentrating on being able to control the horse *when it matters*, and allowing it freedom at other times. However, this presupposes that we have established our authority from the start and that this authority is of the kind outlined above, not the spurious, authoritarian kind.

This philosophy has nothing to do with allowing horses to do just as they please, any more than real freedom is about allowing humans to do just as they please. True freedom comes not with anarchy, but with obedience to legitimate, fair authority. As always, the 'burden of judgement' lies on the trainer/handler, who must decide when it is appropriate to allow horses more freedom, and when it is not. Horses are quite capable of understanding such matters far better than many humans give them credit for!

In spite of this, many trainers/handlers feel insecure if the horse does not obey and respond to absolutely every demand they make. Such people often express the view that if the horse is allowed to 'get away with' something, then somehow the world will come to an end. In *The Nature of Horses* Stephen Budiansky says

> . . . it requires considerable self-discipline to give commands in a consistent fashion and to insist on obedience every time; every rider can think of times when he let his horse get away with something he shouldn't have (break into a canter when he should still have been trotting, cut across the ring, take a few steps after being brought to a halt).[32]

He is perfectly right, of course, about consistency. But how can the horse possibly be expected to obey every single time? A horse may, for instance, break into a canter because he lost his balance in the trot. Indeed, loss of balance is one of the commonest causes of so-called 'disobedience', including bucking – observe how often horses, when galloping around in the field or cavorting about in play, lose their balance and give a great buck to try to restore their equilibrium. If the horse loses his balance under the weight of the rider, which commonly happens, is he to be punished for this? Is no account to be taken of the many factors which might prevent the horse from carrying out the rider's wishes? What sort of rider could possibly insist on such unconditional obedience?

In any case, mere consistency is not enough. If the aids (or, as Budiansky has it, 'commands' – the distinction does matter) are not given in the right way, at the right time, then they are incoherent, and all the consistency in the world will not compel obedience.

As the former Director of the Spanish Riding School, the late Colonel Alois Podhajsky, put it: 'In most cases insubordination is caused by the horse's fear of his rider, by the fact that he does not understand what is required of him, or is unable to execute an exercise for which he is not prepared.'[33] Elsewhere, this wise man – who successfully retrained many extremely 'difficult' horses – says,

> Whenever difficulties appear the first thing the rider must do is ask himself: does the horse not want to execute my demands, does he not understand what I want, or is he physically unable to carry them out? The rider's conscience must find the answer. If there is any doubt it is much better to assume that the horse is unable to carry out the commands and leave it at that, which is much wiser than obtaining the exercise by force. An omission is never of such bad consequence as an injustice.[34]

Vicki Hearne says, 'A refusal to give commands or to notice that commands are being given is often a refusal to acknowledge a relationship, just as is a refusal to obey.'[35] So when a horse refuses to obey (as opposed to being *unable* to obey), he may simply not be listening to us; he may be telling us that our authority is suspect. Youngsters in particular will often challenge the trainer by overt disobedience. This is not, as some people maintain, an attempt at 'dominance'; they are simply questioning our right to command, just as human children and adolescents will. If we have accepted the responsibility for our authority, and it is coherent, then we will survive the challenge; if not, things will go badly for both horse and trainer.

A cheeky foal challenges authority

We must also ask, is unconditional obedience really desirable in all circumstances? Paul McGreevy points out that horses who stand still and refuse to advance may only be wanting to take a good look at something, and this is certainly not a trait we want to eliminate. Horses perceive a great deal more about their surroundings than we generally do; *you* may not notice the black plastic sack in the hedge that wasn't there yesterday, but you can be sure your horse will! Such awareness of their surroundings – a necessary attribute in a prey species – may mean that a horse recognises possible danger long before humans do. McGreevy tells how he and a friend took three horses on an eight-week trek in the Australian bush. One afternoon they found that a bridge across a river they wanted to cross had been washed away, so they tried to ford the river further upstream. Two of the horses refused to approach the bank, so McGreevy jumped on the pack-horse, Mac, who proved more obliging than his companions. Within seconds McGreevy and

Mac were being sucked into a quicksand and had to be towed out by the others. McGreevy comments, 'Although he had been the most obedient, Mac had exposed himself as the least sensible equine member of the expedition. By baulking, the two riding-horses had averted a double disaster because towing them out would have been beyond little Mac.'[36]

As Tom Ainslie says, the horse must be allowed the opportunity to observe and categorise anything unfamiliar in its surroundings, otherwise

> . . . the urgency of the need to do it is expressed in a manner that draws punishment from any impatient or ignorant handler, [and] trouble brews. Not only does the animal's work suffer during the incident but the human-equine relationship worsens in consequence . . . That it sometimes takes the horse a minute or two to satisfy curiosity and add to its catalog is a price that the wise master pays. And a privilege that the contented horse repays.[37]

It must not be thought that I am extolling disobedience in horses or advocating a *laissez-faire* attitude towards handling and training them. There are times when we must be firm, when we must insist that the horse takes notice of us even though he might not feel like doing so. However, the art lies in knowing *when* to do this, and in knowing just how much we can insist on before we provoke resistance and a wearisome battle of wills. As they are mentally geared towards co-operation rather than conflict, horses seldom set out to be bloody-minded for the sake of it (although some undoubtedly do so). We, on the other hand, often provoke conflict by our refusal to see the horse's point of view. One cannot have any kind of meaningful relationship on those terms.

So how does the trainer decide the cause of resistance? Paul Belasik tells a story which nicely illustrates this problem. Belasik was experiencing some difficulties in working a horse in one of the supreme exercises of the High School, the *passage*. While the horse was supple enough in the exercise most closely associated with *passage*, the *piaffe*, he lost all this suppleness when asked for the former exercise and became increasingly rigid and resistant. Belasik felt he would have to change his tactics in developing this movement. As it happened, at this time he had volunteered to take part in some research work into equine locomotion, and this particular horse was fitted with an electrode that relayed his heart rate to some complex equipment. Belasik could actually hear the machine beeping in time with his horse's heartbeat as he rode the Grand Prix dressage test three times, and he could hear the rate climb with some of the strenuous movements and then drop again. When he got to the *passage* where he had been experiencing all the difficulties, although the horse seemed to be making a considerable effort, the heartrate did not go up as he would have expected, it went *down*. It became clear to Belasik that the horse was not getting upset about the *passage*; he was simply holding back.

This bothered him, Belasik says, on two counts: first, because he felt his ability to sort out the horse's problem seemed to have gone so far askew, and second, because he felt that his equine partner had in some way been disloyal. He had been giving his own best effort, but the horse wasn't. This made him wonder if it would ever be possible to know, at all times, what the real level of resistance is. But then he started to ask,

> What if I was fooled by the horse? What if the horse was cheating? What if I unnecessarily changed the course of training when it really didn't need it? Do you need this kind of absolute mind control in order to proceed? It was not as if I was going to quit training the passage entirely – I was just going to change tracks.[38]

If the trainer obeys their own integrity, says Belasik, you have self-respect and mutual respect; and if the trainer does their work well, the horse will probably train well. But if the trainer has given of their best for a long while, and the horse still has not responded, the trainer can do no more. 'The horse has decided not to be trained, and you may have to let go. If you approach training this way, you will give the horse that ultimate respect. You give it a choice.'[39]

Belasik calls this philosophy of integrity 'the code, the way, the life of a trainer'[40]. This code is what the trainer obeys.

> If you are a sadistic trainer, who will you obey? Are you going to demand authority over the horse's action? Are you going to demand that you never be fooled? Will you be humiliated if you arrive on time but your appointment doesn't? Are you going to chain the horse into answering your commands?
>
> If you can never be fooled, neither can you be surprised by the mysteries and gifts that animals can bestow upon you.[41]

Dominique Barbier, a former pupil of Nuno Oliveira, and Richard Maxwell, a pupil of Monty Roberts, have both suggested that the horse and rider (or trainer/handler) relationship should be thought of as a partnership in which the human retains the controlling interest (51 per cent). Barbier goes further and says that when you set out to train a horse, you are effectively asking the horse, 'Do you want to dance with me?' Charles de Kunffy, a classical trainer with a wide equestrian background who is also an FEI judge, says that when green horses lose their balance under a rider, 'The rider has not yet been recognised as the partner who can solve problems and who secures a life in the comfort zone. We have to convince the young horse of our abilities in that direction, and the best way to proceed is to propose a partnership in motion.'[42] In such a partnership, one must lead and the other must follow; but to be in harmony, the one who follows (in this case, the horse) must accept the direction of the other partner. This does not mean that it is a one-sided partnership. The partner who follows still provides input; in the case of human dancers, they might say, 'Don't go so fast, you're unbalancing me,' or 'It might be better if we tried it this way.' If the other partner is truly interested in dancing, and not just in pushing someone else around, they will listen to what their partner suggests. Brigadier-General Albrecht, former Director of the Spanish Riding School and an FEI judge, says that a genuine horseman 'should be happy to climb off his throne sometimes to consult his equine partner'[43].

No need for domination: Lusitano mare Andorinha and rider enjoy a happy, relaxed partnership (Sylva Loch)

De Kunffy says, 'Horse-initiated actions that are not dangerous should be considered as potentially good, desirable and useful, and therefore welcome. For the continued progress both in mental partnership and physical development, pursue the horse's ideas with encouragement.' For, he goes on: 'Riders best develop their "listening" abilities while remaining alert to opportunities the horse presents.'[44]

Suppose, as in Stephen Budiansky's examples, you are trotting and the horse breaks into a canter. Whether it is disobedience, misunderstanding or simple loss of balance, make the most of it; use the opportunity to improve the canter. Pretend it was what you wanted to do anyway. Only correct the horse if his actions are detrimental to his development or to safety; otherwise turn them into opportunities. As Charles de Kunffy says, 'If a horse is often, or always corrected when he volunteers initiative, the rider will break his spirit. A horse cannot conceive of a programmed partnership that does not tolerate spontaneity.'[45]

So when people like Albrecht and de Kunffy talk about the necessity for the horse to recognise human superiority, they are not talking down from some pedestal upon which they have placed the human race. Nor are they invoking some crude and simplistic concept of dominance, or 'showing the horse who's boss'. They are talking about nothing less than the acceptance of true authority – the authority to make decisions for the ultimate benefit of the horse. If we have 'joined up' with the horse, as Monty Roberts would put it, he will want to follow us in the dance, he will be interested in our ideas and will want to share them. If our authority is coherent, the horse will accept it, not because he recognises concepts such as 'boss', but because he feels safe.

Paul Belasik says that how the rider/trainer handles resistance is directly related to the level of their skill, the quality of their horsemanship and their knowledge of different options.

Too many people assume that they have the right to ride the horse without respect for some proper communication. They have the right to this authority without granting any authority to the horse; without any reverence for the process; without any willingness to be ordered or changed by the horse.[46]

This one-sided pseudo-authority, devoid of genuine communication, is one of the things that make horses crazy. But, says Belasik, 'If you acknowledge the idea that you go into training the horse with the possibility that you can be changed and ordered by the horse, you have built in a flexibility in your style, a movability in your system, a freedom in your reactions.'[47]

So horses do understand the concept of authority, then, provided it is the *right kind* of authority; and they are capable of knowing when they have done wrong. This is shown by Monty Roberts's story of the colt and the old dun mare. However, before we can ask them to accept our authority and our rules, we must first understand their frames of reference and establish mutual trust. A friend was once told by the manager of a well-known stud, 'If you are not prepared to trust the horse, why on earth should he trust you?' We must learn to understand equine rules of behaviour and respect these insofar as it is compatible with our safety to do so. How we deal with all this depends on our integrity and the coherence of our authority. The trainer/handler/rider is never, for one moment, relieved of the burden of judgement.

Notes

1 Lucy Rees, *The Maze*, p. 59
2 Tom Pitt-Aikens and Alice Thomas Ellis, *The Loss of the Good Authority* (Viking, 1989), p. 9
3 Pitt-Aikens and Ellis, *Loss of the Good Authority*, p. 9
4 Pitt-Aikens and Ellis, *Loss of the Good Authority*, p. 9
5 Vicki Hearne, *Adam's Task*, p. 3
6 Paul McGreevy, *Why Does My Horse . . .?*, p. 4
7 McGreevy, *Why Does My Horse . . .?*, p. 49
8 McGreevy, *Why Does My Horse . . .?*, p. 53
9 Hearne, *Adam's Task*, p. 130
10 Sylvia Loch, *The Classical Rider: Being at One with Your Horse* (J. A. Allen, 1997) p. 26
11 Loch, *The Classical Rider*, p. 26
12 Loch, *The Classical Rider*, p. 27
13 Lucy Rees, *The Horse's Mind*, p. 199
14 Rees, *The Horse's Mind*, p. 200
15 Rees, *The Horse's Mind*, p. 200

16 Hearne, *Adam's Task*, p. 130
17 Monty Roberts, *The Man Who Listens to Horses* (Hutchinson, 1996), p. 28
18 Roberts, *The Man Who Listens to Horses*, p. 30
19 Roberts, *The Man Who Listens to Horses*, p. 83
20 Roberts, *The Man Who Listens to Horses*, pp. 86–7
21 Rees, *The Maze*, p. 58
22 Hearne, *Adam's Task*, p. 49
23 Paul Belasik, *Exploring Dressage Technique* (J. A. Allen, 1995), p. 107
24 Hearne, *Adam's Task*, p. 66
25 la Guérinière, *The School of Horsemanship*, p. 122
26 Pitt-Aikens, *Loss of the Good Authority*, p. 15
27 Tom Ainslie and Bonnie Ledbetter, *The Body Language of Horses*, p. 57
28 Ainslie and Ledbetter, *The Body Language of Horses*, p. 59

29 Dr Ian Dunbar, 'Should You Let Sleeping Dogs Lie With You?' *Dogs Today*, March 1997 p. 14
30 Dunbar, 'Should You Let Sleeping Dogs Lie With You?', p. 14
31 Dunbar, 'Should You Let Sleeping Dogs Lie With You?', p. 14
32 Stephen Budiansky, *The Nature of Horses*, p. 160
33 Colonel Alois Podhajsky, *The Complete Training of Horse and Rider* (tr. Colonel V. D. S. Williams and Eva Podhajsky, Harrap, 1967), p. 72
34 Colonel Alois Podhajsky, *My Horses, My Teachers*, pp. 118–19
35 Hearne, *Adam's Task*, p. 49
36 McGreevy, *Why Does My Horse . . .?*, p. 153
37 Ainslie and Ledbetter, *The Body Language of Horses*, p. 53

38 Belasik, *Exploring Dressage Technique*, pp. 106–7
39 Belasik, *Exploring Dressage Technique*, p. 108
40 Belasik, *Exploring Dressage Technique*, p. 108
41 Belasik, *Exploring Dressage Technique*, p. 108
42 Charles de Kunffy, *Ethics and Passions of Dressage* (Half Halt Press, 1993), p. 71
43 Brigadier-General Kurt Albrecht, *The Principles of Dressage* (tr. Nicole Bartle, J. A. Allen, 1983), p. 15
44 Kunffy, *Ethics and Passions of Dressage*, p. 74
45 Kunffy, *Ethics and Passions of Dressage*, p. 73
46 Belasik, *Exploring Dressage Technique*, p. 108
47 Belasik, *Exploring Dressage Technique*, pp. 108–9

CHAPTER TEN

Having Something to Say

A good trainer can hear a horse
speak to him. A great trainer can hear him whisper.

MONTY ROBERTS

WHAT IS COMMUNICATION? My dictionary defines the verb to *communicate* as: 'to impart (knowledge) or exchange (thoughts, feelings, or ideas) by speech, writing, or gestures, etc.'[1]; while *communication* is defined as 'the act or an instance of communicating; the imparting or exchange of information, ideas, or feelings'[2]. Scientists studying animal behaviour have variously tried to define communication as the use of specific signals or displays to influence the beliefs of, or modify the behaviour of others. One rather restrictive hypothesis is that communication is concerned with the manipulation of others in the interest of the individual but, as we shall see, such hypotheses do not take account of the fact that communication is not always voluntary. A standard response to such objections is that involuntary signals do not count as communication; but this simply begs the question.

As Dr Marthe Kiley-Worthington points out, the study of communication in horses has been largely restricted to observation of the more obvious displays of body language (e.g. ear signals, biting, kicking, mutual grooming, etc.). Instead of recording the response of other horses to such displays, assumptions have routinely been made about their meaning.[3]

This is now beginning to change. The last few years have seen a remarkable growth of interest in communication with horses. This has partly been a result of the amount of attention being paid to work on communication with other species, notably apes and marine mammal such as whales and dolphins. It has also stemmed from an upsurge of interest in methods of training which rely not on the physical and psychological domination of the horse, but on *communication*. The most obviously successful practitioner of such a method has, of course, been Monty Roberts. However, ever since humankind first had any kind of relationship with horses, there have always been people who have been outstandingly successful in communicating with them. Indeed, as Paul Belasik puts it, 'Horses do not speak to people with words. Yet man has been communicating with horses for some six thousand years. The lexicon of his communication with horses is no less than the story of riding.'[4]

As always, dogma and superstition – whether of the old-fashioned, religious kind, or the modern, scientific kind – intrude to cloud our understanding and block communication. As we have seen from previous chapters, one of the biggest such blocks has been the extraordinarily persistent idea, still supported by a great deal of scientific thinking, that animals are creatures devoid of language and therefore of real, meaningful communication. Even now, when the concept of animals as unthinking, unfeeling brutes is undergoing drastic revision in many quarters, there is still a tendency to regard animal communication as largely a matter of stimulus and response – almost a knee-jerk reaction. But how, for example, can it possibly make sense to describe (as one author does in a popular book on equine behaviour) a horse's vocal communications as 'primitive reflexes'?[5] Anyone who has really observed horses knows that their methods of communication, like their social organisation, are subtle and complex; yet such is the perception of horses as rather simple, primitive creatures, that such statements continue to be made.

But, as Paul Belasik says, horses do not communicate with words. So how do they communicate? The whole question of whether animal communication – no matter how sophisticated – can truly be called language has caused a great deal of fierce debate ever since the 1960s when a female chimpanzee called Washoe was taught the American sign language called Ameslan. Washoe proved extremely proficient in learning the hand gestures and the meaning of the words, and the experiment was extended to include other chimps, again with great success. Not only did the chimps learn to communicate with their human teachers, they communicated with each other, even inventing swear words (which they had never been taught). Not surprisingly, claims that the chimps were talking to each other and to their human handlers provoked strong resistance from those who maintain that language is a uniquely human characteristic. They objected that Ameslan, as 'spoken' by the chimps, is not really language at all because it lacks the structural properties of true language. By this they mean that the chimps do not make rational use of word order to convey meanings. However, as Mary Midgley points out, these arguments are largely concerned with syntax, and as she says, 'If pressed, this kind of argument is liable to prove that a lot of humans do not talk, either.'[6] Midgley goes on to argue that:

Language . . . is perhaps not, any more than reason, a yes-or-no business, a hammer that you are holding or not holding . . . It, too, is a rich and complex range of skills . . . 'Having language' in the sense in which human beings have it is having a large and versatile tool kit. But kits containing some of the same tools are found in much less ambitious quarters.[7]

So if we accept the idea that other creatures besides humans may share part of the same 'tool kit', what tools do horses make use of in order to communicate? If your sole experience of horses came from films and TV programmes, you might be forgiven for thinking that equine communication was mainly vocal as there always seems to be such a lot of neighing and whinnying going on. However, as any experienced horseman or woman knows, horses actually make relatively little use of their voices. They do use a number of what scientists call 'sensory modalities' – in other words, sight, smell and touch – as well as sound; but it is principally by means of their extraordinarily rich and subtle body language that they communicate with each other and with other species, including, of course, humans – a fact that has been known and made use of since at least the time of Xenophon (and almost certainly long before that).

In spite of this, an extraordinary number of people – particularly those with scientific backgrounds – have great difficulty in accepting that horses might actually be *saying* something. According to this way of thinking, one can dismiss most equine communication as a stock response 'triggered' by a specific stimulus – hence the description, quoted above, of whinnying as a 'primitive reflex'.

Mary Midgley challenges this view, pointing out that animals' responses constitute a huge range of behaviour. 'There is no stock item instantly produced, as there should be if "triggering" was an appropriate word. All the details vary according to how the individual sizes up the situation.'[8] Certainly, she says, there are some gestures typical of the response, but that is also true for humans. The instant reaction is *attention* – the creature looks up – but, as Midgley says, this is only a preliminary to a response. The response itself – depending on the circumstances – may take longer, as the animal must understand the message before acting upon it.

All this is as true for horses as it is for apes. There is no such thing as a standard automatic response, no 'stock reaction' as there would be if their communication were simply a matter of reflexes, the stimulus-response sequence upon which behaviourists hang their scientific hats. All equine communication requires *interpretation*. As with human speech, the *context* is all-important – and having to relate something to a context means interpreting it.

Unfortunately for very many horses, the behaviourist view has dominated to the extent that horses are widely regarded among certain groups as having nothing to say (how can they be saying anything worth listening to if they are only capable of stock responses?). Of course, if one refuses to listen to what another is trying to say, to the extent of denying that they are saying anything, eventually they will either give up trying and retreat into a kind of dull unresponsiveness, or they may go quietly (or not so quietly) crazy. Vicki Hearne, writing about working with crazy horses, says,

> The greatest challenges come from horses who have been beguiled by some confused version of behaviorism, or virtually anything from the matrix of academic psychology . . . sometimes such horses might as well be severely autistic for all the talking that is going to go on for a while.[9]

So for any work with horses to be truly effective we must establish two-way communication. As we have seen with Clever Hans, horses have an astonishing ability to read our body language. We, with our greater dependence on spoken language, have to work much harder to understand theirs.

Our task is made much more difficult by the fact that, as I said above, communication may be involuntary. The horse who stands staring into the distance, with his ears pricked in the direction of his gaze, clearly communicates by his body posture that something has caught his attention. Other horses may pick up his signals and react accordingly but, if they do, how can we be sure that this was his intention? If it was not, does this still count as communication? As we have seen, some schools of scientific thought would argue that it does not. However, as Dr Kiley-Worthington says of behaviour that serves as communication:

> That communication is only taking place when the behaviour is performed with the intent of communicating does not appear to be correct, although such communication may be less sophisticated. Is the horse ever going to prick his ears when he wants others to look in that direction when there is *no* interesting stimulus, and if so how are we ever going to know this? Similarly how can we conclude that he is *only* going to prick his ears when he perceives something interesting and it is *never* intended as a communication signal? It would seem more rational to assume that both functions may well be implicit in many of the movements and postures that the horse performs although inevitably our observations will be incomplete.[10]

Something has held Zareeba's attention: is he communicating or merely reacting? Who can tell?

So how do we begin to understand what horses say to each other and what they may be trying to say to us? Most people who regularly deal with horses and who have some empathy with them will quickly learn how to read their basic moods – whether they are tired or full of energy, tense or relaxed, well or unwell, and so on. Most of us will learn pretty quickly to detect signs of anger or aggression, whether towards humans or other horses: there is no mistaking the threatening body posture, the flattened ears, the hoof raised as if to say, 'Do that again and I'll kick you across the field (or out of the stable, or whatever).' Indeed, so obvious are displays of aggression that this may well explain why so many people have assumed that horses are by nature aggressive. Other signals can be equally easy to interpret if we are attentive enough. When our stallion Nivalis is in his stable and his water bucket needs refilling, he will let us know that he wants water by banging on his door; or, if we are filling up another horse's water bucket, he gives a low whicker to remind us to fill his bucket up too. If he is out in the paddock that runs alongside the stable block, he lets us know when his water bucket is empty by going to the gate near where the dogs' water dish stands in the yard, and banging on the gate post on the other side!

However, equine communication goes far beyond these rather basic signals, and although the voice is not their main means of communication, even here horses can make use of a huge range of nuances of expression.

Over a period of about 40 years Henry Blake studied vocal communication between horses. As result he compiled a 'dictionary' of 47 'phrases' and 54 sub-messages. He found that some of these sounds were common to nearly all horses.

> But the more research we carried out, the more we discovered that we could not rely on set patterns as a guide to interpreting the sounds used by horses as a species. It became clear that different horses use the same sequence of sounds to convey different meanings, each horse having its own language, only similar to that of its associates and not identical.[11]

Not only this: the same basic sounds could be used in different combinations depending on the context.

> As an example of the range of variations, the phrase, 'Where is my bloody breakfast?' can be said by a horse in sound alone, by using the basic phrase 'Welcome' and its six imperatives: that is, two degress of blowing through the nostrils, a low whicker, a high whicker, a low whinney and a high whinney. A horse may also use a snort or even a neigh. Then there are a dozen or so signs or combinations of signs and sounds.[12]

Blake describes the stallion as having the greatest vocal range, but a rather limited range of actual messages, 'simply because in his natural state he is concerned only with three things: sex, danger and food. So his messages are confined to these three subjects.'[13] Blake is here writing from a point of view which sees the stallion as living largely outside the herd, a kind of unattached 'herdsman'. But he is mistaken in this. Stallions do take an active part in family life and they are concerned with much more than Blake supposes. For example, our stallion Nivalis is very attached to his daughter Imzadi, and she to him. Whether he is in his box or out in the paddock beside his stable, if Imzadi does not go over to him he will call her to him with a low nicker to which she always responds and which is quite unlike the sound he uses with mares. It is closer to, yet still different from, the soft nicker used by the filly's mother.

Henry Blake points out that contact with humans increases a horse's vocal range. Horses in the wild do not whinny or bang mangers or doors at

Nivalis calls Imzadi over to him; she responds

feeding times, for obvious reasons, not least of which is the fact that food is always there (except in times of drought or very deep snow, when they may have to search for it – and even the densest horse would quickly work out that whinnying and, say, banging on trees or whatever would not make the slightest difference in these circumstances). Many domestic horses do all these things, of course, particularly when dinner is late in arriving. Blake writes that: 'We note from observation that when a horse discovers the messages that he is trying to convey are understood, either by another horse or by man, he will use it again: that is, he extends his own vocabulary.'[14] He notes further that: 'an alteration in the horse's environment has of course considerable consequence for equine communication, since change in his needs and habits means that the horse needs a new and extended vocabulary to meet these new demands'[15] – as, indeed, humans also do in similar circumstances! Several of our horses have proved the truth of this. In particular, Zareeba seldom used his voice until we moved the horses to their present location in 1992. Then, finding himself with more freedom and getting to know a greater variety of horses (for example, the riding school horses next door), he started to use his voice more. In the space of a few weeks, we heard him use sounds we had never heard him use before, and he kept inventing others all the time.

Although they are capable of such a wide range of vocalisations, horses usually use them to communicate with other horses who are out of sight, to announce their approach, or to attract the attention of another horse. In their more intimate dealings with other horses, it is through their body language that they generally communicate.

It is this body language which has formed the basis for Monty Roberts's methods of handling horses. In his observations of feral horses, he took note of how they responded to each other, and these responses enabled him to devise his method of working the horse loose in a round pen, using the same kind of body language as horses themselves use. (For fuller descriptions of how this works, see *The Man Who Listens to Horses* by Monty Roberts; *For the Good of the Horse* by Mary Wanless; and *Understanding Your Horse* by Lesley Bayley and Richard Maxwell.) None of this is new; the most successful trainers and handlers of different cultures have been making use of body language that the horse understands, in their work from the ground and in the saddle, for thousands of years. The main difference is that these handlers and trainers simply used body language that they knew was effective, without bothering to analyse it too much, or even, in many cases, realising that this was what they were doing. Roberts has taken this one step further and interpreted the horse's body positioning, attitudes and gestures. Whether his interpretations are always correct is open to question; some students of equine behaviour are starting to query the significance of such gestures as, for example, licking and chewing. But perhaps in the context of Roberts's own work and that of his pupils, such as Richard Maxwell and Kelly Marks, this does not matter so much. The important thing is that his methods *work*, and their use can only lead to greater understanding of how horses think. They can also help us to understand how often our own use of inappropriate body language sends the wrong messages to the horse and gets us precisely the opposite reaction from the one we want!

In spite of the fact that equine body language is, as I said above, extraordinarily rich and subtle, many people still attempt to reduce it to a rather limited series of oversimplified, rigidly interpreted signals. While this is certainly a starting point, it can never be more than that – any more than learning the vocabulary and grammar of a foreign language can ever provide more than a framework for discovering the subtleties of expression contained within the language. Nevertheless, as with vocalisations, some attempts have been made to describe each signal and to assign to it a specific meaning. For example, in writing of the varied signals conveyed by movements of the extremely mobile equine ear, Desmond Morris calls these signals a 'simple "language" of the equine ears' and suggests that once we have learnt it 'it will help us to tell at a glance the emotional state of our animals'[16]. But it is neither so simple nor so straightforward. In his extremely useful and comprehensive book, *Horse Behaviour*, George Waring depicts over 70 equine facial expressions illustrating gradations of various moods (reproduced in Appendix II); in all cases the whole expression, and not the ear signals alone, must be read in order to interpret the horse's mood correctly. So while the horse's ears can clearly be a very accurate guide to his mood and general mental state, they should never be 'read' independently of the rest of the horse's body language. An example of how misleading attempts to infer a series of simple meanings from a small group of ear signals can be, is afforded by a widespread misunderstanding of the horse's ear signals when he is being ridden. It is often assumed that when the ridden horse's ears are pricked forward he is alert and sharply attentive, and that when his ears are turned backwards this is a sign of fear or ill-temper. Indeed, Desmond Morris goes so far as to say that when the openings of the ears are directed backwards towards the rider, this:

> … indicates a horse that is submissive towards and fearful of its human companion. The
> lateral element of the ear posture reveals the submissiveness and the twisting backwards of

Above Zareeba is interested in Moonlight. Her ear signals say unmistakably, 'Go away!'

Right Zareeba persists in his courtship; Moonlight's ear signals are now less threatening

the apertures shows the animal's need to catch any tiny sound from the fear-inducing figure on its back. This ear posture is common in horses with brutal owners.[17]

This ear position does indeed indicate that the horse is paying attention, but the rest of this statement is hopelessly wrong. Lucy Rees gives a far more accurate analysis: 'Ears turned back are not necessarily a sign of temper, merely of attention focused backwards'[18]; while Sylvia Loch says,

The horse which cares for its rider will always direct its ears in their direction wherever that person happens to be: forward when they are on the ground, turning round and backward when they are in the saddle . . . a highly trained dressage horse is more concerned about his rider than anything else. Turning back his ears is a sign that he is listening and reacting.[19]

Countless spectators at the Royal Horse Gala in 1996 (in which various groups of classically trained horses and riders gave displays) commented on how happy the horses appeared and how joyous their performances were; for much of the time in these performances, the horses' ears were turned back towards the rider in just the manner described above.

The horse whose ears are pricked forward may not be paying attention to his rider, while ears turned back – particularly if they are directed straight back – may indeed indicate a horse that is tense or fearful of the rider; but as always, one must read the whole expression. There is a world of difference between the tense, unhappy expression of a horse that is being harshly ridden and the happy, relaxed attentiveness of, say, the Lipizzaner in the Spanish Riding School.

Michael Schäfer points out the degree to which equids of all species can read the ear signals of equids of other species; for example, a zebra or a donkey will correctly interpret the ear signals of a horse, deducing from them the horse's mood and intentions. Schäfer goes on to say that the fact that humans lack ear signals may be interpreted as a constant threat[20] – a point also made by Desmond Morris, who says that:

> … in horse language this must make us seem very intimidating indeed, and there is nothing they can do – it must seem to them – to change our domineering mood. No matter how submissively they behave, we never prick up our ears in a greeting, or flop them out sideways in dozy subordination.[21]

In the same way, according to Schäfer, the horse may misinterpret the friendly expression of a dog when it puts its ears back and lets all its teeth show in a kind of grin. According to Schäfer: 'horses do not necessarily interpret this as a happy greeting or a challenge to play and it is usually regarded as a terrible menace'[22].

This may explain why some horses can be quite aggressive with dogs – we must remember that canids were once among the principal predators of horses. However, horses, like other animals, can quite easily learn to read the body signals of other species – hence the spectacular results obtained by Herr von Osten with Clever Hans. Horses do this so unerringly that it seems unlikely that they would consistently misinterpret the signals of dogs, much less interpret a lack of ear signals on the part of humans as constant threats. Feral or domestic horses which have had little or no contact with humans may do so, but the horse who has never been mistreated and who has a good relationship with his human handlers is hardly likely to believe that these humans are constantly threatening him. This is especially true when we consider that – as we saw in Chapter 8 – horses tend to move away from threats or to meet them with aggression. If, for example, my horse Zareeba really believed that my lack of ear signals (or the fact that my ears appear pinned back against my head) signified a constant threat, is it likely that he would treat me with the confident and affectionate familiarity usual to him?

It is equally unlikely that horses who are accustomed to dogs and who get on with them misinterpret their body language in this way. Very young foals quickly learn to 'read' dogs and often treat them as playmates. As a foal Toska was fascinated by dogs, although he later reversed his opinion of them when one snapped at his heels. For some considerable time during the writing of this book I derived almost daily amusement from the attempts of our filly foal Imzadi to get our old Doberman, Cooper, and the Jack Russell terrier Rip to play with her. She snuffled at Cooper's back, playfully nibbling at his tail, and made little darts, leaps and bounds in an effort to incite him to play; but the good-natured Dobie simply sat there, clearly bemused by it all, while Rip simply kept his distance. Perhaps horses are better at reading the body language of dogs than dogs are at reading that of horses!

Right Foals often try to make friends with dogs: Toska with Cooper

Below left Imzadi tries to incite Cooper to play

Below right Zareeba makes friends with Cooper

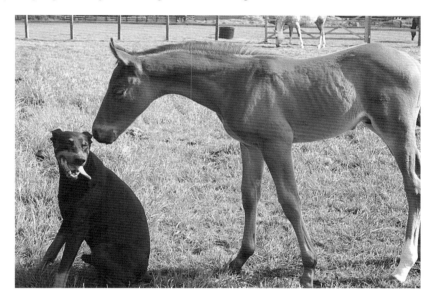

If horses can read the body language of other species so accurately, can they also understand the significance of social gestures peculiar to another species? Many people question whether horses truly appreciate being given titbits as rewards since they do not give each other such 'rewards' or 'presents'. Does such an action therefore have any meaning for them? I believe that in certain circumstances it can.

Most cat owners will be all too familiar with the habit cats have of bringing the results of their hunting activities home, often depositing the pathetic little bodies like an 'offering' at the less than enchanted owner's feet. In my time, I have received countless 'offerings' of such diverse creatures (or parts of them) as birds, mice, shrews, rats, frogs, toads, bats, rabbits and (once) part of a hedgehog. Very often the bringing of such trophies is accompanied by loud proclamations of the hunter's success. Opinions differ among cat experts as to the significance of this gesture. Desmond Morris believes that cats do this because they regard the humans in their lives as extremely inefficient hunters and they are effectively trying to teach us, by example, how to hunt! Other researchers believe it is largely a social gesture, and there is much evidence to support this. Many cat owners, faced with the gruesome remains of their cat's 'kill', have fallen into the error of telling the cat off for bringing in such a noisome mess. The cat's response to this is often to go and kill what she evidently believes to be a more acceptable 'offering'. My mother found this with her cat Squibs. If she told him off for something, he would promptly go out and kill something and bring it back to her in triumph. If she told him off again, he would go and kill something else and bring that back, too – and so on, until she got the message and accepted the occasional 'present' in the spirit in which it was evidently meant.

A few years ago we had a handsome ginger cat who was Zareeba's particular friend. The cat spent a great deal of time with the horse, often lying on his back and grooming his mane near the withers. Tigger would also sleep right next to Zareeba; just near where the horse's head would have been when he lay down, there would invariably be a small Tigger-sized depression in the straw. One day during the winter of 1993–94, Zareeba was stabled up because of bad weather. Our weekend helper Joanne and I, working in the yard, heard the usual loud announcement from Tigger that he had caught something; sure enough he stalked into the yard carrying what looked like part of a rabbit. There was not much of it left, only a small piece of bone with a few shreds of meat and a lump of damp fur attached. Tigger leapt onto Zareeba's half-door, jumped down into the stable, marched over to where the horse was eating his hay and very deliberately deposited the sorry-looking piece of rabbit on the hay in front of the horse. Then he sat down, miaowed once and waited. Zareeba sniffed the 'offering', then gave the cat a very gentle nudge with his nose. Then, as Joanne and I watched pop-eyed with amazement, he took the piece of rabbit in his mouth and started to eat it – fur, bone and all.

Appalled, I ran into the stable and tried to take the piece of skin and bone out of the horse's mouth. Zareeba was having none of this; he showed no signs of actually enjoying it, but he was clearly determined to eat it and would not let me prise it away from him. In front of me and Joanne he ate every last bit of it, bone, fur and all. With visions of colic flashing through my mind I rushed to phone the vet for advice. When he had stopped laughing, he told me not to worry; although I should watch for any signs of colic during the next day or so, he did not think the horse would come to any harm. Nor did he, but he has never eaten anything like that since then, or indicated that he would like to. Why did he eat it? He has never shown any other signs of a depraved appetite. Did he recognise it as an 'offering' from his friend the cat, even though such a gesture is alien to his species? I believe that he did. Why should different species not learn to recognize, and respond to, the social gestures of another species, that may differ from those proper to their own?

Indeed, they do this all the time. Most stable yards have a cat or two about, and, as we saw in Chapter 7, many horses come to enjoy the companionship of cats, sometimes forming very strong bonds of friendship with them. I mentioned there how Zareeba grooms cats whom he likes by licking their backs and necks. As he has frequently seen the cats washing each other, I see no reason why he should not have deduced that this was a social gesture with them as well as serving a practical purpose, just as mutual grooming does with horses.

We still do not fully understand how much information horses can obtain through their sense of smell. The horse's long nose is lined with many layers of scent-sensitive cells. In addition, there is a special structure called the vomeronasal, or Jacobsen's organ, which opens into the back of the horse's mouth; this is found in many other mammals, including cats. When the horse sniffs at something, then raises his head and curls his lip in the expression known as 'flehmen', he is trapping the scent near the Jacobsen's organ and analysing it. All horses do this, but stallions in particular will often spend a great deal of time scrutinising (one might almost say 'tasting') smells in this way, particularly if there are mares about.

When two horses meet, or when regular companions are reunited after a separation, the nostril-sniffing that ensues has

Right above 'Flehmen': Nivalis checks to see whether Roxzella is in season

Right All horses, not only stallions, perform the 'scent testing' known as 'flehmen'. Here Imzadi investigates an interesting smell

'What have you been up to?' Roxzella greets her son Nivalis (here shown as a yearling)

often been interpreted to be part of a ritual to re-establish a hierarchical order. This seems to me a very strained explanation, particularly when it happens after a very short absence. It seems to me far more likely that this is a means of gathering information about what the returning horse has been doing – and, possibly, what his companions have been up to in his absence. Chemical 'messages' carried in the breath and on the skin may tell a whole story about the horse's emotional and mental state, as well as giving indications of where he has been, what he has been doing and (very important in some cases) who he has been with.

At one time, as mentioned in Chapter 8, our stallion Nivalis became very friendly with a little pony called Aero who was turned out in the adjoining field. They sniffed and nuzzled at each other through the fence (the pony was too small to put his head over the top), and spent hours wandering up and down the fence together, grazing side by side with their muzzles almost touching (and sometimes actually doing so). One day one of the bottom rails of the fence came off and Aero suddenly darted into our field. The horses were astonished but clearly delighted: a new playmate! They all pranced and trotted about for a while, with Nivalis keeping a weather eye on the bigger horses to see that they did not crowd his little friend, but there was no aggression whatsoever – in fact, Aero felt relaxed and confident enough to go down and roll, and then wander into the stableyard. Eventually I led him back into his own field while Brian mended the fence. Aero immediately went over to his two closest companions in his own field (a slightly larger pony and a very large Thoroughbred colt) and the other two stood sniffing at the little pony's nostrils for quite some time before they started to graze again. Were they learning all about his experiences? I see no reason why it should not be so.

Anyone who has ever attempted to take exuberant male dogs for a walk will know how frustrating can be their need to pee on every gate, every lamp post, every clump of grass to a degree far beyond the mere necessity for emptying the bladder. This, of course, is the dog's form of scent-marking. Horses do the same: a stallion will dung on top of a pile of dung if it has been left by another stallion; if it was left by a mare or gelding he will urinate on it instead. Lucy Rees describes this in a delightfully humorous way:

> A stallion discovering, or returning to, a dungpile sniffs it with deep concentration and then, with a great deal of flourish and braggadocio, steps over it with high, exaggerated paces to line himself up solemnly and add his contribution. Usually he turns round to smell the pile again afterwards, as if to satisfy himself that he has done it right.[23]

He does this to assure himself that it smells of *him*, that he has eliminated any possibility of confusion about who was the last one in the area.

Scent marking in many species is linked to the defence of territory, but as we have seen, horses are not territorial, although they do have home ranges. Nevertheless, stallions use dunging as a way of denoting their presence. Urinating in dogs and dunging in stallions therefore seem to be ways of leaving a 'signature' – a kind of canine or equine '*Kilroy was here!*'. This makes sense if we consider that horses may need to communicate even when they are out of earshot of each other; if the neigh or the whinny serves to establish the presence and identity of horses within range, the scent-marking may equally be a means, not only of letting others know that 'Kilroy was here', but also of what 'Kilroy's' emotional and mental state was, and what he had been up to.

There remains the possibility that horses make use of another form of communication, one that seems closed to the majority of humans – although many believe our remote ancestors once had the ability to use it. Some decades ago Henry Blake did some experiments with horses which clearly seemed to prove that they could communicate with each other by transmitting mental pictures; Blake called this 'clairvoyance', or extra-sensory perception, to distinguish it from telepathy, although the two can mean the same thing in some circumstances. Over a period of ten years Blake recorded over 30 cases of such communication between himself, his wife and certain horses, although he noted that not all horses could be communicated with in this manner. Much depended on the degree of empathy felt between the communicator and the receiver. These findings have been largely ignored by the scientific community, mainly because of the difficulty of setting up experiments to prove or disprove Blake's findings. However, the fact that something cannot be directly proved does not mean it does not exist (quantum theory is showing that – to misquote Shakespeare – there are indeed far more things in heaven and earth than are dreamed of in our philosophy) and there is a great deal of anecdotal evidence that Blake may well have been right.

In her book *Understanding Horses* Garda Langley tells a story about a stolen horse who was found by telepathy. Gidget, a part-Arabian horse, had a very strong empathic relationship with both her owner and with another horse called Tang. One day Tang was stolen, but although the theft was reported to the police, and although the owner drove around endlessly looking for the horse, there was no sign of Tang. Several days later the owner noticed that Gidget was just standing in the paddock, staring into the distance. Her owner's intuition, sharpened by the empathy she felt for the horse, made her decide to follow the line of Gidget's gaze, even though this meant going straight across country, over fences and barbed wire, over a hill and down into a hidden valley – where, sure enough, she found Tang.[24] Langley says, 'From our point of view, empathy is the most valuable form of communication with the horse, for we not only have insight into how the horse feels, but we intuitively understand the horse's other forms of communication, like verbal messages and body language.'[25]

Many horsemen and women are, indeed, convinced that horses are telepathic. Dick Francis who, before starting his career as a writer was a highly successful jump jockey (becoming National Hunt Champion Jockey in 1953–54), has often written about horses' ability to send and receive telepathic messages to and from their riders. As one of his characters says, 'With some horses, a two-way mental traffic could be almost as explicit as speech'[26]. Whether this is true telepathy or simply an extraordinary empathy which enables both partners to read minute variations in each other's body language, and detect nuances of mood with the kind of accuracy that characterised Clever Hans, is not something we can know for certain; but even if it is the latter, it is still remarkable enough in itself and surely proof of the degree to which communication is possible.

The late Franz Mairinger, one of the wisest of horsemen and for many years a *Bereiter* at the Spanish Riding School in Vienna, says in his book *Horses Are Made To Be Horses*: 'When you have yourself and your horse fully schooled, you just blink and he does it. You may think it's not possible, but it is.'[27] Mairinger describes how he rode his first performance in the Riding School in Vienna doing one of the movements above the ground – the *levade*. This is one of the supreme movements of the High School, in which the horse lifts his forehand off the ground with lowered hocks, at an angle of approximately 30 degrees; Mairinger here refers to it colloquially as 'sitting down'. This requires immense power and collection, as well as great concentration from both horse and rider. On this occasion Mairinger was riding an old horse of Podhajsky's,

> ... who was really fantastic. The Old Instructor [Mairinger's name for his instructor at the school, Chief Rider Polak] said, 'Whatever you do, do not think that he will sit down, because if you think too early, he is going to sit down.' I entered the School and was coming along the wall to the centre line and I was supposed to turn and do the levade in the middle of the School. As I was riding along the wall I was already thinking, 'I hope he doesn't sit down too soon.' That was where I was thinking it, and that is exactly where he sat down. That old horse had been doing that movement for years. He was a very old professor. He knew, 'Now I do my levade, now I walk away.' If you asked him to do it again he

became very annoyed because he knew that he had already done it. This worried me more than anything else, because that old fellow knew more than I did, and I wondered, 'How do I get him to sit down once again?' Well, he did sit down again, thank God, because if he had not I would have been in real trouble. As I came out the Old Instructor said, 'I told you not to think of it.' Whether it was a brainwave or subconscious tension, which it probably was, I *thought* and it happened.[28]

Mairinger is being totally honest here, and not making any claims about telepathy. But even if it *was* subconscious tension, that does not totally explain why such horses not only sense that something is required of them (which, of course, they can pick up from the rider's body posture – a subject that will be discussed in Chapters 12 and 13), but *exactly* what the rider wants (or in Mairinger's case, did *not* want!). It seems likely that several factors are at work here, not least of them the extraordinary sensitivity to tiny signals that is developed by horses trained in the classical High School.

However, many people who believe in the telepathic ability of horses insist that it is *not* just that, but is true telepathy. A number of trainers, including Molly Sivewright FBHS, DBHS and her former pupil Dominique Barbier (who, as mentioned in Chapter 9, also trained with Nuno Oliveira), teach the importance of mental communication with the horse, laying particular emphasis on visualisation, where the rider makes use of mental images. Barbier relates an incident that occurred one day when he was helping his assistant to perform *passage* on one of his stallions, Dom Pasquale. The assistant was experiencing difficulty with the movement and Barbier became very involved with her work. He was sitting on his other stallion Dom Giovanni (with the reins loose), visualising the *passage*. Suddenly, Giovanni began to *passage* even though he had been given no aids to do so. Barbier comments,

I was amazed, since I knew that this horse normally needed considerable readjustment of his balance and position before attempting this movement. Technically speaking, what he was doing was impossible, but he was doing it nevertheless! What an impression that made on me, concerning the power of mental communication with the horse![29]

Barbier goes on to say that, physically, he had not been doing anything.

If you want it badly enough, the horse does it . . . Of course, in the beginning there *is* a physical part, but it is only a reinforcement of the mind. Progressively, it becomes less and less necessary, and ultimately, is not necessary at all. I know what some people want me to say: that when I think of doing a movement I move my body just enough to cause the horse to react. That's *not* what I am saying. The more you develop the mind, the less you need the body.[30]

There is no doubt that horses do have an uncanny ability to 'tune in' to what we are thinking and feeling. Dominique Barbier says, 'Horses do pick up on riders' visualizations, as anyone who has been in trouble or in mental or physical distress can attest. I believe horses give you pictures too, when your mind is open and free enough to receive them. I believe that is the way they communicate with each other as well.'[31]

Why should this not be so? Why should horses not communicate with each other by using parts of their brains that we, too, once used, but have now largely forgotten about? It could be argued that, if this is so, then why do they need other forms of communication? One answer to that could be that they, like Henry Blake, can only do so with horses (or humans) with whom they have a special affinity, or – in the case of strangers – in whom they sense a particular empathy.

Perhaps as a result of the increased interest in 'alternative' methods of handling and training, a number of people have come forward in the 1990s who claim to be able to communicate with horses telepathically – not just in the manner described by people like Henry Blake, Dominique Barbier and Dick Francis, but in a very detailed way. These are the new generation of 'horse whisperers' – a term derived from the nickname given to one of the most famous of the old-fashioned 'horse tamers' who appeared in considerable numbers during the last century – Sullivan the Horse-Whisperer (for a description of these men and their methods, see Henry Blake, *Talking With Horses*, and *The Horse Breakers* by Clive Richardson).

Some of the new 'whisperers' claim to have conversations with horses in which they are told all manner of things about the horse's feelings, experiences and even, in some cases, about the owner! The problem many people have with this is that so much of this presupposes that horses have the same kind of concepts as we do about all manner of things (and not only human concepts, but in some cases typically Western European, culture-specific concepts!) and, moreover, that they understand and can communicate in grammatical English (or whatever language the communicator speaks).

It should be clear by now that I am far from denying that horses can share certain concepts with humans. However, it seems highly unlikely that they would share them to the extent implied by some of these latter-day whisperers. It is even less likely that they would have such a complete grasp of human language (although here, again, their capacity to understand may be far greater than is generally supposed).

Furthermore, 'inside information' of the kind given to some horse-owners by whisperers is sometimes of the kind that skilled fortune-tellers can often glean without the enquirer even being aware of it. Even amateurs can do this. Many years ago I was roped in to act the part of a 'fortune-teller' at a Red Cross fund-raising event. It was all a bit of harmless fun and no one took it seriously; yet, given that the type of people attending were all of a similar age and status, it was astonishingly easy to read a great deal of information just from their mannerisms and external appearance. My 'readings' were inspired guesswork but I was startled by how often my guesses were greeted with, 'How on earth did you know that?'

Nevertheless, there is enough in some of the reports to give one considerable food for thought. While some of the information given is clearly a psychological ploy (and in some cases none the worse for that as the advice given is often very effective), some of it has the ring of genuine communication. Perhaps it is the expectations of the owners that cause some whisperers to describe their communications with horses in such anthropocentric terms; perhaps some of them *do* experience genuine communication. One should not allow healthy scepticism to run riot and cause us to reject out of hand what may be, in some cases at least, the real thing. After all, even if horses do not express themselves in human language and culture-specific concepts, why should they not communicate in other ways? Some horse whisperers, including one of the best known, Nicci Mackay, have reported that in some cases they actually feel the pain the horse is experiencing, while in others they receive emotions, sensations and pictures. Why should an empathic, sensitive person not interpret such signals in terms of human language? Of course, this brings with it the difficulty that they might be interpreting the feelings etc. in accordance with their own preferences and prejudices, but that applies to a greater or lesser extent to all communications we receive, from whatever source – even the written word.

Indeed, there is evidence that humans once communicated with animals in just such a way. Many anthropologists believe that the purpose originally served by the cave paintings of animals, such as may be found in the Dordogne and many other places throughout the world, was as an effigy for magical purposes connected with hunting. This belief is supported by the fact that the Aborigines of Australia and the Native Americans still use such pictures for this purposes. The shaman or 'medicine-man' would go into a trance while contemplating the image, either to 'see' telepathically where the prey could be found or, alternatively, to communicate with the prey and lure it into an ambush.

There are numerous variations on this kind of trance-communication among different cultures, among the best known being the shark and porpoise callers of the Pacific. Here the shamans also put themselves into a trance in which they 'visit' the shark or porpoise people and invite them to their village. And the sharks and porpoises do come, as various Western observers have testified, most notably Sir Arthur Francis Grimble, Land Commissioner in the Gilbert Islands in 1914.

Just as they dismiss the power of prayer, sceptics will no doubt dismiss this kind of thing as wishful thinking; but it has such immediately obvious results that one cannot reject it so easily.

In the end, I think the only sensible attitude towards a subject so difficult to verify or test by experiment is to do as the Hopi advise and keep the tops of our heads open – but not so open that the brains fall out!

The philosopher Ludwig Wittgenstein tells us that if a lion could speak, we couldn't understand him. If this were true, then all attempts at animal training would fail since they depend on understanding and being understood. In *Adam's Task* Vicki Hearne talks about the kind of riding that results when the rider *is* able and willing both to listen to, and talk with, the horse. She describes watching a film of Colonel Alois Podhajsky riding a highly educated horse in some complex dressage movements. There were, she said, even in slow-motion close-up, no visible cues or aids.

Riders whose grammar is contaminated by behaviorism will speak of making constant 'adjustments' of the horse's movement, anticipating with minute accuracy the horse's deviations. But a more traditional and better way is to speak of the wonderfully rich and subtle *conversation* that goes on in this sort of riding.[32]

Finally, we must realise that we can only communicate with horses if we first recognize that they have something to say; and that all of us, if we open our minds, can enter into that 'wonderfully rich and subtle conversation' that the greatest riders and trainers have always maintained.

Notes

1 *Collins English Dictionary*, 2nd edition, 1986, p.319
2 *Collins English Dictionary*, p.319
3 Dr Marthe Kiley-Worthington, *Communication in Horses: Cooperation and Competition*
4 Paul Belasik, *Exploring Dressage Technique*, p. 109
5 Léone Marshall, *Your Horse's Mind*, p. 13
6 Mary Midgley, *Beast and Man*, p. 216
7 Midgley, *Beast and Man*, p. 226
8 Midgley, *Beast and Man*, p. 235
9 Vicki Hearne, *Adam's Task*, p. 126
10 Kiley-Worthington, *Communication in Horses*
11 Henry Blake, *Talking With Horses*, p. 43
12 Blake, *Talking With Horses*, pp. 55–6
13 Blake, *Talking With Horses*, p. 45
14 Blake, *Talking With Horses*, p. 46
15 Blake, *Talking With Horses*, p. 49
16 Desmond Morris, *Horsewatching* (Jonathan Cape, 1988), p. 9
17 Morris, *Horsewatching*, p. 7

18 Lucy Rees, *The Horse's Mind*, p. 72
19 Sylvia Loch, 'Talkback', *Horse & Rider*, February 1996, p. 74
20 Michael Schäfer, *The Language of the Horse* (tr. Daphne Machin Goodall, Kaye & Ward, 1975), p. 166
21 Morris, *Horsewatching*, p. 8
22 Schäfer, *The Language of the Horse*, p. 166
23 Rees, *The Horse's Mind*, p. 109
24 Garda Langley, *Understanding Horses* (David & Charles, 1989), pp. 80–1
25 Langley, *Understanding Horses*, p. 81
26 Dick Francis, *Bolt* (first published in 1986; Pan edition, 1988), p. 10
27 Franz Mairinger, *Horses Are Made To Be Horses* (Rigby, Sydney, Australia, 1983), p. 49
28 Mairinger, *Horses Are Made To Be Horses*, p. 49
29 Dominique Barbier, *Dressage for the New Age* (Prentice Hall, 1990), p. 10
30 Barbier, *Dressage for the New Age*, p. 11
31 Barbier, *Dressage for the New Age*, p. 97
32 Hearne, *Adam's Task*, p. 112

CHAPTER ELEVEN

A Little Learning

For what the horse does under compulsion . . . is done without
understanding; and there is no beauty in it either, any more than
if one should whip and spur a dancer. There would be a great deal
more ungracefulness than beauty in either a horse or a man
that was so treated.

XENOPHON, *c.*400 BC

I
F ONE BELIEVES, as the Victorians did, in the inevitability of progress, one might expect
to find that we have improved vastly on the methods of horse-training used by early
masters such as Xenophon; surely we have learned much more in the intervening 2,400-
odd years? In many respects we have. We have far more scientific knowledge about the actual
processes of learning and the biomechanics of equine movement than Xenophon, or later
masters such as la Guérinière, ever did. So why is it that, with all our modern skills and
understanding of these physical and mental processes, we have not only progressed comparatively little, but actually regressed in some respects? Why, in spite of an unprecedented
number of books, instructional videos and the like, are so many people still ignorant of the
correct principles of training horses?

To understand this, we must not only take into account the cultural prejudices discussed
in Chapters 8 and 9, we must also see how twentieth-century theories about learning have
coloured people's attitudes towards the training of horses.

How do horses learn? A huge amount of research into learning processes, carried on
throughout the twentieth century, has revealed that all mammals – not just horses – learn in
much the same ways. The strengths of some species may lie in different areas of learning than
those of others, but essentially the processes are the same. Different modes of learning have
been identified, all of which are important to everyone concerned with the care and training
of horses.

Early in the twentieth century a school of thought arose in the USA which had a profound influence on the study of animal behaviour. This was the American 'behaviourist school' described in Chapter 2. As we saw in that chapter, the behaviourists insisted that we could not study mind, only behaviour; and, further, that all behaviour was the result of 'conditioning'. Until relatively recently most scientists accepted that learning consisted mainly of 'conditioning', as described by the behaviourists, and little effort was made to explore other possibilities. Then, however, the increase in studies of animal behaviour, not in arid laboratory conditions but in the animals' natural habitats, began to reveal that there was much more to animal learning than the behaviourist model had suggested.

For instance, when a baby animal is born (and this applies to humans too) it goes through a process known as 'imprinting'. This is nature's way of ensuring that a duck knows he is a duck, a goat that she is a goat, and a horse that he is a horse. The image of the mother is 'imprinted' on the baby's brain, so that it knows who she is and will not try to follow either another animal of the same species or an animal of a different species, which in some cases could be fatal. In certain species (notably some birds) imprinting takes place almost as soon as the baby is born, and is irreversible. Such animals, if raised in isolation from their own kind, come to believe that they belong to a different species; Konrad Lorenz gives some amusing examples of this in *King Solomon's Ring*. In mammals the process is neither so swift nor so strong. As Dr Kiley-Worthington points out, foals have a great deal to learn during the first few hours of life. They must disentangle those long legs, learn how to stand without falling over, find the teat, learn how to suckle, etc. – all this as well as how to recognise mother and stay with her.

> In addition there are no guarantees that the foal will follow his mother even after suckling; some will, some will follow another foal or gelding. So even imprinting is not hard, fast, irreversible learning in equines; it takes a good few days for the foal to recognise mum and stay with her, just as in human infants.[1]

So those humans who are afraid that by handling new-born foals they may disturb the imprinting process probably need not worry too much, provided they don't overdo it. What *can* cause problems is the hand-rearing of orphan foals, who then become more completely imprinted on humans. They suffer from species-confusion, not knowing properly how to behave with humans, but at the same time lacking the social skills they would learn from other horses – first from their mothers and then from other horses within the group. As a result they cannot fit into either human or equine society. Unless their human handlers have vast amounts of skill and patience, such foals can grow into truly obnoxious horses, through no fault of their own.

The foal, having learned who his mother is and how to move around without falling over, must then learn all kinds of things about his environment. It was observation of this kind of learning process that made experimental psychologists aware that learning involves much more than just conditioning. We absorb all kinds of information about our surroundings and the people we associate with; so do horses.

We all know that the horse manages to remember routes and particularly the way home. The feral equine *knows* about his home area and where he is in it and much about this has not been conditioned learning; it has been the absorption of information without conditioning. This has been called 'silent learning'.[2]

Horses are particularly good at this kind of learning which is sometimes called 'latent learning'.

They are not so good, however, at what is called 'insight learning', which bypasses normal 'trial and error learning': sudden realisation of the answer to a problem. Humans are great solvers of the kind of problems that require insight, partly because of our manipulative ability, but horses in the wild would have little need to tackle this kind of problem. Their talents lie elsewhere, and we should not judge them as lacking intelligence because of that. However, as Lucy Rees points out, some horses, particularly bright youngsters, sometimes do show insight on being given new cues for the first time. Such horses may readily make the connection between the cue and the required response; much depends on how calm the horse is and how attentive he is to his handler or trainer.

A great deal of what we do with horses depends on a process called *habituation*. We saw in Chapter 7 how horses react instantly to possible danger. Clearly though, no animal can go through its entire life startling and running away from everything in its environment. So horses, like other animals, learn what elements in their environment are worthy of their fear and what may be safely ignored – in other words, they grow accustomed, or *habituated*, to things which would otherwise cause constant alarm.

The sensible handler makes use of this procedure in training horses. Right from early foalhood, the horse may be gradually accustomed to all manner of things and situations which he finds potentially frightening. If he trusts the handler and the latter can inspire calm, he will learn that these 'bogeys' pose no threat to him; that a plastic bag in the hedge will not jump out and eat him, a squeaky pram or bicycle is not a new kind of monster, and the man picking his feet up and doing strange things to them is not trying to prevent him from running away from danger, as there is no danger. Xenophon knew the value of habituation: he says that before the colt's proper training as a ridden horse commences, the groom is directed to lead him through crowds 'to make him familiar with all sorts of sights and all sorts of noises. Whenever the colt is frightened at any of them, he should be taught, not by irritating but by soothing him, that there is nothing to fear.'[3]

The great eighteenth-century master, la Guérinière, mentions that in the past colts newly brought in from pasture to begin their training were given into the charge of persons called *cavalcadours de bardelle*, who were:

… chosen from among those with the greatest amount of patience, industry, spirit and diligence . . . They accustomed young horses to being touched with the hand, fitted with the bridle, the saddle and the girth, etc. They reassured them and made them easy to mount. They never used either sternness or force before they had tried the most gentle means at their disposal; and by this great patience they rendered a young horse familiar with and well-disposed to human beings, imparted to it courage and vigour, rendered it well-behaved and obedient to the first lessons.[4]

How different the approach of these two great horsemen is from the brutal methods which so appalled the young Monty Roberts, and which are still used to a great extent in the American West and certain other countries even today. Yet la Guérinière was writing in the early eighteenth century, and Xenophon nearly 2,500 years ago! About the procedures described in the extract above, the former goes on to say, 'If the conduct of these past lovers

Habituation to strange things: Toska investigates Brian

Habituation: Toska with Brian

Habituation: NOT recommended! This is shown here only to illustrate the degree of mutual trust which can be established. Brian with Toska

Below As for the preceding: Brian with Imzadi

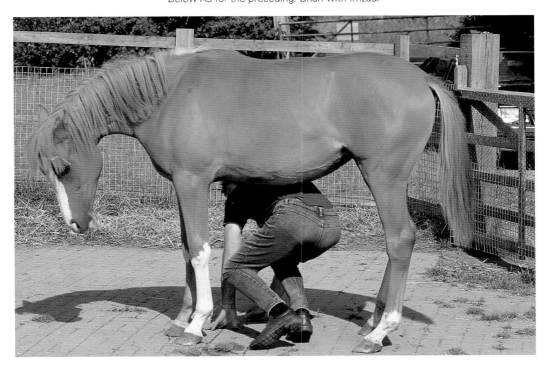

of the horse were imitated today, there would be fewer horses crippled, ruined, intractable, stiff and vicious'[5] – and this is equally true in the late twentieth century.

Clearly, horses learn from their environment, but do they learn from each other? There is a great deal of controversy about whether horses do learn by direct observation. In *The Nature of Horses* Stephen Budiansky says that: 'Experiments have consistently failed to support the belief, firmly held by many, that horses can learn directly from watching other horses (or from watching people).'[6] But this is not strictly true. Relatively few studies have been made of this type of learning; two of these (Baer et al., 1983, and Baker and Crawford, 1986) concluded that horses that were allowed to watch a 'demonstrator' horse perform a task did not learn the task any more quickly than horses which did not watch the demonstrator. A group at the University of Bristol veterinary school designed an experiment to investigate this type of learning (called 'social learning'), which tested the ability of two groups of horses to learn from a demonstrator horse always to choose a certain coloured bucket to eat from, rather than a different one. The test group, which was allowed to watch the demonstrator horse, learned to approach the buckets much more quickly than the control group, which was not allowed to watch the demonstrator. However, their choice of buckets was random, as was the control group's. So although they had learned from the demonstrator horse how to enhance their foraging skills, they had not learned to discriminate between the buckets. Paul McGreevy, who was involved in this experiment, believes that it was possible the experiment was not designed well enough to allow what he calls 'discriminative social learning'; he believes that one day a demonstration system that is more 'user friendly' for the observer horses may well show more positive results.[7] Given the sparsity of such studies, one could scarcely say experiments have 'consistently failed' to demonstrate social learning; the best one could say is that, at this stage, we lack experimental proof one way or the other.

On the other hand, there is ample anecdotal evidence that horses do learn from each other, as well as from humans. Whether they really do copy bad habits from each other, as is generally believed, is difficult to assess, since such habits can arise from such a variety of causes. Biologist Amanda Waters, writing in *Riding* magazine, says,

> There is no conclusive evidence that horses can learn stereotypic behaviour by imitating others directly. If we truly believed horses to be so adept at learning movements by observing others, would we not by now be showing our charges videos of Olympic dressage horses performing the movements that we wish our own to aspire to?[8]

But this completely misses the point on several counts. The author has failed to appreciate that an Olympic dressage test consists of far more than just a series of 'movements' strung together, and that the movements executed by Olympic dressage horses are not simply patterns or shapes performed for the look of the thing. As we shall see in Chapter 12, the movements themselves have various functions, all of which are a means to an end, not an end in themselves. The ability to perform an Olympic dressage test is the fruit of years of gymnastic training and suppling exercises. I shall argue in Chapter 12 that many of the so-called 'dressage movements' can be produced quite naturally by sufficiently athletic horses at liberty, but not all horses have the same degree of ability, and asking them to carry out the same movements under saddle and in a structured, disciplined way is another matter altogether. Even if they wanted to, horses could not learn to perform Olympic dressage movements simply by watching others. I could watch ballet and figure skating (both of which I enjoy very much) until the sun explodes, but merely watching would never enable me to perform an *entrechat, a fouetté en tournant*, a triple *axel*, a *salchow* or any other of the many complex movements found in ballet and figure skating, because my limbs and muscles have not been trained to do so, and I have not developed the necessary balance and agility, which take many years of training and practice to achieve – as well as a lot of basic talent!

Nevertheless, there are convincing cases where horses appear to have learned from watching others being ridden or lunged, as well as by copying each other in the field. We have always encouraged youngsters to watch other horses taking part in these activities, as it must surely be reassuring for them to have seen other horses doing these things before being asked to do them themselves. Nivalis was allowed to watch the other horses being lunged long before he himself started work on the lunge. When my husband came to start Nivalis off, he was amazed at how much the horse already knew. He understood what was meant by the verbal commands, 'Walk on!' and 'Ter-r-ot!; so much so that after only a couple of sessions on the lunge he was working loose, without even a halter of any kind, and responding as precisely as any horse long accustomed to working on the lunge. Of course, this could be partly because he is an extremely bright horse and a very quick learner. However, the real test came when the vet examined him for his stallion licence. He had to canter on the lunge so that the vet could check his heartrate; but up to that time Brian had never asked him to canter, either on the lunge or off it, so he was not sure how Nivalis would respond. As it happened, he popped into canter the first time Brian said, 'Can-ter!', without having to be pushed forward in any way, and he could only have learned that from watching the other horses being lunged in canter!

Nivalis's mother Roxzella, who is also very bright, effectively taught herself to put her forefeet up on a bale of straw. She had never been taught to do anything like this, apart from 'shaking hands' (i.e. lifting a foreleg on request but *not* pawing or striking out). One day when she was in the stable and Brian was about to put some fresh straw down for her, he decided to try an impromptu experiment. He put his own foot on the bale of straw, to see if Roxzella, who had seen her son do this numerous times, would get the idea. Within a few minutes she was imitating Brian and putting first one hoof, and then the other, up on the bale of straw. To see if this could be repeated with another horse, we then tried it with Zareeba – with the same result, although this time a few more attempts were needed. Both horses had repeatedly seen Nivalis do the same thing, and appeared readily to associate what Brian was doing with what they had seen Nivalis do.

Horses appear to learn from others, not only *what* to do but *how* to do it. In the Autumn 1976 issue of the *Arab Horse Society News* John Blundell described how his hunter filly set out, on her own initiative, to imitate the movement of his Arab filly Fiammetta. Arab movement is quite different from that of the hunter types but John Blundell's filly worked hard at her imitation, and by the time she was three she had acquired true Arab movement.[9]

Sylvia Loch describes how one of her horses taught himself *passage* through watching another horse. This horse had never been 'taught' *passage* and he had certainly never offered it (but in view of what I said earlier about horses not learning dressage movements simply by watching, bear in mind that this horse was already capable of working in collection under saddle; the foundations for the *passage* had already been laid). He used to enjoy watching Sylvia school his stable companion, a horse who was already well confirmed in *passage*. Sylvia describes what happened then:

> He is rather jealous by nature and on one particular occasion, hung his face over the fence longingly as though wishing he were in there instead. His turn came that afternoon and, after our warm-up as we prepared for proper work, I realised he was trying hard to do something different. Instead of going forward in his normal collected trot, I felt he was holding against me. His back felt different, round but no longer as soft and swinging, as though he were trying to raise it more. Suddenly he relaxed and it all came through, two or three magical steps! For the first time ever he had offered me passage and it had all come from him. I do believe he had watched and learned.[10]

In fact, when one considers the matter, it would be little short of miraculous if a social species like the horse did *not* have the ability to learn by observing others. How else would they learn so much about what it is to be a horse?

How long does it take to train a horse? The Duke of Newcastle replies,

> . . . it is very difficult to say in what time a horse may be dressed, because that depends upon his age, strength, spirit and disposition; his agility, memory, sagacity, good or bad temper . . . It is therefore as impossible to answer this question, as it would be for the ablest master in the world to say, that all the scholars in the university will become learned at a certain time.[11]

– and as an answer, that could scarcely be bettered.

One ability horses do possess in a high degree is that of 'one-trial learning' – that is, they can learn after only one experience. This is a particularly valuable trait for a prey animal to possess; after all, a predator can make mistakes in hunting and live to hunt again, but a wild horse would need to learn fast which animals and places to avoid and how to escape from danger, otherwise he or she would simply be dead. Second chances, while they may be forthcoming, cannot be relied upon.

This can work for those of us who seek to train horses, or it can work against us. The horse can learn bad things just as easily as he can learn desirable things; and one careless error may affect a horse, in some cases for the rest of his life, in others certainly for a very long time.

One of our horses, a handsome young home-bred warmblood, is a case in point. Well handled since a foal, he will allow himself to be groomed and have his feet picked out without fuss; he will also stand to attention when asked, to allow these jobs to be done. He is a big horse, however, and like many big young horses, at the time of writing he still lacks a little co-ordination and balance. While quite happy to have his feet handled and picked out, he finds balancing for the length of time his feet are being trimmed difficult, and like many such gangly youngsters he tends to fidget. On one particular occasion the farrier – perhaps overtired after a long day – grew impatient as the horse waggled his off-hind leg about. 'Give over!' he shouted at the horse, and gave him a violent dig in the ribs with his elbow. Not surprisingly, the horse took this as an assault and reacted as he would with another horse: he lashed out with a smart cow-kick. The farrier suffered only bruising and some inconvenience, but the horse, who had previously never kicked, had learned to kick out in self-defence if a man (even my husband, who had raised him from a foal and has always treated him gently) approached the side where he had been dug in the ribs. He is gradually being educated out of this, but it is still quite possible that this horse, who never kicks out at other horses, will retain this habit of kicking at humans whenever he is startled. A moment's impatience and lack of thought can do that much damage. Those people who believe that compelling a horse to 'behave' through force and rough treatment is the right way, should reflect that for every problem they 'cure' in this way, they may be creating several others. One of the greatest virtues in anyone handling horses is indeed patience!

Horses seldom forget experiences of this sort, but opinions have varied throughout history about just how good a memory the horse actually has. The great seventeenth-century master Pluvinel, *écuyer principal* to King Louis XIII of France, rather surprisingly believed that horses have a poor memory. His compatriot, the even greater master François Robichon de la Guérinière, disagreed: 'no animal', he wrote, 'remembers better than the horse the first abuses it suffers.'[12] Indeed, although individual horses vary in their capacity to remember, as a species their ability in this respect is remarkable. The twentieth-century Portuguese master Nuno Oliveira, who trained many horses to the highest possible standard, said, 'I cannot stress enough, in the training of the horse, that the fundamental characteristic of his psychology is his memory. Although extremely useful in the horse's schooling, this memory makes any errors in training or violence by inexperienced riders infinitely dangerous'[13].

In spite of this, a surprising number of people – even those who should know better – persist in believing that horses have insufficient brainpower to retain long-term memories. One reader wrote in to the 'Questions and Answers' page of one issue of the weekly magazine *Horse & Hound*, expressing concern that her horse's reluctance to accept being bridled up might stem from a painful experience more than a year before. She was very probably right, but the consultant vet replied that horses 'do not have the brainpower to remember incidents which happened more than a year ago'[14]. But almost every trainer, from Xenophon onwards, has surely been aware that horses most certainly *do* have the brainpower to remember events, often from many years previously. As they have also (as stated above) been shown to be extremely good at one-trial learning, this, together with their phenomenal memory, is why we must always strive to teach them the right things, and as far as possible avoid unpleasant experiences which the horse will never forget. The vet concerned did admit that learned behaviour problems can occur, but it is disturbing to think that such an answer could appear in the pages of Britain's most widely read equestrian magazine. While we must certainly always consider the possibility of present pain or physical discomfort, learned behaviour is at the root of a huge number of problems that horse owners encounter. Were it otherwise, there would be far fewer horses around described as 'problem horses'.

So how does this learned behaviour arise? It is an example of the process already mentioned, which is called 'conditioning'.

The most famous example of this, and the one most generally cited, is that of Pavlov's dogs. The Russian scientist Pavlov, experimenting with dogs in the early part of the twentieth century, found that, while his dogs would normally only salivate at the sight and smell of food, if he rang a bell at the same time, the dogs would eventually come to associate the sound of the bell with the food, and would start to salivate at the sound of the bell alone. This is called 'classical conditioning' and it can occur naturally. The story of the horse jabbed in the ribs by the farrier is a case in point: the horse originally had no reason to associate a man approaching his side with pain, but he now does so following his experience with the farrier. He also thinks that having his off-side rear foot picked up will result in pain. Similarly, a horse who has happily gone past a gateway for years may have a frightening experience there – perhaps a dog rushes out barking, or a plastic bag in the hedge flaps and gives the horse a fright. The horse subsequently refuses to approach that gateway, even though whatever frightened him may no longer be there; he has been 'conditioned' to fear it. Humans too can be affected like this – they can develop phobias about certain places, sights, sounds or smells because they are associated with, although not the cause of, some unpleasant experience. Understanding how a bad experience can result in this kind of conditioning helps to explain a great deal of equine behaviour that otherwise seems incomprehensible to us.

However, while conditioning of this type is clearly extremely influential in shaping a horse's behaviour, it must not be overestimated. For example, while many stimuli can be easily associated with fear, some are more readily associated than others. To take the classic example often used as a stand-in for almost every other species of mammal, rats will easily learn to associate food with illness, and if a certain food makes them ill they will thereafter avoid eating it. However, experiments have shown that no matter how often such unpleasant stimuli as loud noises or electric shocks are paired with induced illness, rats are very unlikely to make the connection. Similarly, conditioning cannot explain many phobias, such as a fear of certain animals or insects, which are experienced by people who have never even been exposed to such creatures, let alone suffered any harm from them. My Arabian gelding Zareeba is terrified of hosepipes. While he will endure having his feet and legs hosed down, it is only on condition that he is allowed to stand as far away from the offending object as possible, and baths are a matter of buckets and sponges rather than hosepipes, no matter how warm the weather. Yet he has never in his entire life had an unpleasant experience with a hosepipe. I believe he thinks the hose is a snake, although he has never seen a snake. Could the source of his fear lie far back in his ancestry – some genetically transmitted ancestral or collective 'memory?'[15] After all, in the desert environment in which Zareeba's ancestors lived, snakes could well have been a significant danger to horses. Another of our Arabians, the stallion Nivalis, shows a similar aversion to hosepipes, although he too has never had a bad experience with one. Both horses are normally sensible, without any behavioural problems. I know of several other people whose Arabs have phobias about hosepipes. In her account of a life with horses, *The Treacle Bucket*, Elaine Dollery describes how they were able to restrict her daughter's Arab gelding Prince to one area of a field simply by placing a length of hosepipe on the ground. 'The poor horse was firmly convinced that all hoses were snakes, and he would shudder away to the opposite end of the field whenever any kind of piping appeared.'[16] So we must be wary of just what we attribute to classical conditioning; things may not always be as they seem.

The other kind of conditioning is known as 'operant conditioning', and it is forever associated in the minds of many people with B. F. Skinner and his infamous 'Skinner boxes'. In these, as we have seen, the 'operant' (which might be a rat, a pigeon, a monkey or whatever) works either to earn a food reward or to avoid a punishment. According to strict behaviourist theory, all learning works on the basis of stimulus-response. Once a 'cue' or stimulus has elicited the desired response, a new stimulus or cue can be 'paired' with the old one by presenting first the new stimulus or cue, then the old one. Eventually the operant will come to associate the new stimulus or cue with the correct response.

The stimulus (or cue) could be almost anything; in the case of a rat in the Skinner box, a buzzer or a light; in the case of a ridden horse, the feel of the rider's leg. The idea is that all the required responses have to be *taught* by means of conditioning, and the response is purely mechanical.

We have already seen in Chapter 2 how this can lead to absurdities. While the idea works well in laboratories, its limitations become apparent when it is applied to the real world, as it then becomes quite clear that no animal can learn everything it needs to know in this manner. Nevertheless, the basic idea of conditioning remains at the root of almost all learning theory that deals with the training of animals.

Conditioning works by means of reward and punishment. The stimulus is presented to the animal; a correct response is rewarded, and – depending on the school of thought followed – an incorrect one is punished. In fact, experiments have shown that punishment is singularly ineffective as a way of training animals in general, and horses in particular. The latter may indeed become obedient as a result of punishment training, but it is the obedience of a robot. Furthermore, as Lucy Rees points out, a horse that is driven by fear may not be safe in situations that he finds more frightening than his rider's punishment. Punishment, says Rees,

. . . can be useful for discouraging bad behaviour that the horse has thought up for himself, like biting, but useless when trying to teach a horse a new action in response to a new cue: punishing a 'wrong' response frightens and confuses the horse and makes him even less likely to cooperate the next time . . . Bad use of punishment causes great resistances in training.[17]

Nuno Oliveira observes that:

The horse will remember when he has been punished in order to force him to carry out an exercise that is uncomfortable for him, and each time that he is asked for that same movement he will become tense, and sometimes rebel in the expectation of punishment.[18]

For this reason good trainers simply ignore incorrect responses and reward correct ones. Indeed, many modern trainers insist that they use reward rather than punishment. Yet one must question the extent to which this is actually true. For example, in one popular book about the horse's mind, even though the book aims to lead to greater empathy and strengthen the bond between horse and rider/handler, the author makes only nine references to reward, and no less than 26 to punishment!

The reward (or punishment) is called a *reinforcement*; it reinforces the training because it increases the likelihood that the animal will repeat the response the next time. In his review of learning in horses C. A. McCall says,

. . . all current equine learning research is based on the assumption that horses learn through stimulus-response-reinforcement chains (trial and error). The stimulus-response reinforcement theory states that a horse perceives a stimulus or cue, such as the rider's legs or seat or a black or white bucket. The horse then makes a random response to this stimulus. If this response is correct, the horse receives positive reinforcement (reward). If the response is incorrect, the trainer can either ignore the response and repeat the stimulus or apply negative reinforcement until the horse makes the correct response.[19]

In Chapter 13 I shall show how the horse's response to the rider's correctly positioned body and legs is far from being 'random', but for now let us see how the process outlined above works.

Positive reinforcement rewards the horse with something pleasant when he makes a correct response.

Negative reinforcement involves removing something the horse finds *unpleasant* as soon as the correct response is made. It should not be confused with *punishment*, as negative reinforcement comes *before* the response and punishment comes *after* an incorrect response.

McCall says, 'Like stimuli, reinforcements can be either natural or "primary" (food, pain, return to herdmates), or learned, or "secondary" (pat on the neck, voice).'[20]

'Secondary' reinforcements are paired with 'primary' reinforcements in the same way as a new stimulus is paired with an old one. A secondary reinforcement (e.g. a pat on the neck) is followed by an old, primary reinforcement (e.g. a carrot or a mint). After a few such pairings, the horse will associate the pat with the food reward. However, this makes assumptions about what is of importance to horses, that are not necessarily correct. The first of these assumptions is that the 'secondary' reinforcements are not natural to the horse and that they are not, *in and of themselves*, important to the horse. But why should a pat (or better still, a stroke or a scratch) on the neck (especially near the withers) not be extremely pleasing to the horse? Certainly a hearty slap, such as one often sees,

Below Nivalis works loose without even a halter

Bottom photo Nivalis is rewarded with a cuddle. Even if he does not associate this with any specific part of the training, he will relate it to the training session itself, which he will then remember as a pleasant experience.

may not be appreciated by the horse, but there is ample evidence that a stroke or a scratch (especially from someone for whom they feel affection) is not only pleasurable but very relaxing to them.

Similarly, while horses themselves may not be very vocal, they do not need 'primary reinforcements' to find verbal praise in itself pleasing, provided it is given in the right tone of voice by someone whose company they enjoy. I proved the truth of this with our filly foal Imzadi. From the earliest hours of her first day of life, she responded to a scratch or a cuddle and the sound of my or my husband's voice. She was taught everything, from walking on when asked, to picking up her feet, with no other rewards than these. Food rewards were not introduced until much later and they proved no more effective than verbal praise and a scratch or a cuddle had done.

Indeed, many trainers never use food rewards and yet they still manage to get remarkable results. One must always gauge what is important to the individual horse. Alois Podhajsky says,

> The tender little soul blissfully accepts the smallest caress, as was the case with Neapolitano Africa, who would have purred like a kitten had he not been a Lipizzaner stallion. The slightest rebuke, however, was a tragedy for him and he became nervous and anxious. The more materialistic horse obviously prefers sugar or other titbits to patting and stroking as if he would say: 'Don't make all that fuss, go ahead and give me the sugar!'[21]

The problem with applying the results of equine learning research to training procedures generally used in the horse world is that a discrepancy exists between the methods used. As McCall points out: 'Trainers mainly utilize secondary reinforcements in horse training, and they use more negative reinforcement than positive. In contrast, most equine learning tests employ primary positive reinforcement.'[22] Circuses (oddly enough in the eyes of some, given the opprobrium generally heaped upon them these days) also tend to use mainly positive reinforcements; good circus trainers can achieve remarkable results with horses using such methods. But what about the general run of horse trainers and riders? Do they, as McCall suggests, principally make use of negative reinforcements? And if so, why?

In aversion, or negative reinforcement, training, the horse is taught to move away from, or react to, something unpleasant. It is widely believed that horses can only be taught in this way, that they will only move forward, for example, to avoid something they dislike or fear, such as the pressure of the leg, a kick, the sting of a whip, a jab of the spur; or that they will stop in order to avoid the pain of the bit.

A huge number of scientists and science writers who have studied equine behaviour certainly appear to believe that this 'negative reinforcement' is fundamental to the training of the horse. While he admits that: 'Much of the early training of young horses involves habituation, exposing them repeatedly to stimuli that might be frightening at first, until they no longer react,' Stephen Budiansky goes on to say that: 'More advanced training typically follows the model that behavioural psychologists term operant conditioning through negative reinforcement. A correct response to an aversive stimulus (relaxing the jaw and backing in response to pressure from the bit) is rewarded by removal of the stimulus (loosening the reins).'[23] Léonie Marshall, a dressage trainer and judge, remarks that: 'As with the group system in the wild where pain is inflicted by the use of the teeth or hooves, so in a domestic situation the way to learn is through various forms of discomfort or pain, followed by a reward.'[24] But pain in the wild is only inflicted as a punishment, to teach the horse what *not* to do. There is evident confusion here between punishment which, as already stated, is useless as a way of training, and negative reinforcement. Yet such confusion is widespread, even among very experienced trainers and riders.

The use of *positive* reinforcement, in preference to methods which entail pain and discomfort for the horse, is rarely mentioned in the general literature, except almost in passing. Although he does mention positive reinforcement, Paul McGreevy goes on to say that:

> Unlike with modern dog and cat training the horse is still largely taught by negative reinforcement – that is, the introduction of an unpleasant event to increase his willingness to perform a given behaviour. This works because the horse learns that to perform a certain response is the only way of avoiding or escaping the unpleasant event. For instance, he will learn to move away from the pressure of leg aids, or he will learn that slowing his speed will ease the force of the bit on his tongue.[25]

Note the words, '*the force of the bit*.' Almost 2,500 years ago, Xenophon warned us that 'anything forced or misunderstood can never be beautiful'; while in the seventeenth century Pluvinel emphasises that it is much more important to train the horse by using gentleness than by using force, 'for the horse who works with pleasure performs more gracefully than the one who is constrained by force'[26]. The great *écuyer* further states that: 'One must avoid using force for I have never seen anything positive come out of a horse if such is the case.'[27]

Yet, now, in the late twentieth century, we have the horse being trained by methods that do use force, by those who are either ignorant of, or who misunderstand, the very principles of gymnastic training as worked out by the great masters of equitation and continually tested in such institutions as the Spanish Riding School of Vienna. A horse may indeed learn to step back in order to obtain relief from the pressure of the bit; but he will certainly not learn to relax his jaw in response to that pressure since the pressure itself creates tension (he may 'give' with his jaw, but that is not necessarily the same thing – often we see horses who are subjected to this kind of pressure opening their mouths in discomfort). He will also tend (unless the rider is very, very skilled indeed) to raise his head and hollow his back, which makes the backing process not only difficult but actually painful for him; and either way he will not use himself properly. Similarly, a horse may indeed slow down when he feels the 'force of the bit', but if he is responding solely to that force the slowing process may be carried out in a biomechanically inefficient manner, as pressure on the bit does nothing to help him engage his hind legs.

How desperately sad for the horse, if we truly believe that the only way we can train him is not by making work pleasurable for him, but simply by removing something *unpleasant*. One wonders what happened to the idea, expressed beautifully by the great Elizabethan horsemaster Gervase Markham, of the 'secret pleasing and cherishing of the horse with the bridle'.

Yet such is the widespread ignorance of the principles referred to above, that many people do believe that horses can only be trained through fear and unpleasantness. Fiske, whose book *How Horses Learn* is often quoted in this context, believed that avoidance conditioning, or negative reinforcement, was the foundation of horse training. But as Lucy Rees observes, 'This is simply untrue. A large number of horses have not been trained in this way, and they are none the less sensitive and responsive.'[28] In his review of learning behaviour in horses, McCall notes that equine learning abilities are similar under primary positive and primary negative reinforcements. He quotes one study where ponies which had learned better than others in a shock avoidance (negative reinforcement) situation were also the better learners in a positive reinforcement situation – which surely tells us that negative reinforcement should be unnecessary! Why use it, when positive reinforcement works just as well? The answer may be that some horses actually appear to learn faster under negative reinforcement schedules. Another study, in which horses were punished for incorrect responses with a CO_2 fire-extinguisher (a method widely used for the 'training' of show horses in the USA), centred on the performance of horses which had previously learned to escape from a maze under primary positive reinforcement. The same horses made fewer errors after the punishment was introduced but spent more time deciding which part of the maze to enter – in other words they were worrying about which choice to make, because they knew a wrong choice would result in punishment.

The results of this study have made it easy for people to claim that horses learn faster as a result of aversive stimuli, and in that way to justify their use. However, these results may be skewed because the same horses had already become accustomed to mazes and had some idea of what was expected of them.

One must also question (ethics aside!) whether any possible time advantage is not cancelled out by the mental and physical damage that may result from a negative approach to training. Many competition horses which have been trained by such an approach suffer from pronounced physical and mental problems. In *Physical Therapy and Massage for the Horse* Professor Jean-Marie Denoix and Jean-Pierre Pailloux remark that: 'It is important to recognize that emotional equilibrium is as vital to optimum sporting performance as the physiological readiness of the underlying mechanical structures, which will not perform on command unless the horse is comfortable and confident.'[29] A number of conditions have been identified (notably by the Russian scientist Kurtsin) which produce neurosis and eventual breakdown in mammals. Among these conditions were long and/or frequent negative (unpleasant) stimulation, and this includes precisely the kind of negative reinforcements commonly used in the training of horses.

As Lucy Rees says,

The more that positive reinforcement – praise and relaxation – is used, the less aversion is

Above Calm and relaxed: Brian lunges Arabian mare Anazar

Right 'Why aren't you taking notice of me any more?' Having enjoyed her training session, Anazar now tries to attract Brian's attention . . .

. . . and succeeds

necessary; and conversely the less praise is used the more aversion is necessary or the horse never learns at all. But unpleasantness breeds fear, fear tension, tension inability to respond and thus resistance – and training becomes a desperate, dangerous and unpleasant struggle.[30]

So any training system which is based on fear – even mild fear, or the avoidance of unpleasantness – and thus creates tension is, in the end, counter-productive. Lucy Rees points out that horses do sometimes make things unpleasant for themselves; she uses the analogy of the young horse that does not respond to the bit but continues to push against it until it becomes uncomfortable. In a similar manner, a green horse may try to avoid work by yanking the reins out of the rider's hand. Instead of yanking back, as riders are so often taught to do, the educated rider will simply firm up their seat to avoid being pulled out of the saddle, fix their elbows to their sides and let the horse make himself uncomfortable. (This passive resistance on the part of the rider works wonders; the horse soon realises that he is getting nowhere – and he has done it all himself.) However, this is a different matter from the deliberate use of aversion (other than in some very exceptional circumstances involving the rehabilitation of horses rendered vicious or crazy by incoherent 'training' and handling. Such cases are beyond the scope of this book and in any case they require a profound understanding of the principles of training as well as of equine psychology. For examples of such rehabilitation work, see Vicki Hearne, *Adam's Task*). Such deliberate use in ordinary circumstances, in the words of Lucy Rees, 'is unnecessary and seems an expression of the worst traits of human nature. There is little that is desirable in a horse that is frightened into dull obedience'[31].

So how, then, do we go about training the horse? Do we – as so much equine behaviour literature suggests – have to proceed as though we were imposing our will on the horse, shaping his behaviour by means of 'cues' or stimuli paired with pleasant or unpleasant experiences, until we achieve the desired response? The main problem with this 'stick and carrot' system is that it is actually a very superficial way of communicating with the horse. Its limitations are quickly revealed when one considers some of the bizarre things that can result from this approach. One of Mary Wanless's pupils was advised (by another trainer) to teach her horse not to charge off while taking a pull on the rein, by hitting him every time he did so. Far from teaching him not to pull on the rein, it simply taught him to run away from the stick immediately after he *had* taken a pull! It would have made far more sense to find out *why* he needed to pull away in this fashion, then to treat the cause, not the symptom. American trainer Vicki Hearne tells a similar story about a Quarter Horse she had been given to retrain. This horse was a confirmed bolter who had been in the hands of numerous other trainers. One of them had tried to teach him to stop by letting him gallop past a hitching post and then jumping off as she tossed the reins over the post. So the horse learned to slow down near the hitching post but, as Vicki Hearne comments, 'otherwise this vaguely behavioristic fantasy of training served only to teach him that perhaps he could get rid of the rider by heading for whatever resembled a hitching post'[32]. In the end Vicki Hearne cured him of bolting by opening his mind to other possibilities – but that story is best read in Hearne's book *Adam's Task*, as is the story of Drummer Girl, the psychotic mare described in Chapter 9. No amount of 'conditioning' could have cured this mare; it required an enormous amount of faith in the horse's ability to respond before Vicki Hearne could restore this crazy mare to sanity. The fact that she did so, however, suggests that there is another, subtler way which taps into the horse's own feelings and makes use of his natural responses.

There is, indeed, such a way, but it is often obscured by the language frequently adopted even by trainers who are aware of these other possibilities. For instance, when most trainers and riders (and certainly most behavioural scientists, even on the relatively rare occasions when they are themselves trainers and riders) refer to the 'aids', they mean cues that the horse has to be taught by conditioning. Sadly, there is currently too little understanding of the original meaning of the term 'aids'. Even the translator of Waldemar Seunig's celebrated book, *Horsemanship*, replaces what he calls the 'antiquated term "aids"' by 'controls' – evidently feeling that this term would be of more use to the modern rider[33]. Unfortunately, this changes the whole meaning of the term 'aids', from something designed to 'aid' the horse in both understanding and in execution, to a concept of control (which suggests a rather one-sided relationship). As Sylvia Loch points out, the verb 'to aid' immediately suggests some kind of positive partnership. The Elizabethan term was 'helps'. 'Thus from the beginning the novice horseman was encouraged to think in terms of helping his horse rather than commanding him.'[34] So we find the Duke of Newcastle saying, 'It is true that patience without knowledge will never do, as knowledge will seldom do without patience: you must therefore treat him gently, and not exert your full power . . . Reduce him by degrees, mixing gentleness with *helps* and corrections, [my italics].[35] But the emphasis nowadays is on 'submission'. This is one of the primary requirements in any FEI dressage test: that the horse should show 'submission'. Sylvia Loch says, 'I have always argued that this term should be prefaced with the word "happy" to indicate that the submission is something which comes from the horse's giving of himself willingly to the rider. Partnership would be a better word to use altogether.'[36]

It is worth noting that the word 'submission' in this context comes from the German *Durchlassigkeit* – an untranslatable word which means that the horse is free from excess tension and is attentive and receptive – that he is 'pervious' to the aids; and this is the sense in which all great classical trainers and riders use it. Brigadier-General Kurt Albrecht (formerly Director of the Spanish Riding School) says, 'Submission is the keystone of impulsion, of straightness, correct carriage and pliability of the hocks.'[37] Used in this way it has *nothing to do with the kind of submission shown by a subordinate animal to a dominant one*. It is therefore unfortunate that, in the absence of a single word to encompass the German meaning, *submission* is now universally used among speakers of English. It leads to a great deal of misunderstanding about the relationship between riders/trainers and the horses themselves.

Lucy Rees points out that our attitude towards the horse's responses can affect the way in which we set about training and riding. 'When the horse "does what he is told" we can look at it in different ways: we can say the horse *submits* to our will, that he is *obedient* to our commands, or that he responds to our signals.'[38]

Using the term 'submission' as it is generally used among English-speaking people, rather than as Albrecht uses it, Rees goes on to say,

> The idea of submission, like the idea of a dominance hierarchy based on aggression, leads to difficulty. It is not the way that horses naturally think about relationships . . . they think in terms of friendship, kinship and signals. It is in competition (one with the other) that they submit, by moving away from each other's threats.
>
> Is moving away, then, to be the basis of our coming together? Is threat to be the framework of our harmonious relationship? For many trainers and horses it unfortunately is, which makes the horses understandably eager to escape the process altogether.[39]

The alternatives are more attractive. With *obedience*, the trainer thinks of reward as well as punishment and aversion. This is the essence of the 'stick and carrot' type of training. If the horse obeys, all will be well; if he disobeys, it will not. 'The disadvantage here', says Lucy Rees, 'is that the horse is left no space. Unable to think for himself, he becomes confused or agitated when faced with new problems. The trainer feels no compunction to take notice of the horse's signals'. We shall see in Chapters 12 and 13 that this is precisely the case when riders indulge in fantasies about manipulating the horse into shape by means of conditioned responses. 'This one-sided process, a stream of commands, is more suited to motorcycles than to living animals, and again it is not the way that horses naturally think.'[40]

'What next?' Toska waits for Brian to ask him to do something

Horses do, however, Rees says, think about responsiveness. They are very good at reading signals which is something they do constantly (remember the story of Clever Hans). So, as Rees says,

> The trainer who thinks in terms of responsiveness is thrown back on himself when the horse does not cooperate: he looks at the mistakes he may be making in his own signals, looks at the horse's signals too, and is more able to make the adjustments that are so necessary when dealing with such varied characters. He can pick up and develop the horse's ideas when he wants to without seeing it as a breakdown in discipline. The horse, freed of the pressures of a bully or a sergeant-major, is interested in the problems facing her and is grateful for any suggestions that help her through them: she does not fight back, nor become an automaton, but uses her mind and indulges in one of her greatest talents, that of responding.[41]

This is precisely the attitude adopted by the very greatest trainers. Owen MacSwiney, who had remarkable success in educating young horses from the ground says,

> The desire is to have the animal work *with* you and to make it *understand* whatever you want of it. People who are afraid of sentimentality and of being accused of 'humanising' their animals, tend to develop a complex that denies them access to the realities of an animal's observation powers, its powers of assessment and its willingness to learn. Because of this, many fall into the trap of believing that they can only achieve results by the imposition of mastery of some kind. It has escaped them that an animal may well enjoy learning, or being ridden, and is capable of actually looking for direction. That, by its posture in given situations, it can literally ask the question 'Well, what next?'[42]

In the next two chapters we shall see how confusion about the horse's responses, and about exactly what we are trying to teach him, can lead to mediocre or even harmful results; and how the teachings of the great masters of equitation can help us to overcome this confusion. For now, let us end with Lucy Rees who, after considering the wise words of Xenophon, says, 'Those Greeks rode bareback into the horrors of war on hot little stallions: how many modern riders could do the same on aversion-trained horses? In over two thousand years, have we regressed?'[43]

Notes

1 Dr Marthe Kiley-Worthington, *Equine Welfare*, p. 100
2 Kiley-Worthington, *Equine Welfare*, p. 80
3 Xenophon, *The Art of Horsemanship*, pp. 21–2
4 François Robichon de la Guérinière, *The School of Horsemanship* (orig. pub. 1733 as L'École de la Cavalerie; tr. Tracy Boucher, J. A. Allen, 1994), p. 83
5 la Guérinière, *The School of Horsemanship*, p. 83
6 Stephen Budiansky, *The Nature of Horses*, p. 163

7 Paul McGreevy, *Why Does My Horse . . .?*, pp. 55–6

8 Amanda J. Waters, 'Stable Advice', *Riding* magazine, 1998

9 John Blundell, 'Do Horses Learn from Each Other?' in *The Arab Horse Society News*, Autumn 1976, no.43, p. 119

10 Sylvia Loch, 'Talkback' *Horse & Rider*, March 1996, p. 90

11 William Cavendish, Duke of Newcastle, *A General System of Horsemanship* (a facsimile of the London edition of 1743; J. A. Allen, 1970), pp. 15–6

12 la Guérinière, *The School of Horsemanship*, p. 83

13 Nuno Oliveira, *Reflections on Equestrian Art* (tr. Phyllis Field, J. A. Allen, 1976), p. 40

14 'Questions and Answers', *Horse & Hound*, June 12 1997

15 For a fascinating theory regarding collective memory, see Rupert Sheldrake, *The Presence of the Past* (Harper Collins, 1994), and *The Rebirth of Nature* (Century, 1990)

16 Elaine Dollery, *The Treacle Bucket* (Dollery Books, 1992), p. 50

17 Lucy Rees, *The Horse's Mind*, p. 167

18 Oliveira, *Reflections on Equestrian Art*, p. 40

19 C. A. McCall, 'A Review of Learning Behaviour in Horses and its Application in Horse Training', *Journal of Animal Science*, no. 68, 1990, pp. 76–7

20 McCall, 'A Review of Learning Behaviour in Horses', p. 78

21 Colonel Alois Podhajsky, *My Horses, My Teachers*, pp. 49–50

22 McCall, 'A Review of Learning Behaviour in Horses', p. 78

23 Budiansky, *The Nature of Horses*, pp. 156–7

24 Léonie Marshall, *Your Horse's Mind*, p. 46

25 McGreevy, *Why Does My Horse . . .?*, p. 53

26 Antoine de Pluvinel, L'Instruction du Roy, quoted in *The Maneige Royal*, Introduction by Dr Hilda Nelson p. XII.

27 Pluvinel, *The Maneige Royal*, p. 93

28 Rees, *The Horse's Mind*, p. 167

29 Jean-Marie Denoix and Jean-Pierre Pailloux, *Physical Therapy and Massage for the Horse* (tr. Jonathan Lewis, Manson Publishing Ltd, 1996), p. 10

30 Rees, *The Horse's Mind*, p.167

31 Rees, *The Horse's Mind*, p.167

32 Vicki Hearne, *Adam's Task*, p.140

33 Waldemar Seunig, *Horsemanship* (tr. Leonard Mins, Robert Hale, 1958), translator's note, p.13

34 Sylvia Loch, 'The Essence of Classical Riding', *Horse & Rider*, December 1994

35 Newcastle, *A General System of Horsemanship*, p. 14

36 Loch, 'The Essence of Classical Riding', *Horse & Rider*, September 1994

37 Brigadier-General Kurt Albrecht, *A Dressage Judge's Handbook* (tr. Nicole Bartle, J. A. Allen, 1988), p. 18

38 Rees, *The Horse's Mind*, p. 168

39 Rees, *The Horse's Mind*, p. 168

40 Rees, *The Horse's Mind*, pp.168–9

41 Rees, *The Horse's Mind*, p.169

42 Marquis MacSwiney of Mashanaglass, *Training from the Ground*, pp. 168–9.

43 Rees, *The Horse's Mind*, p. 168

CHAPTER TWELVE

Can We Teach the Horse How to Be a Horse?

...the horse knows the rider in ways the rider cannot fathom

Vicki Hearne

WE SAW IN CHAPTERS 10 and 11 the diverse ways in which horses learn and communicate with each other. We have seen how their ability to read body language, whether visually or through their sense of touch, is infinitely superior to ours. Yet this last fact is either ignored or underestimated by large numbers of trainers and riders, who persist in blaming the horse for lack of understanding, whereas in fact it is their own body language that is either confusing or misleading the horse as to their intentions. There is also a vast amount of misunderstanding over just what it is we are trying to teach the horse when we school him under saddle. The resulting confusion often leads to frustration on the part of the rider/trainer and to behavioural problems on the part of the horse.

This and the following chapter might be considered to belong more properly to a training manual, but I have included them here in an attempt to clarify some of the communication problems identified above, and to indicate how these might be addressed.

First let us consider how the training and riding of horses is generally approached, in the English-speaking countries at least.

We are often told that horses were not made to carry riders and that most if not all the things we ask them to do under saddle are essentially alien to them. This is especially considered to be the case in the realm of dressage where the manner in which the horse is asked to carry himself, and the movements required, are often regarded as unnatural. It is therefore assumed that a horse's way of going in the dressage arena, as well as all the movements required of him, are things that must be laboriously 'taught'.

This has the effect of distancing the rider/trainer from the horse. Instead of working together in harmony (the Greek image of the centaur – human and horse joined as one being), the rider becomes merely a passenger who gives orders and the horse is relegated to the role of a creature to whom orders are given. There is thus no real communication, other than in a superficial sense. The horse may obey, but it is a mechanical kind of obedience, without that spontaneous gaiety we see in horses who truly become one with their riders. But why should this be so? What prevents us from 'getting through' to our horses? I believe it is the fact that, for the most part, we approach the matter from the wrong end.

As we saw in Chapter 11, most trainers and training manuals emphasise conditioned learning as the means by which we 'teach' the horse to obey our aids under saddle. Let us consider just what it is we are trying to 'teach' the horse.

That great horseman Franz Mairinger asked the question, 'How much and what can we teach the horse?' He came to the conclusion that:

> So far as movement is concerned we can't teach him anything at all, for the simple reason that he can already do everything that we might want him to do. He can walk, trot, canter, stop and turn, jump and change legs, go backwards – and he could do it all as soon as he was strong enough to stand on his legs . . . He learnt it in the same way that we learned to walk . . . Nobody taught us, it just came naturally. The horse learnt it in the same way, all programmed into his genetic inheritance.[1]

If we can't teach the horse anything, says Mairinger, what can we do? 'What must we do to be able to make use of his power and movement, of his ability to go fast, to cover long distances, and jump over all sorts of obstacles? The magic word is "education", which will give us the understanding of the horse.'[2] The sole purpose of that education is to establish an understanding between horse and rider, and to help the horse to regain his balance with a rider on his back. The rider cannot balance the horse, since the load cannot balance the support (although it can, of course, *un*balance it!). The horse must learn to balance himself – but how can he do this? The answer to that question lies within the next chapter, but for now we must consider why things go wrong when people become obsessed with the idea of 'teaching' the horse movements or 'teaching' him how to carry himself.

This applies especially to dressage and showing riders, who seem to have the greatest problems in this area. Long-distance riders, show jumpers (and to some degree eventers, except insofar as the latter have difficulties with their dressage) tend to worry far less about such things; the best of them recognise that flatwork is the foundation of all that the horse does under saddle, but they are much less concerned with appearances than with practicalities. They know what they have to achieve and its purpose (although this does not prevent them, too, from having communication problems). On the other hand, many dressage and show riders (and huge numbers of ordinary riders who do not aspire to 'dressage' but who genuinely want to improve their horses) seem confused about the purpose of dressage. They forget that 'dressage' (a term disliked by the late Colonel Alois Podhajsky, who said it was reminiscent of drilled poodles) is nothing other than the basic education of the horse, by means of suppling and strengthening exercises, to carry himself and the rider with the greatest efficiency and the minimum effort, regardless of the use to which the horse is put. The great German master Steinbrecht says that the aims of dressage are 'to develop the natural forces and capabilities of the horse to perfection through gradual and appropriate exercises'[3]. Now that competitive dressage has become an end in itself, this fact is often overlooked. Riders and trainers forget (if they ever really knew and understood) the purpose of the various movements. So they set out to 'teach' the horse something he already knows perfectly well *how* to do, not understanding that it is his own lack of muscular development and/or the interference of the rider's weight on his back that prevents him from executing it.

Take, for example, one of the most basic movements: the shoulder-in. This is often held up as a complicated movement which horses have difficulty learning. However, although it is undoubtedly a complex manoeuvre, shoulder-in is by no means as difficult as many people suggest. It can be introduced as a suppling exercise at a relatively early stage in the horse's training. Furthermore, horses do *not* have to be taught how to perform it: it is completely natural to them. Our stallion Nivalis has certainly never been taught shoulder-in; yet when he is trotting up and down along the fence trying to impress the mares in a nearby field, he performs a shoulder-in (it is really a counter shoulder-in, or shoulder-out, but no matter; the actual shape of the movement is the same) that conforms precisely to the laid-down definition of a three-track shoulder-in. His dam Roxzella was never 'taught' shoulder-in; she was introduced to it via the shoulder-fore, when my husband, who was riding her, just put his body into the shoulder-fore position – and the mare simply mirrored his movement.

Nivalis in shoulder-out

Of course some horses find it easier than others; it depends how naturally athletic they are. But *all horses*, provided they are sound and of reasonable conformation, have the natural ability to perform this movement; not perfectly at first, certainly, but with the ability to improve as they muscle up and become more supple.

The one thing that is usually forgotten (although not by the most knowledgeable trainers) is that shoulder-in – like any other dressage movement or exercise – should never be thought of as simply something one has to 'teach' the horse if one wants to 'do' dressage. It is – as with dressage in general – nothing other than a means of suppling and gymnasticising the horse in order to make its job of carrying the rider easier. François Robichon de la Guérinière, who is credited with inventing the shoulder-in, did not wake up one morning and decide to create a movement that would show off the horse's training and obedience. He developed the shoulder-in as we know it from exercises that had, in their turn, been worked out by earlier masters such as the Duke of Newcastle. Its value lies in the fact that it has a threefold purpose: it helps to straighten the horse; it helps to engage the hind legs because the horse has to step under itself with the inside leg; and it helps to free and supple the shoulders. This is a very crude explanation; a full description of the virtues of the exercise and how it does all these things would take up a chapter in itself, if not a whole book. However, I think it helps to illustrate *why* the movement is important.

If we isolate the movement from its purpose, so that it becomes an end in itself, we run the risk of misunderstanding it, and of believing that it is something we must laboriously 'teach' the horse to do. So we hear of dressage trainers 'teaching' the horse flying changes, 'teaching' the horse *piaffe* and *passage* – all things that the horse knows perfectly well how to do, indeed, has known from the very day of its birth! Admittedly, even trainers who are very well aware that we cannot teach the horse how to be a horse, often speak of 'teaching' the horse various movements as this saves a great deal of tedious explanation. Perhaps it would be better to speak of 'introducing' the movements.

Some writers have been very sceptical about whether the High School 'airs' do represent natural movement. Evidently finding little to admire in what he calls the 'prancing' horse pose – and, in the process, completely misunderstanding the true nature and purpose of collection – Stephen Budiansky writes, in *The Nature of Horses*, that: 'the truth of the matter is that these collected gaits are not ones that a freely moving horse, or a green horse, or a wild horse, will ever select on its own – unless it is highly emotionally aroused.'[4]

With all due respect, this is nonsense. Steinbrecht, whose wisdom is justly revered by some of the greatest horsemen and women, wrote:

If the trainer wants to have a correct view of the mechanism of the movements, of the activity of the individual limbs, and of the coaction of all the limbs during forward movement, he must diligently observe the young green horse in the pasture. He will then be convinced that mother nature has endowed the foal with everything that he has seen as beautiful and artistic in thoroughly trained military and dressage horses, and this with such freshness and grace . . . In its mischievous games, the young colt will display quite a number of the higher-level movements, from a passage to airs above the ground.[5]

I have frequently seen such movements performed by relatively novice, green, or in some cases completely untutored horses while at liberty; and while it is true that these 'performances' are not as polished as those one might see at the Spanish Riding School, nevertheless they have been technically quite acceptable versions of them. Even as a yearling, our stallion Nivalis could produce a spectacular *piaffe* and *passage* while playing with Zareeba; the latter, while escaping the colt's boisterous attentions, executed canter pirouettes (which he has never been 'taught') that put to shame anything currently seen in international Grand Prix dressage. The stallion's dam, Roxzella, is an exceptionally athletic mare whom I have seen, on at least four occasions, performing a *courbette* that would not disgrace her at either Vienna or the Cadre Noir at Saumur. I have also seen her execute a very creditable *capriole* –

all out of sheer high spirits and *joie de vivre*. The stallion's daughter, Imzadi, was executing pirouettes, *levades* and *croupades* within hours of being born.

The great masters of equitation observed how foals and young horses perform the various 'airs' in their play (from Newcastle, *A General System of Horsemanship*)

I have also seen these movements performed by other people's horses, not just our own. Not long ago we went to see a young Lipizzaner stallion, who welcomed us with much fuss, nuzzling and gentle nibbling. He then decided he would like to show off to us so, after *passaging* exuberantly around, he did a magnificent *levade*. No one had ever taught him to do this; it just came naturally to him. I have seen the same kind of thing in many other places, among equally green horses. One Classical Riding Club member recently told me of her delight in watching her two Lusitano colts dancing about like High School horses, in exactly the same manner as my Arabians.

Even tiny foals perform their own versions of 'airs above the ground': Imzadi at 36 hours old

None of these horses could be described as 'highly emotionally aroused', unless one places in this category sheer high spirits, boisterous play or simple showing off. Yes, horses *do* enjoy showing off, just as they most certainly enjoy athletic movement for its own sake. Behaviourists and sociobiologists may deny this as vigorously as they choose, but this tells us far more about them than it does about the animals they study. As we shall see in Chapter 16, horses can take as much delight in learning to use themselves properly as a human athlete can in the proper use of his or her body. Such exuberance is perfectly natural, especially in young horses!

Stephen Budiansky further says, 'How much of a "spirited" horse's spirit is the consequence of our whipping it into a frenzy remains a valid question.'[6] So it does, if one's concept of a 'spirited' horse is represented by the unfortunate near-lunatics one sees far too often in showrings, particularly in the USA. But this is light years away from the idea of a spirited horse as portrayed by Xenophon and his like, and whipping a horse into a frenzy has absolutely nothing to do with the classical High School as established by Pluvinel, de la Guérinière, Marialva, etc.

'A nervous horse', says Budiansky, 'may prance, but a freely moving, calm horse shifts its weight forward in a dynamically maintained balance.'[7] However, as we have seen, a horse does not have to be nervous to prance. Our Arabian stallion is not in the least nervous; in fact, he is for the most part extremely relaxed. He prances because he enjoys it – and because he likes to show off, especially to mares – he would not be much of a stallion if he did not! To pretend otherwise is to distort what Budiansky maintains he is trying to clarify: the nature of the horse. If we were to carry Budiansky's argument to a logical conclusion, we would have to confine ourselves in riding to a rather leisurely walk, as this is the free-ranging horse's most normal gait! Furthermore, free, calm, *forward* movement has *always* been the aim of classical dressage training, even in the most collected movements.

It is not, therefore, a question of teaching the horse unnatural movements, but rather of evoking and then refining what comes naturally; although it may be that some breeds, such as Spanish horses, Lusitanos, Lipizzaners and Arabs, are more likely to find these movements easy and to produce them naturally than less high spirited or less naturally athletic breeds. It was not a matter of trainers 'inventing' such movements and setting out to 'teach' them to the horse.

Forerunner of the *pesade*: Nivalis confronts another entire (note how deeply his hocks are engaged; this is *not* just a rear, but a true 'air above the ground') (B.Skipper)

It is often supposed that the High School 'airs' were created as medieval battle movements, but the same people who propose this 'invention' then often proceed to cast doubt on the medieval warhorse's ability to execute them! I believe that what happened was this: at some time in the distant past, possibly thousands of years ago, the first people to make full use of the ridden horse in battle recognised the value of certain naturally occuring movements such as the *pesade* (like a controlled rear, the forerunner of the *levade*), the *capriole* and the pirouette, in threatening, challenging and then evading the enemy. These enterprising horsemen then went on to refine the movements the horse produced naturally and to train both horse and rider so as to produce the desired response when needed. There is evidence that such movements have been used by horsemen at many different times and in many different cultures. They were certainly used by the ancient Celtiberians of the Iberian Peninsula, where they are still of great practical use in the mounted *corrida*; by the classical Greeks, as we know from the writings of Xenophon; in Christian Byzantium, in Transcaucasia, in India, by the Turks, and most probably by the Arabs too.

Stephen Budiansky writes, 'The military necessity that created the ideal of the "high school" of riding is another distorting lens that still affects our notions of what constitutes

The High School: the Duke of Newcastle performing a *capriole*

not only the natural behaviour but also the natural movement of the horse.'[8] He concludes that: 'the enshrinement of the high school as an ideal continues to do great mischief to our understanding of the natural movements of the horse'[9].

But this is to misunderstand totally those ideals, as well as the natural movements themselves. As Steinbrecht puts it:

> The opponents of training the horse so that it carries itself in balance argue against a subject which they either do not understand at all, or of which they have gained a completely incorrect view from false disciples of the art who downgrade it by their incompetence and do damage to the same degree that they intend to be useful.[10]

For this is the essence of the High School – that the horse must be *supple and in balance*. Only then can he carry the rider to the best of his ability; and the fact that horses correctly trained in the classical High School stay sound longer (in spite of the strenuous nature of their work) than horses trained any other way is only one proof of this. The High School is nothing more or less than a university for the horse. Not all horses will have sufficient ability to progress this far; but that is no reason not to educate them to the highest possible level without stretching them beyond their natural limits. Even when the nature of warfare changed so that the 'airs' above the ground and the advanced movements on the ground were no longer so essential in battle, they were still recognised to represent the ultimate in the horse's training – the point at which the horse was so supple and collected that he could perform whatever was asked of him with fluent ease – and this has been the aim of all the great masters of equitation, as well as of the few remaining academies such as the Spanish Riding School and the Portuguese School of Equestrian Art. As American trainer Paul Belasik, speaking of a specific High School movement, the *piaffe*, says,

> . . . the real essence is in the process. The idea behind the *piaffe* is not to exhibit some kind of specifically calculated movement, for the sake of exhibition or the rider's ego. It is instead to perform a supreme exercise. The *piaffe's* real value lies in doing it, not in proving anything by exhibiting a trick. The *piaffe's* value is in the cumulative gymnastic effects it has on the horse.[11]

For this very reason, many trainers do not set out to 'teach' such movements. They wait until the horse is sufficiently developed gymnastically and begins to offer the movement naturally – as a confirmation, if you like, of the correctness of the earlier work. As Sylvia Loch says,

> Once the horse has the strength behind to begin to gather himself, and comes more up and through the gaits, the *piaffe* and *passage* should come of their own accord. You just shorten the gait a little as though going into halt, ask a little more from the lower leg further back, and the horse starts to step on the spot; the moment this happens you reward him. He remembers the kindness and the next time, he's eager to offer a little more. If it doesn't happen like that, then he's not ready.[12]

But when the training is dominated by the idea of teaching the horse movements – usually with the aim of competing – very often this natural progression is omitted (if, indeed, it is recognised at all). The trainer sets out to teach the horse the movement by whatever method produces results; and while this approach makes some very poor or

Espada with Sylvia Loch in *piaffe* (Hector Innes)

inadequate riding possible even at high levels of competition, the result, more often than not, is fundamentally incorrect. What we see all too often is a movement that is a travesty of what it should be. This is why the classical masters have always warned against training that merely teaches the horse 'tricks'.

What do they mean by teaching the horse 'tricks'? In the 1950s the psychologist Moyra Williams, who had considerable success in breeding and competing with showjumping horses, tried an interesting experiment with several of her horses. She had been observing how one of them, whom she had been using to teach people to ride, succeeded in ignoring the heavy-handed, clumsy aids of his novice riders; yet, after about a week of being ridden by no one but herself, he managed to regain his former responsiveness. This made her wonder whether the conventional aids were really being applied to those parts of the body most suited to receive them, as many horses seemed extremely insensitive to pressure over the ribs. …'Many people', she wrote: 'find that they have to use spurs before pressure from the legs is responded to at all.'[13] She felt that it would make more sense to train a horse to respond to touch on those areas most sensitive to it. After some trial and error, she decided that the withers seemed much more sensitive to a light touch than anywhere else, and that this would be the part of the horse's body where riding aids would be most effective. A full description of how she set about training a horse to respond to a different set of aids may be found in Dr Williams's book, *Horse Psychology*, and in her chapter entitled 'Look – no bridle!' in *The Horse and the Bit* (ed. Susan McBane). Dr Williams succeeded in training a mare, Nona, and several other horses to associate a series of simple pressure-aids (e.g. a push forward with both hands to go on, a pull back on the mare's mane with both hands to stop, pressure on the right side of the neck to turn left, pressure on the left side to turn right, etc.). 'Within a very short time Nona, and most of her successors in the experiments, showed every sign of knowing what was wanted of her at the different aids.'[14]

Against this undoubted success was the fact that only Dr Williams could ride the horses so trained. As she notes in another book, *Understanding Nervousness in Horse and Rider*, 'I found myself bound (almost literally) to care for and exercise my horses myself, as no one else could communicate with them. This taught me the value of a common set of aids for use between all horses and riders.'[15]

The problem with Dr Williams's idea is that she was starting off under a misapprehension about the nature of the conventional 'aids'. We must understand here that she was writing from the point of view of someone brought up in Britain during the inter-war years, when there was very little interest in academic riding. The reasons for this are several and are admirably discussed by Sylvia Loch in her definitive history of the art of riding, *Dressage: The Art of Classical Riding*. It is sufficient to say here that this lack of interest in the finer points of riding had much to do with an obsession with hunting and cross country riding, the feeling that dressage was unnecessary 'foreign' nonsense, and that horsemen were born, not made. As Anne Grimshaw remarks in her monumental review of British equestrian literature, *The Horse: a bibliography of British books 1851–1976*, there was in Britain between the First and Second World Wars:

… a prevalent attitude amongst those from 'horsey' backgrounds, and even amongst those who had never ridden, that actually learning to ride was unnecessary. The misconception that riders were born and not made was widespread, as was the belief that if one had not begun to ride in childhood then it was useless … There was nothing to learn; it was merely a matter of sitting on a horse, pulling the reins to stop, kicking it in the ribs to go, and that was all there was to it. Riding as an art or science was relatively unheard of by the riding public.[16]

Even Henry Blake, who had considerable success in competition, had a very crude concept of the aids (not to mention his idea of training, which would have sent Steinbrecht into an apoplexy!).

If you sit on a horse and pull the reins, it will stop quite easily – it is trained to stop when it feels the pressure of the bit. When you touch it with your heels it will go forward. You can steer it to the right, you can steer it to the left. You can teach your horse very quickly to do anything it is physically capable of doing.[17]

This uneducated, push-pull attitude towards riding was not universal, of course; there were some serious students of riding as an art or science in Britain at that time. Nevertheless, this simplistic view of what riding and training entailed, together with the absence of any continuous tradition of academic riding, goes a long way towards explaining misconceptions regarding the nature of the aids.

Such misconceptions are evident in Dr Williams's comments on the 'conventional' aids. She wrote,

That the riding aids conventionally used in this country are the result of choice and are not fundamental to the control of the animal is, of course, well known. Certain tribes of Red Indians used to control their animals superbly with nothing but a noseband and a single rein. The cowboy in Western America seldom uses his legs to turn a horse, relying more on a slight flip of a rein or on a change of weight in the saddle.[18]

The first sentence echoes the British tendency to reduce the aids to the use of the hands and legs (mostly the former), ignoring the use of the rider's seat and body position. This is scarcely surprising when one considers the attitudes described above, and the fact that, even today, in many riding schools the use of the rider's seat is hardly mentioned. In the late 1970s and mid 1980s Molly Sivewright FBHS, DBHS, was deploring this situation and attempted to remedy it with her excellent books, *Thinking Riding* (Books I and II). Regrettably, not much has changed since then; the average novice rider may sometimes be told that they should be using their seat, but rarely is it explained to them how they should be doing this. Yet, as we shall see, this ignores the most important means by which the rider communicates with the horse!

In fact, the aids used by the Native American and the true Western rider are those of body-weight and posture, together with the use of the legs – used in the same way as the classical rider uses their body to guide the horse, whether in an eighteenth-century *manège*, at the Spanish Riding School or in the modern Portuguese mounted *corrida*. The conventional British aids, although often crudely taught and applied, are not arbitrarily chosen, but are a somewhat oversimplified version of the universal aids that have stood the test of time. In partial recognition of this, Dr Williams says elsewhere that: 'having a universal set of aids (using whatever technique is fashionable) which is used by everyone in all countries, has the advantage that riders and horses can be interchanged without causing confusion'[19]. As we shall see in the next chapter, however, the technique is not – or should not be – dictated by the whim of fashion. Indeed, if it was, it is difficult to see how the aids could be regarded as 'universal', since fashions might change in one country but not in another, which would be confusing to say the least!

With regard to Dr Williams's original reason for the experiments, she failed to understand how horses learn to protect themselves against crude or harsh riding: some react violently and take refuge in flight; others simply withdraw, seeming to become more and more insensitive. Effectively, they 'switch off'. Even now, a surprising number of very experienced trainers and riders fail to recognise this and persist in believing that horses lack sensitivity in the girth area and over the ribs. They could not be more mistaken, as Chapter 13 will show. Dr Williams's horses regained their sensitivity when ridden by her because their resistances had not been allowed to become habit; with many riding school horses, who are not regularly reschooled by competent riders, this defensive habit may become so ingrained that it will take even an expert considerable effort to coax them out of it (see Sylvia Loch's discussion of this problem in *The Classical Rider: Being at One with your Horse*, Chapter 6).

I have no doubt that Dr Williams's experiments were a success because she was a sensitive, well-balanced rider who built up a tremendous *rapport* with her horses. Nevertheless, interesting as these experiments were, I feel they remain just that – interesting experiments. They are valid in that they show just what can be achieved by teaching horses the conditioned responses so beloved of behaviourists, but this is something that any good circus trainer can do, as Dr Williams herself admitted. Certainly we make use of such responses when lungeing the horse, although good lungeing makes far greater use of body language than even the best trainers normally recognise; in fact, a great deal of lunge-work, carried out correctly, makes use of very similar body-language to that taught by people such as Monty Roberts. Verbal commands, such as 'Walk on!', 'Ter-rot!' and 'Can-ter!' are paired with this body-language, so that eventually the verbal commands can be used on their own. However, in all but the earliest ridden work, 'conditioning' methods are only of very limited use because, as trainer Karin Blignault remarks in *Successful Schooling*, they cannot teach *quality* of movement. In *Ride With Your Mind* Mary Wanless points out that we can indeed teach the horse to go into canter, for instance, whenever we pull his ear, tap his shoulder or whatever; but what kind of transition we would get is anybody's guess. And it is the quality of the transition that matters: sloppy transitions make for sloppy gaits, which may ultimately be damaging to the horse. Falling into canter any old how will not do.

As we shall see in the next chapter, the problem with using conditioned responses is that they take no account of the horse's physical and mental condition, or of all the other things the rider may or may not be doing besides giving deliberate signals. As Sylvia Loch says in *The Classical Rider*, 'Horses do what they *feel* we have asked them to do, not what they guess we are trying to say. How can a horse know we want right lead when our body is actually saying something else?'[20] Regarding another popular type of 'conditioned response' training, using voice commands and rewards, she says that this

> . . . is perfectly proper provided this, in itself, is not the method. Their use can complement the method, but if used in isolation will result in the horse learning to do everything by memory in the way that a dog learns new tricks. What happens later, when the horse changes hands and the new owner says things in a different way or in a different language and there are no instant rewards? The horse will feel lost and bewildered.[21]

All this is what is meant by teaching the horse 'tricks'. The trouble with relying on this kind of training is that once the horse has been taught the conditioned response, and the rider is certain that he has not only understood but is physically able to perform what is required, what then? Does the fact that the horse knows *what* to do and *how* to do it mean that he is always able and willing actually to do it? The rider who concentrates on teaching the horse such 'learned responses' is creating a one-way system of communication. As I said earlier in this chapter, the trainer/rider is reduced to the level of merely giving orders, while the horse, in turn, becomes a subordinate whose role is solely that of execution of those orders. The horse can either obey or not; and if the rider ignores the effects of their own physical interaction with the horse, how can they accurately read the horse's response? Nuno Oliveira has observed that: 'To practise equestrian art is to establish a conversation on a higher level with the horse; a dialogue of courtesy and finesse.'[22] — and even if the rider does not aspire to the level of art, dialogue with the horse is essential if riding is not to be reduced to the level of crude coercion. If the horse can only say 'Yes' or 'No', what kind of conversation is that?

This is not to say that one should not teach the horse other kinds of 'tricks', provided these are not used as a substitute for proper gymnastic training. Teaching different things can help to educate the horse's mind, a subject discussed in Chapter 16. And certainly, we must make use of *some* 'learned responses', both from the ground and in the saddle. The most frequently cited of these is moving away from the rider's leg. It is often said that, logically, there is no reason why a horse should walk forward in response to a nudge from the rider's leg. He has to learn to associate the nudge with the command, 'Walk on!' (or whatever words one chooses to use), which is generally taught at a very early stage in his education. The same could be said of the leg aids which ask the horse to move sideways. So it might be argued that this is something which has to be 'taught'.

Or is it? In the next chapter we shall look at this, together with the problems posed by the kind of training which relies on learned or conditioned responses, and why training – or riding – that is based on the horse's natural responses, is far superior.

Notes

1 Franz Mairinger, *Horses are Made To Be Horses*, p. 32

2 Mairinger, *Horses are Made to be Horses*, p. 33

3 Gustav Steinbrecht, *The Gymnasium of the Horse* (orig. pub. as *Gymnasium des Pferdes*, 1885; tr. of 10th edition by Helen K. Gibble, Xenophon Press, 1995), p. 44

4 Stephen Budiansky, *The Nature of Horses*, p. 70

5 Steinbrecht, *The Gymnasium of the Horse*, p. 44

6 Budiansky, *The Nature of Horses*, p. 68

7 Budiansky, *The Nature of Horses*, p. 70

8 Budiansky, *The Nature of Horses*, p. 69

9 Budiansky, *The Nature of Horses*, p. 70

10 Steinbrecht, *The Gymnasium of the Horse*, p. 46

11 Paul Belasik, *Riding Towards The Light* (J. A. Allen, 1990), p. 109

12 Loch, Sylvia 'Talkback', *Horse & Rider*, September 1994

13 Dr Moyra Williams, *Horse Psychology* (J. A. Allen, revised edition 1985) p. 120

14 Williams, *Horse Psychology*, p. 122

15 Dr Moyra Williams, *Understanding Nervousness in Horse and Rider* (J. A. Allen, 1990), p. 46

16 Anne Grimshaw, *The Horse: A Bibliography of British books* 1851–1976, (Limited edition, The Library Association, 1982), p. 143

17 Henry Blake, *Talking With Horses*, p. 26

18 Williams, *Horse Psychology*, p. 120

19 Dr Moyra Williams, 'Look – no bridle!' in *The Horse and the Bit* (ed. Susan McBane, Crowood Press, 1988), p. 121

20 Sylvia Loch, *The Classical Rider*, p. 232

21 Loch, *The Classical Rider*, p. 40

22 Nuno Oliveira, *Reflections on Equestrian Art*, p. 18

CHAPTER THIRTEEN

The Magic Spot

You can talk to a horse as often as you like but you will
only make him do something for you through the influence
of your position. That is how you talk to him.

FRANZ MAIRINGER

IN FRONT OF ME AS I write is a translation of *Le Maneige Royal*, by Antoine de Pluvinel,
écuyer principal to King Louis XIII of France. This translation, taken from the edition of
1625, is embellished with reproductions of the engravings by Crispian de Pas, which
originally illustrated the book. They all illuminate various aspects of Pluvinel's teaching, but
one in particular catches the eye.

This shows a horse tied between two pillars, a common method of training from the
ground in those days and one which is still used at the Spanish Riding School for practising
certain movements. The horse looks a trifle suspicious, and his whole stance is reminiscent
of a maiden aunt protecting her virtue. On the left of the engraving M. de Potrin stands by
one pillar; on the extreme right stands the young Louis XIII. M. de Pluvinel stands by the
other pillar next to the king, evidently giving him instruction, while in the background M. Ie
Grand hovers rather inattentively with a gaggle of courtiers. Both the king and M. de Potrin
are pointing with long sticks at a spot just above and behind the horse's elbow.

But what can they possibly be doing? Unfortunately, the engraving does not explain, nor
does M. de Pluvinel's text greatly enlighten us, except to explain the role of the pillars in lateral work. Yet one is left with the distinct impression that this picture has something of great
importance to tell us.

By the end of this chapter I hope the hidden message of the engraving will have been made
clear, but for now let us return to the questions left unanswered at the end of the previous
chapter: if conditioned responses are not, after all, the real key to effective riding, then what

The magic spot: M. de Pluvinel instructs King Louis XIII of France

is? The answer lies in that aspect of riding already identified as being, regrettably, most neglected by riding school instruction: the rider's position in the saddle, and the precise application of the aids. Therein lies the secret of what we have already found to be the most effective human-horse communication of all: that of touch.

As Franz Mairinger points out, 'the cornerstone of our success in schooling lies within the horse's ability to re-establish his natural balance under the rider's weight. It is the horse that must find his balance.'[1] How can the rider help him to do that? By *sitting still relative to the horse*. Thus the rider's position in the saddle is of paramount importance. In Franz Mairinger's words: 'position comes first, and everything else comes after'[2].

But does this mean that the rider is totally passive? Not at all; *passive* is not the same thing as sitting still relative to the horse. The latter simply means that the rider makes no extraneous movements that will upset the horse's equilibrium or send confusing signals where none are intended. Being passive, on the other hand, means that the rider is nothing more than a passenger; and indeed this is more often the case than not. This might not matter quite so much where the rider's expectations are very limited, say, if he or she simply wants to go out for a pleasant ride, although it does not make for a particularly safe or responsive horse. In most situations, however, it matters very much indeed. The way in which the horse carries himself and uses his back and limbs is of paramount importance to his well-being; a horse that works correctly under a rider is going to lead a longer, happier life than one which is cramped, tense and restricted in his back, and whose joints, because of this, no longer function effectively as shock absorbers.

Unfortunately, because of the widespread neglect of the rider's position, accompanied by a corresponding lack of understanding of just how much the rider affects the horse's carriage and way of going, there is an equally widespread tendency to blame any problems on the horse. For example, with the upsurge of interest in dressage has come an obsession with 'outline'. Riders worry endlessly about getting their horse to 'go in a correct outline'. Frustrated by their horses' seemingly limitless repertoire of evasions (the commonest being raising the head and hollowing the back, setting the jaw against the hand, or overbending to escape the contact), desperate riders fall eagerly on any advice which promises a cure for their problems. The advice given – whether by instructors, equestrian magazines or animal behaviour experts – usually identifies a number of possible causes and suggests various remedies for such evasions. These range from having the horse's teeth, neck and back checked; having the tack checked (all of which should, of course, be considered as possible causes and appropriate remedial action taken if necessary); changing to a milder/stronger/different bit; more use of the leg to drive the horse forward into the contact, and other variations on the same themes. More often than not – and this has the greatest relevance to our current study – it is assumed that the horse either has the wrong conformation, or that he simply has not understood what is required of him, and that what is needed is more schooling, perhaps using different tactics. The horse, it is assumed, must 'learn' to work 'on the bit'.

The FEI definition of being 'on the bit' is as follows:

A horse is said to be *on the bit* when the hocks are correctly placed, the neck is more or less raised and arched according to the stage of training and the extension or collection of the pace, and he accepts the bridle with a light and soft contact and submissiveness throughout. The head should remain in a steady position, as a rule slightly in front of the vertical, with a supple poll as the highest part of the neck and no resistance should be offered to the rider.[3]

This should, technically, be unambiguous enough. Unfortunately, such is the widespread lack of understanding of the principles involved that all too often it is forgotten that the *horse himself* makes his own outline as a result of being correctly trained and ridden; an 'outline' should *never* be imposed on him. Furthermore, the carriage of the head and neck is the *result*, not the cause, of the hocks being engaged, and the back lifted and rounded. Yet relatively few riders and trainers, in the English-speaking countries at least, appear to appreciate this; most seem to home in on the position of the head and neck as being the key to an 'outline' and the horse being 'on the bit'. Thus we find Paul McGreevy writing that: 'Many horses find that being ridden on the bit (in other words, with the line of the head at right angles to

Zareeba: head carriage maintained through changes of pace and direction:

the ground) is far from comfortable if it has to be held for any length of time.'[4] This is true enough, which is precisely why a horse should never be asked to work 'on the bit' until sufficient muscle has been built up in the right places! The problem is that here the author has reduced 'on the bit' to one simple concept – that of the position of the head and neck.

He goes on to say that: 'While this posture has its origins in display behaviour among loose horses, it is rarely maintained continually through changes in pace and direction.'[5] In fact, loose horses that are naturally well conformed and athletic *do* tend to maintain such a head carriage throughout changes of pace and direction – depending, of course, on what they are doing. It is not merely a part of display behaviour, but a sign of whether the horse is using himself properly. A horse that is 'strung out' and on his forehand is much less able to 'gather' (or, if you prefer, to *collect*) himself for sudden changes of gait or direction than one which has engaged his hind legs, rounded his back, lowered his croup and, as a consequence, raised and arched his neck. The very fact of a horse 'collecting' himself in this way makes his back muscles more able to transmit the 'drive' from the hind legs (and, for our purposes, to carry a rider), ready for instant action in any direction. That, and not the cosmetic appeal of an arbitrarily imposed head carriage, is why it is necessary for the trained riding horse to work 'on the bit'. (For a fuller discussion of what collection and being 'on the bit' entail, see Sylvia Loch, *The Classical Seat* and *The Classical Rider*, Paul Belasik, *Exploring Dressage Technique*, and Mary Wanless, *Ride With Your Mind*.)

Paul McGreevy points out that: 'Every good dressage rider will acknowledge that some horses are easier to "get into an outline" than others. This is not because they have a greater desire to please their owners, but because the posture is easier for them to achieve.'[6] This may be true for some horses whose conformation means that they may not need quite so much by way of gymnastic and suppling exercises to build up sufficient muscle to use themselves properly. However, as we have seen, getting the horse into an 'outline' should never be the rider's aim, since if the horse is correctly trained and ridden he will make his own 'out-line' – even if his conformation leaves a lot to be desired! McGreevy goes on to say that: 'to insist on a regimented relationship between head and neck in every ridden horse is far from realistic'[7]. Of course it is, which is why such a concept has no place in classical riding or training! Furthermore, it has nothing to do with the true aims of dressage. Unfortunately, very many trainers and riders think that it has, which means a great deal of physical and mental anguish for horses forced, whether through harsh riding or restrictive 'gadgets', to carry themselves in a manner that works against the body posture dictated by their current mental and physical state.

Writing about this very problem in *Ride With your Mind*, Mary Wanless quotes a renowned trainer as saying that one of the biggest problems in Britain is sour, resentful horses. 'These poor crea-tures', says Mary Wanless, 'are seething at the indignity and discomfort of the rid-ers' attempts to force them into a certain shape or movement.'[8] The horse can only use his back and hindquarters properly, and come into the correct outline, when the rider is correctly balanced and taking responsibility for their own weight. Otherwise the horse is carrying an un-balanced load, and this will compromise his ability to use his back and hind legs.

Nivalis makes a natural 'outline': quite acceptable for a green young horse

As Brigadier-General Kurt Albrecht, former Director of the Spanish Riding School, says in *Principles of Dressage*: 'An incorrect posture of the rider is the root cause of innumerable dif-ficulties in controlling direction and also of faulty carriage of the horse.'[9]

The best riders all sit in such a way that their high muscle tone helps to keep them in place and distributes their weight so that the pressure is not concentrated on one small area of the horse's back. They do not just sit on the seatbones, but in a balanced position, with their cen-tre of gravity aligned above their base of support (their feet), and with their weight distrib-uted through the entire pelvic floor as well as through the buttocks and the thighs. They are not fixed rigidly in this position, of course, as they make constant tiny shifts of position in response to the horse's movements; but they *appear* to be still. From the horse's point of view, they sit *lightly*, although this is a purely descriptive way of putting it, as the actual weight remains the same. However, it feels lighter to the horse because the balance and weight distribution of the rider make it so much easier for him to engage his back muscles and move correctly. A rider who does not take responsibility for their own weight, who sits like the proverbial sack of potatoes, with all the weight concentrated in one place, will auto-matically be unbalanced. Such riders will not only seem heavier to the horse (even though they may in fact weigh less), they will put far more pressure on the horse's back (who would you rather have stand on your foot – a man in flat shoes or a woman wearing stiletto heels?). Unfortunately for horses, such riders are all too common, since how to sit correctly is seldom taught in riding schools.

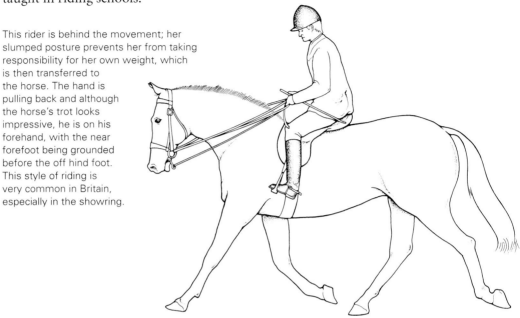

This rider is behind the movement; her slumped posture prevents her from taking responsibility for her own weight, which is then transferred to the horse. The hand is pulling back and although the horse's trot looks impressive, he is on his forehand, with the near forefoot being grounded before the off hind foot. This style of riding is very common in Britain, especially in the showring.

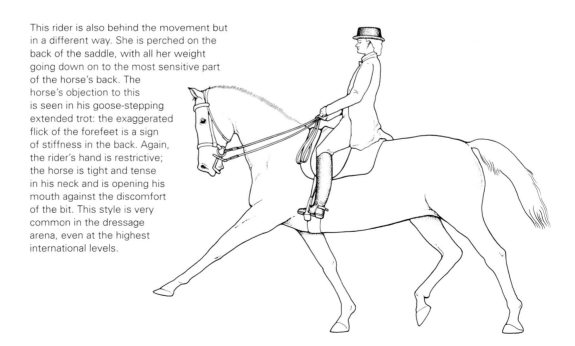

This rider is also behind the movement but in a different way. She is perched on the back of the saddle, with all her weight going down on to the most sensitive part of the horse's back. The horse's objection to this is seen in his goose-stepping extended trot: the exaggerated flick of the forefeet is a sign of stiffness in the back. Again, the rider's hand is restrictive; the horse is tight and tense in his neck and is opening his mouth against the discomfort of the bit. This style is very common in the dressage arena, even at the highest international levels.

This rider is truly in balance with his horse, aligning his bodyweight over his feet and sitting over the strongest part of the horse's back. The hand is soft and giving, and the horse responds by stepping out in a free, relaxed manner. This was drawn from a photograph of Nuno Oliveira riding a Lusitano stallion.

With such riders, who unwittingly increase the pressure they put on the horse's back, the natural tendency will be for the horse to hollow away from the discomfort. This usually results in a raised head, as the pressure from the rider causes the back muscles to contract and shorten, bringing the head and neck closer to the croup along the topline. If the horse is a short-backed type, he may well become extremely uncomfortable to sit on. Longer-backed horses, particularly if they have very flexible backs, may still feel comfortable to the rider, but they will nevertheless be hollow; and in either case the hind legs will not be able to engage properly.

In this situation, any attempts to induce the horse to lower his head, by whatever means, will result either in a horse that fights and tenses even further, or one that gives in, lowers his head and decides to live with the discomfort. He then has to work many times harder to fulfil the demands of his rider. In both cases the basic work will be incorrect and the muscular damage that can result may be severe.

One of our most eminent and respected equine physiotherapists, Mary Bromiley, has this to say:

> It is interesting to note that the head raise/back hollowing reflex can be activated by the pressure caused by a rider sitting too deep. The horse is forced to dip the back and raise the head by a reflex over which it has no control – its brain makes this occur as an automatic response. When this happens the position of back and neck is then incorrect and outline is lost.[10]

Here is the whole point of the matter. The raised head and hollowed back that cause so many riders so much grief have, in most cases, *nothing to do* with whether or not the horse has been 'taught' to carry his head and neck in a certain position. This response is neither a sign that he has not understood what is required of him, nor the result of some cussedness on the part of the horse. Horses do not actually enjoy going around with their noses poked and their backs hollowed; with the added weight of a rider this posture is acutely uncomfortable for them, and the fact that so many of them are permanently ridden in this position – as with forcible riding in an imposed 'outline' – is responsible for a lot of back problems. (For a fuller discussion of the biomechanics of this, see Jean-Marie Denoix and Jean-Pierre Pailloux, *Physical Therapy and Massage for the Horse.*) This hollowing away from discomfort is a natural *reflex*. Unfortunately, those trainers who insist that the horse performs exclusively by means of 'conditioned responses' very often fail to understand that this is what is happening, and try to compel the horse to bring his head down by means of draw-reins, other 'training aids', or good old brute force and ignorance. 'Small wonder', says Mary Bromiley, that 'the animal becomes confused: its brain is giving one command, and the creature's pain another with tension as the immediate result. When this occurs the animal cannot work in a relaxed supple manner.'[11] Raising the head is also a sign of tension; it is part of the 'fight or flight' mode.

It is only when we understand the part played by the rider's posture in dictating the horse's response that we can begin to ride and train him in a manner that works *with* his nature rather than *against* it. When we make the error of assuming that the ridden horse must be taught the correct head and neck position by means of conditioning, we perpetuate a misunderstanding that may cost the horse dear. An increasingly common method of teaching the horse to accept the bit relies on the concepts of 'conditioning' and 'negative reinforcement' described in Chapter 11. In this method, the rider takes up a firm contact, with fairly short reins, and rides the horse forward into this contact at the trot. The idea is that the horse will yield to the pressure of the bit by dropping his nose. The instant that he does, the rider must 'reward' him by releasing the reins. As Paul McGreevy says: 'When the head is in the required position, the absence of pressure on the reins is the horse's reward.'[12] The rider then takes up the contact and repeats the process; in theory the horse should yield more quickly this time, because he will have learnt that yielding means relief from pressure. If the horse resists, the rider persists. 'Don't give until the horse gives!' is usually what the rider is told by trainers and instructors who teach this method. It is stressed that when the horse does yield, even fractionally, he must be instantly – and that does mean instantly – rewarded by the giving of the reins. Otherwise he will learn only to become resistant to the hand.

There are several problems with this method (apart from the fact that it cannot be other than unpleasant for the horse). First, the rider needs to be very powerful, as well as very experienced; they need to use extremely strong forward driving aids to ensure they are not just pulling the horse's head in from the front. Second, it will only work with certain types of horse. The quiet, laid-back, easy-going horse may well adapt to this method with little resistance. Sensitive horses, anxious ones and the fiery or stubborn ones will tend to resist – and resist hard. I have seen a nice part-bred Arabian tanking around an arena, sweating profusely on his neck and shoulders and giving no signs of yielding even after more than an hour of being ridden in this manner. Other horses will simply set their jaws against the bit, using its pressure to gain some relief (in the same way as pressing a finger on the gum can temporarily relieve an aching tooth). Some horses hollow, some overbend; some rear, and others simply run away. Yet a large number of riders and trainers – even those working at the highest level – still insist that this is the only way to achieve true 'lightness'.

Many riders who have been taught to use this method, and whose horses have developed strong resistances as a result, have become disillusioned and, when they have been introduced to more humane and enlightened methods, have then become angry on behalf of their horses. One of the girls who often comes to help look after our horses told me that she, too, had been taught this method at a riding school; all that happened was that the horses became heavier and heavier in the hand, and more and more resistant to the idea of going forward. She sometimes ended a lesson with her hands and wrists almost numb. She felt this couldn't be right but, at 17, thought she lacked the knowledge and experience to argue with her instructor. Like many other riders, she simply assumed the problem lay with her lack of ability. By way of demonstrating to her that this was not so, and that this kind of riding is not only forceful but unnecessary, I first of all rode Zareeba and demonstrated how he could be brought 'on the bit' with the lightest of contacts. Then she rode first him, and finally our supersensitive mare Roxzella, on the lunge and felt for herself what could be achieved simply by adopting the correct posture and giving the aids correctly and sensitively. She said afterwards that she had had no idea riding could be like that, and she felt angry that she and the horses she rode had been put through such an unpleasant, forceful process. 'I just wish', she said to me, 'that there was some way I could go back to those horses and say I'm sorry.'

There is another, far better way of teaching the horse to accept the bit, which does not put any pressure on him, and which involves the rider gently 'sponging' the reins with the fingers to encourage

Lorraine discovers how her position in the saddle helps Roxzella to step out freely

the horse to relax his jaw. There is not room here to describe this method, which is used by all good classical trainers; the reader who wants to learn more should read the excellent descriptions of this method given by Sylvia Loch in *The Classical Rider* and Karin Blignault in *Successful Schooling*. Blignault says that: 'This method is by far the easier and more logical way of creating lightness, balance and roundness. *It is within the grasp of all riders and horses*'[13] (my italics). It is simply not true to maintain, as some trainers do, that with certain types of horse the more forceful method is the only way to get them to accept the bit. It may be that in *exceptional individual circumstances* such a method, used very briefly by an extremely educated rider, may be more effective; but the watchwords here are *exceptional* and *educated*. The latter quality is by no means as widespread, even at the highest levels, as one should hope to see.

And at all levels, but particularly when it comes to more advanced training, truly skilled horsemen and women can bring a horse 'on the bit' without any rein pressure whatsoever — and without the need for any 'conditioning'. This is done by means of the rider's posture and body-language in the saddle, making use of infinitely subtle, almost imperceptible signals which evoke a natural response in the horse. This explains how the great Nuno Oliveira could, in the words of Sylvia Loch: 'collect and balance a young, fit, unschooled horse within seconds . . . a passable piaffe and passage could be extracted from untalented riding hacks before unbelieving eyes'[14]. There was no 'conditioning' involved, and no 'tricks': simply a great horseman holding, as he said, a 'conversation on a higher level'.

Unfortunately, relatively few trainers and riders seem to understand the nature of this dialogue with the horse (although many may achieve it without really knowing how they have done so). On attempts to 'teach' the horse to carry himself in an 'outline' (whether by gadgets or the aforementioned brute force and ignorance), Mary Wanless says in *Ride With Your Mind*: 'this assumes that the horse can be made to look beautiful through being subdued,

Force is simply not necessary: Joanne with Roxzella on the lunge shows how a polite contact is all that is required

Nuno Oliveira and Ansioso. The master recognised that not all horses can carry their heads in the same position, and that some must be allowed to have their noses in front of the vertical

manipulated, and made to be obedient; that he can learn, through domination and reason, to hold his body in a certain way'[15]. She goes on:

> The sad truth is that the rider's attempts to 'teach' him the correct posture inevitably provoke resistance, until she discovers the part she unwittingly plays in perpetuating the cramping and deadening reflexes: the ways in which horses actually respond – seeking or retracting from the rider's seat, hand and leg – are far, far more complex than mere obedience to a system of signals which she, in her infinite wisdom, deigns to teach them.[16]

Finally, she says that:

> . . . even when the horse can be taught to give the right response to an aid, and he has a conscience, and he does what he knows he ought to, he will do it in a carriage which is determined not by how well he has learned his lessons, but by how much he is protecting himself – through his own unconscious mechanisms – from the rider's indelicacies.[17]

In other words, no matter how much the horse has understood what is required of him, and no matter how hard his back end works to send him forward to the bit, in the end the way he carries himself will be determined by the state of his back and neck. If his back is cramped or restricted by a badly balanced or rough rider (not to mention, of course, a badly fitting saddle), or he is held in at the front by harsh hands, then all the 'conditioning' in the world will not help him to work correctly.

As we have seen, the truly skilled rider makes use of the equine understanding of body-language, both to communicate and to gain a response. They do this by means of tiny, subtle shifts of bodyweight and the almost imperceptible contraction and relaxation of certain muscles. But how does the horse interpret what they mean?

At the end of the last chapter I queried whether even the horse's response to the rider's leg was as much of a conditioned response as we would like to believe. Let us return to the engraving I mentioned right at the beginning of this chapter. You will recall that I asked: what could M. Potrin and the young King Louis possibly be doing? What were they pointing at? Molly Sivewright, head of the renowned Talland School of Equitation, has a name for it. She calls it 'the magic spot'.

She first became aware of this when in 1962 Major Boltenstern, Chief Instructor of the Swedish Cavalry, came to Talland to run an Olympic dressage course for the British Horse Society. One of the things that struck Mrs Sivewright was the use the Major made of what came to be called by her family 'Uncle Gosta's little folk dance'. In this, he worked the horse quietly in hand in what Molly Sivewright describes as 'a kind of mobile turn on the forehand, with a few steps of leg-yielding added at intervals, both movements being used to complement each other to remove any constraint and to loosen the horse'[18]. The work was much more subtle than this, of course, involving a combination of forward and restraining aids. One thing that particularly intrigued Mrs Sivewright was the way in which the Major would use the butt-end of the schooling whip, softly or firmly, depending on the individual horse, to press the horse's side just in front of the girth and approximately 20 cm above the elbow. Curious about this, and about the very evident improvement that resulted in horses worked in this way, she wanted to know more. A clue came when she watched Taffy Jenkins, a noted equine manipulator, working on the back of a horse that had been injured. When Mr Jenkins was satisfied that the horse was straight and level, he asked Mrs Sivewright to put her hand on top of the horse's loins, to check his reaction. He then poked the horse in the very same spot that Major Boltenstern did during his 'folk dance' exercises. Mrs Sivewright could feel the reaction – every time Taffy Jenkins poked the horse, his loins sprang up. Mr Jenkins explained that, just where he was pressing, there was a nerve very close to the surface, and that it sparked off a spontaneous signal to the muscles under the lumbar vertebrae, arching and stretching those above the spine. (American paleontologist Dr Deb Bennett demonstrates the same action in her video *Secrets of Conformation*). Mr Jenkins also explained that this nerve connects with the muscles which bring the hind leg on the same side forward. This same nerve (often referred to as the 'intercostal' nerve) also activates the external abdominal muscle, which plays such an important part in lifting the horse's ribcage as part of the mechanism of raising and arching the back. In fact, it would be more correct to speak of a whole group of 'intercostal nerves'. Udo Burger, a noted veterinary surgeon as well as a great horseman, does not mention these intercostal nerves, but instead refers to the external oblique abdominal muscle arising from the ribs. He writes, 'Stimulation of the cutaneous muscle by one leg or spur will cause it to contract, flex the hip joint and draw the hindlimb forward.'[19] (See also Sara Wyche, *Understanding the Horse's Back*, p. 51.)

The value of working the horse in hand in the way described by Molly Sivewright has been known and understood for centuries in the various classical schools of Europe, notably those of the Iberian Peninsula and of Vienna; although, in fact, it is really a shoulder-in practised on the ground. But did the great masters of the seventeenth and eighteenth centuries, upon whose teachings those of the modern classical schools are based, understand the location and effect of the intercostal nerves? If we look at the engraving which started this discussion, I think it very probable that they did. What else could M. de Pluvinel be teaching the young king? However, that is not the end of the story. There is still the consideration of how the action of the intercostal nerves can be used to stimulate responses in the ridden horse.

In 1994, a lively debate on certain aspects of riding was carried on in the letters page of the magazine *Horse & Rider*. One area of debate concerned the term 'on the girth'. One participant objected that this term was a fallacy because if the leg were literally 'on the girth', the toe would be well in advance of the knee, and the rider would therefore be unbalanced. This objection is not new; it was voiced by Mary Wanless in her book *Ride With Your Mind Masterclass*, where she says, 'how can the rider have her body aligned with a vertical shoulder, hip and heel, *and* have her lower leg "on the girth" at the same time? The two are mutually exclusive.'[20]

It gets worse. If we look at the most classical riders of all, the riders of the Spanish Riding School, or masters such as Nuno Oliveira or Egon von Neindorff, we see that their heels are down and back, so that the lower part of the lower leg is quite some way *behind* the girth (this leg position is also specified in the handbook of the German Equestrian Federation). This means that they are actually balanced over their own base of support, i.e. their feet, and can take responsibility for their own bodyweight, instead of handing over that responsibility to the horse – hence the importance of the shoulder/hip/heel line (although the description should really be shoulder/hip/*ankle*, emphasising that the heel is fractionally further back under the seat, otherwise the rider is not truly in balance – try standing with your knees bent as if in the saddle and the heels themselves in line with the shoulder and the hips, and you will see what I mean. See the illustration of Nuno Oliveira on page 213, and that of Arthur Kottas on page 295). However, this poses the problem of how the leg aids are given. Many trainers insist – and they are quite right – that using the leg too far back (except as a specific aid, e.g. for lateral movements, flying changes or advanced collected movements) is likely to upset a sensitive horse and deaden the response of a more phlegmatic one. So how do we reconcile this leg position with that advice?

The answer is that classical riders make use not of the heels, but of the whole lower leg, depending on what they are trying to achieve. As a normal aid to ask the horse to go forward, they use the inside of the lower leg near the top of the boot – which is not only more or less 'on the girth', but actually lies nearer the intercostal nerves which stimulate the correct muscles of the back and hind legs. British trainer Toni Cherrett, who spent six years studying with Hans Riegler, one of the Chief Riders of the Spanish Riding School, says, 'The rider's leg is applied to the horse's sides on the inner area of the lower leg, near the top of a long riding boot.'[21] In 1996 I was asked by an equestrian magazine to write an article on 'forward movement' and how to achieve it. I asked Sylvia Loch (who has also written about the intercostal nerve and its effects) about the use of the leg in this way. 'Oh, yes,' she said immediately. 'My late husband Henry used to use his leg just like that, near the intercostal nerve.' (Lord Loch, an ex-cavalryman, was an exceptional horseman and one of the few Britons to be accepted as an equal by the very classical horsemen of Portugal.)

One of Britain's top dressage riders, renowned for his long, elegant legs, took part in a demonstration not too long ago where one of the horses he rode lacked depth of girth, so that the rider's legs hung down below the horse's barrel. One lady asked him, did it not matter that he could not use the lower part of his lower leg? 'No,' replied the rider, 'why should it?' The more I watch them, the more I am convinced that even some riders who are not aware of using the leg in this way actually do so, while many others, such as the riders mentioned above, use it consciously.

But as this use of the lower leg is not widely taught, how did the term 'on the girth' come into usage? Molly Sivewright provides the answer.

> M. de la Guérinière directed that the rider's lower leg should be on the girth with his spurs touching the horse's sides a hand's breadth, no more, behind the girth. It seemed strange, to the point of contradiction, that M. de la Guérinière, who wore long-necked spurs and trained horses up to high school work, should use his legs comparatively so far forward. Yet all his horses showed true collection of a very advanced standard, and he was most insistent that aids must be invisible, which makes it unlikely that he would countenance riders swinging their legs back and forth. He must have had a feeling for the intercostal nerve even if he did not know its name or its exact whereabouts.[22]

We must also remember that in the seventeenth and early eighteenth centuries a more straight-legged posture was adopted. This was a practical solution for the cavalryman: in conjunction with the high-pommelled, high-cantled saddle, which held the rider in place, a long-legged posture, with the feet thrust against the stirrups, prevented the rider from being lanced out of the saddle in combat. Much more use was made of the thighs and knees as aids; in fact, la Guérinière lists them before the aid of the lower leg. In addition, riders made far greater use of the back, abdomen and thighs to stabilise and lighten the seat than most modern riders do. However, as the needs of the cavalry changed, it was no longer so imperative that the rider should be immovable in the saddle. He needed more freedom of movement in order to use his bodyweight more subtly. M. de la Guérinière himself modified the *selle royale*, then in general use, to a form more like that still used at the Spanish Riding School today. This also meant that the rider needed to be balanced more over his feet, so the lower leg position gradually became modified so that the knees were bent, and the heels were brought back under the rider. But the principle stayed the same: the leg was used where it would produce a natural response.

This can be taken further. I mentioned above how la Guérinière listed the aids of the thighs and knees before those of the lower leg. With sensitive horses these can be used as a very subtle aid to lateral work, or even to aid forward impulsion, as Sylvia Loch mentions in her book *The Classical Seat*. I have found them invaluable with my Arabian gelding, whose thin-skinned ticklishness means the lower leg has to be used with great tact. (*The Classical Seat* also gives a wealth of practical information about how the rider's leg may be used in different positions to obtain different responses.)

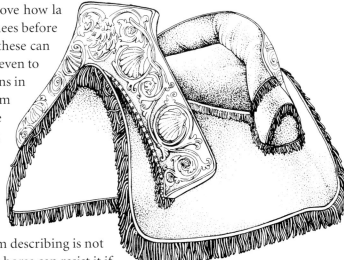

The *selle royale*

We must recognise, however, that what I am describing is not a totally automatic reflex like a knee jerk. The horse can resist it if he is too tense; if the action of the leg or spur is too harsh, when he will tend to lean against it (or in some cases retract his side away from the pressure); or if it is not positive enough he may merely find it annoying, and twitch the skin as if trying to get rid of a fly. As Bürger says, it must become an 'educated reflex which the rider can utilise to stimulate the engagement of each hindleg alternately. A small area of the skin, just behind the girth, can be made so sensitive to the slightest pressure of the lower leg that it is often called the "neuralgic spot," '[23] – a somewhat unfortunate term to use, as it implies pain, and that is the last thing we want to cause the horse (and certainly the last thing Dr Bürger would have intended!). Indeed, if the rider uses the leg sensitively, the horse should feel no pain or discomfort. A much better concept is that of the 'magic spot'!

We must also remember that the precise positioning of the leg is essential – neither too far forward (which apart from anything else unbalances the rider), nor too far back. McTimoney chiropracter Dana Green, who has spent many years treating horses, says,

> . . . the leg position of the rider in relation to the horse's back is of the utmost importance. It is where the back raises . . . that is the crux of the matter. If one wishes the back to raise at and just behind the withers then it is essential that the muscles covering the ribs connected to those vertebrae are stimulated. The resulting expansion of the ribcage, in conjunction with the lifting of the abdomen, raises the horse's back. Thus a leg placed too far behind the girth will encourage the horse to raise its back behind the rider's seat which tends to place the horse on its forehand.

– hence my own emphasis on the use of the leg near the top of the boot, just on the girth. Dana Green goes on to say, 'When one has ridden a horse which comes up underneath one's seat the experience is magical and never to be forgotten.'[24]

The great classical masters have always recognised that the deepest, most effective form of communication with the horse is that which comes from the many tiny, subtle signals between horse and rider, i.e. body language interpreted kinaesthetically in the case of the rid-den horse, and visually as well as kinaesthetically in the case of training from the ground. This is why the old masters have always placed such enormous emphasis on the rider's posi-tion in the saddle. The rider 'talks' to the horse through his body. Karin Blignault, who has studied occupational therapy and neuro-developmental therapy, calls this 'facilitation and inhibition of movement', from two concepts developed by Dr Carl Bobath and his wife Berta in their remedial work which encourages normal movement in spastic children. She describes facilitation of movement as:

> . . . the term used to describe the manner in which we encourage the horse to produce the correct movement – in other words, the aids. We explain to the horse, with our body, what to do with his body. Thus it is a body language which explains, very specifically to the horse, which muscles to contract. We use the aids in a very specific way to influence the horse's natural balance and righting reactions and therefore facilitate the movement we want . . . In the same way we use aids to inhibit (prevent) unwanted movement by relax-ing the muscular activity. This unwanted movement in horses is caused mainly by tension and anticipation. The movement we try to avoid most is hollowing of the horse's neck and back. Through inhibiting the action of the neck and back extensor muscles, we can pre-vent this hollowing.[25]

(For a fuller understanding of what the author is saying here, see *Successful Schooling*, Chapter 4 'The Nervous System and Relaxation'.) Of course, there is still conditioning of a sort involved, since reinforcing an appropriate or correct response by rewarding the horse helps to ingrain that response in his mind until it becomes, as it were, second nature. But this is a far more complex – and effective – concept than the rather simple-minded stimulus-response model we are usually offered. The truly effective rider co-operates with the horse's natural responses, reading his reaction and responding to it in a subtle, intimate conversa-tion, rather than merely giving orders. This is the difference between evoking the horse's nat-ural movements and teaching him 'tricks'.

You will recall that in Chapter 11 we looked at different approaches to training the horse, and at Lucy Rees's analysis of what happens when a horse 'does what he is told', the results varying depending on whether we think in terms of *submission, obedience* or *responsiveness*. 'Each of these attitudes affects the way we go about riding or training.[26] Although the great classical trainers have frequently spoken and written about submission and obedience, in practice they have paid far more attention to the horse's responsiveness. As Sylvia Loch says,

> The ancient riding masters who developed the system which is still used in the classical schools of the world today worked out which signals would aid or help the horse the most. They studied the horse's responsiveness and his involuntary and voluntary actions. They found that certain parts of the horse's anatomy were more sensitive than others; they dis-covered similarly that other parts were weak and could not cope with much weight. That is why the 'correct' placing and application of the aids has become so important to us, not

because it is correct for us, but because it is correct and comfortable for the horse if he is to retain a modicum of his own graceful, economic way of moving.[27]

The key, then, to riding and training the horse is *responsiveness*. This does not mean that we pay attention only to the horse's *physical* responses; we *must*, if we are to be successful, obtain the willing co-operation of his *mind*. Without that, the horse can block all our attempts at influencing him via the aids. We must first establish communication on a mental and emotional level. Writing about the very subject discussed earlier in this chapter, Sylvia Loch observes that: 'no horse can be forced to give his back if he does not want to. An illusion of rounding may indeed be achieved mechanically but lightness has also to involve a giving of his mind.'[28] In other words, before we can even think of rounding the horse's back and engaging his hind legs, we must first engage his mind!

This, in effect, is the whole essence of the real art of riding: not teaching the horse movements and commands, nor demanding total submission, but gaining a response through two-way communication. What, then, is more effective – an elaborate system of training by learned responses, which places the burden of comprehension wholly on the horse; or a system of riding which makes use of his natural responses, to work with him rather than against him? The latter approach does not treat him as an unthinking robot. On the contrary, it liberates him, to be himself, to engage in subtle conversation in the medium he best understands – body-language and response.

Notes

1 Franz Mairinger, *Horses Are Made To Be Horses*, p. 32

2 Mairinger, *Horses Are Made To Be Horses*, p. 31

3 FEI Dressage Rule Book, Object and & General Principles, Clause 107

4 Paul McGreevy, *Why Does My Horse . . .?*, p. 187

5 McGreevy, *Why Does My Horse . . .?*, p. 187

6 McGreevy, *Why Does My Horse . . .?*, p. 187

7 McGreevy, *Why Does My Horse . . .?*, p. 187

8 Mary Wanless, *Ride With Your Mind*, p. 125

9 Brigadier-General Kurt Albrecht, *Principles of Dressage*, p. 35

10 Mary Bromiley, *Natural Methods for Equine Health* (Blackwell, 1994), p. 171

11 Bromiley, *Natural Methods*, p. 171

12 McGreevy, *Why Does My Horse . . .?*, p. 187

13 Karin Blignault, *Successful Schooling*, p. 42

14 Sylvia Loch, *Dressage: The Art of Classical Riding* (Sportsman's Press, 1990), p. 183

15 Wanless, *Ride With Your Mind*, p. 123

16 Wanless, *Ride With Your Mind*, p. 124

17 Wanless, *Ride With Your Mind*, p. 123

18 Molly Sivewright, *Thinking Riding*, Book 1 (J. A. Allen, 1984), p. 234

19 Udo Bürger, *The Way to Perfect Horsemanship* (first pub. in Germany as Vollendete Reitkunst, 1959; tr. Nicole Bartle, J. A. Allen, 1986), p. 240

20 Mary Wanless, *Ride With Your Mind Masterclass* (Methuen, 1991), p. 53

21 Toni Cherrett, 'On The Bit', *Classical Riding Club Newsletter*, no. 2, June 1995

22 Sivewright, *Thinking Riding*, p. 240

23 Bürger, *The Way to Perfect Horsemanship*, pp. 240–41

24 Dana Green in a letter to *Dressage* magazine, January 1998, and in conversation with the author

25 Blignault, *Successful Schooling*, p. 10

26 Lucy Rees, *The Horse's Mind*, p. 168

27 Sylvia Loch, 'The Essence of Classical Riding', *Horse & Rider*, September 1994

28 Sylvia Loch, *The Classical Rider*, p. 261

CHAPTER FOURTEEN

Are Horses People?

Temperament: an individual's character, disposition, and tendencies as revealed in his reactions.

Character: the combination of traits and qualities distinguishing the individual nature of a person or thing.

Personality: the sum total of all the behavioural and mental characteristics by means of which an individual is recognised as being unique.

COLLINS ENGLISH DICTIONARY

O HORSES HAVE personalities, then?' my friend was asked recently at a party. 'Er, yes, of course they do,' she replied, taken aback. It had never occurred to her that anyone could think otherwise: after spending most of her life with horses, she had known so many of them, all with widely varying characters, that the idea of horses not having personalities seemed almost insane.

Some people may object to the use of the word 'personality' in referring to horses or any other non-human animals, but in fact it is quite proper to use the word 'personality' in this context. The word *person* did not originally apply only to human beings, although it is now mostly used in this way: it meant a character in a play – the Latin *persona*, a mask. Hence the word *impersonation*, often used by critics in its true context: an actor *impersonating* a character gives that character life and meaning, effectively bringing it into *being*. *Person* thus refers to a unique individual, one who is unlike any other. We could only sensibly object to calling a horse a *person* if we had irrefutable proof that there were no differences in character or temperament between individual horses – and as we shall see, the very opposite is true.

Yet as Chapter 3 showed, many ethologists and animal behaviour scientists refused, until quite recently, to acknowledge that the 'variability between individual animals' which they could scarcely avoid noticing in the animals they studied, amounted to 'personality'. Even among 'horsey' people there exists a surprising number who have never noticed personality traits in the horses they deal with; or, if they have, they have in many cases firmly discouraged the expression of such individuality. For an even larger number of those involved in the scientific study of horses, the question simply does not arise. So it is that a great deal of the literature concerning the behaviour, handling and training of horses tends to give the impression that all horses will behave in the same manner, with little if any variation; and that, as far as the management and training of the horse is concerned, the same methods must be used regardless of the horse's individual character traits. Indeed, a candidate for examinations awarding recognised qualifications will fail miserably if he or she deviates even slightly from the methods laid down by the examining body. There is no room for consideration of the horse as an individual, let alone for the tailoring of training or management methods to suit the needs of that individual.

So instructors and stable managers are indoctrinated with a 'system' which, while it may be adequate for comparatively straightforward characters with few quirks, simply does not prepare them to deal with cases requiring more understanding. Some, of course, overcome this limitation by virtue of their own independently gained knowledge and understanding; but many others do not, and the results can be very distressing. In the July 1997 issue of *Horse & Rider* a reader described how they had recently removed two horses from one of Britain's leading teaching equestrian centres. Although one of the horses was in excellent condition, the other – a completely different type – was underweight, unhappy and 'no more educated than the day he arrived . . . In short, there was no room at the centre for a horse which did not fit standard rations, standard work, standard rest, standard attention and grooming.' We are, says this reader, 'falling well below standard by continuing to churn out instructors who know very well how to train, load, feed and exercise the bog-standard brown horse, but nothing else.'[1]

Unfortunately, instruction manuals, veterinary training and a great deal of animal behaviour literature all tend (with a few notable exceptions) to reinforce the view of the horse as a creature with a set range of behaviour. Although it is recognised that horses are unpredictable, this is too often set down to external factors, and while that elusive quality known as 'temperament' is sometimes discussed, this is very often reduced to a consideration of whether or not the horse is easily trainable, and it is rarely recognised that horses have greatly differing personalities, just as humans do. The personality of every horse, and every human, reflects the sum of their genetic inheritance plus their lifetime experience, but it is also much more than this: it is that indefinable quality that makes each individual unique. In other words, each horse is more than the sum of his or her parts!

But if we recognise that horses are individuals, how do *they* recognise individuality? We saw in Chapter 10 how horses may leave scent-messages, the equine equivalent of 'Kilroy was here'. However, to leave messages identifying oneself presupposes that one *has* a sense of identity. To many people who are in daily close contact with them it might seem obvious that of course horses have such a sense of identity. Owen MacSwiney suggests that animals, and very young children, do not think of themselves in the first person singular. His two-year-old step-grand-daughter Philippa did not say, '*I* want teddy'; she said '*Lippa* wants teddy,' – her name was thus her personal identification. In the same way, he suggests, horses identify

Kilroy was here!

themselves with their given names, 'or the name used in relation to it. The name becomes the first person to the animal.'[2] So do horses have names for themselves and for each other, apart from those given to them by humans? At first sight, this might seem a fanciful question. After all, if they do not have language as we know it, how can they have names?

But is a spoken language necessary? Donald Griffin, a pioneer in the study of animal cognition, considers that animals might have names for each other, even though these would not, of course, be expressed in words. And we have already seen, in Chapter 5, that actual words are not always necessary for even advanced conceptual thought. We have also seen how scent-marking could be considered a form of 'signature', and considered the possibility that horses might think in images, rather like the concept of pictograms. Might such an image not be the equivalent of a name?

Or what about sounds? Konrad Lorenz observes that:

Among several species of birds that mark their territory acoustically there is great individual difference of sound expression, and some observers are of the opinion that, in such species, the personal visiting card is of special significance. While Heinroth interpreted the crowing of the cock with the words, 'That is a cock!' Bäumer, the most knowledgeable of all domestic-fowl experts, heard in it the far more special announcement, 'That is the cock Balthazar!'[3]

In the same vein, might a horse's whinny not serve also as a name? Each horse has a very distinctive whinny which clearly identifies him or her to other horses. Humans too, if they know the horse well enough, can identify the voice, just as we recognise the voices of human friends and acquaintances. If we know the latter well enough, and they telephone us, we may very often not even need to be told who is speaking, because we know their voices so well. Exactly the same can apply with horses. If I am working in the stableyard out of sight of the field and I hear a horse call out, I know instantly who it is. Roxzella has a loud, rasping call that in a human could, for the most part, only be achieved by many years of overindulgence in alcohol and tobacco. Tiff's whinny might best be described as sounding like the bleat of a demented nanny goat through a megaphone. Kiri's is a loud, but more demanding, truculent tone. Toska, her son, has a high-pitched, babyish-sounding voice; Kruger's is not quite so high-sounding, and with many variations in pitch and tone. Nivalis, the stallion, has (like many stallions, except when they are roused) a rather wimpish, high-pitched whinny with undertones of his mother's seductive rasp. His daughter Imzadi has a high-pitched squeal;

and finally, Zareeba has a voice which ranges from a *basso profundo* (when he wants his dinner) to a melodious *coloratura soprano*.

In his celebrated *Narnia* chronicles, C. S. Lewis makes imaginative use of this idea. In *The Horse and His Boy* the talking horse Bree tells the boy Shasta that his full name is Breehy-hinny-brinny-hoohy-hah — which sounds like exactly the kind of name a horse would have. Is there any good reason why horses should not identify themselves – and others known to them – in such a fashion?

Yet to a surprisingly large number of people, even those who do deal with horses on a regular basis, this idea would seem incomprehensibly twee or fanciful. The effect this kind of negative thinking has on our relationships with horses can be seen in a number of ways, one of the most curious of which is precisely this general attitude to the naming of horses.

If we meet a stranger only briefly, we are not generally perturbed by the idea of not knowing their name. However, if we need to talk to them for any length of time, we tend to feel uneasy if we have no means of addressing them directly. Being able to call them by their name confirms their 'personhood' and establishes them as someone we are able (we hope) to talk to. It seems inconceivable that we should work with someone for even a short space of time and not know their name. If I should inadvertently call someone, whose name I ought to know, by the wrong name, I feel disturbed because I have done them a discourtesy; I have failed to pay sufficient attention to *who they are*. Before we can communicate meaningfully, we need to know who we are talking to; and that means not confusing them with someone else or disregarding their identity, their *personhood*, if you like.

Few people would seriously attempt to train a dog without first ensuring that the dog knew, and responded to, its name. Yet there is still a tendency for people to believe that horses do not respond to their names as dogs do and that it is therefore unnecessary to call them by name. An example of this was afforded by the late Moyra Williams. In her book *Horse Psychology* we find the following statements:

> In view of the undoubted quickness with which horses learn to distinguish verbal commands, it may seem surprising that they do not learn to come, like dogs, when they hear their names. If a group of horses is grazing together and one is called, it never shows any sign of recognition; nor, if a stable is entered and a particular horse's name is mentioned, will there be a single individual response. Admittedly, the clang of a bucket will cause all heads to be raised and will arouse generalised whinnies of expectancy. But no single whinny will sound for a single bucket; no single horse comes forward to a single name.[4]

When I first read this I found it extraordinary, and still do, having no idea why Dr Williams should have had this experience with horses when my own (and that of many other people) has been almost entirely the opposite. All our horses know their names and will respond to them both inside the stable and out of it. The late Colonel Alois Podhajsky, Director of the Spanish Riding School for 26 years, mentions several instances of horses responding to their names. In his moving tribute to the horses he had worked with in the course of a long career,

Podhajsky recalls the Thoroughbred Bengali, the last charger he rode in the Austrian army. Bengali's life was saved by his response to his name. The horse had fallen into the Danube near a dam while they were out riding, and it seemed inevitable that he would be carried away by the fast current.

> Instinctively I called his name – it seemed a weak attempt to interfere with inevitable fate. But the familiar voice worked wonders. Bengali lifted his head, neighed hoarsely, and began to fight the current with all his strength in order to reach the bank where I stood. It was quite a task to drag him up the steep and slippery dam to safety.[5]

On another occasion Bengali and Podhajsky were going across country when Bengali unseated his rider by putting in an unexpected buck jump. Bengali set off for home, but his rider did not relish the prospect of a long walk back. 'As loud as I could I yelled "Bengali", but without much hope, for he was rapidly disappearing in the distance. When he heard my voice, however, he turned around and came toward me in a large circle and was calm and willing when I mounted into the saddle again.'[6] Podhajsky later describes an episode involving another of his horses, the great Nero, with whom he gained the bronze medal in dressage at the Olympic Games of 1936. Podhajsky had been away for some time, and on his return he went to see Nero, as he always did after an absence from home. However, while Podhajsky was away, Nero had been taken to the stables for sick horses, which housed some 40 other horses as well. In the dim light Podhajsky could not find him. 'Disappointed and sad I was about to leave when as a last attempt I called him by his pet name, "Burschi". Immediately Nero answered by neighing softly from the far corner of the stables.'[7]

Owen MacSwiney, who spent many years training horses from the ground, says that: 'It is evident that every horse identifies itself with its name which it regards as peculiar to itself.

Our horses come when called: Zareeba gallops to greet Brian

Responses to the name may be vocal even when the familiar voice calling it is out of sight.'[8] Indeed, this has been our experience. If my husband is out of Nivalis's sight and calls the latter's name, he and he alone will answer. If I go out into the field and call 'Zareeba!', he will look up and amble or trot over for a scratch or a mint, or simply to rub his head on me by way of greeting. None of the others will respond, unless their own names are called (or unless they sense that mints are in the offing but then I rarely take mints or other titbits out into the field).

Kruger comes when called, but Zareeba *(left)* wants to join in

Here, I think, is where Dr Williams made her error in the experiment she tried, to see if she could train horses to respond to their names. She attempted to get two horses to come in response to their names for a reward of carrots; but no matter how often she tried, both horses would come running up to her, nudging her hands and pockets for the carrots they knew were there. When it comes to titbits, in such situations horses can be very socialist in attitude. They seem to feel that if one gets a titbit, all should get one regardless of whose name was called. Dr Williams blamed the horses for their 'obtuseness'; it did not seem to occur to her that it might have been her experiment that was inappropriate.

For whatever reason, many other people feel as Dr Williams did, to the extent that naming horses, and getting them to respond to their names, is somehow seen as unimportant. This tells us a great deal about prevalent attitudes towards relationships with horses. Sylvia Loch describes how, during the course of a clinic, she was shocked to find that a woman taking part in the clinic had had her horse for six months and had not yet named her. Sylvia immediately named the horse for the woman, and by the end of the lesson the horse was responding to her new name. 'I could not contemplate working with an animal even for half an hour without giving it the security and identity of a name . . . Horses, like people, need names. Only with a name can you feel singular, unique, special. How can a relationship blossom and grow if there is no sense of identity?'[9]

Indeed, in many cultures it is considered of the greatest importance that horses should be given a name and that they should know and respond to it. The Arabs have been particularly insistent on this point. In her journal, Lady Anne Blunt of the famous Crabbet Arabian Stud describes the *bedawin* rituals that followed the birth of the colt foal Ibn Mesaoud in Egypt, 1892.

Khuddr said, 'What have you named him? Is he not Mesaoud's son?'. 'He is,' we said, 'but we have not yet given him a name.' 'Oh but you ought,' Khuddr replied, 'he ought to learn his name at once so that he should know it and he must be called Mesaoud', and before anyone could protest the huge fat figure of Khuddr had rushed at the foal, thrown two sausage like arms round its neck and was bellowing into its ears 'Mesaoud, Mesaoud . . .' in deafening tones which drowned the feeble voices of those who tried to expostulate. 'Now,' drawing himself up in triumph, said Khuddr, 'he will never forget *that*.' No indeed, I should think he *never* would.[10]

However, in the Western world at least, the whole business of naming horses illustrates how ambiguous attitudes to them really are. Many names seem to be merely a label for a piece of property, vying with those given to pedigree show dogs for daftness and lack of euphony. Most horses, of course, have stable names which often bear no relation to their registered or given names. But it is the way in which even these names are expressed that the ambiguity really shows up.

It is a convention in some parts of the world to enclose the name of a horse in double quotation marks – so my horse Zareeba would appear in print as "Zareeba" (e.g. Mrs L. Skipper riding "Zareeba"). This was a convention I had always found mildly irritating, but I had never really understood the reason for my irritation until I read Vicki Hearne's book *Adam's Task: Calling Animals by Name*. In this splendid, often difficult but always rewarding book, Hearne points out the way in which this convention seems designed to deny horses any real sense of identity. The very fact of enclosing the name in what she calls 'scare quotes' serves to indicate that these are not real names, and the creatures behind them have no true identity. To illustrate this she tried an experiment on her husband, the philosopher Robert Tragesser. She asked him to look at several sentences, such as the following: 'I am married to "Robert".' In each of the sentences, as in this one, his name was enclosed in double quotes. As he looked at them, Tragesser felt a jolt of uneasiness: 'as though what had been a name for a person – his person – had suddenly become something like a label, and the uneasiness – the dis-ease – is the uneasiness of someone the labeler can't and won't talk to'[11].

And as we have seen, this question of communication – of 'talking' or 'not talking' – is at the root of much of this negative thinking about horses. How can you talk to someone you don't believe has a real identity? It would surely be like talking to the furniture.

Apart from the question of their own identity, how well do horses recognise and remember individuals of either their own or other species? Opinion is divided on this question. While it is generally accepted that horses can remember and recognise old equine friends even after many years of separation, a significant number of people question whether horses have the same capacity to remember human acquaintances. Although she acknowledges that horses may often remember other horses very well (and, of course, their human handlers when they are in regular contact with them), equestrian writer Susan McBane says that:

. . . horses' memories of people after a considerable separation, say months or years, are either not so good or else horses soon 'get over' the parting and are not particularly both-ered about renewing the association. My own horse's breeder came to visit him six months after I had bought him and he showed no sign whatsoever of even recognising her, let alone being pleased (or otherwise!) to see her, yet she had done virtually everything for him, and seen him more or less every day of his life since he was born. Similar happenings have also occurred in other people's experiences.[12]

I do not think we should draw any hasty conclusions from this about horses' abilities to recognise human individuals after a long separation. For every instance of apparent non-recognition, one could probably cite a case that showed the opposite. My own Arab gelding Zareeba had not seen *his* breeder for a number of years. Then one day the breeder came to see us unexpectedly. Zareeba was out in the field, at least 200 metres away from the field gate. When George walked into the field, Zareeba looked up, whinnied out, and trotted straight over to him with every sign of pleasure and affection. Although he is a friendly soul who loves visits from humans, whether strangers or not, he does not normally whinny out to just anyone in this way. He clearly recognised George as someone who had been special to him, and treated him with an affectionate familiarity far beyond what he would have extended to a stranger.

Alois Podhajsky once took over the training of a difficult mare, Judith, with whom he developed a tremendous rapport. Unfortunately, to Podhajsky's distress, when Judith's train-ing was sufficiently advanced her owner took the opportunity to sell her abroad. Podhajsky did not see her again until he went to a horse show in Switzerland a year later. Judith's new owner showed her to Podhajsky.

> She stood apathetically in her box, not paying any attention to her surroundings. I called her by the pet name I had used with her. As long as I live I will never forget how she lifted her head and pricked her ears as if searching her memory for the owner of this voice. Slowly she turned around, came towards us, and greeted me with a soft neighing, rubbing her nose on my shoulder in a familiar gesture. Her owner watched with amazement and murmured: 'How funny, never has this strange creature come towards me. I could have called as often as I wanted!'[13]

Henry Blake tells the story of Darwi, a pony he bought for his daughter Paddy when she was about three years old. As Darwi was so small, Blake got his neighbour's young daughter, Doreen, to back him. Darwi and Doreen quickly developed a great affinity for each other. In due course Darwi was also ridden by Paddy, and then, after she had outgrown him, he was sold on. No more was heard of him for eight years; the Blakes moved to Wales and Doreen got a job and also moved away. Then one day Henry Blake's father was at a gymkhana where he was greeted by none other than Doreen, who had a very distinctive voice. They had been talking for a few minutes when they realised that a pony at the far end of the field was whin-nying its head off. The next thing, a pony with a very small child on its back came galloping towards them. The pony skidded to a halt just where Mr Blake and Doreen were standing. 'My father rescued the child, and the pony proceeded to greet Doreen. After eight years he had recognised her voice from the other side of the field. I do not suppose Doreen had handled Darwi for more than three or four months. But a bond was there between them even after eight years.'[14]

Cheryl Proctor, who runs a riding stables in the Lake District, recounts a story about an old pony they had on loan when she was a young girl. The pony, Tessa, had been with the same family for many years before Cheryl's family took her on permanent loan; she had been the first and only pony of a girl who had since grown up, married and was living in Australia. She and Tessa had not seen each other for a number of years.

Then one summer Tessa's owner turned up unexpectedly to visit her. Cheryl recalls, 'I have never seen such a reaction from a horse – when she saw her old owner she was so happy to see her, she whinnied and whickered and nuzzled'. One interesting thing that came to light was that, as a child, Tessa's owner had taught the pony to say 'please' by lifting up a front leg. 'We never knew this and it wasn't until Tessa saw her old owner that she said "please" so enthusiastically that she nearly fell over. It was a lovely sight to see, and we were all quite overwhelmed with Tessa's sheer joy.'[15]

The reasons why some horses appear not to remember people after long separations, while others clearly do, may lie in the different personalities of the horses involved, as well as – perhaps – the degree of empathy which existed between those involved. Perhaps they don't always choose to show their recognition. Perhaps they really don't remember the person involved. Who knows? After all, *we* sometimes forget the names and faces of people we have not seen for a long time. What is important is that we realise that horses in general *do* have this ability to remember and recognise humans after a period of time, whether or not *all* horses are able (or willing) to do so.

While appreciation of this ability is important to our understanding of our relationships with horses, it can also lead to some very strange conclusions. Stephen Budiansky says, 'The ability of horses to recognise individuals may also explain why some riding horses appear to know – and put to the test by disobedience – unfamiliar riders, and why some horses can be successfully managed only by certain people.'[16] Well, certainly riding horses know when they have an unfamiliar rider on their backs. Given their ability to recognise individuals by sight, smell and the sound of their voice, not to mention their incredible sensitivity to body-language, in particular with relation to touch, it would be very odd indeed if they did *not* recognise a different rider! (Equally odd is the assumption that 'disobedience' automatically means the horse is putting the rider to the test. As previous chapters have shown, there may be many reasons for 'disobedience', including faulty communication!)

Horses whose personalities have not been repressed but allowed to flourish often show a degree of curiosity about human proceedings that goes far beyond any simplistic stimulus-response effect. In many cases the initial interest seems to develop into a lasting fascination. Classical Riding Club member Sam Tobias reports that her Arabian gelding Ali (who, very sadly, had to be put to sleep before this book was finished) used to love watching football and rugby matches. On match days she would turn him out of her gate, let go of him, and he would walk into the car park of the local Rugby Club and stand and watch the game. Perhaps it was the sounds and movement that fascinated him; perhaps it was the atmosphere. Or maybe, as he was a horse who adored human company, he simply liked being with a lot of people. Who can say?

In fact, Ali liked to share in whatever human activity was going on around him. If the farrier had a cup of tea, Ali would have one too; he also liked sandwiches and fizzy drinks, even a can of lager if he could persuade people to share such goodies with him. The same horse also loved human children; he would stop dead in his tracks at the sight of them and put his head down for them to pet him. If he saw a pushchair he and Sam had to stop so that Ali could see the child. Sam did not encourage him in all this; it was just something he did of his own accord.

Any number of horses develop idiosyncratic tastes for human food. Several of our own horses have shown such inclinations: Zareeba likes most non-meat-based human foods, especially salt and vinegar crisps and cheese sandwiches, although if all that is on offer is cheese and ham, he will carefully eat the cheese and the bread and spit out the ham! His girlfriend Roxzella

Ali adored human company (Samantha Tobias)

adores Batchelors Spicy Mexican Tomato Soup; Nivalis, her son, is partial to a cup of coffee, as is his daughter Imzadi – and all like those extremely strong, fiery throat lozenges called Fisherman's Friends. Like Sam Tobias, we did not deliberately set out to create such tastes in them; they revealed them spontaneously by showing curiosity about what we were eating, and asking – in that inimitable way horses have – to share it. Zareeba is a past-master at this, having quickly learned that humans find his facial expressions irresistible. When he was quite young I taught him, as part of his education, to take a mint from between my lips without snatching. In order to see where my mouth was (as horses cannot see directly in front of their noses) he had to tilt his head up and to one side, which gave him a very comical expression. He soon found that humans were enchanted by this, and turned it into a sure-fire way of coaxing goodies from them!

Having established, then, that horses have very well-defined personalities, how can we begin to determine what *type* of personality a horse possesses?

Numerous ways of assessing this have been put forward over the years. Dr Moyra Williams believed that differences in temperament linked to coat colour might be associated with the distribution of sensory nerve-endings in the skin.

Some horses develop peculiar tastes: Arabian filly Princess Carmara shares Joanne's glass of cider

In albinos there is no doubt that sensory deficiencies in the eyes coincide with a lack of pigmentation in the skin, so that the lack of pigmentation in greys as a whole may well be accompanied by a sparsity of sensory nerves in the skin, making them frequently docile and easy to handle.[17]

There are several problems with this ingenious theory. First, the eyes of albinos tend to show more, not less, sensitivity to certain stimuli, notably sunlight. Second, there is the fact that the gene which causes greying in horses is quite different from those genes responsible for the forms of 'albinism' found in horses – cremello and perlino, well as the true (and rare) white. These three all have pink skin, whereas greys have dark skins (except under true white markings, where the underlying skin will usually be pink). Finally, there are probably as many 'fiery' greys as there are 'fiery' chestnuts; one only has to think of eventer Ian Stark's famous 'grey boys', Glenburnie and Murphy Himself. Few people who remember the great Murphy in his heyday would call him 'docile'!

Still, there appears to be something immensely attractive to many people in the idea that a horse's (or a human's) personality can be attributed to external, easily recognised factors. One intriguing example of such wishful thinking is that of the pseudo-science of phrenology. At the beginning of the nineteenth century a man called Gall believed that there was a connection between an individual's character and the bumps on the outside of their skull.

This 'science' was named phrenology, and Gall claimed that the degree of development of the skull bumps could indicate the corresponding level of development of different qualities in various areas of the brain.

Unfortunately for this ingenious hypothesis, it did not fulfil its promise, since specific qualities that Gall identified (such as a love of children) are not governed by correspondingly specific areas of the brain. Although phrenology enjoyed some popularity through-out the nineteenth century (and has been resurrected several times since then), it gradually faded into obscurity. Gall did attempt to apply the principles of phrenology to horses, but the results have more curiosity value than any practical use as a guide to equine personality.

It is often said that a person's character may be read from their features, and various attempts have been made to give this belief a scientific basis. Perhaps the best known of such attempts was made by the nineteenth-century Italian criminologist Cesare Lombroso, who studied the facial characteristics and skull shapes of the inhabitants of

Zareeba knows humans find his facial expressions irresistible

state prisons. Lombroso cited the high incidence of small skulls, heavy jaws and pointed ears as evidence that these features denoted a 'criminal' type. The problem with this hypothesis – which was quickly pointed out – was that there were many people outside the prisons who also had these facial characteristics but who were not criminals or of 'criminal tendencies'; and that there were also many others who *were* criminals who certainly did not conform to this type.

This is the weakness of this approach: that it provides convenient 'labels' for preconceived stereotypes which may bear little or no relation to reality. Nevertheless, such an apparently easy method of assessing character has continued to be popular, whether the subjects are humans or horses. Jan May, for example, divides horses into what she calls 'three distinct hierarchical categories'[18]. These are:

Group 1   dominant;
Group 2   responsive;
Group 3   indifferent.

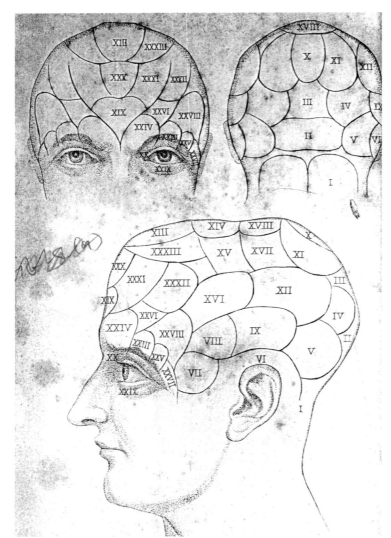

Gall & Spurzheim divided the human brain into areas which supposedly governed various faculties

I	Organ of amativeness
II	philoprogenitiveness (*love of offspring*)
III	inhabitiveness?
IV	adhesiveness
V	combativeness
VI	destructiveness
VII	constructiveness
VIII	covetiveness
IX	secretiveness
X	self-esteem
XI	love of approbation
XII	cautiousness
XIII	benevolence
XIV	veneration
XV	hope
XVI	ideality
XVII	conscientiousness
XVIII	firmness
XIX	individuality
XX	form
XXI	size?
XXII	weight and momenta?
XXIII	colouring
XXIV	locality
XXV	order?
XXVI	time?
XXVII	number
XXIII	Organ of tune
XXIX	language
XXX	comparison
XXXI	causality
XXXII	wit
XXXIII	imitation

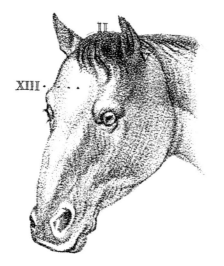

Gall & Spurzheim also tried to apply this principle to horses

After setting out this rather simplistic group of categories, she goes on to describe what can be learned of the horse's state of mind from its facial expressions (e.g. the expression of the eye, the ears, the mouth and lips, etc.) and tail carriage. However, while – as we have already seen – all of these are indeed a reliable indication of the horse's mental and emotional state, all they really tell us is what those states are at any given time. They do not provide more than a passing indication of the horse's real character or personality. As with humans, those can only be accurately gauged by close observation of how the horse behaves and reacts in a variety of situations.

Even so, many people insist that a horse's character can be read accurately from its outward appearance. Linda Tellington-Jones, for example, has devised a system of judging a horse's temperament by the position and type of the various whorls (or swirls, as she calls them) which appear in the horse's coat hair.

Every horse breeder or owner who has ever had to complete an identification form for breed registration, or who has watched a vet complete an identification chart for vaccination documents, will know how complex these patterns of whorls can be. Linda Tellington-Jones maintains that they are the equine equivalent of fingerprints, each pattern of whorls distributed throughout the body being unique to each individual. This is somewhat contentious, as some scientific authorities believe the equine equivalent of fingerprints to be the leg chestnuts, which may be equally unique to each horse. To my knowledge this has never been thoroughly established, but both ideas may indeed be correct – maybe the horse has two sets of 'fingerprints'! However, Tellington-Jones goes further and states that the type and positioning of whorls on the face can be used as a reliable means of determining a horse's personality. She says that this method was used by gypsy horsemen for centuries, and further cites the lore of the *bedawin* who, she says, placed much significance on the interpretation of swirls. Unfortunately for this latter example, it depends largely on which tribe is considered, as *bedawin* lore regarding desirable markings in horses (whether hair swirls, white markings or whatever) is (or was, as a great deal of such lore is now gradually being forgotten among the *bedu*) largely a matter of fashion, and there are almost as many contradictory *bedawin* sayings about desirable markings as there are horses left in the desert!

Nevertheless, Linda Tellington-Jones clearly believes that a study of such swirls can give a valid 'reading' of the horse's character type. She cites the case of a horse who was so vicious he was about to be put down. Tellington-Jones looked at the horse, and from the swirl on his face, which extended several inches below his eyes, concluded that the horse was not by nature aggressive, as horses with such swirls generally tend to be friendly. She decided that there must be some specific cause for his aggressive behaviour. She examined the horse (who had to be cross-tied before she could do so), and found that the horse was in considerable pain from a sore neck and back. Remedial body work (see Chapter 17) relieved his pain and he became a changed horse. Linda Tellington-Jones says, 'Now, if that horse had not had long swirls, I wouldn't have been so quick to think the problem was a physical one, but his behaviour was extremely uncharacteristic for the type of swirl he did have, so I looked for pain in his body.'[19]

But surely any observer who knows anything at all about equine behaviour and psychology would *always* consider the possibility of physical pain before condemning a horse as 'vicious'. They would also consider what psychological as well as physical experiences might have rendered the horse so difficult to handle. There is no need to look at facial swirls before considering such possibilities. This is not to say that genuine 'rogues' – the equine equivalent of the human psychopath – do not exist, but they are very rare, for the simple reason that true psychopaths are rare in non-human animals anyway. In the wild, among such intensely social creatures as horses, they would seldom survive, let alone be allowed to reproduce, as they would disrupt the cohesion of whatever group they attached themselves to and would almost certainly be driven out. However, thanks to human interference in natural patterns of reproduction and survival, they *do* occasionally crop up in domestic horses. As William Steinkraus says,

> . . . as a rider's experience expands he will begin to recognise the telltale gestures and expressions that distinguish the rogue, or the genuinely dishonest horse, from the variously spoiled and frightened horses that present some of the same symptoms. When a true rogue is encountered, the best advice is probably to dispose of him, no matter how beautiful he is, or how wonderfully he can go 'when he wants to'. However, such horses are very rare – and should a rider find he is encountering very many truly stubborn or unwilling temperaments, he should examine his own skills and find what he is doing that has made him such a bad horseman.[20]

To be fair, Linda Tellington-Jones does say that swirls should not be read on their own when analysing personality, but as one of numerous contributing factors. However, the problem with attributing such importance to external features is that it encourages people to ignore factors that may be of much greater significance in determining the cause of problems. For example, Tellington-Jones cites the case of a professional rider whose horse was giving her a very hard time. Although she had bought him to train for dressage, she felt she was making no real progress with him.

> I took one look at the horse and thought, well, no wonder she's feeling frustrated. The horse had three clustered swirls on the forehead, short ears set close together, very narrow nostrils, small eyes and an extremely short mouth. The ear, nostril, eye and mouth characteristics formed a picture of a resistant horse with low intelligence, and the three swirls added a factor of unpredictability.[21]

But how can one make such a snap judgement without taking into account the many other factors which might play their part in creating the horse's resistance? I can immediately think of several which might explain such problems: a horse with narrow nostrils, small eyes and a very short mouth might be experiencing problems with breathing, defective eyesight and incorrect bitting for his type of mouth. That is without even beginning to consider whether the rider's training methods were suited to this horse and whether she was a sympathetic, well-balanced rider (the fact of someone being a professional is no guarantee of any of these things). How can one possibly judge a horse's intelligence in such a cavalier way, without close, detailed and impartial study?

Tellington-Jones advised this rider to sell the horse to someone who would be intrigued by a complex character and who wanted a challenge. She reports that the rider was relieved to hear that the fault was not with her training. I expect she was. Riders and trainers usually are relieved to hear advice which lets them off the hook, which effectively takes away from them that 'burden of judgement' which I described in Chapter 9. It is not clear whether, in the instance just described, any attempt was even made to assess whether the training method being used was suitable for this horse. It is so much easier to blame the horse, for being stubborn, resistant, intractable, vicious, stupid or whatever – anything, in fact, which relieves people of the responsibility of treating the horse as an individual, of learning what makes that individual 'tick' and then matching their approach in training and riding to his or her character.

Failure to accept this responsibility can have tragic, or near-tragic, results. One horse for whom such failure almost ended his career before it had properly begun is Immortal, a Lusitano gelding. Immortal was bought in Portugal by a lady who had fallen in love with the breed. After a long search, during which many wonderful horses were considered and rejected, she found Immortal – not the schoolmaster she had been looking for, but a totally green four year old. Undaunted, and convinced that this was *the* horse for her, she bought him and arranged for him to be backed and ridden away in Portugal. Some weeks later she returned to Portugal to ride the horse herself for a week at the schooling yard where he had been backed. She describes this as quite an experience. She rode her green horse in the school with six or seven stallions, and found his manners to be perfect. In due course Immortal was brought to the UK where his behaviour continued to be exemplary. His owner rode him both in the school and out hacking, and she says that he was 'immediately bomb-proof in traffic'. For three months she continued to ride him, during which time they had a few exciting experiences but nothing more than one would expect from a totally green young horse.

At the end of this time, Immortal's owner had to go abroad for a couple of months, so she arranged for him to go to a local couple who were well known and had a great deal of experience in schooling young horses. She did not expect to find a perfectly schooled horse on her return, but she did think his schooling would at least have advanced during the time she was away. To her horror, when she returned to this country she was informed that the horse was a killer and that she must not ride him. She was told to get rid of the horse and that she must be careful if she sold him because he might kill someone. The people with whom she had left him had ridden Immortal, but considered him so dangerous that they refused to let any of their staff ride him. Apparently he had been so touchy that they were unable to tighten a girth or adjust a stirrup leather while sitting on him. They had tried cantering him in the school non-stop for an hour on each rein but could not tire him out or quieten him.

Immortal's owner was devastated. Her dream horse had turned into a potential killer, and she was being advised to get rid of him! She took him home and poured out her troubles to her teacher. Fortunately, the latter was very sympathetic, and said that even though she had not seen the horse since his return, she would ride him and assess him. She did this and reported that he was fine; she could even, while riding him on the road, adjust both the girth and the stirrups. The problem was that by this time his owner, unnerved by what she had been told, was terrified of him; but she loved him so dearly that she felt they simply had to try to form a partnership.

With the help of Lucy Rees, who hacked the horse out and, in the words of Immortal's owner, 'had a lot of fun looking over gates and hopping up and down banks', Sylvia Loch who nursed Immortal and his owner through a three-day clinic, and sympathetic instructor Carolyn Morgan, the partnership did, eventually, start to materialise. After six months his owner felt confident enough with him to start riding him out alone. 'During this time', she says, 'he became less tense, more relaxed but needing extreme care in handling – a slightly tight rein and he would tense, too strong an aid and he would worry. Success depended upon a very correct classical seat, calm, calm hands, still legs and loose rein.'[22] All aids had to be extremely subtle – a question of slight shifts of position or contraction of the muscles. Perseverance paid off. Since then, Immortal and his owner have gone on to compete successfully in both dressage and endurance events; the horse who was branded a killer is now loved and admired by everyone who comes to know him.

But why did the genuine (if green) horse who came out of Portugal turn into a potentially lethal neurotic? It would be facile – and incorrect – to suggest that, as is often the case with horses that change hands, his 'true' nature did not reveal itself until he had settled in. Throughout the time when he was first bought, backed and ridden away, there was nothing in his behaviour to suggest that he was temperamentally suspect. Nor was there anything to indicate that some experience during that time had unhinged him. On the contrary, apart from the stress of a long journey to the UK (from which he had had three months to recover) Immortal had suffered no traumatic experience that would account for his sudden change. True, he had a lot of changes to cope with in those three months, but most horses do not turn killers overnight in such circumstances. So what went wrong?

The people who declared him to be a killer were not monsters. They did not beat him up or mistreat him in any way that would be generally recognised as mistreatment. Theirs was simply a failure of understanding. Having had some considerable success with certain types of horse, they did not sufficiently recognise the differences in character, temperament and personality that one might expect to find in a sensitive, hot-blooded horse. They rode him exactly as they would have ridden a more phlegmatic horse, with disastrous results. Immortal's problem was that he was not only very sensitive (as Lusitanos tend to be), he was also very willing. He wanted to do his best to please, and while he was ridden and handled in a manner that took into account his sensitivity, and while he understood exactly what was expected of him, he was fine. It was when he encountered people who did not know how to cope with a character such as his that – like Lucy Rees's Lipizzaner stallion, described in Chapter 9 – he felt he was fighting for his life. Ridden in a style to which he was not accustomed, with a very tight, short rein and much stronger aids than the very light, subtle aids to which Portuguese horses are trained, pushed into an endless canter in futile attempts to tire him out (instead of being allowed the balance and calm which he so badly needed), he felt restricted, confused, worried and – when there was no release from this tension – increasingly desperate. Like most horses who feel themselves under unendurable pressure, he tried to escape: bolting was his way of trying to find release. Other equally sensitive horses might have reacted differently; my Arab mare Roxzella, for example, might well have taken refuge in rearing, as that is her response to even a hint of too much pressure on her mouth.

The lesson Immortal teaches us is that while the fundamental principles of horse-training remain the same, the method used must vary according to each individual horse. As Alois Podhajsky says, 'Without the subtle variations and adaptations of the method to the individual, riding would remain a sport limited to the level of a handicraft without ever rising to the sphere of art.'[23] Podhajsky goes on to compare the type of horses usually ridden in dressage competitions (and often in other types of competition too) with the Lipizzaners with whom he worked for over 20 years. He says that:

> . . . they do not have the pronounced individuality of the Lipizzaner stallions and surrender more readily to their rider. They submit more philosophically to the rider's will and so are easier to ride and may be ridden in a more primitive way. If, however, one of these creatures rebels against unjust treatment, he is quickly labelled 'outlaw' or 'rogue' and given up to disappear in the mass of unhappy horses.[24]

Sadly for horses such as Immortal, this is also the fate of many sensitive, hot-blooded horses who simply do not conform to rigid ideas of how horses should react to training. Podhajsky's comments on the Lipizzaner apply just as much to any other intelligent, sensitive, high-couraged horse: 'His intelligence, together with his physical power, demand a thorough understanding of his mentality and an individual approach to his training. In other words, his education must not follow a rigidly set pattern.'[25]

So, if we reject the rather crude attempts to 'categorise' equine personality types mentioned above, is there any other way in which we can attempt to describe and understand the different types of equine character?

The famous Russian scientist I. P. Pavlov (he of the 'conditioned reflexes') made detailed studies of experimentally induced neurosis (achieved by creating conditions of chronic conflict) in dogs. He found that certain dogs became savage, some withdrawn and anxious, while others simply ignored the conflict. Pavlov concluded that the dogs' ability to cope with conflict had a great deal to do with their personality type, and he classified them into four types:

- **choleric** – aggressive, hasty; reacts to conflict by becoming overreactive and savage;
- **melancholic** – gentle and timid; reacts to conflict by withdrawing, becoming afraid of everything;

- **sanguine** – strong, bold and lively; continues to respond even in the face of conflict;
- **phlegmatic** – strong and easy-going; deals with conflict by ceasing all reaction.

These types may be recognisable as those used to classify human character types ever since classical times. Lucy Rees says,

> We can recognise these types among horses, too: the choleric types, bold and irritable, are easily turned vicious; the melancholics are those timid, unconfident, miserable ones that turn barn sour and hopelessly nervous; the sanguine ones are the 'honest' horses that continue to try in all circumstances, while the phlegmatic type is most often seen in the duller type of cob (and in many riding schools).[26]

However, we should resist the temptation to use this as yet another 'easy' way of categorising horses that will enable us to evade our responsibilities. As with humans, we may find intermediate types who do not fall easily into one specific category; there may even be a considerable overlap of types, where horses that display what could be called a choleric temperament in some situations, are sanguine and well adjusted in others. Or horses that seem phlegmatic may, in some circumstances, display all the characteristics of a melancholic type. As Lucy Rees warns us,

> . . . a well-trained horse of whatever character will perform reliably at home (when seen by a prospective buyer, for instance), and, if only seen when handled, give little clue as to his future potential in different and changing circumstances. Similarly a badly trained or handled horse will give a poor account of herself, no matter how adaptable her character. At the moment it is only years of experience, often hard won, that teach us the difference between the two.[27]

Moreover, we should be wary of dismissing specific character types – such as choleric or melancholic – as undesirable. These types may be more 'difficult' than the sanguine or phlegmatic ones, but as Vicki Hearne says of the many 'difficult' characters brought to her to train or re-train, 'I never encountered a horse in whose soul there was no harmony to call on.'[28]

If we always seek to make life easy for ourselves with horses, we may miss some of the most rewarding experiences that training and handling them may bring.

Notes

1 J. Loftus, Readers' Letters, *Horse & Rider*, July 1997
2 The Marquis McSwiney of Mashanaglass, *Training from the Ground*, p. 53
3 Konrad Lorenz, *On Aggression* (originally published in 1963 as *Das sogenannte Böse, Zur Naturgeschichte der Agresion*; tr. M. Latzke, Routledge, 1996), p. 27
4 Dr Moyra Williams, *Horse Psychology*, p. 112
5 Colonel Alois Podhajsky, *My Horses, My Teachers*, p. 111
6 Podhajsky, *My Horses, My Teachers*, p. 111

7 Podhajsky, *My Horses. My Teachers*, p. 112
8 Marquis of Mashanaglass, *Training from the Ground*, p. 53
9 Sylvia Loch, *The Classical Rider*, p. 19
10 Lady Anne Blunt, quoted in *The Crabbet Arabian Stud*, by Rosemary Archer, Colin Pearson, Cecil Covey and Betty Finke (new ed. Alexander Heriot, 1994), p. 84
11 Vicki Heame, *Adam's Task*, p. 169
12 Susan McBane, *Behaviour Problems in Horses*, p. 73
13 Podhajsky, *My Horses, My Teachers*, pp. 98–9
14 Henry Blake, *Talking With Horses*, pp. 24–5
15 Cheryl Procter in a letter to the author, November 1996
16 Stephen Budiansky, *The Nature of Horses*, p. 86
17 Dr Moyra Williams, *Understanding Nervousness in Horse and Rider*, pp. 33–4
18 Jan May, *Equus Caballus*, pp. 6–15
19 Linda Tellington-Jones, *Getting in Touch With Horses*, Kenilworth Press 1995/(extract given in 'Whorls Apart', Horse & Rider, September 1995, p. 29
20 William Steinkraus, *Riding and Jumping* (Doubleday, New York, 1969), p. 76
21 Tellington-Jones, *Getting in Touch With Horses*, extract in *Horse & Rider*, September 1995, p. 29
22 In a letter to the author, October 1996
23 Podhajsky, *My Horses, My Teachers*, p. 129
24 Podhajsky, *My Horses, My Teachers*, p. 130
25 Podhajsky, *My Horses, My Teachers*, p. 130
26 Lucy Rees, *The Horse's Mind*, pp. 193–4
27 Rees, *The Horse's Mind*, p. 195
28 Hearne, *Adam's Task*, p. 146

CHAPTER FIFTEEN

Do Horses Dream?

Let it be said, and never forget, that the horse
is endowed with intellectual faculties which your
vanity alone prevents you from recognising.

FRANÇOIS BAUCHER

W E ARE OFTEN TOLD that only humans have the gift of imagination; and surely the ability to dream implies imagination, as when we dream we are visualising scenes that exist only in our minds (since even the most familiar location some- how seems different in dreams) and experiencing events that are real only to the dreamer. To visualise something not immediately present *is* to imagine it. Yet horses do dream.

Most people who share their lives with dogs will have seen them twitching in their sleep as if running, giving little whimpers and yips as they do so. Horses will often do the same, twitching their legs and giving subdued little whinnies; adults, youngsters and foals will all do it, although it is much more easily observed in foals as they spend far more time lying flat than older horses do.

But how do we know they are dreaming? Sleep falls into several categories, depending on the level of brain activity. Paradoxical or rapid eye movement (REM) sleep is characterised by patterns of brain activity which indicate dreaming. This is the kind of sleep referred to above, but according to the research into sleep in domestic animals carried out by Y. Ruckebusch, REM sleep only occurs in horses who are lying flat. We are sometimes told that horses do not need to lie down in order to sleep and it is quite true that they can sleep without lying down, thanks to the stay apparatus in their legs, which enables them to stand upright without any muscular effort. This does not mean, however, that they never need to lie down. In fact, they spend on average about 10 per cent of their time lying down, whether partially upright with their legs curled up, or flat out. Horses lying down are vulnerable, as getting up takes some effort for such big animals, so in the wild one would seldom see all the horses in a group lying down at the same time. In domestic situations, however, if the horses concerned feel secure in their surroundings, it is not uncommon to see whole groups lying down together. In the summer we have frequently arrived at the stables early in the morning to find not only our own horses, but all the horses in the field belonging to the riding school next door, lying down together in their various groups!

Lying down therefore seems to be psychologically, if not physically, necessary for horses as it is only when lying flat that they can dream. It is believed that paradoxical (REM) sleep is essential to mental health, and indeed Michael Jouvet has found that animals who have been experimentally

Foals spend more time lying down than older horses: Zareeba as a foal stretches out in the sunshine (Anita Chadfield)

deprived of REM sleep have developed severe psychological disturbances, or even died, as a result.[1] Lucy Rees says, 'Paradoxical sleep appears to be concerned with sorting out the impressions and experiences of waking life. It is interesting to see that youngsters sleep more than adults, and that stallions, which are generally more alert and active than mares, also sleep flat more than mares do.'[2]

Disturbed dreams have often been reported in horses which have been in battle. So it seems that horses do think about, and possibly relive, earlier experiences in dreams. If they recreate such experiences (and possibly imagine things which have never happened) in their dreams, may they not also do this in their waking moments? There is really no good reason to suppose that they do not.

Do horses have a sense of past and future? Many people believe that horses exist only in the present, but that cannot be so, as they have such excellent memories and clearly remember – and perhaps think about – past events. Indeed, if they did not we could scarcely train them, since we rely on this memory in training, and also on their ability to think about what they have learned. We don't know, of course, the extent to which they think about the past; but given their ability to dream, there seems no reason to doubt that they do think about it.

What of the future? Again, it is often confidently asserted that horses do not think about the possibility of future events, because 'animals have no concept of the future'. But what mysterious power gives us the right to make such assumptions? Such beliefs are often based on the most perverse reasoning. For instance, Paul McGreevy, in *Why Does My Horse . . .?*, dismisses the idea that a pony might be refusing to lie down because he is worried about not being able to get up again. He says in response to an enquiry from an anxious owner: 'Fears about getting up are not the reason for your pony's resolve to remain standing, because horses do not seem to worry about future events.'[3] He goes on to say,

I can say this with some confidence because the horses that have the greatest trouble rising are the ones that get cast (trapped against the side of the box while trying to get to their feet). And these poor characters get cast time and time again because they never learn to avoid lying in boxes that are too small for them to get up in.[4]

However, if it were true that horses 'do not seem to worry about future events', then a vast proportion of the problems people encounter with them would simply not occur. They would not, for example, worry about what might happen when they encounter situations where something unpleasant has happened to them on a previous occasion. A classic example of this is the reluctance to load into a horsebox typically shown by horses who have had a bad experience in one. Our stallion Nivalis used to load without any fuss until one day he slipped on the ramp of the horsebox, inuring his knee. Although the injury was more painful than severe, he refused point-blank to walk up the ramp again until we had placed the wagon next to a rise in the ground so that the ramp was quite level. Once Nivalis was satisfied he could step on it without slipping, he went in happily (although not before we had convinced him it was safe by letting him watch his mother go in and out of the wagon first and letting him follow her in); until then he was not prepared to risk slipping again.

As for horses that get cast, there is some evidence that the size of the stable has little if anything to do with this phenomenon. I have seen a small foal become cast in a huge foaling box, and only a couple of weeks before I wrote this, Kruger got himself cast against a fence while loose in the *manège*, simply because he chose what seemed like the most comfortable place to roll and then misjudged the amount of space he had in which to do it. It seems that this, and not the lack of space, may be what causes some horses to get cast regularly; in some boxes the practice of banking straw up against the sides (supposedly to help prevent horses from getting cast) may actually be the indirect cause. The horse chooses what seems like the most comfortable place to lie down – the softest part, where the bed is deepest – rolls, and finds that he has misjudged the amount of room necessary to avoid getting jammed up against the stable wall (there may, of course, be other reasons for horses getting cast but this is the commonest one I have observed). Lack of ability to anticipate the future does not necessarily come into it, because for some horses, the need to lie down may outweigh any fears they may have about getting cast – just as in some humans (even some very intelligent ones) the need to smoke, or consume alcohol, is greater than any fears they may have for their health. For this reason I don't think we can make any judgement about the level of intelligence of horses who repeatedly get cast!

So horses do have a sense of the future, even if they do not necessarily look too far ahead. Whether they can project thoughts further into the future is not something we can know until some means has been devised of measuring that possibility. In the wild they would probably not need to do so, as the cyclical nature of their existence means that forward planning would not be necessary other than to consider something on the lines of: 'It's getting colder, we'd better start moving over *there*' – 'over there' possibly being south, or wherever is warmer, has better grazing, and so forth. However, lack of the need to plan ahead does not automatically mean they have no capacity to do so. It may just be that, like the ability to reason in depth, it is a faculty that lies dormant until developed!

Another faculty often denied to horses by those who profess to know them is that of empathy. Many people who have studied animal behaviour have expressed the belief that animals in general lack the capacity to feel compassion because they are unable to empathise with others. But in order to believe this, we have to ignore the role that empathy plays in social interactions.

Empathy is more than sympathy: one may feel sympathy for another without entering into the feelings of the 'other' in any way. Empathy is basically an awareness of, and a sharing of, the emotions of others. It is something that even babies can feel; they show distress when another child is hurt or appears upset. The more empathic a person is, the more he or she will be attuned to the subtleties of manner and expressions which tell us how another person is feeling. It seems almost inconceivable that horses, with their hyper-sensitivity to body-signals and to the moods of others, could fail to be empathic. Psychologist Daniel Goleman has characterised lack of empathy as a kind of emotional tone-deafness; a horse that lacked the ability to 'tune-in' to the emotional states of other horses would be a social misfit, just as humans with a similar disability tend to be.

Even so, many people believe that horses lack the capacity for empathy, and therefore compassion, as compassion flows from empathy (the 'Rosenthal effect' may also be at work here, since you are scarcely likely to look for something if you don't believe it exists – as with the anthropologists who consistently failed to observe romantic love even when it was right under their noses). Yet horses who are emotionally well adjusted and who have been allowed to form strong bonds with their handlers and/or with other horses, do show both empathy and compassion.

This can sometimes take the form of protectiveness. Dr June Alexander, already mentioned in Chapter 7, once suffered an accident in one of her fields. Badly winded, she lay on the ground. One of the mares came over to her and protectively chased the other horses away. The mare next stood still while Dr Alexander clung to the horse's forelegs, using them to haul herself painfully to her feet. The mare then obligingly acted as a 'crutch' to support Dr Alexander as she hobbled to the field gate.

Several winters ago, I foolishly spent an entire afternoon shovelling gravel for the *manège* drains in the middle of a snowstorm while suffering from a severe chest cold. The result was a nasty bout of bronchitis, but I could not do what common sense dictated and stay in bed. The horses had to be seen to, and my husband was working long hours that week. So for several days, in spite of a racking cough which left me feeling exhausted, I somehow managed to struggle though the various stable jobs. One day, having got everything done and feeling like a wet rag, I collapsed gratefully into the corner of Zareeba's stable – the warmest place in the yard – to wait for Brian to come and take me home. Immediately Zareeba came over to see what was the matter. He must have wondered why I was lying down, as he had never seen me do that before, although I had often sat in the corner of his stable. He might even have thought I was dead, because he nudged my leg a few times until he saw me move. He stood

Protectiveness: Zareeba and Dandy

over me, sometimes touching me with his nose, ignoring his hay and everything else that might normally have claimed his attention, for at least an hour and a half. Not until Brian arrived did he finally move away.

What was he thinking about? Was he merely curious or did he realise I was ill, and was he trying to protect me? If he had just been curious, he would probably have moved away after a while (as he had done on previous occasions when I had gone and sat in his stable), since even he cannot maintain his interest in something that does not move for that long. On the other hand, the protectiveness he shows towards foals and vulnerable youngstock makes me wonder whether he sensed my temporary weakness and felt it behoved him to stand guard, just as a mare would over a sleeping foal.

In the autumn of 1996 Zareeba's half-brother Kruger suffered an injury which resulted in temporary radial nerve paralysis. Fortunately he recovered the use of the affected leg very quickly, but for a couple of weeks he was not quite his usual ebullient self. As he frets when turned out alone, we put him out with the other horses, because we knew none of them would harm a convalescing horse. The mare Roxzella, however, was not convinced of that. Although the other horses had not shown the slightest inclination to be aggressive towards Kruger, or take advantage of his relative weakness, Roxzella took it on herself to protect him from real or imaginary harm. She followed Kruger everywhere, not allowing the other horses anywhere near him. When he wandered into the stableyard for his ritual look around and 'clean up' (described in Chapter 6), Roxzella came with him and several times they ended up in the same stable. When this happened she – who would normally have challenged him for any food going – simply kept watch over Kruger until he had finished rooting around, then accompanied him out again. She did not stop this protective behaviour until Kruger was quite clearly back to normal – his usual cheerful, bumbling self, barging around like a Sherman tank.

Sometimes the empathy between horse and owner can be so intense that one suffers pain and distress when the other does, just as some men suffer all the pangs of childbirth when their wives are in labour! Ali, the Arabian gelding whose liking for rugby matches was described in Chapter 14, had such a close relationship with his owner that this exchange of physical and mental sensations occurred numerous times. On one occasion Ali had been diagnosed as suffering from pain in his neck, withers and shoulders. That night his owner was struck down by the worst backache and shoulder pain she had ever had. On another occasion she had left Ali in good health at 5 p.m.; but at 6.30 p.m. she suddenly felt a horrible sensation. Without really knowing why, she raced back to his stable, to find Ali in the throes of a really bad colic. On other occasions, when Sam was going through a period of emotional distress, Ali felt this to such a degree that he became physically ill. The latter could be dismissed as coincidence, except that the bouts of illness invariably happened at the same time as his owner's spells of emotional stress. It seems that Ali was indeed empathising with her.

When Annie, the mare whose problems with mud-fever were described in Chapter 7, witnessed her companion Millie suffering the agonies of grass-sickness, Annie showed signs of considerable distress. However, horses do not necessarily have to feel friendship for another horse or a human before they can show sympathy and act in a compassionate manner. Many horse owners report that when they are depressed or upset their horses seem to understand this, and some go out of their way to show extra affection. A rather cynical explanation of this might be that these horses sense that they are not receiving their owner's full attention and are seeking to claim it, but there are many cases where this cannot be true. Jane Littlefair, whose Arabian gelding Sultan was described in Chapter 7, had an old mare, Sorrel, who was almost impossible to catch. She treated it all as a game and towards the end of her life her behaviour in this respect became even worse. To cap it all, Sorrel was never in the slightest bit affectionate.

Then one day Jane was riding a very difficult Thoroughbred mare who reared up and deposited her rider in a ditch, narrowly avoiding falling on her and crushing her. Jane was naturally very shaken up and went into Sorrel's field trembling from the reaction to her fright. To her amazement, Sorrel came up to her – something she had never done before – nudged her affectionately and then refused to leave Jane's side until the latter had calmed down and stopped shaking. That was the only demonstration of affection Sorrel ever gave.

Sometimes compassion can come from the unlikeliest sources. Robin was an 11 hh pony who was rescued from a sale. On arriving at his new home he immediately made friends with an aged pony, Billy, who was then 35 years old. The two became inseparable and Robin, who felt quite insecure (possibly because of earlier experiences), would panic if Billy was out of sight for some reason. The two stayed close together all the time and were often to be seen some distance away from the rest of the horses. Among these other horses was a mare called Cher, a large Thoroughbred x Cleveland Bay. Cher was not particularly sociable with the other horses and was often seen to bite and kick out at them. She was further discouraged from social contact with them by her boyfriend, a big hunter gelding who did not like to see other horses near her. So Cher never gave little Robin a second glance.

Then one winter Billy began to fail, and finally had to be put to sleep. Robin was present when this happened, as his owners felt it was important that he knew what had happened to Billy and did not just think he had been taken away. Clearly, Robin could not be left on his own so they tried to introduce him to the rest of the horses, who were some distance away as Robin and Billy had always stayed near the farm towards the end. Robin's owner tells the rest of the story:

As we got near the horses Cher came purposefully towards us so we let go of Robin – she walked up to him, and off they went together, side by side, almost touching like a mother and foal. She took him away from the herd, back to where he and Billy had spent their last few days together. For the next three days she stayed by his side; sometimes the other horses came near them, and finally they joined with the herd again. Robin made friends with our donkey, Bobby, and they too are now inseparable, so he is obviously the type of pony that needs one close friend. But for that short time, Cher stood by him in his grief, and looked after him. It was so out of character for her . . . She was never seen with Robin again after those few days. To me this was incredible and I would never have believed it as I am not really sentimental and would never have thought horses would behave in this way – now I know better.[5]

One of the most compelling stories of a horse displaying empathy for another creature must surely be that of Capricho, an Andalusian x Arabian whose owner, Sara Crozier de Roca, rescued him from the most appaling ill-treatment. Rehabilitated, Capricho became a different character from the panic-stricken, virtually unmanageable horse Sara first saw dripping with sweat in a dealer's yard in Mallorca. He grew extremely tolerant of the stable cats, allowing one of them to sleep curled up on his rump. What makes his story (which will be continued later on) relevant to this part of the chapter is his reaction to a wounded hen that used to come and stand beside him at feed time. Several people repeatedly observed how, when the hen came to stand beside him, Capricho would fill his mouth with food, lower his head and deliberately deposit the food on the ground for the hen to eat. The hen eventually recovered and reared a brood of chicks in Capricho's shelter.[6]

The protectiveness some horses show towards other horses, or to their riders and handlers, is especially marked in some individuals. As I remarked earlier in this chapter, my gelding Zareeba has always been very protective towards foals and those he considers vulnerable. Although Zareeba's half-brother Kruger is a year younger, being part warmblood he is considerably bigger than his pure Arab brother. However, when we first brought Kruger, as a three year old, home to our yard, Zareeba decided that his brother needed protecting against the other horses (who in fact accepted him very well after the ritual squealing and pulling of faces). In the process of protecting his 'little' brother, Zareeba – who had always backed away from any confrontation – suddenly developed a courage he probably never knew he had. At the slightest hint of any aggression towards Kruger, he would go charging in, not attacking the aggressor but simply getting between the latter and Kruger so that any attack would be directed at himself instead. This happened numerous times until he evidently decided that Kruger was able to look after himself. They have tended to grow apart slightly as Kruger has become more independent and as Zareeba has acquired new friends, but they are still very close and woe betide the horse – or human – who tries to harm Kruger while Zareeba is about!

This very evident protectiveness brings us to another aspect of equine behaviour which is often overlooked: the vexed question of altruism, which we discussed in Part I. If you follow the popular sociobiological argument that altruism is 'designed' to maximise the survival of one's own genes through helping one's close relatives to survive, then Zareeba's concern for Kruger (being his half-brother) fits in very neatly with this. But as we saw in Part I, this view confuses motives with long-term effects, and it breaks down at every turn. It does not begin to explain why Zareeba, as well as protecting his half-brother, should also show a very strong tendency to protect foals, youngstock or indeed any other horse whom he perceives as weak and in need of such protection. He demonstrated this very well with Nivalis when the latter was a foal. The first time Nivalis was turned out with the other horses, Zareeba immediately (as he did with Kruger) stepped in to prevent the other horses from molesting him. For some considerable time, whenever the horses were enjoying a bit of boisterous play, it was Zareeba rather than Roxzella (Nivalis's dam) who would step in to protect Nivalis when things got a bit rough; he always kept himself between the foal and the other horses. But Zareeba, although a pure-bred Arabian, is only very tenuously related to Roxzella and Nivalis so protection of his own genes could scarcely come into it except in a very roundabout way. Moreover, he was first introduced to Roxzella and her foal when he and Roxzella were both six years old and the foal five months old, so he was not even 'related' to them by any sense of group identity. One can only conclude that he was responding to some deeply felt sense of responsibility towards young and vulnerable creatures.

This same sense of protective responsibility has been shown by Roxzella, as we have seen in her behaviour towards Kruger when he was injured. Curiously, she has always been less protective of her own son – perhaps because, from an early age, he showed his independence. However, her concern for other horses has been quite remarkable, as the following story shows.

When my husband's mare Kiri gave birth to her first foal, Toska, she was extremely protective of him (although she trusted us sufficiently to let us handle him and she was not 'foal proud' in the way some possessive mares are). However, when we eventually started letting Roxzella out with them, Kiri would quite happily relinquish Toska to Roxzella's care while she went off to graze or simply to have a wander around free from the attentions of her off-spring. Toska readily adopted Roxzella as his 'aunt', even though she did not make a big fuss of him (certainly not in the way his own mother did). Her role consisted more of generally watching over him and administering discipline whenever he got a bit 'uppity', as colts will.

In time, we introduced the other horses to Toska and his mother, but as Kiri was present at all times Roxzella's protection was not necessary. However, when the time came for Toska to brave the company of the other horses without his mother, something interesting happened.

His mother was nearby, watching from her stable, which has a back door opening out into the field. Toska took a few tentative steps into the field. The other horses looked up, saw him, and Zareeba and Kruger started to amble over out of curiosity.

Immediately Roxzella stepped in to intercept them. Whether she thought Toska had inadvertently strayed away from his mother I do not know, but one thing was certain: the other horses were not going to get a chance to molest him. Putting herself between Toska and all possible harm, she drove the other horses away quite aggressively, even turning on her boyfriend Zareeba and her own son Nivalis. Once satisfied that none of them would dare approach her and her 'charge', she then shepherded Toska back to his mother's stable, taking him right up to the door, where she stopped, as if to say to Kiri (who had been observing all this without the slightest sign of agitation), 'Here he is; I've brought him back to you.'

Later on the same day we let Toska out once more with the others, again alone, to see what would happen. This time Roxzella, while monitoring the situation cautiously, was less overtly protective: she kept a weather eye on the other horses, always putting herself between them and Toska, until she was sure none of them was going to molest him. Only then did she relax and start grazing, although always near to her 'charge'.

Roxzella clearly suspected that the other horses might prove aggressive to Toska (although, in fact, none of them have); and she was prepared to risk possible injury to herself in order to protect him. Protecting her own genes did not enter into the matter; not only is she not related to Toska in any way, she does not even belong to the same breed of horse. She is a pure-bred Arabian, while Toska is by a Belgian warmblood stallion out of a Thoroughbred x Cleveland Bay mare. Nor is it likely that she was acting out of a purely maternal instinct. Although she produced her son without any fuss, and looked after him well enough, she could hardly have been described as the 'maternal' type. 'Dutiful' would be a more appropriate description. Unlike Kiri, who seems to revel in the whole business of producing foals and caring for them, Roxzella shows no enthusiasm for motherhood. And given the fact that she had already had a foal, and knew very well how to care for him, it could not even be argued that she was 'rehearsing' for the role of motherhood – as some ethologists have suggested may be the case with those primates observed to take on the role of 'aunting'.

Zareeba has similarly stepped in to protect Toska when the horses have been enjoying a gallop about. If he thinks things are getting a little rough, he will often place himself between Toska and the other horses, even though they have never shown the slightest sign of attacking him; and like Roxzella, he is not at all related to Toska!

I would suggest that the only explanation that makes any real sense is that Roxzella and Zareeba are simply exercising an evidently well-developed sense of responsibility. There is no need to evoke some contorted and contrived 'selfish gene' theory to account for this; in evolutionary terms, it makes perfect sense, as such a sense of responsibility benefits both the individual (do as you would be done by, or face the consequences, and be done by as you did) and the group as a whole.

Again, it could be argued that a sense of responsibility is 'only' another instinct. That may be so up to a point; a mother's instinct to protect her young often does not seem to have anything to do with a consciously willed effort. But this does not explain the very evident feelings of responsibility demonstrated by any number of horses towards their riders.

Richard Adams's delightful novel *Traveller* is a kind of military 'Black Beauty', the autobiographical story of Traveller, the horse who belonged to the great Confederate General Robert E. Lee during the American Civil War. Long since retired from the horrors of war, in the comfort of his stable and paddock (and relishing occasional forays into the countryside with his beloved 'Marse Robert'), Traveller tells his story to the stable cat. One of the great themes in the book is how Traveller discovers his sense of responsibility towards his master. He describes seeing horses bolting with their riders, or simply running out of control, and concludes that he does not want to be that kind of horse, with no sense of who he is or of where his duty lies. No matter how frightened he may be, he always endeavours to stay calm. He recounts his sense of shame at being the unwitting cause of an accident that befalls 'Marse Robert': startled by something, he jumps away, causing General Lee to fall forward onto his hands which are badly damaged (this incident actually happened and is well documented). Even though it was not deliberate, he blames himself for 'Marse Robert's' injuries, and ever after that tries his best to atone for his lack of responsibility.

To some people, who pride themselves on their objectivity, this may sound like anthropomorphic slush; but in fact Adams captures the essence of how many horses *behave* as if they think. As it is unlikely that they are deliberately fooling us, are we mistaken in believing they think this way? If a human friend behaves as though she feels responsible for looking after me, even though she does not say so (and this has happened to me), am I misguided in thinking that she really does feel a sense of responsibility towards me, just because l cannot know precisely what she thinks?

One of the most moving sights I have ever witnessed was at the Great Yorkshire Show some years ago, during a display given by the Riding for the Disabled Association. The famous Lloyds Black Horse, Downlands Cancara, was ridden by a young woman who – although the precise nature and extent of her disability was not clear – could scarcely hold the reins in her hands. It was also quite apparent that her aids were virtually non-existent. Yet this horse – a powerful, high-spirited Trakehner stallion – carried her with grace and dignity around a large showring, to tremendous applause. It would be easy to reduce this to an example of a very well-trained horse conditioned to perform in a certain way. However, to anyone not trapped in the straitjacket of behaviourist dogma, this was something far more than that. Cancara's whole demeanour spoke of his pride in his task and his empathy with his young rider. He knew exactly what he had to do, and he did it superlatively well. Does this not argue a sense of responsibility?

If we accept this, it should come as no surprise that so many horses do get on remarkably well with the disabled and the mentally disadvantaged. Autistic children, in particular, have often benefited immensely from being with horses; and I know of one Arabian stallion who was regularly ridden out by an autistic child in perfect safety.

Throughout the history of horsemanship, there have been innumerable instances of horses exerting themselves far beyond their natural strength in order to save their riders. This cannot be explained by the convenient method of dismissing such efforts as the result of the rider's coercion; nor can they be explained by some vague reference to 'herd instinct' or 'flight responses'. Horses, like humans, have finite resources. If a horse is exhausted then all the spurring or flogging in the world will not induce him to travel a step further than his physical strength allows, while fear will only take a horse so far (so-called 'blind panic' is rarely involved in such cases). But if the horse and his rider are united by a strong bond of mutual trust and affection, then the horse's sense of responsibility may, for a time, enable him to exceed the limits of his strength. Alois Podhajsky describes how his life was saved by his horse in a battle during the First World War.

> Neger saved my life by his huge bounds at the canter. He had been wounded by shrapnel and yet did his duty until his last breath. I am not ashamed to admit that tears came into my eyes when I bid farewell to this brave and loyal creature. I had lost a teacher and a friend.[7]

From India comes a story which there is no reason to doubt, as it is well documented. Almost legendary in Rajastan (formerly Rajputana) in northern India, are the exploits of the sixteenth-century Maharana Pratap of Mewar and his charger Chetak against the forces of the Moghul Emperor Akbar under the Raja Man Singh. At the battle of Haldi Ghati on 17 June 1576, Maharana Pratap, on Chetak, engaged Raja Man Singh, on a war elephant, in single combat. Chetak sprang up alongside the *howdah* in a tremendous *capriole*, and Maharana Pratap thrust at Man Singh with his lance. Man Singh ducked, however, so Pratap wheeled Chetak around to spring up again in a *courbette*, and drum his hooves on the great war elephant's

Chetak: from a painting at the Chetak Chabutra, Haldi Ghati, Rajastan (S.H.A.A. Imam)

head, while Pratap cut down the *mahout*. If he had been able to kill Man Singh too, the Maharana would probably have won the battle, but the war elephant turned and fled. At that point Moghul reinforcements arrived, and Maharana Pratap was defeated and forced to flee the field. Wounded in the battle and pursued by two Moghul chieftains, galloping over rough terrain, Chetak carried his chain-mail-clad rider for 6 kilometres up towards the pass of Haldi Ghati where the way was barred by a torrential mountain stream. Rapidly losing blood, Chetak gathered himself for one final, tremendous effort, and with one great leap cleared the churning torrent, to collapse, dying, on the far bank. The truly astounding thing about this heroic flight was that Chetak accomplished it on *three legs* – his off-hind foot had been severed at the fetlock joint. He died with his head cradled in his master's arms; at Haldi Ghati an altar was raised, known as Chetak Chabutra, in memory of this deed of heroism.[8]

Following on from concepts of empathy and responsibility is that of *justice* – a concept which many people believe horses do not have. Paul McGreevy says, 'Horses have no regard for "fair play" or "justice"; they do what they have to in order to ensure that their genes survive.'[9] No, they don't. I say it yet again – no creature does *anything* in order to ensure the survival of their genes, although that is one of the results of their actions. It is not – and cannot be – a motive, or even any kind of aim, except from an exceedingly remote evolutionary viewpoint. *Now* is what is important to horses (and, for that matter, to humans). Individual survival may come into it, although as individual survival for horses depends largely on the cohesion of the group, one must ask how a group of individualists concerned solely with their own survival could possibly maintain that cohesion.

In fact, if we look back to Chapter 9 and recall Monty Roberts's observations of how the wise old mare taught the colt that his manners were unacceptable, we can see that this *is* a concept of justice. For what is punishment for crime? Not merely revenge (although it is sometimes that), but *justice*. Such behaviour is not acceptable: reform it or face the consequences. Do as you would be done by, or be done by as you did – such concepts are just as valid in the world of horses as they are in that of humans. The mare in Monty Roberts's story stepped in to prevent the colt from committing any further 'crimes', even though she herself was not being attacked. That is justice put into action. Furthermore, the colt accepted his punishment, even to the point of voluntarily banishing himself from the group following a lapse in his newly found manners: he knew it was *just*.

If one opens one's eyes, one may see countless examples of how this works in equine societies. Where a bully makes a real nuisance of himself, other horses in a group will often develop their own methods of dealing with him. In *The Treacle Bucket* Elaine Dollery describes an amusing incident of this nature. One horse she knew, called Russet, was a terrible bully with a habit of biting other horses hard just above the root of the tail. It did not matter how big or small his victim was; Russet would attack any other horse in this way. The other horses in the field eventually grew fed up with this treatment. One day when Russet had sneaked up on one of them, ready to bite, the gelding Prince came up behind Russet and bit hard at his tail, enabling Russet's victim to escape. At the same time, the two biggest horses, Brutus and Barona, came up on each side of Russet and prevented him from getting away, as he was facing the fence. Brutus and Barona held Russet in place while Prince continued to bite him, and this went on for about 20 minutes before they let Russet go.[10] He was not seriously injured, but he never bit another horse.

Horses show their resentment of unfair treatment by humans, too. Whether they really do wait for an opportunity to 'get back' at the perpetrator of the injustice or bad treatment is not clear, but they certainly remember such injustice and some act on that memory when they get a chance. Susan McBane tells the story of a Thoroughbred stallion who had spent his racing days in the north east of England. He had been harshly treated and had developed a vicious temper as a result. After he was retired to stud, sympathetic handling improved his outlook on life, but he had learned to hate people with the distinctive accent of the area where he had raced; he associated the accent with his bad treatment. One day a visitor from the north east came to the stud. The visitor was warned that this horse would react violently to the sound of his accent, but he forgot and ended up standing with his back to the stallion. The latter, hearing the detested accent, lunged over the door of his box and took the back off the hapless visitor's jacket![11]

If the horse's training has been based on establishing mutual trust and understanding, so that the horse knows what is expected of him, he will not resent being told off for something that the training has established as being unacceptable. He will, however, resent punishment unfairly given. Franz Mairinger cites the case of a horse called Coronation who would not take sugar for three days after he had been hit for stumbling when it was not his fault.[12] Alois Podhajsky tells how his great horse Nero would also refuse sugar if he had been unjustly treated. Nero loved his sugar so much that:

> If . . . he refused to take any sweets from me I knew that the worst had happened, that I had done him wrong in the course of the training or had demanded too much from him. It was his manner of disapproving the philosophy of 'sugar-bread and whip'! To me this behaviour was a serious warning that I had made a mistake and that I should be more moderate in my demands.[13]

If horses have a sense of responsibility, and of justice, do they take a pride in any of the feelings that accompany these concepts? We cannot, of course, be sure, but few people who have observed horses with an open mind can doubt, seeing their attitude and bearing, that in appropriate circumstances they can and do feel pride.

What is pride? It is often confused with arrogance and vanity, but these are not necessarily involved in feelings of pride. My dictionary says that among other things pride can be 'a feeling of honour and self-respect; a sense of personal worth' or 'satisfaction or pleasure taken in one's own or another's success, achievements etc.,'[14] while 'proud' may mean 'having a proper sense of self-respect', 'stately or distinguished', 'bold or fearless'[15]. Horses can certainly be bold or fearless, but can they take pride in their achievements? Can they have a sense of self-respect, a sense of personal worth? I shall argue in the next chapter that they certainly can take a pride in achievement. If we recall the story, cited in Chapter 9, of the stallion who felt so humiliated by bad treatment that he turned to self-mutilation, I think it is clear that they do have a sense of self-respect.

Stallions can suffer from injured pride perhaps more than most. The lighter aspect of this is described amusingly by Tom Ainslie:

> The guileless candor of the horse is most charmingly demonstrated in its proudly pompous self-satisfaction. Horses seldom try to mislead other horses, and they do not intentionally mislead human beings. But they sometimes fool themselves. The strutting stallion discovers after a close encounter that another stallion is even noisier and more pugnacious. It runs off and stops strutting until the psychological wounds heal. Or the same stallion is cut down to size by an unreceptive mare.[16]

Sometimes the psychological wounds do not heal so quickly. Nivalis became quite ill as a result of an incident which happened shortly after his first foal, out of my husband's mare Kiri, was born. A well-grown Thoroughbred colt escaped from his nearby field, broke through into one of ours and set off in pursuit of Nivalis's mother Roxzella, although she was not in season and would most likely have rejected him even if she had been. Nivalis and Zareeba, who were both in the field with her, galloped after them and the result was a terrifying wall-of-death chase. Although fast horses of their type, neither Nivalis nor Zareeba, at 14.3 hh each, was any match for a large Thoroughbred hell-bent on having his wicked way with a mare. Roxzella herself – more long-striding than her son or her boyfriend – only just kept ahead of the would-be ravisher. Fortunately, my husband managed somehow to chase Nivalis and Zareeba into the adjoining field before any serious damage was done; by the time the colt caught up with Roxzella he was too worn out to do anything about it, so Brian was able to catch him quite easily and restore him to his home. However, although Nivalis had miraculously escaped any injury more serious than a few superficial scrapes, he was utterly exhausted both mentally and physically, to the point of suffering from muscle tremors. A severe chill was averted by quick action, but although he recovered physically within a few days, he fell into a depression from which he could not be roused. He would not eat properly, showed no interest in exercise or in the loose schooling that he loves, and received all attempts to rouse him out of his lethargy with indifference.

Then one day the colt who had caused all the fuss committed another 'crime'; he escaped from his field again and this time got among some mares belonging to some other neighbours. This was too much; the delinquent was banished to another part of his owners' property, where Nivalis could no longer see him. With his rival out of the way, Nivalis was restored to mental equilibrium. His appetite returned, his usual high spirits re-asserted themselves, and he once again began to take an interest in life.

His depression appeared to have been caused not by his physical distress, but by the fact that he had been powerless to protect his family – not only his mother, but Zareeba (a member of Nivalis's family by extension), as well as Kiri and the foal. The mere presence of another entire male was enough to constitute a threat in Nivalis's mind, even though the colt

Nivalis challenges a rival

had shown no interest in any of them but Roxzella. Nivalis felt badly about the whole incident because he had not been able to defeat the intruder. What made it worse was that he could still see the colt in the latter's field nearby and was always conscious of the potential threat. He was unable to enjoy peace of mind knowing this. In the wild he could have herded his family away from danger; here he could do nothing. Fortunately the situation resolved itself; but if it had not, such conflict might have resulted in a complete breakdown if no steps were taken to remove the source of the conflict.

In other words, Nivalis's pride was hurt. As well as the fear of another horse harming (or stealing) his family, his sense of self-esteem suffered because he could do nothing about the situation – could not, in other words, fulfil the role nature appointed for him.

As we have seen, the role of protector is not confined to stallions; Zareeba and Roxzella have both shown strong protective instincts. But this aspect of a stallion's nature should never be underestimated in assessing what is important to them. Dr Kiley-Worthington tells the story of a stallion she took to a show on one occasion, together with some of the mares he normally lived with. This stallion was normally very well behaved and could be safely out ridden with either his own mares or strange mares, whether or not they were in season. On this occasion, however, when he saw his mares going off to take part in different classes, and he was left with strange horses in his ridden class, he behaved atrociously. What made him create such a fuss, says Dr Kiley-Worthington, 'was not his mares going away, which is mildly upsetting but something he was very used to, but them going off with *other* horses without him being able to do anything about it!'[17].

It was in part his 'unbending pride' that made Lucy Rees's Lipizzaner stallion – described in Chapter 9 – such a difficult character. He resisted violently attempts to subdue and dominate him, because his pride would not allow him to submit to coercion. Yet we may recall Lucy Rees's words describing the change in his attitude once he no longer felt under pressure to maintain his self-esteem at all costs: 'his remarkable gentleness and nobility made it almost impossible to believe he was the same horse'. Gentleness, pride, courage – which Maestoso Sitnica certainly had – and magnanimity are all qualities bound up with that elusive quality, nobility. Most of us are familiar with the term, 'the noble horse'; but is 'nobility' a word we can legitimately use in connection with horses, or is it just another projection of human values onto a non-human creature?

Stephen Budiansky quotes one of the knights of the Emperor Frederick II as saying, 'No animal is more noble than the horse, since it is by horses that princes, magnates and knights are separated from lesser people.' Budiansky comments,

> The unavoidable expense of horses made them something only the richest members of society could afford; given the nearly universal belief that wealth equalled nobility, and given what Piggott calls "the ever latent anthropomorphism of antiquity", the association with nobility made the horse itself a Noble Animal.[18]

However this is a half-truth, a projection of our present-day perceptions which takes quotations, such as the one given above, out of context and uses them to misinterpret the whole *ethos* of the *chevalier*, the equestrian knight. According to this ethos it was the *man* who was ennobled by his association with the horse. To be an equestrian was to practise *virtue* in its fullest sense, as only the man who humbled himself, who set aside all vanity and arrogance, could truly master the training and riding of a horse. As Charles de Kunffy says, 'For centuries, horses were a means to educate the elite in all societies where the horse was known. They were man's partners, enhancing his status not only by their imposing sight, but by conveying to the beholder that in the saddle an equestrian, in all his virtue, was enthroned.'[19] It was this *virtue* that masters such as Pluvinel and la Guérinière sought to instil in their pupils. 'For it was only through the training of a horse, through riding one, that the virtues of a man could emerge . . . The horse could and did give man a total education. He had to be tamed and befriended, and could not be fooled by honeyed words.'[20] These virtues could only emerge if the student recognised that the horse too had virtues; if he recognised the innate capacity of horses for *nobility*.

There are horses who demonstrate their nobility through their generosity. Recall Capricho, the horse rescued from ill-treatment, who shared his food with a wounded hen. Capricho proved his generosity in many other ways, all the more remarkable because of what he had been through. When Sara Crozier de Roca first saw him, Capricho could hardly walk, because his hooves were so overgrown. He was sweating, his nostrils flared in panic, and he had to be sedated before the vet could examine him. His nose was badly scarred. His tongue had at some time been almost severed through, and had healed with a slight twist and lump. The inside of his mouth had been injured by his sharp, neglected teeth. His sides bore scars caused by sharp spurs, and he had been gelded by the truly barbarous (and illegal) method of trapping the testicles between split canes.

Capricho was, not surprisingly, very difficult to handle. Sara's first priority was to sort out his health problems and make life more comfortable for him. He became panicky if shut in a stable, but would attack other horses who came near him, so he had to be given a separate pen and a shelter out in a field. When he eventually came to be ridden, he was extremely nervous, continually shying, and bolting whenever he found the opportunity. By means of a huge amount of tact and patience, Sara managed to persuade Capricho that being handled and ridden did not mean he would be subjected to pain, as always seemed to have been the case in the past.

Capricho, his health and faith in human nature restored (Sara Crozier de Roca)

After two years he was a changed horse who no longer bolted or attacked other horses. Sara writes,

> Throughout our relationship, I have been amazed by the nobility and gentleness of horses in the face of ill-treatment . . . He is so gentle that he never bites, and will hold his feet up in turn for my seven-year-old daughter to pick out his hooves. He loves to snuffle along my arms or rest his head against me whilst I pull his ears or play with his nostrils . . . He loves to play, looking at me and then dropping the grooming brushes off the wall one by one, or taking the hose in his mouth when I shower him and closing his teeth so that the water spurts all over me instead of him.[21]

Eighteen months after she acquired Capricho, Sara developed an allergic reaction which caused her legs to swell, and she was unable to ride or even go near a horse for several weeks. When she did manage to go and see Capricho, he set up a tremendous fuss by way of greeting. 'When I led him up to the stable yard, he ran his nostrils up and down my arm, gently caressing it and occasionally pushing at me with his head.' Sara tacked him up very gingerly because the skin was still very tender on her arms and legs, and mounted up. Previously, Capricho had always started off with a lively jog before settling down, but on this occasion, Sara says, 'He was so careful, quiet and considerate of me that he reduced me to tears!'[22]

Generosity following the most inhumane treatment might cause sceptics to conclude that this proves how stupid horses really are. However, such generosity is a feature of humans too. Any number of people who survived the death camps of the Second World War have expressed, and demonstrated through their actions, their forgiveness towards those who used them with a brutality that almost beggars belief; and these include some very intelligent and gifted people indeed. Some horse-whisperers, who claim to be in touch with the inner feelings of horses, report that the latter (like many survivors of the death-camps) are able to feel such generosity towards their tormentors because they believe such people act from ignorance. Who can say whether this is true? It certainly seems that horses like Capricho – himself a horse of great intelligence – do possess a remarkable capacity to forgive past wrongs once they are restored to a sense of security and peace.

If part of the essence of nobility is, besides generosity, a combination of pride, courage and loyalty, then some of the most outstanding examples of this nobility may be found in the *corridas* of Spain and Portugal. I refer not to the bullfight on foot, where the only horses involved are the unfortunate, broken-down horses of the *picadors*, but to the mounted

It takes courage for the horse to face an Iberian fighting bull, even, as here, a tame one. The horse is ridden by Eleanor Taylor (Roger Taylor)

The *cavaleiro* is literally riding for his life (courtesy Arsenio Raposo Cordeiro)

Below The bullfighting horse must show relish for the fight: Antonio Ribeiro Telles on El Viti (courtesy Arsenio Raposo Cordeiro)

bullfight (in Spain this is referred to as the *rejoneo* to distinguish it from the bullfight on foot; in Portugal it is the only form of bullfight, and is there known simply as the *corrida*).

This is not the place to discuss the ethics of bullfighting; it is sufficient to say that while in Spain the bull is still killed in the *rejoneo*, in Portugal he is spared. In the Portuguese *corrida* the fight is not so much a pitting of wits against the bull as a test of the skill and courage of the *cavaleiro* and his horse combined – the idea of the partnership being paramount. The *cavaleiro* must be able to rely utterly on his horse's unswerving courage and loyalty, for he is literally riding for his life, and the slightest hesitation may prove fatal. It is a testimony to the skill of these horsemen – a skill which dates back to ancient times – and to the valour of their horses, that injuries to horses are very rare, and it is considered a terrible disgrace for the *cavaleiro* to allow this to happen.

Sylvia Loch, describing the exploits of these daring horsemen, says, 'Great bullfighters, who at the height of their summer season, daily court death with their beautiful horses, are unreservedly emotional about the relationship they share with their fighting horse.'[23] Alvaro Domecq, one of the most renowned *rejoneadors* of this century, fought many bulls with his great mare Espléndida. It is very rare for a mare to be ridden in the mounted bullfight; stallions are used almost exclusively. But every now and then such a mare as Espléndida will overturn tradition. Domecq says of her:

> But what a good heart toward her rider, proven on so many difficult occasions! Espléndida . . . would have preferred that they kill her rather than that anything should happen to me. She was a model of fidelity and loyalty, she understood me so completely.[24]

In attributing such qualities to their horses, it is highly unlikely that riders such as Domecq have been mistaken. Examples of horses performing prodigies of valour on the battlefield may sometimes be attributable to the horse's sense of self-preservation or that vague quality known as 'herd instinct'; but neither of these can be invoked in the case of the bullfighting horse. In Portugal, home of some of the most renowned bullfighting horses, the bullring is relatively small. The horse has room to manoeuvre but cannot escape. Nor can he take refuge in a group; there is no group. There is only himself, his rider – and the bull. And this is no placid domestic cow, but a full-grown Iberian fighting bull, bred for his power and aggression. Yet not only does a good bullfighting horse face the bull with immense courage, he does so with every sign of relish. Indeed, a bullfighting horse who did *not* relish the fight would not only be useless, he would be a liability, since his rider could not rely on his steadfastness. For the same reason, coercion is out of the question; a horse who is afraid of his rider cannot be trusted in a fear-inspiring situation.

And fear-inspiring it is. Alvaro Domecq tells how he realised that Espléndida was pregnant 'because, for the first time, she trembled before going into the ring, but she controlled herself and fought better than ever. She was a mare of pure gold. Valiant, which is more than not being afraid; it is overcoming fear . . . resolute . . . the heart to face and cheat death.'[25]

Notes

1 For a brief description of Jouvet's work see Steven Rose, *The Conscious Brain* (Weidenfeld & Nicholson, 1973), pp. 244–5

2 Lucy Rees, *The Horse's Mind*, p. 105

3 Paul McGreevy, *Why Does My Horse . . .?*, p. 210

4 McGreevy, *Why Does My Horse . . .?*, p. 210

5 Cheryl Procter in a letter to the author, November 1996

6 Sara Crozier de Roca, 'Capricho's Story', *Horse & Rider*, June 1997, p. 58

7 Colonel Alois Podhajsky, *My Horses, My Teachers*, p. 24

8 S.H.A.A. lmam, *Chetak Or A Tale of a Man and a Horse* (The Indian Heritage, 1994), pp. 8–10

9 McGreevy, *Why Does My Horse . . .?*, p. 194

10 Elaine Dollery, *The Treacle Bucket*, pp. 164–5

11 Susan McBane, *Behaviour Problems in Horses*, p. 80

12 Mairinger, Franz, *Horses Are Made To Be Horses*, p. 55

13 Podhajsky, *My Horses, My Teachers*, p. 95

14 *Collins English Dictionary* 2nd ed. 1986

15 *Collins English Dictionary* 2nd ed. 1986

16 Tom Ainslie and Bonnie Ledbetter, *The Body Language of Horses*, p. 69

17 Dr Marthe Kiley-Worthington, *The Behaviour of Horses*, p. 135

18 Stephen Budiansky, *The Nature of Horses*, p. 73

19 Charles de Kunffy, *Ethics and Passions of Dressage*, p. 43

20 Kunffy, *Ethics and Passions of Dressage*, p. 43

21 Crozier de Roca, 'Capricho's Story'

22 Sara Crozier de Roca, in a letter to the author, July 1997.

23 Sylvia Loch, *The Royal Horse of Europe* (J. A. Allen, 1986), p. 134

24 Alvaro Domecq in *El Caballo en España*, quoted by Sylvia Loch in *The Royal Horse of Europe*, p. 134

25 Alvaro Domecq, *El Caballo en España*, quoted in Loch, *The Royal Horse of Europe*, p. 148

CHAPTER SIXTEEN

Developing the Horse's Mind

The intelligence of the horse increases rapidly with
education. An intelligent master or trainer can make an intelligent
horse. It is a stupid trainer that makes the so-called stupid horse.

COLONEL R.S. TIMMIS DSO, *c*.1915

I AM SORRY TO TELL you that I am seriously contemplating the gelding of Rose of
Sharon's 1906 colt by Harb, that I named Rodan. He is a magnificent appearing colt,
but has a nasty temper, something entirely new in our experience with Arab horses.
From a very young colt he has been ready to kick or strike any one who came near him,
and I am afraid he may hurt some of my men as he gains in strength. No one can touch
him to groom his quarters, neither kindness nor discipline affects him . . .[1]

Thus wrote Colonel Spencer Borden in May 1907 to Lady Anne Blunt of the famous Crabbet
Arabian Stud from which the colonel had bought several horses. Lady Anne replied, 'Surely
it is too soon to despair about the Rose of Sharon colt. I have never met with a bad-tempered
Arabian horse in all my thirty years' experience.'[2] She had consulted with her stud manager
in Egypt, she said,

. . . an Arab of the Muteyr, the most famous horse breeding tribe in the S. Eastern Nejd,
about your colt. He declared that no Arabian horse could be innately or permanently ill
tempered, although young colts may sometimes be violent to begin with, from being
above themselves and to let off high spirits, 'before their intelligence is developed', as he
expressed it.[3]

She went on to tell Colonel Borden about a colt that the stud manager, Mutlak el Battal, had
dealt with when working for the late Ali Pasha Sherif in Cairo. This colt had started life very

much like the Rose of Sharon colt, by behaving savagely, but he had been cured by exercise and work (it is important to realise here that Mutlak did *not* use coercion – just a vast amount of patience and persistence). Lady Anne's remedy for Rodan was similar. 'Of course,' she wrote, 'Rodan is too young to be mounted but all the preliminary processes could be gone on with and the sooner the better. No "discipline" other than the firmness necessary to keep him in check and never to let him have his own way.'[4]

Colonel Borden took Lady Anne's advice; part of his course of action involved changing Rodan's groom for another. 'This latter, a Portuguese, is very gentle with him, but patient and firm, never letting him get the upper hand, persisting always until the colt does what he wants him to do. He never raises his voice, Rodan likes him, and is a changed animal.'[5]

On being told the story of Rodan, Mutlak, the *bedawin* stud manager, said, 'Ah, I like to see them nice and bold.'[6]

This passage is interesting on several counts. First, there is the wisdom shown by both Lady Anne and her stud manager in not attributing Rodan's 'nastiness' to any inherent bad temper, but rather to the bumptiousness of a young colt who had simply, as Mutlak would put it, got 'above himself'. Then, one is struck by the way in which both Mutlak and Lady Anne took it for granted that horses *have* an intelligence to be developed. Finally, there is the absence of any suggestion of 'breaking' the colt's spirit in order to tame him; this was to be done by awakening and expanding his mind by means of work suitable to his age and level of physical maturity.

None the less, the general belief still persists that horses basically dislike work, and that they only respond to our demands either to avoid unpleasantness or because they are rewarded (for responding) or punished (for not responding).

This is a very short-sighted and limiting attitude. In my book *The Arabian Show Horse* I touched on this subject when discussing the reasons why so many horses in ridden classes fail to produce more than a very mediocre performance. I wrote there:

> A large number of people believe that horses basically dislike work, and that being ridden is for them at best a chore, for which their sole reward is their dinner bucket. I believe that to start training a horse in this frame of mind is an almost certain recipe for mediocre results. It is as if a teacher, lacking the conviction that pupils can find the learning process stimulating and the pursuit of knowledge fascinating, sets out to teach with the basic attitude of, 'Well, I know you're not going to enjoy this which means it's going to be hard work for me, but we both have to do it anyway so let's just get on with it.' Such a teacher – and there are all too many of them – is hardly likely to inspire anything but the very boredom he or she fears. And so it is with horses.[7]

In other words, if you believe that a pupil (whether equine or human) is either too dull or too unresponsive to learn, then your attitude and your teaching methods will reflect this, and the pupil really *will* be dull and unresponsive. Classroom experiments have confirmed that this is precisely what happens when teachers prejudge their pupils.

Whether or not a horse finds work boring or stimulating, a chore or a pleasurable experience depends not only on the character of the individual horse (just as with humans, some like work, others are basically lazy), but also on the skill of the teacher. However, it can also depend on the extent and type of early handling the horse has received.

In the past, it has too often been the case that young horses have been left virtually unhandled until they were mature enough to be ridden. They have then suddenly been expected to accept handling and all the accompanying restraints, not to mention the shock of discovering that, after all the freedom to which they have been accustomed, they must now accept the discipline of learning to work under a rider. It is as if a human adolescent, never having been to school, is suddenly put through a course of higher education and expected to master it in a relatively short time. No wonder so many young horses have been ruined both mentally and physically by such unreasonable demands. And, of course, it is the resistances provoked by precisely these unreasonable demands which have made so many people believe it is necessary to use force in 'breaking' horses.

The dangers of expecting too much from horses which have been inadequately prepared have been recognised for centuries. The great master of the eighteenth century, François Robichon de la Guérinière, says,

> The origin of the greater part of the horse's defences does not always lie with Nature; one often requires of them things of which they are incapable, desiring to accelerate too greatly their learning and to teach them too much; this coercion renders exercise odious to them, strains and exhausts their tendons and sinews, whose elasticity is the very foundation of suppleness; and often they are ruined when one believes they are trained; then, no longer having the will to resist, they obey, but with ill-will and without any vigour whatsoever.[8]

La Guérinierè's comments are just as valid today as when they were written. Fortunately, the practice of leaving youngstock almost unhandled until their third or fourth year is now much less common, as horse breeders have begun to realise that any benefits, such as time saved by simply turning youngstock out virtually unhandled, are cancelled out by the increase in difficulty experienced later when the time comes for the horses to be trained under saddle. (Of course, many breeders do not back and ride away their own stock, so they never face this difficulty, which is then passed on to someone else.) Indeed, there have always been breeders and trainers who have recognised this; it really should not have needed the publicity surrounding Monty Roberts's 'quick start' techniques to bring this to the attention of the horse-minded public.

Almost 2,500 years ago Xenophon understood the principles recently restated by Monty Roberts and others: that the horse should understand that his comfort and security lie with his human handlers. 'For if this be done, colts must not only love men, but even long for them.'[9]

The education of a young horse can and should start as soon as the foal is born. The foal can learn to accept being touched all over, as well as gentle restraint. We believe in handling

Above Foals should be accustomed to being handled: Brian and Toska

foals every day; they can learn all kinds of things during the first few weeks of their lives, such as having their feet picked up, walking on and then halting when asked to; tolerating gentle grooming and many other simple things which will henceforth be part of their lives. There is always the danger that foals which are overhandled may become too familiar and boisterous with their human handlers, but this can be avoided by setting the ground rules for behaviour right from the start. Californian veterinary surgeon Robert Miller has developed his own technique for educating newborn foals, which he calls 'imprinting', although, while it is based on the biological imprinting described in Chapter 11, this is not quite the same as that process. (For a detailed description of this technique, which requires absolute understanding of the underlying process, see Mary Wanless, *For the Good of the Horse*, pp. 279–84.) It also helps if foals can be introduced into a group of other horses of mixed age and sex as early as possible. They then learn that bumptious behaviour will not be tolerated.

Colts – like Spencer Borden's colt Rodan – can be rendered much easier to handle if they are given something to think about. Too often boisterous and even

Below Brian with Toska

aggressive behaviour on the part of colts is excused on the grounds that this is only 'coltish-ness', or that they are 'feeling their feet'. One has to realise that if they are healthy colts are nat-urally full of high spirits and energy. If they are turned out with other horses, especially if a group contains other colts or young geldings, they may work off some of this energy in play, which they indulge in not only as a form of release for excess energy, but for its own sake, for the sheer pleasure of it. It also brings the benefits of helping to strengthen their limbs and improve their co-ordination. However, this does not necessarily make them easier to handle. As they begin to mature sexually, many will start to become 'nippy'. This is not necessarily, as most people believe, a sign of aggression, but an expression of the stallion's innate tendency to mouth at objects. There is a widespread belief that stallions will bite mares during mating, but well-behaved stallions, who have not been rendered psychotic by isolation and/or mis-handling, generally only use their teeth to grip mares if the mare is so tall or her barrel so round that the stallion feels unbalanced and needs something to hang on to!

It is, of course, true that stallions use their teeth in fighting more than mares or geldings do, but it is necessary to read the horse's body-language and to judge whether real aggres-sion is involved: is a colt or stallion who nips or bites angry or annoyed? If so, why? Is he bit-ing from frustration caused by an unnatural lifestyle; is it simply playful nipping caused by a lack of mental stimulation and/or a need to mouth at something? Or is it just bad man-ners on the part of a horse who has never been taught the limits of acceptable behaviour? Many colts start off with playful nips that are misinterpreted as actual aggressive biting. The usual 'cure' for this (normally a whack across the nose) does not, in fact, cure anything because while it may discourage the horse from nipping (although in my experience it sel-dom does), it does nothing to remove his reasons for doing so. It may actually make the sit-uation much worse and turn a 'nipper' into a really vicious biter. Lucy Rees cites the case of an Arabian stallion who neither disliked nor feared people. However, he was a vicious biter when handled. He was cured by being worked in a round bull-pen, using a technique simi-lar to that of Monty Roberts but developed independently by Ray Hunt. The stallion had to be worked hard and fast to get his attention. When he was allowed to approach the trainer he soon started to bite when he was rubbed and stroked. When this happened he was driven angrily away. He soon learned that he was allowed to nuzzle and lick the handler but that biting was not acceptable. Lucy Rees says, 'His delight in finding an acceptable way of mak-ing contact with people was almost laughable: he even licked the vet tenderly.'[10] She goes on to say,

> Fire's need to make contact with his mouth is typical of stallions. As often happens, it had
> built up to such a point that, combined with the certainty of punishment, it was expressed
> violently. In a herd, older mares teach colts how to approach and nuzzle politely in exactly
> the same way, by driving them away angrily when they are too rough. But when a horse is
> restrained by a lead rope, he cannot go away, and so cannot learn.[11]

Another Arabian stallion, very well bred, was turned into a vicious biter by inappropriate handling. A very boisterous colt, he did well in the showring but his bad behaviour made his owners afraid of him. He spent the first six years of his life virtually a prisoner in his stable. He was eventually bought by someone who realised that his viciousness was the result of bad management rather than any innate faults of temperament. Although he could be ridden, he tried all kinds of stratagems to get rid of his rider (such as the unpleasant trick of trying to scrape her off along the walls of the *manège*); and he still bit. Kindness alone was not enough to reform this character; his mind had to be re-educated. Eventually, though, he began to realise that life was infinitely more interesting than it had been. Not only was he allowed out to grass (which he had scarcely seen for years), he also got about more as his rider hacked him out (discovering in the process that, against all reasonable expectation, he was virtually bomb-proof in traffic). As his education under saddle progressed and he found his work enjoyable and stimulating, he gradually stopped biting altogether and is now a pleasure to handle and ride. Not long before I wrote this, he was being ridden safely by a twelve-year-old girl.

Zareeba and his half-brother Kruger were both very 'nippy' as young colts. This was caused by nothing more than youthful exuberance and a need to explore things with their mouths. One must remember that, for a horse, the mouth, with its extremely mobile lips, is his only means of manipulation. Sometimes the nippiest, 'mouthiest' colts are the cleverest when it comes to undoing stable doors and untying the knots in the ropes with which they are tied up. We found that Zareeba and Kruger were not nippy because they were being aggressive, but because they needed to play with things with their mouths. Zareeba in particular could never resist the kind of puffy padded jackets often worn around stables in winter. He would also pick one's pocket, and several times I have had to rescue a pair of gloves that were being well and truly chewed! His favourite trick (which he will still do, given half the chance) was to whip my woolly winter hat off my head, wave it up and down a few times, then lower it to the ground and proceed to wipe the floor with it. (Is this evidence of an equine sense of humour? One does wonder.) But puffy jackets were always his greatest temptation. If I (or any other unsuspecting person) walked past too close to his stable door while he was looking out, we might find our progress suddenly arrested as a playful colt grabbed a sleeve in his mouth. On one occasion he took this a little too far. His breeder's small daughter was standing near him one day when he casually picked her up by the hood of her anorak and lifted her clear off the ground! There was absolutely no malice or aggression in any of this; it was simply born of a need to mouth at things and play with them, and it would have been stupid as well as wrong to punish it. I ignored well-meant advice to 'give him a good clout whenever he nips'. Instead, I worked at diverting his mind by teaching him things: simple 'tricks' like shaking hands, as well as giving him things to play with (the often recommended turnip was a great success, with only one problem – it lasted all of five minutes). I taught him that if he wanted to mouth at my hand or my arm – licking, nuzzling, mouthing with his lips, or even a gentle nibble – that was fine, but if he nipped, he would be pushed away and all attention withdrawn. Eventually he stopped nipping altogether, although even now, after a number of years, he still likes to lick and mouth at people' s hands and arms.

Smacking would not have cured him (it had already been tried, and had failed, before I bought him); in time it might well have turned him into a real, frustrated biter. Being gelded did not cure him either. If colts are gelded after they have already developed 'coltish' behaviour, then gelding will not necessarily make them forget that behaviour. What he needed was some outlet for his need to mouth and nuzzle at people and other animals, as well as something to occupy his mind. Lungeing, long-reining, being taken for walks through the woods (where he learned to ignore the 125 Express that came screaming past only a few metres away from the path on its journey out of Darlington Station), as well as teaching him a few basic tricks, helped to develop his mind to the point where being boisterous and nippy were no longer such attractive options as they had once been. We have since tried the same tactics with a number of other 'nippy' colts, with great success.

I have to say here that while in some instances all that is needed to cure a 'nipper' is more freedom and social contact with his own kind, in others this is simply not enough; what is needed is mental stimulation. Very often, as with a naughty child, anti-social behaviour is attention-seeking. If the child (or horse) behaves badly and the parent (or handler) responds with punishment, then even although the result may be discomfort, this is secondary to the fact that the child or horse has got what he or she wanted: attention. So the action which produced the response is likely to be repeated. This is not to say that either children or horses *like* being punished; simply that if their lives are mentally and/or emotionally impoverished, punishment for bad behaviour is better than no interaction at all. (It is this kind of feeling that keeps many embattled married couples together: for some people even domestic strife is better than loneliness.) If this situation persists for too long, the naughty child or the badly behaved horse may not only be confirmed in their anti-social behaviour, they may become locked in a vicious cycle that becomes very hard to break. We must, therefore, not only teach them that anti-social behaviour is unacceptable, but show them an alternative. Experiments with children whose anti-social actions have turned their parents' and teachers' lives into a nightmare have shown that if the children are treated *positively*, i.e. shown an alternative to their bad behaviour, instead of simply being punished for it, the success rate is extremely encouraging. The model of substituting 'do this' for 'don't do that' can be successfully transferred to our dealings with horses.

Rather than simply punishing horses for nipping or barging or whatever form of bad behaviour they dream up, we must seek the reason for such behaviour and then educate them out of it. This is not to say, of course, that more drastic measures may not sometimes be necessary where biting or nippiness is caused by bad manners rather than lack of mental stimulation or distress. As always, one must read the individual horse and the context!

Many people who believe that bad behaviour must never be tolerated and must be instantly (and consistently) punished, are missing the point when they insist on this. This is that the horse, too, has a point of view. To him, his behaviour may be perfectly justified. Take the case of the horse who lashes out in fear. Few horses will kick out for no reason, but there are many situations where they can be frightened into doing so. One such incident was described in Chapter 11, where I told how a young warmblood had learned to kick out when frightened. In that instance, we did not punish the horse for kicking out. How could we have done so? Instead, we have had to educate him out of this tendency gradually, by showing him that a human approaching his off side is not going to attack him. We do this by progressively extending the boundaries of what he will tolerate, instead of asking him to accept being touched along his sensitive side all at once. We do not put him under any pressure, as this would only reinforce his conviction that something unpleasant is about to happen. If, in the process, he does kick out, or threatens to kick, we can still let him know verbally how much we disapprove without resorting to physical punishment. As we have seen, horses do have a sense of justice. Is the horse to be punished for an action which, to him, is not only natural but essential to survival? How coherent does that make our authority seem to the horse?

By adopting the line that education is always better than punishment, we can increase our horses' brainpower, and with it their capacity to cope with the demands we make upon them in their training (this, of course, means taking that training – as well as the horses themselves – seriously). It has been shown in experiments that animals which live in an enriched environment, with plenty of diversions and interesting activities, actually become more intelligent than those in an impoverished environment lacking these mental stimuli. One such study concentrated on 'rich' and 'poor' rats. These rats were litter-mates, reared in two groups in two different environments. The 'rich' rats were kept in cages where a variety of activities were available to them, such as treadmills, ladders and other toys and objects for exploration. They also had social contact with each other, and were frequently handled. The 'poor' rats lived in similar cages, but in a barren environment with little sensory stimulation, social contact or handling. After several weeks the rats were killed and their brains examined. The 'rich' rats had developed a thicker cerebral cortex because their neocortices had developed a more complex network of neuronal circuitry. They also had altered concentrations of certain brain enzymes. Measurable differences were found as a result of even one hour a day of exposure to such an enriched environment. In similar experiments, the intelligence of the 'rich' rats in solving problems became measurably greater than that of the environmentally impoverished rats. Comparable results have been obtained with monkeys, and there is no reason to suppose that the findings are not applicable to most, if not all, mammalian species.

Horses are intensely curious creatures, a quality which we should cultivate and make use of in our training programmes. Owen McSwiney says in this context that whereas some may say horses are curious, he says they like to be *informed*.

Horses are possessed of what some people call curiosity; what others, like myself, would term a lively interest and a constant need of information. They want to know what is going on, what things are, how they smell, what will happen if they go near them. They look, they memorize, and will do so repeatedly if in doubt about something. They combine very clearly what is being demanded of them with the situation in which it is being demanded. If their grasp is good and their tutor is explicit, they will learn the fundamentals of anything we try to teach them, with often remarkable willingness, even eagerness, providing we do not make it a bore by senseless repetition.[12]

Above 'What are you doing?' Imzadi expresses her curiosity
Below Zareeba cannot resist investigating strange objects

So by providing horses – especially green young horses – with an environment which enriches their mental experience, we can actually increase their learning capacity. There are many ways in which green young horses can be educated before they are old enough to be ridden. Apart from the basic education of foals, mentioned above, we can take youngsters for walks as I did with Zareeba. When he was two, and his companion, a Connemara foal, was seven months old, my husband and I used to take them to the bottom of the lane to graze on

'Shake hands!' Nivalis with Brian

the wide grass verge and watch the traffic going past on a busy main road. In this way they learned not to be afraid of even the heaviest traffic. Youngsters can be taught simple 'tricks', such as shaking hands; there need be no fear that this will lead to striking out, even with colts, so long as only the correct action is rewarded. They can learn to stand still when the handler says 'Stand!'; and they can learn some circus tricks, which are not only a wonderful way of educating the horse to think about what he is doing, but also of developing the *handler's* patience and strength of character. Contrary to what many people believe, good circus training has nothing whatsoever to do with coercion. The best circus trainers have always recognised what so many ordinary horse trainers and riders have failed to grasp: that an animal trained through fear or aversion cannot be trusted in circumstances more frightening than the source of its aversion, whereas an animal trained through pleasure and reward will often display outstanding courage and intelligence. When you are dealing with animals with the size and power of elephants, for example, you cannot afford to make too many mistakes in this respect; a frightened elephant is even more dangerous than a frightened horse.

One may teach horses almost any kind of trick; those most often seen in high-class circus acts are described in *Classical Circus Equitation*, by Henrik Jan Lijsen. This excellent book takes the reader through liberty work, High School (at its best, no different in principle from the classical High School of the *manège*), quadrilles and vaulting. The liberty work is perhaps most relevant to our subject as much of it can be taught to relatively young horses. A lot of this work is quite easy; Nivalis virtually taught himself to stand with his front feet on a bale of straw. (This is *not* recommended, however, as the front feet can easily get caught in the baling twine if it is not absolutely taut. If you are going to try this, it would be better to construct a wooden pedestal, as described by Lijsen on page 34 of *Classical Circus Equitation*.) Liberty work, properly done, is invaluable in giving young horses something to think about. They can develop such powers of concentration that they forget all about whatever normally distracts them or about 'acting up' in order to gain attention. As with any aspect of their training, one must be careful not to ask too much of them or to make the training sessions too long. However, if it is done in a relaxed way, they will not feel pressurised and most will learn amazingly quickly. Effectively, they 'learn to learn'. As a result of education, like the 'rich' rats in the experiment, they actually become more intelligent. There are benefits, too, for the handler. Working with a horse in this intimate way can help to strengthen the bond that should always exist between the horse and his trainer. As Lijsen says, 'There is no better way of getting to know animals than by training them. It leads to mutual understanding, a fine appreciation of animal reaction – and, you will find, it greatly improves your patience. One soon discovers that humans, too, can make mistakes.'[13]

But if horses can derive mental stimulation from such education at liberty, what of the sort of education they receive under saddle? Is it – as many people suggest – totally for our benefit? Or can horses, too, derive pleasure from ridden work? More than this: can they actually take pride in doing so? There is a common belief that horses cannot possess any kind of inner motivation; that they will seek only their own comfort. Karin Blignault says, 'Although horses, by their submissive nature, show a certain willingness to learn, they cannot possess

Nivalis enjoys his circus tricks

an inner motivation to perform an action correctly. Such motivation is present only in the human being with his highly developed cortical brain.'[14] But this ignores the fact that, as we have seen, the horse, too, has a 'highly developed cortical brain'! Such a sweeping dismissal of the possibility of inner motivation in horses can severely limit what we achieve with them, as well as making an unwarranted assumption. How do we know for certain what may or may not be possible in non-human brains? The only certainty here is that if we proceed from the conviction that something is *not* possible, we will almost inevitably prove ourselves correct. Nevertheless, Blignault is certainly right when she points out that we should work through what is comfortable for the horse, asking only a little at a time. However, we must not take this to extremes; if we never 'stretch' the horse, neither we nor he will ever find out what he is capable of achieving. What we have to do is work mainly within what is often referred to as the 'comfort zone', and gradually make that zone wider by progressively asking for a little more than the horse is naturally inclined to offer, as soon as we feel he is capable of extra effort.

It is true that, at the very outset of his education, the horse will generally not possess a great deal of inner motivation, except that he may enjoy exercise for its own sake, just as many children enjoy the challenge of learning for its own sake. However, he may not see the point of some of the fairly simple exercises we may ask him to do. When we set out to train a very green horse, there is no way we can explain to him that what we are asking of him is (provided we are following correct principles) for his own good. We cannot say, 'If you do as I ask, you will grow more athletic, have sound limbs and live longer' – even if we could, there is no guarantee that he would accept what we say. Vicki Hearne comments on what she calls 'the extraordinary power of denial' of the ghetto student who said, 'Whaffo I wanna read no *Tale of Two Cities*?'[15] At this stage, the green horse might say, through his resistances, 'Whaffo I wanna trot in no circles?' The trainer (having hopefully ruled out any physical cause for the resistances) can only say something on the lines of, 'Because it will please me if you do.' (In the kind of training I am talking about here, which is of the sort that goes on in places like the Spanish Riding School, there is no place for the type of coercive training that says, 'Do as I say, or else!') In *My Horses, My Teachers*, Alois Podhajsky writes of 'riding an indifferent horse briskly forward in order to awaken him by changes of speed and make him take pleasure in his own movement'[16]. Of course there is very much more to it than this, but the power of frequent transitions – from one gait to another, as well as changes of speed and direction – to engage the horse's interest is quite remarkable. Instead of just slopping along, they have to think about what they are doing and where they are putting their feet. Zareeba used to be quite lazy until we started to make more use of school figures (which should never be performed for their own sake, but as gymnastic exercises for the horse). The first time we executed a shoulder-in, he became so animated that, in human terms, he seemed to be saying something like, 'Wow, that was fun, let's do it again!' When he is first ridden after a break of any length, he is almost invariably excitable and inattentive to begin with, so I start off by riding small circles (voltes), demi-voltes, serpentines, etc., progressing to turns on the haunches and demi-pirouettes – all in walk. After a few minutes of this he is concentrating so much on what he is doing that he forgets all about being spooky and explosive and by the time we come to trot work, he is relaxed and able to work correctly without tensing or hollowing his back.

This concentration on (and enjoyment of) his work means that Zareeba and I have been able to resolve a number of conflicts which otherwise might have damaged our relationship. You will recall that, in Chapter 9, I mentioned the dislike many horses have of stepping into puddles. Zareeba is one of these; apart from anything else, he simply hates getting his feet wet. However, if what he is doing is sufficiently meaningful to him, he will happily ignore such discomforts and phobias as puddles. I was told years ago by a well-qualified person that I should insist on him going through the puddle which accumulates in one corner of our arena after heavy rain. But the more I insisted, the more he resisted, until we were locked in a futile battle of wills. In the end I grew sick of wasting so much time and effort that could be better spent doing more constructive things, so instead I concentrated on school exercises, and whenever we came to that corner, instead of insisting that Zareeba went through it, I deliberately rode him round it. As he became more absorbed in the exercises he forgot about avoiding the puddle, and gradually I was able to ride him closer and closer to it until he would trot through its shallow edges without fuss. Eventually, when he realised it was no great matter after all, he would happily splash through the deepest part without any resistance whatsoever. This is the strategy I have adopted ever since and we no longer have battles of wills about it.

By approaching the training in such a way that it engages the horse's mind, by rewarding the slightest sign of compliance, and withholding such rewards when compliance is absent, the trainer gradually instils in the horse the idea that life is actually more interesting this way. Eventually, because his muscles have been strengthened and his body made more supple as a result of the training, movement becomes more effortless, and the horse starts to take the same pleasure in exercise for its own sake as do many human athletes. At this stage he begins to see the point of all the strengthening and suppling exercises and looks forward to his work. His motivation then becomes not so much any reward the rider may offer him (although that, too, is still important), but his inner motivation to perform well – to move to the best of his ability. This is not, of course, something that we can prove; but many horses make it clear, through their whole demeanour and bearing, that this is important to them. Sylvia Loch describes her ex-bullfighting horse, the Lusitano-Arabian stallion Palomo Linares, as:

> . . . one of the finest horses I have ever ridden. His spirit is indomitable, his generosity humbling. Every step he takes is made in the pursuit of excellence. Nothing is shoddy; he tries with all his might to make each movement perfect and often gives riders the benefit of the doubt because, in his wise old way, he knows how it should be done, and how it should be ridden.[17]

And no one who knows Palomo could doubt that this is so.

Palomo Linares and Sylvia Loch: even when, as here, Palomo is simply having fun, he still strives for excellence (Sylvia Loch)

One of Sylvia's other horses, the Lusitano x Thoroughbred Espada (who is as sharp as his name, which in Portuguese means 'sword') takes pride in his abilities in a different way. At a Classical Riding Club Open Day, Sylvia and Espada were demonstrating some of the more advanced dressage exercises. Suddenly, without any prompting from his rider whatsoever, Espada put in a very neat series of flying changes. The reason: having discovered he can do them, Espada simply loves doing flying changes! Such spontaneity in horses should be encouraged, as we saw in Chapter 9. How unfortunate it is that this would be unacceptable in competition dressage which, sadly, often serves to stifle that which it should be developing.

Espada also takes a delight in performing the Spanish walk, a movement often decried by purists who say it is an unnatural circus movement. Correctly done, however, it can be beneficial in helping to free the shoulders. I have actually seen horses out in a field perform a very close approximation of the Spanish walk in displaying to one another. Espada clearly loves showing off *his* Spanish walk!

One winter, several years ago, my husband and I witnessed what looked like a spontaneous display of self-schooling. The fields were very boggy, so Zareeba and Nivalis (then rising two) had been turned out in the arena together for exercise. To our surprise and delight, we saw Zareeba, closely followed by Nivalis, trotting round with great concentration, executing per-

Espada likes showing off his Spanish Walk (Hector Innes)

fect circles, demi-voltes and figures of eight, with all the solemnity and dignity of a venerable professor imparting his wisdom to a pupil. What impressed us was the sheer precision of the work: this was not merely normal horse-play, but the deliberate execution of school figures. And it was not merely mindless repetition of exercises regularly carried out, because Zareeba introduced variations of his own that we had certainly never practised together. The look of utter concentration on his face, and that of Nivalis (whose solemn demeanour matched that of his mentor), told us that this was something they were doing quite deliberately, for its own sake.

When horses have reached the stage where they not only derive pleasure from their own movements, but insist on performing those movements with precision, then they may become great teachers themselves. Such horses will very often not accept anything less than the same kind of precision from the rider. Alois Podhajsky's great mare Nora, who had to be retired from competition following an injury, continued her army career as a school horse during Podajsky's spell as an instructor at the Cavalry School. 'She helped me to explain the correct application of the aids. She simply did not take any notice of wrong or inexact aids and by her constant behaviour and precise reactions she soon gained the reputation among my pupils of the best school horse of the institute.'[18] In the same way, the horses of the Spanish Riding School do as much of the teaching as the chief riders do. Apart from some very basic directives, little that is taught in that great academy of equestrian art is actually written down. Instead, it is handed down from generation to generation. The young apprentice rider joins the Riding School where he first learns on fully schooled horses, the 'professors'. In time, with guidance from the Chief Riders, he will go on to train his own horses who will, in turn, become 'professors', who will teach other young apprentices . . . and so on.

Many horses will put up with sloppy riding and imprecise aids and muddle through as best they can or, like Palomo, they are wise and forgiving and gently point the way for the rider to understand what is needed. Some others, however, like Podhajsky's Nora, will not accept such a lack of precision in their riders. It matters to them not only physically, but mentally. Such horses will sometimes cause themselves acute discomfort rather than respond to what are not 'aids' in the true sense of the term, but imprecise signals. On the lunge, Zareeba will halt immediately from a walk or a trot on hearing the words: 'Whoa, Zareeba!' Under saddle, if the rider has not learned how to halt using the back, seat and legs rather than the reins, he will march doggedly on, deaf to all verbal commands and seemingly oblivious to anything the rider does with the reins. Nothing is preventing him from halting (even though in the circumstances it would scarcely be a correct halt); he simply won't do it unless the rider gets it right. Similarly, like Nora, he will ignore any aids incorrectly given (except on the odd occasions when he interprets a slightly overemphasised leg aid in trot as an aid to canter). This is *not* naughtiness, as some people might insist, but a strong conviction that things should be done properly or not at all. It's as though the horse is saying, 'No, no; this is not how we do it!' As I said above, this is not something I can prove; it is simply a matter of knowing one's horse. Such horses can teach one so much; only recently I advised a young friend who was riding Zareeba to concentrate on feeling what was happening under the saddle. 'Learn to "listen" with your body,' I said. 'He'll soon let you know when you've got it right!'

This whole question of motivation is one area where, as earlier chapters have shown, the interpretations of behaviourism or cardboard Darwinism become completely derailed. One can always reduce the actions of others to a single motive, particularly if that motive fits in well with a specific view of the world in general. But, in fact, behaviour and actions seldom have only one motive; there are generally several layers of motivation, all interacting. Above all, to do something really well, you must *want* to do it. If it is done out of a sense of duty, or simply for gain, there will be missing from the result that element of inspiration which sets aside the truly great from the merely good or the mediocre. University of Chicago psychologist Mihaly Csikszentmihalyi, following the careers of 200 artists for a period of 18 years after they left art school, found that those who had gone on to become serious painters were those who, in art classes, had painted for the sheer joy of it. Those who had been motivated solely by dreams of wealth and fame had not found a successful career as artists after graduation. Csikszentmihalyi concludes that: 'Painters must want to paint above all else. If the artist in front of the canvas begins to wonder how much he will sell it for, or what the critics will think of it, he won't be able to pursue original avenues.'[19] Horses, of course, are immune to dreams of financial reward, but they may nevertheless be motivated by tangible rewards such as food. What this cannot be, in horses whose performance is outstanding, is their *only* motivation. Certainly, at the very beginning of their training, one cannot expect green horses to *want* to do any of the exercises that will develop their bodies. And, as we have seen, coercion won't do, although for some people it is all too easy an option. We must first earn the horse's respect, then his complicity. Some horses may never progress beyond this compliance with the trainer's wishes. Others, such as Palomo or Nora, may develop an inner motivation to perform to the utmost of their ability which far transcends any simple response to the rider's aids.

Frequently, however, our understanding of such responses is hampered by the reductionist approach which denies animals any inner motivation. The language used by trainers who understand how motivation works is sometimes explained, rather patronisingly, in what one might describe as neo-behaviourist terms:

> To say that a dog responds to praise because it wants to please us is, in fact, a more useful way of thinking about it in the practical, day-to-day business of training than describing it as appeasement behaviour in response to a threat from a dominant member of the social hierarchy would be.[20]

But need we regard the dog's response as 'appeasement behaviour' anyway? Undoubtedly in some cases that is just what it is. In others, however, it certainly is not. We recently took on a Doberman (to replace our old Dobie who, sadly, had to be put down in autumn 1997) who had been rescued by the RSPCA. Max had been well fed and was in general good health but he had evidently had very little meaningful contact with humans. In spite of this, like many

Dobies, he has a wonderful temperament. A mature dog, he had spent most of his life in a compound, and had never been taught even the most basic obedience. He did not know how to sit or stay on command, or even to come when called, although he knew his name. We quickly found that if we raised our voices, or used body-language that Max considered in any way threatening, he would simply scuttle back into the safety of his sleeping-quarters and huddle down in his bed. The only way we could teach him anything was by making ourselves as unthreatening as possible and ensuring that the whole experience was stress-free and pleasurable for him. Otherwise he did not respond at all, but lay cowering in his bed. After a relatively short time he had learned to come when called, to sit, to come to heel, to lie down, and the rudiments of sit-stay; at the time of writing he continues to improve, and clearly enjoys this work which has added a whole new dimension to his life.

None of this would have been possible had we believed that the dog's response was really *only* appeasement behaviour. The important thing here is the *belief*: people who tend to use what scientists call 'anthropomorphic language' generally do so because they *believe* the horse or dog is capable of a meaningful response and that this is not simply 'appeasement behaviour' or whatever might be appropriate in behaviourist terms. People who believe otherwise, who insist, for example, that while it might be useful to express oneself in anthropomorphic terms, this is only a convenient way of talking, will almost inevitably approach training without the necessary conviction that something meaningful can emerge. Talking about training dogs, Vicki Hearne comments,

> To the extent that the behaviorist manages to deny any belief in the dog's potential for believing, intending, meaning, etc. there will be no flow of intention, meaning, believing, hoping going on. The dog may try to respond to the behaviorist, but the behaviorist won't respond to the dog's response; there will be between them little or no space for the varied flexions of looped thoughts. The behaviorist's dog will not only seem stupid, she will be stupid.[21]

Furthermore, when it comes to training horses, we have to remember that, as far as our body language goes, we cannot fool them at all. Here, absolute belief in their capacity for response is essential. Horses know when we are not taking them seriously.

Some horses take themselves – and their work – so seriously that a mistake can seem like the end of the world to them. Alois Podhajsky's Lipizzaner stallion Neapolitano Africa was an outstanding example of this. Podhajsky says he was:

> . . . very good natured and willing to learn but as touchy as a prima donna. Any small trifle was enough to excite him and make him nervous. If he happened to make a mistake he was beside himself so that I had to calm him by patting and caressing and to comfort him by giving him to understand that everybody makes mistakes now and then and that there is nothing tragic about them. I called him my 'sensitive little soul' and treated him with even more care and tenderness than my other horses.[22]

At this point the behaviourist is probably saying, 'Aha!', and pointing out that Neapolitano Africa had no doubt learned that if he made a mistake he would be 'rewarded' by being fussed over. However, common sense rules this out. First, there is absolutely nothing to suggest that Neapolitano Africa possessed such a calculating streak; second, given the tendency of horses to repeat actions they have found to be successful in the past, it would surely have resulted in Neapolitano Africa becoming unreliable in the school, as he might deliberately make mistakes in order to get attention. In fact, the opposite was the case and he was one of Podhajsky's most reliable horses. Nor can it have been that he felt he had displeased Podhajsky, since the latter always took care to reassure him. His mistakes were genuine, momentary errors on the part of a sensitive horse to whom what he did mattered very much indeed.

Vicki Hearne speaks of dogs and horses whose minds and bodies are educated to the point where absolute mutual trust and obedience (in the best sense of the latter, as described in Chapter 9) are the result, as having an 'enlarged vocabulary'; the trainer who respects language – in this case the language of mutual understanding – can have a meaningful conversation with them. The ultimate that one can share with a horse with whom such talking is possible, is that state of grace where horse and rider forget their individual existence and seem to merge into one. At this point their mutual performance becomes so fluid and harmonious that they really seem to embody the Greek idea of the centaur.

The sensation this engenders has been described by Mihaly Csikszentmihalyi as 'flow'. It is the feeling experienced by countless people in virtually any field of activity one could name, when they find themselves performing effortlessly and at their peak of excellence, in whatever activity they find satisfying. Daniel Goleman describes the feeling of 'flow' eloquently:

> That experience is a glorious one: the hallmark of flow is a feeling of spontaneous joy, even rapture. Because flow feels so good, it is intrinsically rewarding. It is a state in which people become utterly absorbed in what they are doing, paying undivided attention to the task, their awareness merged with their actions . . . Flow is a state of self-forgetfulness, the opposite of rumination and worry: instead of being lost in nervous preoccupation, people in flow are so absorbed in the task at hand that they lose all self-consciousness . . . And although people perform at their peak while in flow, they are unconcerned with how they are doing, with thoughts of success or failure – the sheer pleasure of the act itself is what motivates them.[23]

When horse and rider are in this state, all manner of things are possible because there is no longer any resistance between them. As Goleman says, it is the pleasure of the act itself – not any peripheral rewards – that motivates them here; and that pleasure is all the more intense because one is not only sharing it with another creature, but with one belonging to another species. The so-called species barrier has been transcended.

Some riders may never have such an experience, no matter how many horses they ride. Others, some of the truly great riders, may experience it relatively frequently. Most of us have

Above John Whitaker and Milton (Bob Langrish)

Right Chief Rider Klaus Krzisch and Siglavy Mantua I (J.A.A. Hohmann Photography)

to make do with occasional revelations of what such ultimate communication can be like. But even the occasional revelation is worth all the effort that goes into forging such an understanding. Once one has felt such a sensation with one's equine partner, no matter how briefly, recapturing it becomes one's most powerful motivation for riding horses, far above any other.

And what of the horse? There is no such thing as absolute certainty, but watching the inner incandescence of such partnerships as John Whitaker and the great showjumper Milton, or of Chief Rider Klaus Krzisch of the Spanish Riding School and his stallion Siglavy Mantua I, one can scarcely doubt that horses are equally capable of feeling the intense pleasure that the sensation of 'flow' can bring.

Those who are so inclined may, of course, construct some other explanation to account for the apparent motivations of both horses and their riders, which fits in with their general world-view. The reductionist attitude is summed up by Joseph Wood Krutch:

> Suppose you had heard at the opera some justly famous prima donna singing, '*Voi che sapete*' . . . or even Mary Martin washing that man out of her hair. You have assumed that the one genuinely loves music and experiences some emotion related to that which Mozart's aria expresses, also that the other in some sense enjoys her performance. But a scientist of another kind – an economist – comes along and says, 'I have studied the evidence. I find that in both cases the performer really sings for so many thousand dollars per week. In fact she won't sing in public unless she is paid quite a large sum . . . You may sing in the bath because you are happy and you like to do it. But so far, at least, as professional singers are concerned, they sing for nothing but money.' The fallacy – and it is the fallacy in an appalling number of psychological, sociological and economic 'interpretations' of human behaviour – is, of course, the fallacy of the 'nothing but' . . . There is nothing in human experience or knowledge to make it seem unlikely that the cardinal [songbird] anouncing from the branch of a tree his claim on a certain territory is not also terribly glad to be doing it, very joyous in his realization of his own vigor and artistry . . . Whoever listens to a bird song and says, 'I do not believe there is any joy in it' has not proved anything about birds. But he has revealed a good deal about himself.[24]

For those who deny that horses can delight in learning, in using their bodies athletically, or in the execution of precise ridden work, I would recommend watching a good, classical, circus liberty act, a properly trained Western horse working cattle or a Portuguese bullfighting horse practising a *sorte* with a tame bull. Or they should attend the morning schooling sessions at the Spanish Riding School. If they then cannot see the quiet pleasure – Shakespeare's 'gentle majesty and modest pride'[25] – that such horses take in their work, it can only be because they are perversely determined not to do so.

Notes

1 Blunt, Lady Anne, *Journals and Correspondence 1878–1917* (ed. Rosemary Archer and James Fleming, Alexander Heriot, 1986), p. 437

2 *Blunt, Journals*, p. 437

3 *Blunt, Journals*, p. 347

4 *Blunt, Journals*, p. 437

5 *Blunt, Journals*, p. 438

6 *Blunt, Journals*, p. 438

7 Lesley Skipper, *The Arabian Show Horse* (J. A. Allen, 1997), p. 89

8 François Robichon de la Guérinière, *The School of Horsemanship*, p. 82

9 Xenophon, *The Art of Horsemanship*, p. 21

10 Lucy Rees, *The Horse's Mind*, pp. 209–10

11 Rees, *The Horse's Mind*, p. 210

12 Marquis of Mashanaglass, *Training from the Ground*, pp. 46–7

13 Henrik Jan Lijsen, *Circus Equitation* (originally published in Dutch as *De Hooge School*, 1949; tr. by Anthony Hippisley-Coxe; foreword by Sylvia Stanier; J. A. Allen, 1993), p. 20

14 Karin Blignault, *Successful Schooling*, p. 67

15 Vicki Hearne, *Adam's Task*, p. 69

16 Colonel Alois Podhajsky, *My Horses, My Teachers*, p. 49

17 Sylvia Loch, *The Classical Rider*, p. 306

18 Podhajsky, *My Horses, My Teachers*, p. 78

19 Mihaly Csikszentmihalyi, Interviewed in *The New York Times*, 22 March 1992, by Daniel Goleman. Quoted by Goleman in *Emotional Intelligence*, p. 93

20 Stephen Budiansky, *The Nature of Horses*, p. 79

21 Hearne, *Adam's Task*, p. 58

22 Podhajsky, *My Horses, My Teachers*, p. 138

23 Daniel Goleman, *Emotional Intelligence*, p. 91

24 Joseph Wood Krutch, *The Best of Two Worlds* (William Sloane Associates, New World, 1950). Quoted by Masson and McCarthy, When Elephants Weep, pp. 201–2

25 William Shakespeare, *Venus and Adonis*

CHAPTER SEVENTEEN

Living Together

Your horse is the mirror of your soul

ARAB SAYING

I N OUR QUEST to discover what we can about the horse's mind, we have come full circle. We must now ask again the question posed at the beginning of Chapter 1: can horses think?

The answer must surely be: yes, certainly they can think. We have seen that they have a well-developed cortical brain, feel a wide range of emotions, are capable of learning and remembering to a high degree, that they have a rich and complex social life and a varied and subtle system of communication. They have widely differing personalities and motivations, likes and dislikes. In every respect, they bear very little resemblance to the stereotype of a creature wholly moved by instinct and devoid of rational thought or any but the most basic emotions.

This has enormous implications for all of us who own, ride, train or handle horses. We control – or believe we control – virtually every aspect of their lives. We decide where they shall live, what they eat, where they go, what their activities will be, even who they have as companions. We determine whether, with whom and how often they mate; they are rarely given a choice in the matter. They work for us, often participating in activities which would have little or no meaning for them in their natural state. If they were human, we should have no hesitation in calling them slaves.

But, of course, they are not human, and so their situation cannot be judged by human standards. Or can it? If they are not simply creatures of pre-programmed, automatic reflexes, but beings with well-defined minds of their own, capable of a wide range of complex feelings (including the power of forming strong personal bonds), can we not apply the same kind of criteria as we should when judging the quality of life of humans in similar circumstances?

Many people do, of course, apply the same criteria; and this has led some of them to proclaim that all domestic animals (and this includes household pets, together with horses) exist in a state of slavery. They believe that this is completely unacceptable, and some of the more extreme holders of such views are determined to ensure that the keeping of domestic animals (including pets) is 'phased out'.

To those of us whose lives revolve around our animals, such an idea is unthinkable. Surely, we feel, the proponents of such extreme 'animal rights' views have a wholly distorted view of the kind of lives led by domestic animals. There is, in fact, nothing inherently degrading, or exclusively human, about the idea of pets (or to use a more acceptable term, 'companion animals'). Other animals may themselves have the equivalent of 'companion animals'; chimpanzees and gorillas in captivity have frequently sought and enjoyed the companionship of animals of other species, especially cats. We have only to see the evident pleasure that a great many horses take in the company of other species such as cats, sheep and goats, actively seeking them out even when they have ample companionship among their own species, to realise that cross-species friendship may be far more common throughout the animal world in general than we realise. With regard to pets or companion animals kept by humans, even when we recognise (as the more aware among us surely must) that factory farming methods as applied to cows, pigs and hens, etc. are quite unacceptable and need to be replaced by more humane methods of husbandry, we tend to feel that the same criticisms cannot be applied to the way we keep our household pets.

Yet the horrific numbers of cases of cruelty to, and neglect of, domestic animals of all kinds that the RSPCA are daily called upon to deal with tend to make the thinking animal lover wonder whether the animal rights people may not be right after all. If so many of us are incapable of caring for the animals we choose to believe we 'own', should we – any of us – keep animals at all?

Let us put this in perspective. While many of the cases dealt with by the RSPCA and other rescue organisations are the result of deliberate, sickening cruelty, most are caused by ignorance, and in some cases a reluctance to assume responsibility. Both cruelty and a lack of responsibility appear to be part of the problem identified in Chapter 9: if people are brought up to hold all forms of authority in contempt, and at the same time to deny other people any respect, should we be surprised if cruelty (which often stems from a lack of respect for others, as well as an inability to empathise with them) is sometimes the result? If, at the same time, people are indoctrinated with the idea that acceptance of personal responsibility is somehow weak and an infringement of personal freedom, then it is almost inevitable that a fair number of them will indeed abdicate that responsibility in their dealings with humans and non-human animals alike. The answer is not to ban the keeping of pets, but to educate people, not only in the practicalities of caring for them, but in respecting them and having a sense of responsibility towards them.

This would involve teaching people in general to recognise that animals – whether horses, dogs, cats or whatever – are not simply alien beings with whom we have nothing in common, nor furry toys (or, in the case of horses, furry bicycles), but individual, sentient creatures, with thoughts, needs and feelings of their own, which we shall need to take into account in dealing with them. Indeed, as far as cats and dogs are concerned, most thinking 'owners' already do take account of such things (note the quotation marks – I shall return to the vexed question of ownership later).

But what about horses? Do we have sufficient respect for them? Can we justify what we do with them? If so, how? First, we should consider that the animal rights views set out above maintain that contact with humans means that animals will have to behave in ways that are not natural to them, and that they will inevitably suffer as a result. If this means that we must keep ourselves apart from non-human animals, so be it. Dr Kiley-Worthington calls this *animal apartheid,* and in *Equine Welfare*, she sets out her reasons for opposing such an idea. Desmond Morris also puts the idea of animal apartheid in a proper context. He says, 'By maintaining our working relationships with domestic animals, even though they are no longer economically essential, we encourage that close bond of intimacy that lets us know other animals and ensures that we continue to care about them.'[1] Morris goes on,

> Domestic animals cannot be freed like human slaves. They have no wild homes to go to, so that to de-domesticate them would be to destroy them. The swollen human popula- tions have already pushed back the remaining wild animals to a point where for most peo- ple they are nearly invisible. We would end up in an animal-free zone of isolated human existence. The animal world would be out of sight, out of mind, and before very long, out of space. We need the constant presence of animals as a reminder to ourselves of our ani- mal nature . . . Cruel animal partnerships are an abomination, but benign ones are a joy to behold: the world would have a narrower horizon and a bleaker landscape without them . . . We need more intimate contact, or our children will eventually become so dis- tanced from all animal life that they will start to view it merely as another exotic fiction flitting across the television screen.[2]

To me, a world without animals would be a bleak, joyless place indeed. Like Dr Kiley- Worthington (who expresses similar sentiments in *The Behaviour of Horses*), I count the horses, dogs and cats with whom I share my life as among my best friends. They express their affection for me and my husband in a multitude of ways; who has the right to say that we have not enriched their lives as much as they have enriched ours?

In *Equine Welfare*, which considers in depth this very question, Dr Kiley-Worthington says that she does not believe that contact with humans *inevitably* has to cause prolonged suffer- ing to equines or any other animals. Much depends on how the equines are looked after, managed and trained. She asks,

> Is doing unnatural things necessarily bad and going to reduce the quality of life for human or animal? After all humans learn to read and write and we all agree that they should do

so. This is not *natural* but it is considered to enrich life. Correctly done, so that there is no suffering, learning different and new things could presumably also enrich the life of equines . . .[3]

I believe that it does enrich their lives. Certainly, in many cases, the lifestyle we select for our horses leaves a great deal to be desired from their point of view. They may spend too much time confined in stables, with insufficient opportunities to satisfy their physical and psychological need for fibre intake, movement and social companionship; in particular they may be denied the opportunity to form sexual bonds or to maintain family ties. Foals may be weaned abruptly, creating psychological trauma which may only reveal itself in later behavioural problems. We separate friends and family without, in many cases, any regard for the emotional upset it can cause. Many horses survive all of this because their nature is adaptable: this, after all, was one of the very qualities which enabled humans to domesticate them in the first place. However as I said earlier in this book, they are not *infinitely* adaptable, any more than we are. Some cope far better with a human-imposed lifestyle than others.

All these potentially stress-inducing aspects of husbandry are something we can alleviate. If we are aware of the problems inherent in some of the ways in which we keep horses, we can alter – or at the very least adapt – our husbandry systems in ways that will minimise stress to the horses in our care. We can, in most cases, take steps to ensure that they are able (in the language of behaviourism) to perform most, if not all, of the behaviours necessary to their well-being (see Appendix I, Stereotypes, for a brief discussion of these behaviours and how stereotypes can develop where horses are prevented from performing them. See also Dr Kiley-Worthington's *Equine Welfare* and Lucy Rees's *The Horse's Mind* for some constructive ideas on how to provide our equines with an appropriate lifestyle.) And let us not fool ourselves into thinking that a horse mainly or wholly turned out in a field, or a wild horse, is necessarily better off than one who has the security and shelter of a stable when he needs it but who is allowed plenty of freedom and exercise, as well as ample opportunities to socialise with his friends. The horse permanently out in the field may have all the space and exercise he needs; he may have all the food he wants and can eat, but his environment and his mental life may still be impoverished. While horses in the wild have undoubted advantages in that their free-roaming lifestyle and the constant presence of familiar companions may make them better-adjusted individuals, they often suffer physical hardships because of extreme weather conditions. If they fall ill they may suffer considerably before they either recover or die (apart from anything else they are likely to suffer from chronic parasite infestation), and injuries which in a domestic horse would not even be considered serious could mean the difference between life and death for a feral horse. Just because something is 'natural' (i.e. it would be normal for horses in the wild) does not automatically mean it is what they prefer. I once read a magazine article which warned against assuming that because we humans tend to like a soft, warm bed, horses must necessarily also want the same. After all, said the writer, in the wild they would have to lie on the hard earth! This is true much of the time, but given the opportunity, many of them do prefer – and will seek out – a soft and preferably warm bed. Several years ago, when we were constructing a couple of new stables, a heap of sand, left over from the foundations, was dumped in the field. Morning after morning when we arrived, there would be my husband's hunter mare and her boyfriend curled up snugly together on their bed of soft sand!

More recently still, the riding school next door to us laid a new surface in their indoor school. They spread part of the old woodchip surface over a marked-out area in one of their fields to serve as a temporary riding surface. Sure enough, the morning after it was put down, there were four or five horses lying down on the soft new surface.

Our part-bred Arabian filly Imzadi goes a stage further – she snuggles down on the top of the muck-heap!

All of this does not mean that horses are necessarily better off in domestic situations, any more than they are necessarily better off in a completely free-ranging lifestyle with no human interference. It depends what criteria we use to assess what being 'better off' means; and this can vary immensely with individuals. Some horses cannot tolerate being stabled; others are quite happy to spend most of their lives in a stable so long as they have a modicum of freedom, plenty to occupy their minds and a rich and varied social life. So before we make blanket judgements about the quality of life necessary to keep equines healthy, happy and stress-free, we should consider their individual natures. Not all horses thrive in the same kind of environment, just as not all humans do. While there may be parameters which define an acceptable lifestyle, within those parameters there may be room for a huge range of variation. As the old Russian saying has it, what's health to the Russian is death to the German!

Above all, if we enrich the horse's mind, we can compensate, at least partly, for the unnatural lifestyle we impose upon him. The horses of, say, the Spanish Riding School, lead a pretty unnatural life from most points of view, not least because for most of the year they are housed in the centre of a large European city. Yet these horses stay sound and continue to

Although they do lie down in the field, given the choice Kiri and her daughter Imzadi like to come into the stable to lie down on a soft bed of straw

work until well into old age. This is not only because Lipizzaners are, in any case, a long-lived breed, but because of the correctness of their training, which never seeks to rush them beyond their natural pace of development, and also because of the emotional richness of their lives. Although kept stabled, they can still see and touch one another. They have the constant company of their own kind, with whom they form strong bonds and attachments. They also form deep and lasting bonds of respect and affection with their grooms, and in particular with their riders. Restraint is kept to a minimum; you may recall from Chapter 6 that Pluto Theodorosta was able to go for his little walk across the road into the Winter Riding School because the door of his box was always open. And their minds are kept occupied: with their work and with the activity which goes on around them, as well as by their periodic trips abroad. While behavioural problems are not unknown, they are relatively infrequent; visitors are constantly impressed by the look of calm contentment on the faces of the famous white stallions.

If we cannot always keep horses in the conditions most natural to them, then we can make up for this to some extent by providing an enriched environment. We can educate the horse's mind by teaching him new things, taking him to different places, and allowing him to indulge his natural curiosity about new objects and places. If we take the trouble to learn how to communicate with him (whether from the ground or in the saddle) in his own subtle visual-kinaesthetic language, the task of training will not only be much easier, it will be much more pleasurable for all concerned.

However, a number of people these days (among them many of the animal rights proponents mentioned above, but also including many ordinary men and women without any connections to the animal rights movements) maintain that it is cruel to train animals, that it restricts their natural freedom, etc. But mere freedom from human-ordained discipline is not freedom to do as an animal wishes; in the wild animals are always constrained by the ever-present need to find food, shelter and safety from predators or rivals for prey. Nature is no innocent paradise where all live in harmony and security, free from the contaminating interference of humankind. Even if humans were to disappear off the planet, this would still be so. Dr Kiley-Worthington, while arguing for as natural a lifestyle for domestic horses and ponies as we can possibly arrange, nevertheless asks, is a so-called 'natural' lifestyle the only way all horses should live? Should we interfere with a sentient being just to 'educate' him, even if it is done in a way that is pleasurable to him? Is it not just an infringement of his freedom? She points out that:

> If we adopt this attitude for humans in our everyday lives it would mean ensuring that the 'natural' and personality behaviour of each individual would not be encouraged to adapt and fit in with the existing conditions and society, even for pleasurable experiences and long-term benefits. In other words, 'cultural' experiences and education would not exist. It would not seem to be a desirable approach to foster the development of a 'fulfilling' life for a human. Why then is it considered the only acceptable way for equines (or other species) to live?[4]

However, many of the views expressed by the proponents of 'animal apartheid' appear to stem, like so much else in a similar vein, from a dreary kind of pseudo-Marxism which sees the world principally in terms of coercion and exploitation. Sadly, as several chapters of this book have shown, too many of those who train and ride horses appear to confirm this dismal view, which concurs with that put forward by psychologist Oskar Pfungst and quoted in Chapter 6. But as we have seen, this has not always been the case; in the past there have always been great horsemen and horsewomen who have seen the horse as a friend and partner rather than as a slave. Even now, when the obsession with competition which afflicts so much of the equestrian world means that, for very many people, the horse is little more than a piece of living sports equipment, there is a growing number of people who seek more enlightened means of communicating with, training and riding horses. Hence the surge of interest in what are often referred to as 'alternative' therapies and training methods: methods which seek to work with the horse's nature rather than simply imposing an alien system from outside.

As we have seen, the greatest masters of equitation have always used such methods, although they may not have realised that this was what they were doing. Allied to the interest shown by an increasing number of people in the methods of people such as Monty Roberts and his pupils Richard Maxwell and Kelly Marks (as well as of others who have independently developed similar ways of communicating with and training horses, such as Ray Hunt and Pat Parelli), there has been an immense increase of awareness of, and interest in, the heritage of the masters of equitation referred to above, which is often called *classical* riding and training. I defined this in the Introduction; suffice it to say that the Classical Riding Club (see Appendix III), set up in 1995 by Sylvia Loch, now has a worldwide membership of like-minded people, bound together by a love for the horse and a wish to preserve the classical traditions which seemed in danger of becoming swept away. These include some very prominent horsemen and women, but in the main they are ordinary horse owners and riders who feel that there have to be better ways to ride and train horses than those they generally see in practice.

Then, too, there are the various therapies with which their practitioners set out to improve domestic life for the horse: acupuncture, herbalism, homoeopathy, holistic medicine, aromatherapy and a host of others, including some very effective massage therapies which seek to release hidden tensions, mental as well as physical. One of the best known of these is the therapeutic bodywork carried out by Linda Tellington-Jones, which employs a variety of sophisticated massage techniques, and very successfully too. (For a fuller discussion of these various therapies and techniques, see Mary Wanless, *For the Good of the Horse*.)

The main problem with all these assorted therapies and techniques is that, as Mary Wanless found when she came to research her book *For the Good of the Horse*, there is no unified 'theory of everything' which would enable us to integrate all the various treatments and methods. So we find inherent contradictions: X says that so-and-so is the cause of Dobbin's apparent back problem, while Y says it is something else. The problem is that both of them may be right! In fact, this is no worse a situation than we find with conventional methods of treatment, where one vet may contradict the findings of another. There is no such thing as an infallible 'method'; in exploring the exciting developments of such alternative therapies, as well as the training methods of Monty Roberts and others, and even the time-tested principles of the classical schools, we must not fall into the trap of allowing one kind of dogma to be replaced by another, or seeking easy 'universal' solutions to problems. As always, we must ask questions, observe and learn, and not shirk the responsibilities entailed by acceptance of that ever-present 'burden of judgement'.

Even with all this, what about the implication that, at best, we are condemning our horses to a life of slavery? We must ask, what is meant by 'slavery'? As always in such situations, we must have recourse to the dictionary. Mine defines a slave as: (1) a person legally owned by another and having no freedom of action or right to property; (2) a person who is forced to work for another against his will; (3) a person under the domination of another person or some habit or influence.

If we look at (1), then it seems that horses are indeed our slaves, as we obtain them by means of an exchange of money and they certainly have no right to property (but then such a concept would be meaningless to them anyway). Also, they have precious little freedom of action.

Points (2) and (3) are less problematical. We can only say that horses are forced to work for us against their will if we can show that they dislike such work and would not do it of their own free will. However, as we saw in Chapter 16, horses who work in partnership with their handlers and riders can and do come to enjoy their work, even to look forward to it; and the fact that they can do this has been the cornerstone of centuries of educated horsemanship. So while it would be true to say that *some* horses are forced to work against their will, it is not true for a great many horses, particularly those who perform to very high standards (and I am not necessarily talking about competition horses here). As for the idea of the horse being dominated, we have already seen what a bogus concept that is. If, then, we train and handle our horses in such a way that work becomes a pleasure for them, and do not fall into the trap of equating legitimate authority with tyranny or domination, we can truthfully say that, according to definitions (2) and (3) above, horses are not our slaves.

But what about definition (1)? Does the fact that we legally 'own' our horses mean that we do in truth own them? Are they really only so much property? In the eyes of the law, the answer is, unfortunately, yes which has led to a great many horses being treated as if they were just so many living assets. However, the same law also acts to protect horses; because they have no legal or moral status of their own, they need such protection in order to ensure that someone bears the legal responsibility for caring for them. The animal rights argument here would be that we should accord horses legal status as persons in their own right, but while this is an attractive idea, it won't do, for reasons which a very little thought will make clear. To have such status in our world they would have to be fully informed of the rules and concepts by which our societies operate, since the notion of rights without responsibilities is not only incoherent but ultimately destructive – as our late twentieth-century Western societies are now discovering to their cost. (The fact that there are exceptions to this rule – as in the case of certain mentally ill people or those otherwise incapable of making decisions for themselves, is no argument against this general principle.) This is not to say that animals can't have rights – a concept explored admirably by Desmond Morris in *The Animal Contract* – simply that we can't accord them full and equal rights within the law.

Does legal 'ownership' of our horses automatically render them our slaves? I don't think it need do so. I certainly don't consider that I 'own' my horses in anything but this legal sense (although I do sometimes think they definitely 'own' me!). They 'belong' to me and to my husband in the same way that we 'belong' to them: they are part of our family group (which also comprises several dogs and cats). Our authority over them stems from precisely this familial relationship, in the sense in which authority is used in Chapter 9. In a way we are their 'foster-parents'. Indeed, a video film of the Spanish Riding School refers to the riders of the school in just such a manner: as foster-parents of the horses in their charge. To some this might seem demeaning, as though we are seeking to maintain our horses in a perpetual state of foalhood (and, as the pseudo-Marxists might say, thereby to exert control over them), but this is not at all the sense in which it is meant here. It implies nothing more or less than complete acceptance of responsibility for them: not only for their physical care, but for their intellectual and emotional development. Human par-

Part of the family: the author with Nivalis aged five months

ents do not cease to be parents just because their children have grown up. In many cultures throughout the world, where the wisdom derived from age and experience is not devalued as it is in so many Western cultures, children continue to defer to their parents even when the former are grown up and have children of their own. They see nothing demeaning in this; it is the respect due to people who have nurtured and cared for them and, in a very real sense, given them being.

There is nothing at all new or revolutionary about the idea of extending the concept of 'family' to include the non-human animals who share our lives. In her book *Equine Welfare*, Dr Kiley-Worthington suggests that those humans who first domesticated horses might have formed very strong emotional bonds with them.

> Raising young animals in the home generally results in emotional bonds being formed between the humans and the animals . . . they become familiar with and often fond of one another. When humans were raising foals, perhaps some might even have suckled them if they were very young; people certainly suckled piglets and in some parts of New Guinea they still do.[5]

In the seventh century AD, Omar, friend and companion of the Prophet Mohammed, was

instructing the faithful to treat horses as they would their own children: 'Love horses and look after them, for they deserve your tenderness; treat them as you do your children; nourish them as you do friends of the family and blanket them with care. For the love of God do not be negligent for you will regret it in this life and the next.'[6] The mares and foals of the *bedawin* shared in the family life, even to the extent of wandering into the family tent for a scratch, a drink of precious water or a handful of dates.

To some the concept of admitting the horse into one's family in this way might seem sentimental, and therefore rather suspect. However, I have never understood the rather irrational fear of 'sentiment' which seems to afflict a great many people who deal with horses. *Excessive* sentiment might indeed cloud our judgement, as would an excess of any emotion. But an absence or deficiency of emotion is equally detrimental to our understanding. Love for the horse has been the great *leitmotiv* that unites true horsemen and women of all eras: the fiercest *bedawin* warrior, the toughest German or Russian cavalryman, the proudest and most fearless *cavaleiro* or *rejoneador* – these have never been

'Love horses and look after them, for they deserve your tenderness; treat them as you do your children, nourish them as you do friends of the family and blanket them with care.' Tiff as a young foal (Lynn & Sara Debnam)

Below A horseman or woman should never be afraid to demonstrate their love for their horses. Here Brian shows his affection for Nivalis after a training session

afraid to admit to the deep love they have felt for their horses, nor to express their emotions freely. An old Austrian cavalry manual states quite unequivocally: 'The cavalryman loves his horse more than he loves himself' – and that was frequently no exaggeration. Alois Podhajsky has written of the deep love he felt for the many horses who shared his life, in particular the plain mare Nora, whose supreme talents transcended her ugliness so that observers forgot all about her plain appearance. But as Podhajsky says, 'To me she had never been ugly because I knew her wonderfully straight and decent character, her tenderness and her loyalty, and because I loved her.'[7]

If, then, we accept our horses into our 'family circle', even though we may not share our homes with them, we acknowledge more fully their personhood and their individual needs. The fact that we restrict their freedom then becomes of secondary importance. For even our freedom, while undeniably far greater than theirs, is also circumscribed by the necessities of daily life: of earning a living, raising a family or whatever. Most of us have both far less, and far more, freedom than we realise; the greatest freedom of all is not defined by physical boundaries but by mental ones.

For those horses who have such relationships with those who care for them, I think there can be no question of slavery. However, in order to have such a relationship, we must first recognise that the horse, too, has a point of view, and that he may see things from a different perspective. As Lucy Rees says,

If we, with our infinitely superior intelligence and imagination, cannot put aside our anthropomorphic value-systems of competition and power, of home dens and discrete, hard-won meals, of the giving of presents as signs of friendship, all of which are the heritage of an animal that spends at least part of its time hunting, how can we expect a horse not to be hippomorphic? How can he understand that his very size seems threatening, his vegetarian teeth alarming? How is he, who relies on love, trust and freedom to escape, to realize that we want him to tune into our desires despite the fact that we constrain and hurt him?[8]

The answer lies in giving our horses as much freedom of choice as is compatible with their personal safety and ours. The more we take the trouble to build a relationship based on mutual trust, respect and affection, the more freedom we will be able to allow them. As with dogs, the greater their 'vocabulary' (in the sense in which the word is used in Chapter 16), the more we can trust our horses to take responsibility for their own actions: in other words they enter the sphere of moral life. So the horse who has an 'enlarged vocabulary' – a horse, for example, such as Pluto Theodorosta – can be trusted with a degree of freedom unthinkable to a green young horse fresh from the field, because he knows what actions are acceptable in what circumstances, where his safety lies and whose authority he may trust.

As earlier chapters have shown, the training ethos which makes such mutual trust possible rejects any notion of the bridle as an instrument, as Vicki Hearne puts it, 'of the kind of subjection that, in my experience, exists only in the fantasy lives of people who have bizarre notions about the nature of power. Abandoning such notions is essential to conversing with horses.'[9] Unfortunately, as Hearne also points out, many people do fear the abandonment of such power fantasies; this fear – which is often linked to fears about loss of control – may also, Hearne suggests, be what she calls 'a terror of genuine power', as such power entails enormous responsibilities. This fear of losing control is at least partly what makes so many people subject their horses to excessive restraint and harsh training methods. As Paul Hunting, who runs the highly successful 'Ride For Your Life' workshops, says,

> Most of the time our attempts to control life don't work and we get upset and hurt. Then, usually, we tighten our grip . . . we become more committed to controlling, more creative at it – even qualified in it! And so the endless spirals of frustration, stress and failure continue . . . We live in a world that seems to be addicted to 'control'. Our fear of losing control often runs (and ruins) our lives.[10]

Minimum restraint: Joanne with Mo (the feed scoop undoubtedly helps!)

Instead, Hunting stresses the value of what he calls taking 'response-ability' for the manner in which we attempt to control things in ways that don't work. 'The horse mirrors this accurately.'[11] — hence the truth of the Arab saying quoted at the head of this chapter. 'He is also our partner in revealing to us when we have changed our inner attitude.'[12] You will remember that, in Chapter 13, I pointed out that the horse's carriage is ultimately determined not only by how well the rider 'facilitates' his movement, but by his mental state at the time: as Sylvia Loch says, no horse can be forced to give his back to the rider if he does not want to (or, one might add, if a mental blockage is preventing him from doing so)! Exactly the same applies to the rider. Paul Hunting remarks that the rider's physical position on a horse is controlled by their attitude. 'And this, in turn, is under the domain of our spiritual position: our altitude! Therefore the higher we can get in our "spiritual altitude" the more empowered we are to balance the physical position with our horse!'[13]

But this requires letting go of our fears about losing control – whether it is control over our lives or control over our horses. This 'letting go' entails some risk. What if it doesn't work? What if the horse 'takes advantage' and runs away with the rider? This is where our much vaunted 'superior intelligence' gets in the way of understanding and genuine communication. We saw in Chapter 6 how the Cartesian scientific and philosophical concept of 'reason' is actually a very narrow one: as Mary Midgley points out, it defines reason largely as a capacity for mathematical logic. So great are our abilities in this respect that we tend to forget that it is only one form of knowing and understanding. It enables us to manipulate the world around us, but it can also be immensely destructive. On its own, such mathematical logic does not give us the maturity to use our knowledge wisely; the overwhelming scientific and philosophical imperative to do something just because we can may, in the end, make us the only species which has systematically brought about its own extinction.

As far as leading a rich and full mental life is concerned, this kind of analytical ability is by no means the most important factor. As psychologist Daniel Goleman points out, emotional intelligence is at least as important. So too is the power of perception, which is something that horses possess to a high degree. However, the highly developed (some might say overdeveloped) analytical side of our human brain insists on interfering with *our* perceptions, interposing our fears of loss of control between ourselves and genuine communication with the horse.

Children do not seem to suffer from this 'interference' in anything like the same way, which is probably one reason why there are numerous accounts of youngsters being able to handle large, fractious horses who consistently defeat the attempts of adults to control them. Because the child's brain has not yet fully developed its analytical powers, this aspect of the mind has not yet 'hijacked' the rest of the thought-processes.

A good example of this can be found in Fred Zinneman's delightful film *My Brother Talks to Horses*. In this film, a pre-adolescent boy, something of a loner, discovers that he can communicate with horses and dogs. He does not hear them 'talk' in words; he listens to their thoughts. This ability proves very useful on the racetrack where he can 'ask' the horses who is going to win, or who is having an off day – and, of course, they tell him. In the end, though, he finds that as he grows up he can no longer 'talk' with dogs and horses; but he finds consolation in the fact that he can now communicate with girls – hitherto an alien and despised species.

The moral of this charming fantasy is that as he grows up he loses his child's whole-brain sense of unity with, and perception of, the universe, which enables him to be receptive to the thoughts of other creatures. As he starts to enter adult life, his analytical thought-processes start to take over, circumscribing his view of the world and limiting his understanding to empirical 'knowledge'.

I am not suggesting that we abandon this 'analytical mind'; simply that we should recognise its limitations and how it can interfere with our perceptions. Many people never find that true unity with their horses which they so desperately seek, because they are waiting for proof of its possibility.

In helping people to achieve that unity, Paul Hunting coaches them in finding ways to connect with, and trust, their true power. He calls this the power of *enthusiasm*: a word derived from a Sanskrit root meaning literally 'one with God's energy'. Enthusiasm can empower people to raise their spiritual 'altitude', as Hunting puts it.

> Horses respond very differently toward us when we are being our true selves. Because, when we are authentic, the soul releases an impulse. We feel this impulse as enthusiasm … Often we call it joy and it seems that horses feel and enjoy it too. They respond by sharing energy with us more willingly and working with us in greater harmony and cooperation.[14]

This enthusiasm, this 'inner power' is what characterises the very greatest riders. The intense concentration one sees on the faces of riders such as Arthur Kottas-Heldenberg, First Chief Rider of the Spanish Riding School, is what Vicki Hearne calls 'the incandescent gaze of unmediated awareness'. Such riders have accepted in full the 'burden of judgement' and the immense responsibilities this entails; their awareness of the horse's capabilities is also an awareness of the power of his mind and of what he can teach us. They have achieved that true oneness with the horse, embodied by the Greek concept of the centaur.

As I have noted elsewhere[15], even the humblest, least pretentious of riders can strike a note on the same scale as riders such as Arthur Kottas – lower down on that scale, perhaps, but it is the same scale nevertheless. In order to do this we must abandon fantasies of power, of control, even of superiority. We must accept the horse as a partner and friend. As Nuno Oliveira says, 'Make him a companion, and not a slave, then you will see what a true friend he is.'[16]

Above all, we must abandon any notions of training the horse by force, despite what we are told by so many trainers and behavioural scientists. As riders such as Oliveira and Kottas, and trainers such as Monty Roberts, have demonstrated, force is simply not necessary if we first engage the horse's mind. Again, we must heed the wisdom of the master, Oliveira: 'If the horse is happy, everything will be all right; if he is constrained everything will go wrong. And

Arthur Kottas-Heldenberg, First Chief Rider of the Spanish Riding School, with one of the school stallions. Horse and rider combinations such as this bring to life the Greek vision of the centaur (Henric Brabec d'Ipra)

in case that it is necessary to use force, then one enters a domain that does not fit the equestrian art, neither for that matter, in the circle in which civilised people dwell.'[17]

In the end, we must accept that the horse does have a mind, that he has thoughts and feelings and a point of view of his own. If we can respect these, and at the same time ally our powers of analysis to the horse's powers of perception, then we have a partnership that is indeed greater than the sum of its parts. From there, all kinds of wonders and delights await us.

That is the horse's great gift to us. In return, we must repay him with understanding, respect — and love.

Notes

1 Desmond Morris, *The Animal Contract* (Virgin Books, 1993), p.166
2 Morris, *The Animal Contract*, p. 167
3 Dr Marthe Kiley-Worthington, *Equine Welfare*, p. 18
4 Kiley-Worthington, *Equine Welfare*, p. 27
5 Kiley-Worthington, *Equine Welfare*, p. 9
6 Elwyn Hartley-Edwards, *Horses: Their Role in the History of Man* (Willow Books, 1987), p. 34
7 Colonel Alois Podhajsky, *My Horses, My Teachers*, p. 76
8 Rees, *The Maze*, p. 60
9 Vicki Hearne, *Adam's Task*, p. 114
10 Paul Hunting, 'The Power Within', *Your Horse*, January 1998, pp. 4–5
11 Hunting, The Power Within', p. 6
12 Hunting, 'The Power Within', p. 6
13 Hunting, 'The Power Within' p. 6
14 Hunting, 'The Power Within', p. 6
15 In *The Arabian Show Horse*, p. 223
16 Nuno Oliveira, *Reflections on Equestrian Art*, p. 36
17 Nuno Oliveira in *Notes sur l'enseignement de Nuno Oliveira* by Jeanne Boisseau,1979, quoted by Henri van Schaik in *Misconceptions and Simple Truths in Dressage* (J. A. Allen, 2nd ed., 1989), p. 46

Appendices

Appendix I: Stereotypes

The word 'stereotype' is usually used in a behavioural context to denote a range of behaviours characterised by meaninglessly repetitive actions, such as the ceaseless rocking back and forth often observed in severely disturbed children (such behaviour is frequently described by the slightly different term 'stereotypy' (plural stereotypies) to distinguish it from either the printing process known as 'stereotyping' or from the concept of a stereotype as being a standard, fixed idea or range of ideas shared by a particular social group, often about other social groups). This fixed, repetitive behaviour is often seen in caged animals who are deprived of the ability to behave in ways that would be natural to them in a free-ranging situation: a common example is that of the caged tiger who, unable to hunt or partake of any of the other normal 'tigerish' activities, paces endlessly up and down in his cage. When such obsessive, repetitive behaviour is seen in horses and ponies (as in weaving, box-walking, crib-biting, windsucking, etc.), it is usually described as a 'vice' and must be declared if the animal is sold.

However, the term 'vice' implies that the behaviour is caused by some kind of character fault, as vice is defined as 'an immoral, wicked or evil habit, action or trait'[1]. When applied to animals it is 'a bad trick or disposition, as of horses, dogs etc.'[2]. Even now, when we are at last beginning to understand some of the causes of such behaviour, it is still described in much equestrian literature as a 'vice'.

The perception of such stereotypes as defects of temperament (possibly hereditary), and the supposed acquisition of stereotypes as bad habits from watching other horses who exhibit such 'vices', has led in the past to all kinds of stratagems to prevent the horses concerned from indulging in their 'vice'. Weavers, who resemble the disturbed children referred to above in their habit of rocking from one forefoot to the other, and at the same time weaving their heads and necks from side to side, have often been confined behind 'anti-weave' grids – a grille with a V-shaped opening which fits over the stable door so that the horse can still look out but can no longer weave his head from side to side. This does not cure the weaver, of course; in most cases the horse simply retreats inside the stable to weave. The box-walker, who, as the term implies, may spend hour after hour ceaselessly walking around his box, often oblivious to all external stimuli, may find his stable suddenly infested with rubber tyres, the theory being that these will prevent the horse from walking round and round. They don't, of course; most horses in this situation will continue the habit, simply learning to avoid the tyres (or move them). Crib-biters and windsuckers may have their stables painted with foul-tasting substances to put them off chewing the wood, or they may have collars fitted to stop them from swallowing air. They may even have operations to cut certain muscles in their necks to prevent them from windsucking.

None of these attempts at controlling the problem ever really work, because — as is so often the case — it is a matter of treating the symptom rather than the cause. In the past the difficulty has lain in identifying the cause accurately, and this is where modern scientific investigation really comes into its own.

As a result of a number of studies carried out on stereotypic behaviour, most behavioural scientists now believe – and the evidence supports their conclusions – that most, if not all, stereotypical behaviour is a response to an inadequate environment, and that it occurs almost exclusively in horses who are stabled for long periods. This may be a stable in which the horse either suffers from too little, or too much, sensory stimulation, as in yards where there is either no activity – or in some closed barn systems where the horses can see only the horse stabled opposite – or in noisy, bustling yards where there is constant coming and going and excessive sound levels. In addition, stabled horses, especially in racing yards or high-level competition yards, may be fed mainly high-energy concentrate feed, with insufficient fibre. While the horse's needs may be met from a purely nutritional point of view, from a behavioural point of view this is highly unsatisfactory. The feral or free-ranging horse spends approximately 50–60 per cent of his time eating when the grazing is good; in winter, or on poor pasture with little nutritional value, this period may extend to up to 70–80 per cent. Horses are often referred to as 'trickle-feeders'. Their stomachs are relatively small, having evolved to cope with a more or less continuous intake (the grazing times referred to above may be spread over 24 hours). In addition, they are constantly on the move while grazing. Even although, for long periods, this movement may consist of little but a slow progress from one area to another, a grazing horse can still cover a considerable number of kilometres in one day.

If, however, the horse is confined to a stable and fed on a diet low in fibre, these normal behaviour patterns do not form part of his life, and as a result he feels frustration and discomfort. If, in addition, his opportunities for social contact are restricted or even absent, such frustration may be greatly intensified to the point where it is expressed in behavioural abnormalities such as stereotypical behaviour, or in some cases aggression. Paul McGreevy cites the result of one study which revealed that out of 4,468 Thoroughbred racehorses in training, 11 per cent showed stereotypical behaviour.[3] Crib-biting accounted for 5.5 per cent of this behaviour. McGreevy investigated further and found that the reason attempts to 'cure' crib-biting have met with little success appears to be that crib-biters, whose stereotype has its origins in an attempt to compensate for a diet high in concentrates but low in bulk fibre, actually become addicted to their stereotype.

This ties in with the findings of other scientific investigators, notably a team of researchers at the University of Utrecht, who, in the 1980s, discovered that 'twitching' a horse causes the horse's brain to produce chemicals known as endorphins, which are many times more powerful than morphine. It is the production of these natural painkillers which allows a wounded animal (and this, of course, includes humans) to run (or crawl) away to safety even when severely wounded. There are countless stories of soldiers wounded in battle, or civilians who have suffered horrific injuries, being able to carry on for some time as if nothing had happened. This 'period of grace' results from the flood of endorphins released as a result of the trauma or stress. In the case of the Dutch study, horses were first twitched and then injected with Naloxone, a drug which blocks the effect of the endorphins. When this took effect, the twitched horses became agitated as if they had not been twitched at all.

Naloxone has also been tested on pigs kept in battery conditions; such pigs show a high incidence of stereotypical behaviour similar to that observed in horses. However, when experimental pigs were injected with Naloxone they no longer performed the stereotypes. This suggests that stereotypical behaviour acts to release endorphins and that the animal performing it is on a permanent 'high' as a result of this endorphin 'fix' – the non-human equivalent of a junkie. It might be tempting to use drugs such as Naloxone to block such endorphin release, but this would only drive the problem even deeper. This seems even more probable when we consider that as well as acting as powerful painkillers, endorphins also cause a numbing of the emotions. If the hypothesis outlined above is correct – and it seems the most likely explanation in view of the evidence so far – then such an addiction may well be the horse's only way of dealing with an inadequate environment (as, indeed, is often the case with the human junkie). To deprive him of this means of coping – however distressing it may be to us – could well turn a horse that is just hanging on to his sanity into a real psychotic. Unless the horse's health is being compromised to a significant degree, it would seem far better to leave him alone to have his 'fix' and cope with his situation as best he can.

Indeed, it would be much better to try to eliminate the need to perform stereotypes altogether by improving the environment. Unfortunately, this is sometimes easier said than done; the horse who is confirmed in a stereotype may well prove impossible to cure, although an improvement in his management could well reduce its severity and its effects on his health. Milder cases, or those not yet so deep seated, could well respond to a better environment: greater freedom to graze and exercise his innate need for movement, more social contact (whether with horses or humans, but preferably both), as well as a diet consisting of greater quantities of forage. (It is significant that stereotypes seem to occur far less frequently in horses who are fed ad-lib hay or haylage, even where these are stabled for a considerable proportion of the time.)

Another problem lies in identifying which aspects of an individual horse's environment cause stereotypes to emerge. Different horses respond in so many different ways to similar situations that one simply cannot say that horses kept in X kind of environment will invariably tend to develop stereotypical behaviour. Sometimes the character and attitude of the person or persons handling and riding the horse seem to have as much influence on the development of such behaviour as the actual physical environment itself. Heredity is sometimes singled out as a factor, but while a tendency to develop such stereotypes may run in some families, it remains only a tendency, and in some cases it may simply be that such families belong to a breed frequently kept in a restricted kind of environment (e.g. Thoroughbred and Arabian racehorses, Arabian show horses, etc.). In some cases stereotypes can be the result of stress caused by the horse being at what is often considered the 'peak of fitness' (again, as with racehorses and some eventers). While such a degree of 'fitness' is often held up as an ideal, it can actually be highly stressful to the organism in question, as human athletes find to their cost. Extreme fitness for an extreme athletic effort may get the job done but it can have deleterious effects on the horse's or human's general health.

So as with almost every other problem that arises in the course of our relationship with our horses, there is no easy answer. We must look to our management systems and ask, how does the horse's present lifestyle compare with what he would have in a free-ranging situation, where stereotypes have never been observed to occur? If there are deficiencies, can they be compensated for in other areas? For example, the horse who has to spend a considerable proportion of the time stabled may still be kept happy by an enriched environment, ample provision of forage such as ad-lib hay or even good quality clean straw, social companionship, mental challenges such as 'toys' which require him to think and work at solving a problem, etc. A little ingenuity works wonders. Prevention, as always, remains better than cure!

Notes

1 *Collins English Dictionary* Sense (1)
2 *Collins English Dictionary* Sense (6)
3 Paul McGreevy, *Why Does My Horse . . .?*, p. 111

Appendix II: The Facial Expressions of the Horse

Although Monty Roberts and others have directed much attention to the importance of body language in horses, the importance of facial expressions is still somewhat underestimated. Indeed, one often hears the view expressed that horses do not have facial expressions as such! While they do not have the mobility of features that characterises primates, they can and do express a great deal through subtleties of expression, as well as by clear signals (e.g. the position of ears). In his comprehensive study of equine behaviour, entitled *Horse Behaviour*, behavioural scientist George Waring identified over 70 facial expressions which he and his students grouped together according to the context in which they were observed, and then placed these groups in sequences showing the different contexts in which each expression occurred. The illustrations of the facial expressions used in *Horse Behaviour* are reproduced here by kind permission of Dr Waring.

As always, caution is needed. While Waring's identification of such expressions is extremely comprehensive and takes far more account of subtleties than most behavioural studies have done, one should still be wary of trying to identify the moods of individual horses from such identifications alone. The horse's whole posture must be read, as well as the specific facial expression. As the great stoic philosopher, the Roman Emperor Marcus Aurelius, tells us: always look at the whole of a thing!

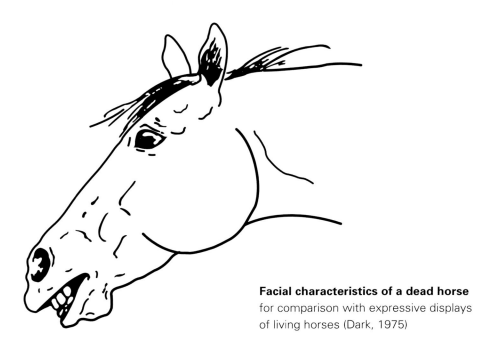

Facial characteristics of a dead horse
for comparison with expressive displays
of living horses (Dark, 1975)

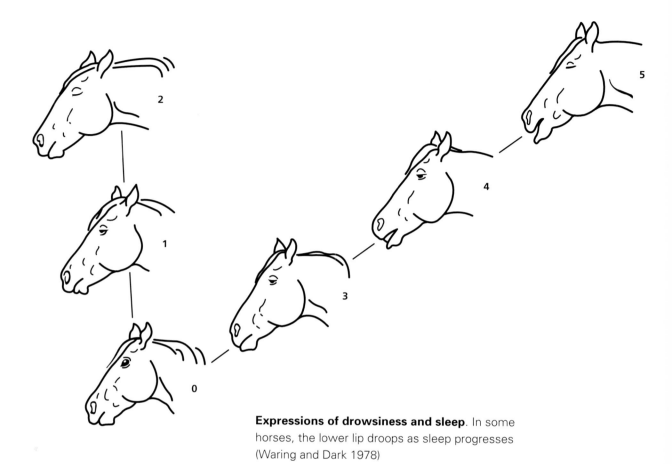

Expressions of drowsiness and sleep. In some horses, the lower lip droops as sleep progresses (Waring and Dark 1978)

Expressions of forward attention (Waring and Dark, 1978)

0 and 0–5 Horse standing or moving in alert manner

0-1-2-3-4 Investigation or manipulation of material on or near the ground

4-3-2-1-0 Ceasing of feeding to observe something in the surroundings

0-5-6-1 and 0-1 Inspection, such as naso-nasal greeting or when handed food

0-5-6-7 Sexually aroused stallion; horse activated while on a halter line

0-8-9-10 and 0-8-11-12 Displayed during energetic locomotion (tail often elevated)

8-9-10 Horse actively avoiding an object on or near the ground; horse yielding to bit pressure

0-8-11-12 Horse approaching a jump

Expressions of lateral attention (Waring and Dark, 1978)

0-1-2-1 Horse in relaxed walk; pattern also occurs when shaking

0-2-3-4-5 Lowering of head durng quiescent grazing; reverse sequence occurs during pauses

0-6-7-8 Play fighting, often while facing opponent and achieving periodic head and neck contact

0-6-9 Tractable horse at ease with rider

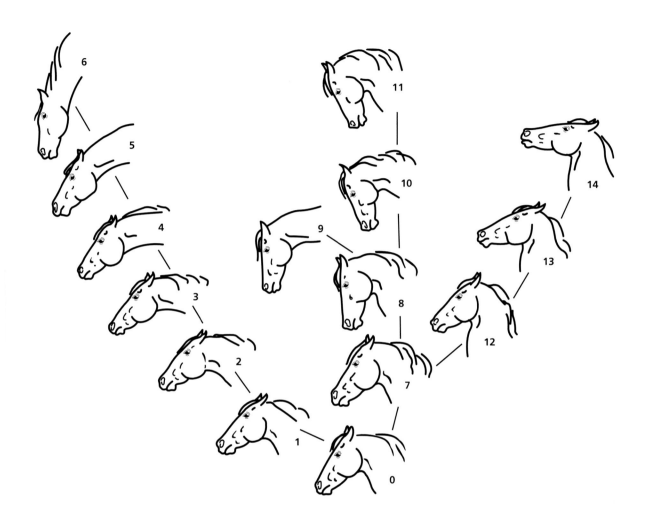

Expressions of backward attention (Waring and Dark, 1978)

6-5-4-3-2-1-0 Sequence shown by a grazing horse that is approached from behind. Reverse sequence occurs with continued vigilance as grazing progresses

0-1-2-3 Horse pushing against a restrictive barrier

3-4-5 Horse physically exhausted or in discomfort

4-5 Facing downwind during a severe storm

0-7-8-9 Tugging at bit and reins to succeed in release of rein tension from rider

8-10-11 Occurs during strong tension on reins when tack limits head elevation

0-7-12-13-14 Variations during head tossing, baulking, or bolting often in response to harsh handling by rider

Expressions of alarm (Waring and Dark, 1978)

0-1-2-3 Frightened horse in locomotion
0-1-2-3-4 Horse being subjected to roughness by rider when restrictive equipment
suppresses head extension and elevation
0-1-5-6-7 Alarming stimulus beside or below horse
0-8 Horse approached by suspicious object

Expressions of aggression (Waring and Dark, 1978)

0-1-2-3-4 Expression during biting and bite threats

0-1-2-3-5 Horse driving or dispersing others, often while swinging head in snake-like manner

0-6-7-8-9 Vigorous approach of stallion toward another male

0-6-10-14 Pattern shown during aggression with rider, during bucking, and in male-male fighting

0-10-11 Expression during kicking and kick threats

0-10-11-12-13 Displays occuring with foreleg striking, rearing, pushing, and avoidance. Occurs when handler strikes head of horse with quirt or whip

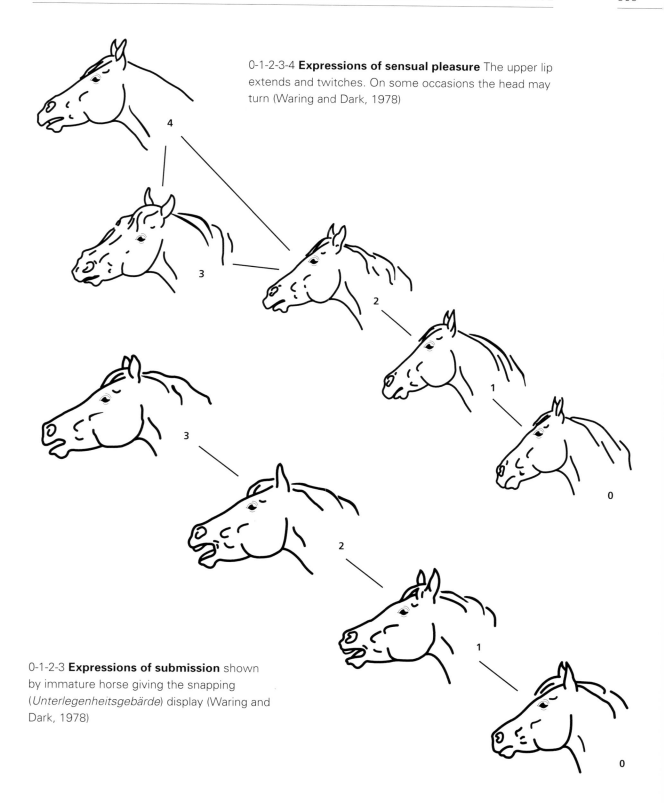

0-1-2-3-4 **Expressions of sensual pleasure** The upper lip extends and twitches. On some occasions the head may turn (Waring and Dark, 1978)

0-1-2-3 **Expressions of submission** shown by immature horse giving the snapping (*Unterlegenheitsgebärde*) display (Waring and Dark, 1978)

Tail postures and displays (Waring and Dark, 1978)

0 Relaxed position while standing

1-2-3-4-5 Variations progressing from a leisure walk to faster gaits, including jumping while at ease

0-1-2-6 Sequence prior to defecation

1-2-6-7 Display typical of mare in oestrus as well as during urination and copulation

1-2-6-8-9 Tail twitching at insects and prior to kicking, striking, bucking, and balking. Some lashing in the vertical plane may occur in aggressive displays

1-2-6-10-11-12 Display during intense exuberance or excitement, usually accompanied by snorting or blowing and energetic trotting or galloping

2-6-10-11 Tail display of stallion during mounting and copulation

0-13-14-15 Display of aggression, alarm or when horse is not at ease with a handler

0-16-17 Display of extreme fear or submission, prolonged pain, or while facing downwind in severe weather

Appendix III: Useful Organisations

The Equine Behaviour Forum

The Equine Behaviour Forum (formerly known as the Equine Behaviour Study Circle) was founded in 1978. Currently chaired by Dr Francis Burton of the University of Glasgow, the EBF is an entirely voluntary, non-commercial, non-profit-making, international group of people interested in equine behaviour. Its membership comprises vets, scientists, professional and amateur horsepeople, breeders, casual riders and horse owners, serious competitors and also people who have no access to equines or who simply prefer to observe them from a safe distance! To enjoy the forum, all you need is a genuine interest in horse behaviour.

The EBF produces a journal, *Equine Behaviour*, edited by author Susan McBane, which comprises members' letters, articles, views and experiences, some scientific papers, book reviews and much more. It organises optional projects for members to carry out, informal talks and discussion groups and visits to places of interest in the horse world.

The forum is very much a member-participation group. Without the active participation of its members, in particular in relation to the contents of its newsletter, it cannot exist.

If you are interested in joining the EBF, please write to: the Membership Secretary, Mrs Gillian O'Donnell, 63 Chaigley Road, Longridge, Lancashire, England PR3 3TQ Tel./Fax 01772 786037

The Classical Riding Club

The Classical Riding Club was started in January 1995 by Sylvia Loch as a means of bringing together like-minded people who were interested in a more philosophical approach to riding. This approach puts the happiness and pride of the horse above all else: even above winning and being seen to be successful. This does not mean that the CRC is anti-competition; on the contrary, it recognises that competition, when participated in for the right reasons, can be a very healthy way of giving oneself and one's horse a goal to aim for and of proving the correctness of training and riding. However, the CRC also recognises that the pressures of modern equestrian sport have all too often meant that the great classical values and traditions seem in danger of being forgotten or swept away, and it is these values and traditions that the CRC seeks to communicate and to help preserve.

The Classical Riding Club membership is composed of people from every walk of life, and with widely differing equestrian backgrounds and levels of ability. Members range from those who do not own or even ride horses but simply have an interest in the classical philosophy, to those working at High School level, with every possible combination of ability and level of knowledge in between. Although the bulk of CRC members are resident in the UK, there are members as far afield as the USA and Australia, as well as mainland Europe. The

CRC welcomes everyone with a genuine interest in the classical ethos but, above all, its aim is to bring this ethos to the everyday rider to enhance our understanding of the horse.

The tangible benefits of the CRC are: a quarterly newsletter which contains instructional articles, book reviews, members' letters, articles by members, details of demonstrations, seminars, open days, teach-ins, lectures, etc. Membership also gives members access to a general equestrian helpline, as well as expert advice via the network of regional Liaison Members. No matter what your query, you can be assured that some CRC member, somewhere, will have the answer. In addition, membership gives discounts on CRC publications and entry fees to certain CRC events, plus information on new dressage tests (see below), as well as all events being held on behalf of the CRC.

There is also a list, available at a nominal charge, of trainers/instructors who have signed a declaration to say that they promise to teach under the classical principles and ethos as laid down in the club's charter. This does not necessarily indicate that the club either knows or approves of these people, but at least it gives members a chance to find like-minded trainers in their area.

Also available is a series of dressage tests, devised by Sylvia Loch in consultation with a number of other experts. These are, more properly speaking, training tests, as their aim is to provide a true test of the correctness of a horse's (and rider's) training. Less emphasis is placed on accuracy of figures and more on the horse's way of going and particularly the manner in which it is ridden. These have been received very enthusiastically by both riders and judges. Copies of the tests are available from the CRC, again for a nominal charge.

The CRC is very fortunate in numbering some internationally renowned trainers among its members. Among them is Paul Belasik (author of *Riding Towards The Light* and *Exploring Dressage Technique* – both inspiring books); and has welcomed as honorary members such illustrious persons as Arthur Kottas, First Chief Rider of the Spanish Riding School and Brigadier-General Kurt Albrecht, formerly Director of the Spanish Riding School.

The Classical Riding Club is a very friendly, informal organisation whose members have proved more than willing to share ideas and information. Every member, no matter who they are or what they do, has something to bring to the organisation, as well as the potential to benefit from it.

If you wish to join, please write to: The Classical Riding Club, Eden Hall, Kelso, Roxburghshire TD5 7QD

Ride For Your Life Workshops

As mentioned in Chapter 17, the Ride for Your Life workshops aim to assist riders to overcome their fears and release their inner potential. In helping to remove the mental blocks that people create for themselves, these workshops have proved highly successful, enabling many riders to achieve far more than they had previously believed possible.

Paul Hunting, who runs the Ride For Your Life workshops, may be contacted on 01252 843163 (telephone and fax).

Glossary

airs above the ground (aires relevés)
Movements in which the horse either leaps or raises his forefeet off the ground, e.g. levade, capriole.

animism
The belief that all natural phenomena possess souls; or, in philosophical thought, that an immaterial force animates the universe.

bedawin
Term describing the nomad tribes of the Arabian Peninsula, their customs, traditions, etc.

bedu
Collective term for the nomad tribes of the Arabian Peninsula.

Bereiter
Rider at the Spanish Riding School.

capriole
One of the airs above the ground. La Guérinière defines it as follows: 'When the horse is in the air with forehand and hindquarters level, it gives a vigorous kick, with the hind legs kept together and extended as far as possible.'

cavaleiro
The mounted bullfighter in the Portuguese corrida or the Spanish rejoneo.

corrida
Bullfight – in Portugal it refers to the mounted bullfight, which in Spain is called the rejoneo, to differentiate it from the bullfight on foot.

courbette
A series of jumps on the hind legs.

croupade
A leap in which, when the horse has all four legs in the air, the hind legs and hooves are drawn under the belly so that the soles of the feet are not seen from behind.

écuyer
A riding master. More properly used to describe someone recognised as a master of equitation.

High School
The highest level of training of the horse, which includes the extremely collected gaits, piaffe, passage and the airs above the ground.

howdah
A seat, usually with a canopy, fastened to an elephant's back.

levade
An air above the ground in which the horse lifts his forehand off the ground with lowered hocks, at an angle of approximately 30 degrees. Up to the nineteenth century the movement was performed with the horse's body at an angle of 45 degrees from the ground; this older movement was known as the pesade and it would be this air that was performed by horses trained by M. de la Guérinière and his contemporaries.

mahout
An elephant driver or keeper.

manège
Arena, ring or other enclosed area where horses are schooled. The baroque or classical manège was considerably smaller than the modern arena as the emphasis was very much on the highly collected movements.

passage
Defined by la Guérinière as 'a measured and cadenced walk or trot'. Now used exclusively to mean a cadenced, elevated trot in which the moment of suspension is clearly defined.

pesade
See levade.

piaffe
'A passage in place' (la Guérinière).

rejoneador
Spanish equivalent of the cavaleiro (q.v.).

sorte
Portuguese term (the Spanish equivalent is suerte) for the various movements and passes which occur in the corrida.

volte
A small circle.

Bibliography

Works Specifically Relating to Equine Behaviour

Ainslie, Tom and Ledbetter, Bonnie, *The Body Language of Horses*, Kaye & Ward, 1974

Bayley, Lesley and Maxwell, Richard, *Understanding Your Horse* David & Charles, 1996

Berger, J. & Cunningham C., 'Influence of familiarity on frequency of inbreeding in wild horses' in: *Evolution*, 41, 229–31, Jan 1987

Berger, Joel, 'Organizational systems and dominance in feral horses in the Grand Canyon', *Behavioural Ecology and Sociobiology*, 2, 1977 (pp. 91–119)

Blake, Henry, *Horse Wisdom*, Souvenir Press, 1986

   Talking With Horses, Souvenir Press, 1975

   Thinking With Horses, Souvenir Press, 1977

Boy, Vincent and Duncan, Patrick, 'Time-budgets of Camargue Horses' in *Behaviour*, 71, 1979 (3–4), pp. 187–202 and *Behaviour*, 72, 1980 (1–2), pp. 26–49, Leiden

Budd, Jackie, *Reading the Horse's Mind*, Ring Press, 1996

Budiansky, Stephen, *The Nature of Horses,* Weidenfeld & Nicholson, 1997

Clutton-Brock, T.H. Greenwood, P.J. & Powell, R.D. 'Rank and relationships in Highland ponies' in *Zeitschrift für Tierpsychologie*, 41 (1976), pp. 202–16

Duncan, P., 'Time budgets of Camargue Horses' in *Behaviour*, 72, (1980), pp. 26–47

Duncan, P., Feh, C. et al. 'Reduction of inbreeding in a natural herd of horses' in: *Animal Behaviour*, 32, 520–7, May 1984

Feh, C. and de Mazières, J., 'Grooming at a preferred site reduces heart rate in horses', *Animal Behaviour*, 46, pp. 1191–4, Dec 1993

Feist, J.D. and McCullogh, D.R., 'Behaviour patterns and communications in feral horses', in *Zeitschrift für Tierpsychologie*, 41 (1976), pp. 337–71

Groves, C.P., Horses, *Asses and Zebras in the Wild*, David & Charles, 1974

Grzimek, B. (ed.) *Grzimek's Encyclopedia of Mammals*, vol. 4 (entry: 'Horses', by Hans Klingel), McGraw-Hill, 1990

Kiley-Worthington, Dr Marthe, *The Behaviour of Horses in Relation to Management and Training*, J. A. Allen, 1987

   Communication in Horses: Cooperation & Competition, Eco-Research and Education Centre, University of Exeter, Publication 19

Langley, Garda, *Understanding Horses*, David & Charles, 1989

Marshall, Léonie, *Your Horse's Mind*, Crowood, 1996

Mason, G., 'Grooming reaches the parts . . .' in *New Scientist*, 141, p. 16, Feb 5 1994

May, Jan, *Equus caballus: on Horses and Handling*, J. A. Allen, 1995

McBane, Susan, *Behaviour Problems in Horses*, David & Charles, 1994

McCall, C. 'Review of learning behaviour in horses and its application in horse training', in *Journal of Animal Science*, 68 (1990), p. 75

McGreevy, Paul, *Why Does My Horse . . .?*, Souvenir Press, 1996

Michael, Beatrice (tr. D. Kreuzer), *Horses: Their Life in Pictures*, Sunburst Books, 1993

Morris, Desmond, *Horsewatching*, Jonathan Cape Ltd, 1988

Pfungst, O., *Clever Hans: The Horse of Mr von Osten*, Holt, New York 1911; reissued by Holt, Rinehart and Winston Inc., 1965

Rees, Lucy, *The Horse's Mind*, Stanley Paul, 1984; paperback ed. 1993

Schäfer, Michael, *The Language of the Horse*, tr. Daphne Machin Goodall, Kaye and Ward, 1974

Schramm, Ulrik, *The Trouble With Horses*, J. A. Allen, 1988
    The Undisciplined Horse, J. A. Allen, 1986

Self, A. & Seaman, J., 'Horse sense' in: *New Scientist*, 148, pp. 52–3, Nov 4 1995

Self, Margaret Cabell, *The Problem Horse and the Problem Horseman*, Arco, 1977

Smythe, R.H., *The Mind of the Horse*, J. A. Allen, 1974

Tudge, C., 'They breed horses, don't they?' in: *New Scientist*, 122, pp. 66–7, June 3 1989

Tyler, S.J., 'Behaviour and Social organisation of New Forest ponies' in *Animal Behaviour* (1972) Monograph 5, 85–196, Baillière Tindall, London, 1972

Vines, G., 'Shrill stallions make the best fighters' in: *New Scientist*, 134, p. 17, June 20 1992

Waring, George, *Horse Behaviour*, Noyes, 1983

Wells, S.M. and Goldschmidt-Rothschilde, B. von, 'Social behaviour and relationships in a herd of Camargue horses' in *Zeitschrift für Tierpsychologie*, 49 (1979), pp. 363–80

Williams, Moyra, *Horse Psychology*, J. A. Allen, 1976
    Horse Psychology Methuen, 1956
    Understanding Nervousness in Horse and Rider, J. A. Allen, 1990

General Equestrian Literature

Albrecht, Brigadier Kurt, *A Dressage Judge's Handbook*, J. A. Allen, 1988
    Principles of Dressage, J. A. Allen, 1987

Archer, Rosemary, *The Versatile Arabian Horse*, J. A. Allen, 1996

Archer, Rosemary; Pearson, Colin; Covey, Cecil and Finke, Betty, *The Crabbet Arabian Stud: its History and Influence*, Alexander Heriot, 1994

Archer, Rosemary and James Fleming (eds.) Lady Anne Blunt: *Journals and Correspondence 1878–1917*, Alexander Heriot, 1986

Barbier, Dominique, *Dressage for the New Age*, Prentice Hall Press, USA, 1990

Beamish, Huldine, *Cavaliers of Portugal*, Geoffrey Bles, 1966

Belasik, Paul, *Riding Towards the Light*, J. A. Allen, 1990
    Exploring Dressage Technique, J. A. Allen, 1994

Bennett, Deb, *Principles of Conformation Analysis, Vol. I*, Fleet Street Publishing, 1988

Principles of Conformation Analysis, Vol. II, Fleet Street Publishing, 1989

Principles of Conformation Analysis, Vol. III, Fleet Street Publishing, 1991

Blignault, Karin, *Successful Schooling*, J. A. Allen, 1997

Bromiley, Mary, *Equine Injury, Therapy and Rehabilitation*, 2nd ed. Blackwell, 1993

Natural Methods for Equine Health, Blackwell, 1994

Bürger, Udo, *The Way to Perfect Horsemanship*, J. A. Allen, 1986

Cordeiro, Arsenio Raposo, *The Lusitano Horse: The Son of the Wind (O Filho do Vento)*, Edições Inapa, Lisboa, 1991

Denoix, Jean-Marie and Pailloux, Jean-Pierre, *Physical Therapy and Massage for the Horse* (tr. Jonathan Lewis), Manson Publishing Ltd, 1996

Dollery, Elaine, *The Treacle Bucket*, Dollery Books, 1992

Geddes, Candida, *The Horse*, Octopus, 1978

Grimshaw, Anne, *The Horse: A bibliography of British books* 1851–1976, with a narrative commentary on the rôle of the horse in British social history, as revealed by the contemporary literature, The Library Association, 1982

Guérinière, François Robichon de la, *The School of Horsemanship*, originally published in 1733 as L'École de la Cavalerie, tr. Tracy Boucher, J. A. Allen, 1994

Handler, Colonel Hans, *The Spanish Riding School in Vienna*, Thames and Hudson, 1972

Hartley-Edwards, Elwyn (ed.), *Encyclopedia of the Horse*, Octopus, 1977

Horses: Their Role in the History of Man, Willow Books, 1987

Kiley-Worthington, Dr Marthe, *Equine Welfare*, J. A. Allen, 1997

Kunffy, Charles de, *The Athletic Development of the Dressage Horse*, Howell Book House, 1992

Ethics and Passions of Dressage, Half Halt Press, USA, 1993

Lijsen, Jan, *Classical Circus Equitation* (originally published in Dutch as *De Hooge School*, 1949), tr. Anthony Hippisley-Coxe; foreword and commentary by Sylvia Stanier, LVO, J. A. Allen, 1993

Loch, Sylvia, *The Classical Seat*, Hyman Unwin, 1988

The Classical Rider: Being at One with your Horse, J. A. Allen, 1997

Dressage: The Art of Classical Riding, The Sportsman's Press, 1990

The Royal Horse of Europe, J. A. Allen, 1986

Mackay, Nicci, *Spoken in Whispers: The Autobiography of a Horse Whisperer*, Mainstream Publishing, 1997

Mairinger, Franz, *Horses Are Made To Be Horses*, Rigby, Sydney, Australia, 1983

Mashanaglass, Marquis McSwiney of, *Training from the Ground*, J. A. Allen, 1987

McBane, Susan (ed.), *The Horse and the Bit*, Crowood Press, 1988

McBane, Susan and Douglas-Cooper, Helen, *Horse Facts*, Stanley Paul, 1990

Nelson, Hilda, *François Baucher: The Man and his Method*, J. A. Allen, 1992

Newcastle, The Duke of, *A General System of Horsemanship*, facsimile of the London edition of 1743, J. A. Allen, 1970

Oliveira, Nuno *Reflections on Equestrian Art*, translated by Phyllis Field, J. A. Allen, 1976

Oliveira, Nuno, *Classical Principles of the Art of Training Horses*, Howley & Russell, Australia, 1983

Pluvinel, Antoine de, *The Maneige Royal*, tr. of the 1626 edition by Dr. Hilda Nelson, J. A. Allen, 1989

Podhajsky, Colonel A., *The Complete Training of Horse and Rider*, tr. by Colonel V. D. S. Williams and Eva Podhajsky, Harrap, 1967

   My Horses, My Teachers (originally published 1967 as *Meine Lehrmeister die Pferde*), tr. Eva Podhajsky, UK edition, J. A. Allen, 1997

Rees, Lucy, *Riding: The True Techniques*, Stanley Paul, 1991

Ridgeway, W. *The Origin and Influence of the Thoroughbred Horse*, London, 1905

Roberts, Monty, *The Man Who Listens to Horses*, Hutchinson, 1996

Seunig, Waldemar, *Horsemanship*, tr. Leonard Mins, Doubleday & Co Ltd, 1976

Simpson, G.G., *Horses*, OUP, 1951

Sivewright, Molly, *Thinking Riding Book 1*, J. A. Allen, 1984

   Thinking Riding Book 2, J. A. Allen, 1985

Skipper, Lesley, *The Arabian Show Horse*, J. A. Allen, 1997

Steinbrecht, G., *The Gymnasium of the Horse* (originally published as *Gymnasium des Pferdes*, 1884, tr. from the 10th German edition, 1978, by Helen K. Gibble), Xenophon Press, USA, 1995

Steinkraus, William, *Riding and Jumping*, Pelham Books, 1971

Wanless, Mary, *Ride With Your Mind*, Methuen, 1987

   Ride With Your Mind Masterclass, Methuen, 1991

   For The Good Of The Horse, Kenilworth Press, 1997

Wyche, Sara, *Understanding the Horse's Back*, Crowood Press, 1998

Xenophon, *The Art of Horsemanship*, tr. by M.H. Morgan, J. A. Allen, 1962

General Literature on Animal Behaviour, Evolution, etc.

Benyus, J., *Beastly Behaviors: A zoo lover's companion*, Addison-Wesley, Reading, Mass., 1992

Bostock, Stephen S., *Zoos & Animal Rights*, Routledge, 1993

Darwin, C., *Expression of the Emotions in Man and Animals*, Greenwood Press, 1868

   The Descent of Man and Selection in Relation to Sex, London, 1871

   The Origin of Species, London, 1859

Dröscher, Vitus B., *The Magic of the Senses: New Discoveries in Animal Perception*, (tr. by Ursula Lehrburger and Oliver Coburn), W. H. Allen, 1969

Evans, Peter, *Ourselves and Other Animals*, Century Hutchinson, 1987

Friedrich, Heinz, *Man and Animal*, Paladin, 1972

Goodall, Jane, *Through a Window*, Weidenfeld & Nicholson, 1990

Griffin, D.R., *The Question of Animal Awareness* (revised and enlarged edition), The Rockefeller University Press, New York, 1981

Griffin, Donald R. *Animal Minds*, University of Chicago, 1992

Hafez, E. S. E. (ed.), *The Behaviour of Domestic Animals*, Baillière Tindall, 1962

Hearne, Vicki, *Adam's Task: Calling Animals By Name*, Heinemann, 1986

Humphrey, N., *Consciousness Regained*, OUP, 1984

Kiley-Worthington, Dr Marthe and Rendle, C.C., *Animal Handling and Animal Educational Psychology*, Eco-Research and Education Centre, University of Exeter occasional paper no. 9a
    An Investigation into the Effectiveness of Improved Handling and Teaching Techniques in Five Specific Cases of Large Herbivores, Eco-Research and Education Centre, occasional paper no. 96

Kiley-Worthington, M., *The Behavioural Problems of Farm Animals*, Oriel, 1977

Leyhausen, Paul, *Cat Behavior: the Predatory and Social Behaviour of Domestic and Wild Cats*, (tr. B. A. Tonkin), Garland STPM Press, 1979

Linzey, Andrew, *Animal Theology*, SCM Press Ltd, 1994

Lorenz, Konrad, *King Solomon's Ring*, Methuen, 1952
    Man Meets Dog, Methuen, 1964

Manning, Aubrey, *An Introduction to Animal Behaviour, 3rd ed.*, Edward Arnold Ltd, 1979

Masson, Jeffrey and McCarthy, Susan, *When Elephants Weep: The Emotional Lives of Animals*, Vintage, 1996

Midgley, Mary, *Animals and Why They Matter*, University of Georgia, 1984

Morris, Desmond, *The Animal Contract*, Virgin, 1993
    Animal Days, Jonathan Cape, 1979
    Dogwatching, Clio Press Ltd, 1987

Pirinçci, Akif and Degen, Rolf, *Cat Sense: Inside the Feline Mind*, Fourth Estate Limited, 1994

Rollin, B. E., *The Unheeded Cry: Animal Consciousness, Animal Pain and Science*, OUP, 1990

Romanes, George, *Animal Intelligence*, Kegan Paul, Trench, Trubner & Co, 1898

Rowell, T., 'Beyond the one-male group' in *Behaviour*, 104 (1988), p. 189

Singer, Peter, *Animal Liberation* (2nd ed.), Jonathan Cape Ltd, 1990

Singer, Peter (ed.) *In Defence of Animals*, Blackwell, 1985

Syme, G. T. & Syme, L.A., *Social Structure in Farm Animals*, Elsevier, Amsterdam, 1979

Tinbergen, Niko, *Social Behaviour in Animals*, Methuen, 1963

Tudge, Colin, *Last Animals at the Zoo*, Hutchinson Radius, 1991
    The Engineer in the Garden, Jonathan Cape, 1993

Wood-Gush, D. G. M., Dawkins, M., Ewbank, R., eds. *Self-Awareness in Domesticated Animals:* proceedings of a workshop held at Keble College, Oxford 7th & 8th July 1980, The Universities Federation for Animal Welfare, 1981

Walker, S., *Animal Thought*, Routledge and Kegan Paul, 1985

General Background Literature

Bakker, Robert T., *The Dinosaur Heresies*, Longman Scientific & Technical, 1987

Bernstein, I.S., 'Dominance: the baby and the bathwater' in *Behavioural and Brain Sciences 4*, 1981, pp. 419–29

Carruthers, Peter, *The Animals Issue: Moral Theory in Practice*, Cambridge University Press, 1992

Chalmers, N. R., 'Dominance a part of a relationship' in *Behavioural and Brain Sciences, 4*, 1981, pp 437–8

Cox, Brian, *The Great Betrayal: Memoirs of a Life in Education*, Chapmans, 1992

Dawkins, Richard, 'In Defence of Selfish Genes' in: *Philosophy*, vol. 56, no. 218, Oct. 1981, pp. 556–73

    The Selfish Gene, Oxford University Press, 1976

Goleman, Daniel, *Emotional Intellience*, Bloomsbury Publishing plc, 1996

Gould, Stephen Jay, *Bully for Brontosaurus*, Penguin, 1992

    Eight Little Piggies, Jonathan Cape, 1993

    An Urchin in the Storm, Penguin, 1990

Hall, Susan J., *Basic Biomechanics* (2nd edition), Mosby, 1995

Imam, S. H. A. A., *Chetak Or a Story of a Man and a Horse*, Indian Heritage, 1994

Leakey, Richard and Lewin, Roger *The Sixth Extinction*, Weidenfeld & Nicholson, 1996

Lorenz, Konrad, *Evolution and Modification of Behaviour*, Methuen, 1966

Lorenz, Konrad, *On Aggression* (originally published in 1963 as *Das sogenannte Böse: Zur Naturgeschichte der Agresion*), tr. M. Latzke, Methuen. 1966

Midgley, Mary, *Beast and Man* (rev. ed.), Routledge, 1995

    'Gene-Juggling' in: *Philosophy, vol. 54, no. 210*, October 1979

    'Selfish Genes and Social Darwinism' in: *Philosophy, vol., 58*, 1983

Penrose, Roger, *The Emperor's New Mind*, Vintage, 1990

Pitt-Aikens, Tom and Thomas Ellis, Alice, *Loss of the Good Authority*, Viking, 1989

Rees, Lucy, *The Maze: Through Hell to Hopi*, Bantam Press, 1995

Rose, Steven, *The Conscious Brain*, Weidenfeld & Nicholson, 1992

    Lifelines: Biology, Freedom, Determinism, Allen Lane, The Penguin Press, 1997

Sheldrake, Rupert, *A New Science of Life*, Blond & Briggs Ltd, 1981

    The Presence of the Past, Harper Collins, 1994

    The Rebirth of Nature, Century, 1990

Shreeve, James, *The Neandertal Enigma*, Viking, 1996

Smuts, B. 'Dominance: an alternative view' in *Behavioural and Brain Sciences*, 4, 1981

Spurzheim, J. G., *The Physiognomic System of Gall and Spurzheim*, Baldwin Cradoch & Joy, 1815

Stevens, Anthony, *Private Myths: Dreams and Dreaming*, Hamish Hamilton, 1995

Stove, David, 'So You Think You Are a Darwinian?' in: *Philosophy, vol. 69, no. 269, July 1994*

Suzuki, David and Knudtson, Peter, *Genethics: The Ethics of Engineering Life*, Unwin Hyman Ltd, 1989

Various *The Encyclopedia of Prehistoric Life*, Mitchell Beazley, 1979

Wilson, Colin, *Starseekers*, Book Club Associates (with Hodder & Stoughton), 1980

    From Atlantis to the Sphinx, Virgin Books, 1996

Wilson, E. O., *Sociobiology: The New Synthesis*, Harvard University Press, 1975

Periodicals (Other than Scientific Publications Cited in the Text)

Classical Riding Club Newsletter
Dogs Today
Dressage
Equine Behaviour: The Journal of the Equine Behaviour Forum
Horse & Hound
Horse and Rider
Riding
Your Horse

Works of Fiction

Adams, Richard, *Traveller*, Hutchinson, 1988
Francis, Dick, *Bolt*, Pan, 1988
Lewis, C. S., *The Horse and His Boy*, Geoffrey Bles, 1954
Shakespeare, William, *The Merchant of Venice*
    *Venus and Adoni*s

Index